SCHOOL READINESS
Behavior Tests Used at the
Gesell Institute

Books of the Gesell Institute

SCHOOL READINESS

Behavior Tests Used at the Gesell Institute

New Edition

FRANCES L. ILG
LOUISE BATES AMES
Gesell Institute of Child Development

HARPER & ROW, PUBLISHERS
NEW YORK, EVANSTON, SAN FRANCISCO, LONDON

To the Fund for the
Advancement of Education
whose various members have borne with us,
believed in us,
and made this volume possible.

SCHOOL READINESS: BEHAVIOR TESTS USED AT THE GESELL INSTITUTE (New Edition). Copyright © 1964, 1965, 1972 by Gesell Institute of Child Development Incorporated. All rights reserved. Printed in the United States of America. No part of this book may be used or reproduced in any manner whatsoever without written permission except in the case of brief quotations embodied in critical articles and reviews. For information address Harper & Row, Publishers, Inc., 10 East 53rd Street, New York, N.Y. 10022. Published simultaneously in Canada by Fitzhenry & Whiteside Limited, Toronto.

STANDARD BOOK NUMBER: 06-012154-8

LIBRARY OF CONGRESS CATALOG CARD NUMBER: 65-10421

CONTENTS

‖‖

LIST OF TABLES

TABLES IN APPENDIXES

ACKNOWLEDGMENTS

This is a work that has been years in the making. Without the continuing long-term support of the Fund for the Advancement of Education, dating back to 1957, this task might neither have been started nor completed. We wish to extend thanks especially to Alvin Eurich, Lester Nelson, and Edward Meade, all of whom showed us how a responsible foundation can become an effective supporter and critic of the projects it supports.

In the gathering of materials thanks are especially due to the hundreds of children whose eager cooperation made us feel more confident in our developmental battery of tests. Teachers and administrators, although on the sidelines, always made us feel welcome, and were most cooperative about rearranging their schedules to fit our needs. Special thanks go to Edward Summerton, Superintendent of the Hurlbutt School, and to Charles St. Clair, Superintendent of the North Haven schools. Also to the two North Haven principals, Mildred Wakeley and Elizabeth Doyle, both of whom saw us through our standardization study and chose to continue working with us in the application of the school-readiness program. Our two developmental examiners for this program, Joan Scranton and Rosemary Zeoli, have courageously and deftly given us a taste of a school-placement program in action.

Among the members of our own staff who carried out these testing programs, thanks are due to Richard J. Apell, Evelyn Goodenough Pitcher, Richard N. Walker, Marjean Kremer, Mary Elizabeth Bourgeois, and Marilyn Knowles. The laborious analysis of the standardization records was undertaken by Judith August, Tordis Ilg, and Marilyn Knowles, and for this we extend our deep thanks. Judith August also contributed patient editorial assistance. Last but not least was the typing of the manuscript so expertly accomplished by Joan Janicki and Marie DePoto.

FRANCES L. ILG
LOUISE BATES AMES

xiii

PREFACE TO THE NEW EDITION

||||||||||||||||||||||||||||||||||||||||||||||||||||||||||||||||||||||||||||||||||||||||||||||||||||||||

Seven years have passed since the publication of this book. We are happy to report that it has had a slow but steady distribution and influence on educational practices. It is not an easy book to read, but has become a valuable book for those who wish to look at each child in his own right in relation to his developmental or maturational age of functioning.

We feel that the distribution of *School Readiness* may have been hampered by its remaining within the textbook department of its publisher, Harper & Row. We recognize its textbook potentials, but we are even more concerned about putting it into the hands of that single reader who is ready to absorb its message and to put it into operation. We are happy to report that this reprinting will make this book more available by placing it in trade, allowing it to stand side by side with our other volumes on any open bookstore shelf.

We know that *School Readiness* could not have been conceived and written without the background and documentation of our previous work. We also know that it will have a more limited appeal than many of our other writings, especially *Child Behavior,* and the trilogy which attempted to encompass the years from birth to sixteen. In the latter three (*Infant and Child in the Culture of Today; The Child from Five to Ten;* and *Youth: The Years from Ten to Sixteen*) we ranged widely into the total life of the child, at least as far as we could fathom it. In contrast, in *School Readiness* we have zeroed in on the focal mechanism that will, it is hoped, reveal at what level each child is operating maturationally.

There was an initial burst of interest in our concept of school readiness and developmental school placement, especially during the affluent years of 1967–70 when federal money was readily available. Innovation was the catchword and our program was initially judged as innovative.

This federal money helped some school systems to get started by training developmental examiners and having us come in to supervise their programs. Some schools in this period produced strong lasting programs with their own power of growth. But others could not survive without the continued support of federal funds.

It is hard for us to judge at this time the extent of the influence of developmental thinking on various school systems. But we do know that our greatest influence has been produced on either seacoast, and that the states showing the strongest interest are New Hampshire, Pennsylvania, Georgia, Montana, California and Washington. Our closest contact has been through our training workshops conducted both at the Gesell Institute three times a year (October, March and June) and regionally.

Regional workshops have soared to fourteen a year in the past two years and have ranged widely over the United States. All in all, more than 2500 persons have attended these various workshops since the first one was held at the Gesell Institute in 1962. The participants in the workshops have come from various walks of life, but each one was bound up in some way with the educational welfare of the child. Many have reported that it was not until they attended a workshop that our book, School Readiness, came alive.

In our closer contact with school systems, both through workshop participants and consultation assignments, we have come to realize that we have acquired both friend and foe. Teachers are our greatest friends, especially those who have struggled through all too many years of trying to teach the unready child, often with minimal success.

There was a time when these teachers might have blamed themselves for their lack of success. Now they have come to realize that they were working against insurmountable odds. The concept of developmental placement has made sense to them. It is what they had been waiting for. When a developmental program was established in their school, these teachers knew the very first day of school, or certainly within the first week, which children were not ready for the work of the grade they were in.

When teachers queried those in authority as to why these unready children had been placed in their classrooms, the answer often hinged on a parent's insistence. This is why we cannot emphasize enough that parents need to be informed about a developmental program, how it works and what it can do for their child. Often we solicit the help of parents who after initial resistance have come to realize how much it has helped their own child to be placed where he should be. Such parents can speak from experience and thus can become a very positive influence.

The demanding parent is, fortunately, in the minority. The truly perceptive parent, more often a mother than a father, knows where her child is functioning. She rightly wants to protect him and to place him in a situation where he can succeed and have enough energy left over to express his own creative urges. More and more parents, especially on the East Coast, and in New Hampshire in particular, are holding their children out of kindergarten or first grade when they feel they are not ready, even though their chronological age would make them eligible. We have found over and over that such parents have made a wise choice and we thank them for making the work of the educator so much easier.

Some teachers and administrators have also put up roadblocks of their own to the carrying out of a developmental program. The seasoned teacher often does not wish to change her ways and is more bound up in teaching the child than in fostering his learning process. At the same time, these same teachers may be somewhat possessive of their children, not wishing to release them to the level where they can function best, and pushing them ahead at the end of the year to give them a "chance." These teachers are looking at the child through their eyes of desire as much as the parent is. They allow the truth about the child's capacity and development to escape them. Perceptive parents who have wanted over a period of years to re-place their children have been up against the judgment of these teachers and administrators. But with greater understanding of the growth process, and after seeing a developmental program in operation, even these educators slowly change.

Part of the unreadiness we are finding is simply related to age—the child is too young or the legal entrance age is too advanced. Fortunately the tendency at present is to put the entrance date back to September first from its previous date of December thirty-first or even later. Thus in many states the child is now required to be fully 5 when he enters kindergarten or 6 when he enters first grade. Here we would wish to compliment those Southern states which have their cutoff dates closest to September first.

But even with a September first cutoff date there are many children who are still behind and who need extra time—six months, one year or even two years. That is why each child needs to be examined individually. And that is why the school needs to provide a meaningful curriculum. If a child is still functioning at a 5-year level though he may be 6 or 6½, he should be placed in an advanced kindergarten situation rather than in a 5½-year-old group. And if he is two years behind, he should not enter first grade until he is 8 years of age. To see one of these older-in-age first graders in action may someday convince us that the European tendency to have children enter first grade at 7 years of age is a valid one.

We are not alone in our research findings as to the importance of behavior age in determining school placement. Confirmation of the usefulness of the Gesell Developmental Tests comes from a number of sources. One of the most impressive confirmations comes from Arthur R. Jensen of California, who comments that "Readiness in the cognitive sphere is largely the ability to conceptualize the learning task, to grasp the aim of one's efforts long before achieving mastery of the task.

"The relative ineffectiveness of shaping one's behavior to external requirements as compared with internal requirements is perhaps seen most dramatically in the child's efforts to copy geometric figures of varying difficulty. Unless the child can internalize conceptual representations of the figure, he cannot copy it, even though the model is directly before him. Partly for this reason, as well as for its correlations with school readiness, the Ilg and Ames figure copying test is probably one of the most convincing and valuable measures of cognitive development in the preschool years and throughout the primary grades. It shows very clear-cut age differences, and the ten figures come close to being a true scale in the Gutman sense."

We have often been asked how our work compares with that of Piaget. We have always been deeply interested in Piaget's writings. Our point of view is extremely similar to his, though the emphasis is somewhat different since we do not separate out cognition as such from the rest of behavior.

Alan Kaufman of the Psychological Corporation has recently carried out a study to see whether the clinically developed tasks of Gesell and Piaget stand up to the rigors of psychometric analysis and also to check on the reliability of these tests. His study showed that the Gesell Scale does demonstrate reliability. He also found a rather high correlation (.64) between performance on a battery of Piaget tests and on the Gesell Developmental Scale. Further follow-up studies by Kaufman are now checking on the predictive validity of our tests. Preliminary results suggest that they do provide an effective prediction of school readiness.

If we ourselves had to choose one special part of our test battery to determine the readiness of a child we would choose the Incomplete Man Test. We have known distraught developmental examiners, such as the one who was suddenly deluged with thirty-seven new pupils in the early grades the first day of school. She decided just to give them the Incomplete Man Test. Before the day was out she had placed all thirty-seven by means of this one test alone, and later discovered that she had missed out on the placement of only two children.

This developmental examiner's success has been corroborated by Joan Chase of Ohio in a computerized attempt to determine which clinical measures correlated most highly with the actual promotion decisions of a group of first-grade teachers. The clinical data reviewed by her were voluminous. The most highly predictive of all the measures used was the Gesell Incomplete Man Test.

All our findings suggest that no matter how good the instruction and how adequate the school situation, boys and girls still need to have attained a certain level of readiness or of behavioral maturity before successful learning can take place. The demands of the learning situation must match the child's behavioral maturity.

The practical application of this concept is beginning to bear fruit and is triggering considerable research. A recent report comes from a town in California where a developmental program has been in force for a period of two years. Three schools were compared, one with a traditional program, a second with an Elementary and Secondary Education Act program, and a third with a developmental placement program. The traditional school started out the highest in kindergarten. The ESEA and the developmental placement school were closely matched. By the beginning of first grade, however, the ESEA school had definitely lost ground and the developmental placement program was far out in front, especially in the extended first-grade program. The traditional school, which had been in the lead to begin with, had lost considerable ground. Therefore this particular community is planning to extend the developmental placement program to all of its elementary schools. But we must emphasize that the success of such a program is dependent upon the groundwork laid down and the inclusion and cooperation of all those involved—teachers, parents, administrators.

Our own greatest lack has been our inadequacy in advising schools and teachers as to what to do with their children after they have placed them developmentally. We know that 4½-year-old groups need pretty much of a nursery school regime. We know that 5½-year-old groups should not be treated as first-grade groups, though they often are.

Fortunately, one of our New Hampshire contingents, *The New Hampshire School Readiness Project,* Title III of ESEA 1965, has written a pamphlet entitled *School Readiness, One Piece of the Puzzle,*[1] in which they not only discuss the readiness concept but also give a full accounting of their 5½-year-old groups (which they classify as pre-first grades). They give some very specific ideas as to how to facilitate an environment for learning at this pre-first-grade level. We highly recommend the reading of this pamphlet for anyone seriously interested in starting a developmental placement program. It is now for us to do further research on developmental curriculums at least from 4½ to 8 years of age, with the intervening ages of 6½ and 7½ not to be forgotten.

We know that much help and support needs to be given to any school system that is contemplating starting a developmental program. We recommend a slow start preceded by informing both parent and teacher groups, preferably in small units of eight to ten persons, as to what the program is about. Initially only one school in a school district should be chosen, as a pilot school. Without a principal who is committed to the program, no success can be anticipated. A developmental examiner,

---

[1] This publication is available gratis from New Hampshire State Title III Office, 64 N. Main Street, Concord, New Hampshire, 03301.

preferably chosen from the teacher ranks of the school in question, should be trained and given an office, however small, with a telephone on a jack to be disconnected when she is examining. This is no part-time job. It needs full attention.

Unfortunately it is a job so far without background, without certification, and without sources of training except through in-service facilities and self-learning on the job. Each developmental examiner (more often a woman than a man) must make the job her own. She needs to move slowly from grade to grade, one year at a time, knowing each child not only individually through the developmental examination but also as a member of his group. She needs to interview each teacher about each of her children at the end of every year. All of the teachers at a grade level need to be involved in the ultimate placement of each child for the upcoming year.

It is a complicated process, in which the child's scholastic achievement is considered as only one part of his total growth. A child may be achieving very well but still be very immature emotionally and unable to cope with the social functioning of his group. Proper placement demands a sound judgment on the part of principal, teacher, and examiner as well as the use of the usual achievement scores.

It takes at least five years to produce a growing, smoothly running developmental placement program. The first two years are the hardest. With an informed parent and teacher group, possible resistances of both groups slowly evaporate. Parents often report a child changed for the better at home when he is no longer under the stress of overplacement. Teachers report that for the first time they feel like teachers. They no longer need to spend so much time on discipline and noise level. They can now spend their time freely and happily teaching children or responding to their pupils' needs. Those teachers who may have resisted a curriculum assigned to them now find that this same curriculum works well as long as their children are ready for their assignments.

To be sure, most good teachers are exhausted by the end of the day, but they now report that they are happily exhausted because they have been so successful. This has been especially true at one of our oldest strongholds, Cheshire, Connecticut, where a developmental placement program went into operation in 1965 and now has been extended to all five elementary schools.

To assist the developmental examiner in her long, slow self-training, we have made available two sets of cards—one on the Copy Forms, the other on the Incomplete Man Test. These cards depict typical responses from 4½ to 10 years, and will, it is hoped, prove a useful supplement to information given in the present text.

A companion volume, *Is Your Child in the Wrong Grade?* (Harper & Row, 1967), was written primarily for parents, but has also proved helpful to teachers who need to make parents aware of the importance of school readiness and correct grade placement. Another book, *Stop School Failure,* by Ames, Gillespie and Streff (Harper & Row, 1972), may add a new dimension to this total field with its chapters on perception and vision.

As the reader will see, our work is never ending. We hope to simplify the execution of the developmental placement program in time. The child speaks out very clearly in many different ways. It is for us to have ears to hear what he is saying, and eyes to see what he is doing. Even now we are working on a new projective task of "draw a colored tree," which rarely takes a child more than five minutes to accomplish and can tell us much.

It is the developmental point of view that guides us and carries us through this demanding task of evaluating and properly placing each individual child. May this volume be only the beginning of a long and successful quest.

FRANCES L. ILG
LOUISE BATES AMES

New Haven, Connecticut
February 23, 1972

"*Unfortunately, we are too inclined to talk of man as it would be desirable for him to be rather than as he really is. . . . True education can proceed only from naked reality, not from any ideal illusion about man, however attractive.*"

CARL JUNG

PART I
INTRODUCTION

CHAPTER 1

A POINT OF VIEW

||||||||||||||||||||||||||||||||||||||||||||||||||||||||||||||||||||||||

Education sometimes seems to be interested in everything except the child.

This statement may sound both harsh and blatantly untrue. Many educators may be shocked by both its impact and its implication. Yet it contains at least a suggestion of truth.

In this post-Sputnik era since 1957, American education as a whole has been subjected to sharp criticism. The various curricula have been scrutinized and found wanting. The adequacy of teachers and their training has not fared much better. Our school systems have been compared with foreign systems, most often to our disadvantage. The fact that we were comparing similar grade levels with no concern for the fact that some foreign countries do not allow their children to enter first grade before 7 years of age has not modified the critics' reports. The child in his own individual right, which includes his own rate of growth, has been neglected in these evaluations. What was being taught received first consideration.

There was a time when the educator was very much concerned about the child. He often spoke of the "whole child," thus expressing his interest in the child's total development. But the something needed to give this concept sticking and growing power was lacking in this early period of concern. The educator ended up by giving only lip service to his beliefs. The child himself seemed to be actually no better off than he was before. If anything, the concern for the whole child which was on the verge of arriving at a truth, stimulated lively opposition. Ground that had been gained was lost and so controls were tightened in an effort to hold the child up to ever stricter standards.

Neither of these two approaches, one emphasizing the demands of the child, the other the demands of the environment, took into sufficient

5

account a third most important factor—the growth stage and capacity of the individual child. It is the meshing of these three factors—first, the child at a certain age or level of growth; second, the child as a unique individual; and lastly, the child living in a certain environment—which any educator must keep in mind in order to be successful.

In our own research we have given major and primary attention to developmental expressions of age. We have been astonished by the recurrent comparable expressions of developmental age, and by the recurring similarities of behavioral patterning as it changed from age to age. Though we also have great concern for variations in timing and quality of expression in different individuals, we can only allude to these incidentally in the present volume. A fuller treatment of individual differences is needed at a later date.

As to the third factor, the impact of the environment on the child, we need to elicit the help of the educator whose laboratory is primarily concerned with this factor. We would wish to give help in revealing the child in his own right, regarding both his developmental age and his individual expression, so that the educator may more effectively provide an environment which can easily mesh with the child and with his capacity to receive.

The need for accommodation of the environment to both age and individual differences becomes evident from the moment of a child's birth. We found it especially evident in our research on infant feeding. As hard as a mother may try to impose a rigid schedule on some infants, she is not successful unless she responds to their individual demands. These demands are most marked in the first 12 weeks. The success of feeding in this period depends upon the environment's capacity to accommodate itself to the child.

By 12 to 16 weeks the need of the environment to accommodate grows strikingly less, and a certain predictable order can be established. The parent who has been rigid in her demands, who has doggedly lived through those first 12 weeks imposing her will in the form of a rigid scheduling, may misinterpret her success at 12 to 16 weeks by concluding that her baby has had a successful learning experience. She does not realize that growth itself has taken over and that by her rigid early demands she has missed, in those early weeks, the potential give and take between herself and her child. Both mother and baby will have come through this period, but both are in danger of coming through with a potential deficit.

A mother needs to attune herself to the two facets expressed by her child—that of demand and that of adaptation. If these two are allowed to come into balance, they can produce a self-regulation which allows the child to express himself in his own right. At one time the demands of the individual, influenced by his age and his individuality, will be in the ascendancy. At another time his response to the demands of the environment is dominant. It is necessary for the environment to be responsive to these changing expressions of the growth process.

This demand of the adult—parent or teacher—that he accommodate to all of these different needs of the child, may seem too complicated and bewildering to some, who may feel more comfortable in caring for the child through one of the two extremes of either rigid control or of loose permissiveness. What is worse, they may vacillate between the two, thus failing to give the child a chance to grow within the limits of his own reality. They remain ignorant of or unresponsive to the laws of growth. They choose what is to them the easiest way. In the end it may turn out to be the hardest way for the child, who is thus deprived of the opportunity to find himself.

It is for us in child development to make the adult's task easier and more within his reach. We need to simplify basic concepts so that we can translate them into meaningful examples that the adult can understand and can compare with his own experience.

There is no more rapid learner than a parent or a teacher living with a growing child. We need, if we can, to unlock the door of insight so that the adult can see the child more clearly. But we as child specialists must ever check ourselves, knowing that the idea or the theory can never be substituted for the reality of the lived experience. It is the lived experience between the child and his parent, the child and his teacher, the child and his friend (and also his sibling), the child and his dog, the child and himself that becomes important.

By studying and documenting what we see and interpret, we hope to provide paths or blueprints to guide parents and teachers. But it is the child through his multiple relationships who alone can travel the path. We cannot live for another person, but he in turn cannot live in a vacuum. He moves through people and experiences and makes them his own.

Stages and Cycles of Growth

One of our blueprints which we have revised repeatedly over the years deals with stages and cycles of growth. Those who are conceptually minded may find this description of ages and stages of practical interest and use. Others may find it less meaningful, but should at least be comforted to know that striking growth changes do occur, that a child does move through stages—some better, some worse.

In our initial work with the preschooler our sights were spotty. We could identify certain stages but not the total flow of development. Thus we recognized the 2½-year-old in his ambivalent stage of wanting to go in two directions at once and, when this turned out to be impossible, exploding in temper. We recognized the happy, well-adjusted 3-year-old, the querulous, unsure 3½-year-old, the out-of-bounds 4-year-old. Somehow we felt that there must be a flow of relationship between these various stages—a basic ground plan which would pull them all together in a unified pattern.

It was not until our work with the child from 5 to 10 that a clearer order began to emerge. How to express this order became our problem. At first we used words to summarize the ages:

> 6 years: initiation
> 7 years: impression
> 8 years: expression
> 9 years: exploitation

However, such description was inadequate since it still did not give a flow of development. And also it did not cover four salient age periods —5 years, 5½ years, 6½ years, and 10 years. A next step was to use some form or analogy which would include all the stages as we saw them. The golf stroke came to mind:

> 5 years: a focal stage with the eye on the ball
> 5½–6 years: a breakup stage of reposturing, getting ready for the stroke
> 7 years: the backstroke, building up power to drive through
> 8 years: the drive through
> 9 years: the landing of the ball, the culmination of all previous stages
> 10 years: ready to tee off again

This analogy was more satisfactory, but we felt it did not do full justice to the important stages of 5½, 6, and 6½, a breakup and reorganization period when emotions well up to meet and fuse with new intellectual interests.

It was then that we thought of the wave in all of its phases of movement—of calm, of boiling, of form into trough and crest, and return to calm. Here was an expression of nature which could be seen in rapid, successive phases. The growth of the individual seems to express the same phases or stages even though much more slowly, since the stages in this instance require months or even years. This concept of the wave has served well to cover behavior changes in the age range from 2 through 16 years.

The following diagram expresses graphically the form of the wave as it indicates the ages of the changing stages in three cycles of growth which correspond to each phase of the wave in action:

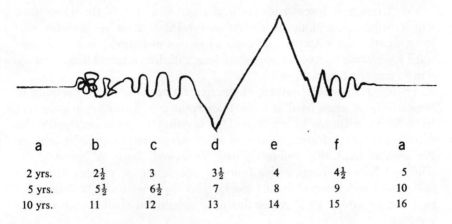

a	b	c	d	e	f	a
2 yrs.	2½	3	3½	4	4½	5
5 yrs.	5½	6½	7	8	9	10
10 yrs.	11	12	13	14	15	16

This analogy of the wave is of course only a descriptive aid. It is useful to have a form to measure against, but we must remember that it is only a description and not a reality. However it is healthy and helpful to know that a child does go through stages. Such knowledge can forewarn us about "bad" stages and, what's more, can enable us to look forward to and eventually enjoy the "good" stages.

In summary, these six successive stages which occur repeatedly in the years from 2 to 16 may be described as follows:

a. This is a stage of calm, of integration, of meshing with the environment. Who is more delightfully affectionate than the 2-year-old, nicer to have around than the 5-year-old, more casual and appreciative of his parents than the 10-year-old?

b. Stage *a*, however, is the calm before the storm of stage *b* when boiling and bubbling begins to occur. Two-and-a-half may well earn his name of King or Emperor, five-and-a-half, of devil or angel, and eleven of spitfire. But it is from this matrix of growth, of tapping new sources, that a child's future growth emerges.

c. What a pleasant change occurs at stage *c* when an organization of opposites takes place! The 3-year-old becomes ready for nursery school, the 6½-year-old is judged to be a pleasure in the classroom, and the 12-year-old is spoken of as mature, even though this maturity may be only a passing phase.

d. Nothing is static, or should be, in growth. Thus the inwardizing of stage *d*, the trough of the wave, follows naturally the *c*-stage when forces were in better balance. At each repetition of this phase, the child withdraws in his own way. Three-and-a-half wants to stay in the house, seven wishes a room of his own, and thirteen wants to set up housekeeping in his own room, and seldom emerges. This can be a difficult stage, but it provides a needed time for the building up of new forces.

e. These new forces rush forth at stage *e,* a crest-of-the-wave stage which brings marvelous expansion and release. It is no wonder that FOUR, EIGHT, and FOURTEEN all tend to go out-of-bounds. But what outward joyousness in contrast to the anxious withdrawn mumblings of stage *d* in its trough of inwardness!

f. Stage *f* is one of return, of reorganization, of intricate meshing of forces. Who is more hard at work than FOUR-AND-A-HALF separating fact from fancy, wanting to grasp reality, wanting to make ready for the demands of more formal schooling in kindergarten? And who is more the scholar than the well-integrated 9-year-old, busy in knowing the why and how of things in his fourth grade activities, curious about all things and independent in his work? This 9-year-old self is catapulted to a higher power at 15 when learning should be challenging and rewarding.

And so it goes, stage following stage and cycle following cycle. To help the child grow more fully through these stages, one must have a better idea of what the child is going through so that one can better accommodate him by knowing when to make a firm stand and when not to. It is also important to recognize when complaints on the part of the child are real, and when they are possibly imaginary. The sore throat complaints of the 6-year-old may well be valid, but the multiple complaints of the 9-year-old often disappear when they are overridden.

(It is important to note that growth is slowing down as it moves through succeeding cycles. In the cycle from 2 to 5 years of age, 3 years elapse, 5 years from 5 to 10, and 6 years from 10 to 16.)

Individuality

Not all children, however, go through all of these stages, even though perhaps the majority do. When a parent reads in one of our books about a child of a certain age level and reports, "You have described my child exactly," then we know that this is a child who is moving through the usual stages of development fully and with clarity. Such children are usually well constituted. Their timing is accurate, or relatively so. They do what is expected of them at certain times. They have good grasping mechanisms and know when to start. They have equally good release mechanisms and know when to stop, to let go—so that they can move on into new territory. These are the children who are easy to teach. These are the children who are often self-taught. They are constantly in the process of discovering. They are a joy in the classroom.

Other parents complain that they can't find their child in the usual age descriptions. These are often the children who are highly individuated. They are always themselves rather than their age—at least so it seems. Their timing as well as their pattern of growth is their own.

This individuation may of course be expressed in many different ways. There are, for instance, those children who show an impulsive nature with a rapid grasp and release mechanism which doesn't allow them to travel the path of growth needed to integrate inner and outer forces into a firm fabric or foundation. Their behavior is like the sudden turning on of an incandescent light which radiates in all directions. Just as suddenly the light can burn itself out. This type of individual is often spoken of as brilliant, but along with this compliment may come the complaint that the child lacks sticking power, that he wants to succeed too quickly. If he doesn't succeed quickly he is apt to give up. Without help in developing sticking power and putting forth effort, these individuals may come to adult life with all sorts of separate brilliant pieces that haven't been integrated into a useful whole.

An almost opposite type of individuation can occur when there is slowness of grasp and release rather than speed. Such children may be slow to grasp but when they have once secured their hold, they go on and on, elaborating their paths, restricting them to be sure but traveling long distances unless they get into a perseverative rut, which is their danger.

When they can move positively they may become the early experts. This is the 21-monther who can identify 300 birds, the 4-year-old who encompasses music through his records, or the 5-year-old who knows the names of all the fish in the seven seas. Rather than being incandescent bulbs radiating their light widely though briefly, these individuals are like lasers with coherent light that concentrates but shows no tendency to spread. They are exasperating in a different kind of way from their incandescent friends. Rather than releasing too quickly, they hold on too long. It can become very wearing to have to bow to their interests, to feed them their restricted diet, to restrict so much of their living to satisfy their demands. Such children need help both in grasping new areas before it is too late, and in releasing too prolonged behavior before it takes over in an automatic way.

These are only two of countless possible individuations showing extremes of behavior. Any such highly individuated persons are over-balanced on the inner side of growth. They move primarily from themselves outward. That is why they are so often dubbed egocentric or selfish. They suffer from a lack of self and thus they cling tenaciously to the little self they possess. It is only as this self grows that they can reach out to other selves or respond to the environment around them. We need to satisfy their inner-self urge while at the same time holding a firm hand, since they do not respond to their environment in an expected way, especially in their early years. More often than not stimulation from without is too much for such children to absorb. It rather tends to set them in wild movement, making them go faster and faster until they fall into pieces themselves or produce such chaos in the environment that they need to be removed from the presence of others.

These highly individuated children who seem moved almost entirely by their own inner forces can be the disruptive children in the classroom. These are the ones for whom placement in the group needs to be very carefully considered. Maybe entrance into school should be delayed, or such reduced attendance as only two mornings a week in kindergarten, or Wednesdays off in first grade, should be considered. Special laws and rules need to be laid down for them. Daily reminders need to be used as props. Such children need to learn that a certain kind of behavior cannot be tolerated and that one earns the right to go to school.

A third method of growth is one that moves neither through the usual stages nor through strong individuation. It just does not move as we might wish and expect. It is responsive, but without the inner emotional support one would hope to find. These are the children we speak of as being "reality-bound," the ones who learn through doing, who are dependent upon being shown very specifically, who, as their name implies, are bound down by reality in its most literal sense.

These are the children who so frequently need remedial help. We need to know more than we do about the method and rate of growth of such children, and to face the reality of our findings, however low they may be. We need to find out how to tap the inner sources of such children, how to discover their individual interests, which can be very strong if only they can be identified. We need to set up a whole new timetable, however slow it may be, which will fit their growth and behavior.

Implications for Grouping

Various forms of grouping of ages have been tried out in our schools and have been adhered to with varying levels of passion and success. Some have worked out, some haven't.

We believe there could be more natural cleavage points than are sometimes used, especially when careful and correct grade placement has been exercised as the basis for grouping.

In this age period from 5 to 10 years it seems to us that a natural cleavage point comes at 8 years, another at 11 years. Therefore we would favor two clusterings of grades in this period, the first to include the 3 years from kindergarten through second grade, and the next the 3 years from third through fifth grade.

In looking at these groupings more carefully it becomes apparent that the child of 5 to 7 doesn't have the stamina in energy or adaptability that he will develop by 8 years of age. Children of these earlier ages would profit by some reduction in school attendance. But more important, these younger children need to be allowed to progress at their own rate. They need to find their place. They need to be made ready for the rigors and the greater demands of the 8- to 10-year grouping.

It is understandable that the concept of an ungraded setup has arisen for this age group of 5 to 7. Such an approach has some definite advantages. However we would prefer to place the child in this age range more selectively and more specifically, since a child needs not only to go at his own pace, but also benefits from the stimulation of others who are progressing as he is. He thrives on an environment geared to him. When he is in a group that is operating more as a unit, his own adjustment is more easily discerned.

Within this initial 3-year period the child should be helped to find his place in a group suited to him. The rate and method of growth of most children can be picked up in kindergarten. Some, however, do not reveal themselves clearly until the more demanding learning situations of first grade. And still others may not expose their difficulties in putting forth effort and completing their assignments until they meet the more rigorous demands of second grade.

By third grade, if we accept and apply our developmental findings about each individual child, there should ideally be no misfits or failures, except perhaps in a matter of degree. This means that a child should not be passed into third grade until he is more or less at a full 8-year-old level developmentally (regardless of his age in years), and ready to accept the demands both of the age and of the grade. Academic demands will be even more strenuous in the fourth grade, wherefore he will need to be even more ready to accept them.

Most children can be placed in regular class grouping according to their rate of growth. But there will be some who will stand out clearly in this early 3 years as unsuited to the regular stream of education. There will come the time when any regular class group can no longer absorb them, when they will need to be sidetracked at least for their academic training.

This adjustment should definitely be made before third grade. It is for such children that we recommend an ungraded setup—a group of about 15 children or even fewer, from the ages of 7 or 8 to 12 or 13 years. This group would include the extremes of the "reality-bound" child with normal potentials and of the highly individuated child, often very brilliant, who cannot adjust to the demands of the regular school group.

Though this book does not deal with the older ages, we would like to comment on school grouping for the years 11 to 15. We feel that the very real preadolescent upheaval changes that occur in the 11-year-old relate him more to the 12- than to the 10-year-old. We believe, however, that he is not ready to move out into the community by joining an unwieldy large group at a junior high school level. We doubt that TWELVE or THIRTEEN shows himself ready for such a move, either. We would prefer to keep these three ages of 11, 12, and 13 together, related but partially separated from their elementary school unit, with opportunities to intercommunicate with similar grades in other schools.

It is FOURTEEN who is ready to expand, to go out into the community. But since he tends to go out of bounds, he is best held in a smaller unit of just 14-year-olds. With such an arrangement, which has already been tried successfully in some communities, his strong desire to socialize can be more easily contained. At this time, an important decision can be made as to whether he should pursue an intellectual or a practical course or even go away to school in the tenth grade. Such an arrangement of putting FOURTEEN by himself both enriches his life and allows a decision to be made about his future within the context of a good successful school experience.

In these introductory statements we have hoped to express a point of view and to suggest its possible implications for primary school education. We hope that this chapter will have oriented the reader's thinking so that he will be receptive to what is to come. Our aim is to arrive at some unifying method of viewing the child so that we shall always see him as a whole, see him as himself. In the past, educational methods have too often fragmented him or have restricted their appraisal in judging him to some single aspect of his growth.

It is through developmental thinking and the use of certain tools that reveal the developmental process, that we have reached our present point of view. It is through this same developmental thinking and through these same tools, more specifically the developmental examination as described in this volume, that we hope the child will be enabled to reveal himself as a total individual, telling us about his level and method of growing and his state of readiness for the different stages of the educative process.

Possibly the greatest single contribution which can be made toward guaranteeing that each individual child will get the most possible out of his school experience is to make certain that he starts that school experience at what is for him the "right" time. This should be the time when he is truly ready and not merely some time arbitrarily decided upon by custom or by the law. In the succeeding chapter we shall discuss various possible criteria for determining when the child shall start his school career.

CHAPTER 2

CRITERIA FOR SCHOOL ENTRANCE

Over the years there have been many different measures used for determining a child's readiness to start school. Before the advent of the kindergarten, first grade entrance was generally associated with the age of 6 years and the eruption of the 6-year molars. The problem did not seem very difficult in earlier days. The level of success of different children was expected to vary, but groups were small and there was time for individual attention.

When formal legislation began to make school attendance compulsory, classes became larger and problems raised by those children not actually ready for the grade to which age assigned them became more serious. If there were no kindergarten facilities available in a community, the tendency was to allow an increasing number of children who seemed ready to enter first grade before they were 6. This trend may well have been stimulated by parents, moved either by pride or by an inadvertent tendency to push their children. The schools accommodated, and kept changing the age of entrance into first grade until, in some, it reached March 1 of the previous year, thus allowing a child of $5\frac{1}{2}$ to enter first grade.

Fortunately, the evidences of failure or strain on the too-young child soon became sufficiently apparent to most educators so that they began slowly to reverse this trend toward a younger entrance age. Thus the age of school entrance has steadily increased in most communities in the United States through the slow reversal of the date line.

The main weakness of chronological age as a criterion for school entrance is that even if we could determine exactly the age at which the average girl or boy is ready to start kindergarten or first grade, any *average* would still imply that only 50% of any group of children might be expected to fall close enough to this average to insure their reasonable readiness. There would still be a great many exceptions to any general rule.

However, chronological age still remains the chief criterion for school entrance in most schools. At present it varies from a child's being permitted to enter first grade if he is 6 by September 1 to his being permitted to enter first grade if he will be 6 by the succeeding January 31.

Table 1 summarizes the current entrance requirements among the

TABLE 1   *Age Required by Different States for Entrance to First Grade*

Required Date	Age at Entrance	Number of States
No date set		11
Local decision, no statewide policy		6
6 by January 31	5^7	1
6 by December 31	5^8	11
6 by December 1	5^9	3
6 by some time in November	5^{10}	5
6 by some time in October	5^{11}	6
6 by September 1 or 15 (or merely 6)	6	9
Total		52^a
Median for those with a state-wide date	5^{10}	
Mean for those with a state-wide date	5^9	

^{a} This includes District of Columbia and Puerto Rico.

different states. Though a goodly number tend to admit children to first grade on the younger side (12 states at 5^7 and 5^8), the trend is toward delaying their entrance until they are 5^{10} to 6 years (20 states). This is a healthy trend and shows a good awareness of the importance of adequate age.

If chronological age alone must be used as an entrance criterion, our experience favors the older age allowed by a September 1 date line. However, even this does not allow for the fact, generally accepted, that the development of boys in this age range is slower than that of girls.

As an entrance date line became more fixed and rigid, parents' demands for exceptions to the rule became more and more pressing. Some new criterion seemed needed to determine whether a child younger than the date line requirement might still be ready for the demands of any given grade.

This need of some method of determining possible exceptions arose at a time when the intelligence test had come into high favor and the so-called IQ was being considered an all-important factor in measuring a child's ability. An apparently logical conclusion was thus drawn that if the intelligence of a child was found to be superior, he must be moving at a more rapid rate than average, and even though on the young side, he was thought to be able to compete with older children in the school situation. Entrance into school was thus determined in many communities by the IQ rating. A child with a high IQ was often allowed to start school even though he might not be legally old enough to do so. The belief was that his intelligence would carry him through.

It soon became evident, however, that intelligence is only one part of the child's total personality. A mere intelligence test does not and cannot attempt to measure a child's level of maturity. A child may be of clearly superior intelligence but may at the same time be behind others of his age in either physical or behavioral maturity. This combination is so common in boys that we have coined the term "superior-immature," which indicates that a child is well above average in intelligence but below average in behavioral maturity.

When neither age nor intelligence was found fully adequate as a school-entrance criterion, the educator became more concerned about finding other possible measures of a child's readiness. Thus, school-readiness tests were devised, many of them with special emphasis on determining readiness for reading. We ourselves were much interested in Marion Monroe's battery of Reading Aptitude tests, and found two of these tests so valuable that we have included them in our present series of developmental tests. The Metropolitan test is another good readiness test still used extensively and with a fair amount of success.

But these and other so-called readiness tests in actual practice proved to fall considerably short of an evaluation of the total organism. Some measured only reading readiness as such. Others turned out to correlate more closely with the IQ than with the total developmental level of each individual child. Thus a child who reads at or even considerably above his age level might still be merely at age or even below in other areas of behavior.

What we really need to know in determining readiness for school entrance is a child's *developmental level*. We need to know at what age he is behaving as a total organism. This is not a measure of his level of physical maturity, though physical maturity or immaturity can provide supporting evidence. More often than not physical immaturity, such as slow teething, does go along with behavioral immaturity. Similarly, physical maturity may go along with behavioral maturity. We are aware, however, that any such correlations, though helpful, are subject to many exceptions and must be used with great caution.

Fifty years of experience in the use of a battery of developmental tests has shown that the child's developmental level can be determined through the use of such behavior tests. We shall present in this volume normative portraits of behavior which can be expected at each age level from 5 to 10 years, so that educators can match any given child's performance against these age norms. Though any child's behavior level may be somewhat uneven—that is, he could be performing on some tests at a higher or lower level than on others—it is possible for a trained examiner to make a reasonably objective evaluation of the general level at which any given child is responding.

The child's behavioral level may, of course, be at, above, or below the level of his chronological age. But it is his behavioral level rather than his age in years which we consider to be the correct clue to good grade placement.

We agree with current school-entrance practice in that it assumes a 5-year-old level of behavior to be necessary before a child can effectively carry out the work expected of a kindergartener in most schools; a 6-year-old level of behavior necessary before a child can do first grade work.

Where we disagree with current school-entrance practice is in its implied assumption that a chronological age of 5 guarantees 5-year-old behavior. We prefer to reckon 5-year-oldness in terms of behavior rather than in terms of age in years. Thus regardless of age in years, we consider that a child's general *performance* needs to be at a 5-year-old level before he enters kindergarten, and at a 6-year-old level before he enters first grade.

We propose that every child be given an individual behavior examination and that his level of performance be determined at the time he is being considered for school entrance, and if possible, whenever promotion to a succeeding grade is being considered.

Our first experience in giving a battery of behavior tests to determine the extent to which school performance level corresponds with chronological age was a research study conducted in the Hurlbutt school in Weston, Connecticut. It is reported in the following chapter.

CHAPTER *3*

THE WESTON STUDY: HISTORY OF OUR INTEREST IN CORRECT GRADE PLACEMENT

||||||||||||||||||||||||||||||||||||||||||||||||||||||||||||||||||||

The Weston study, our first school-placement study of any scope, can now be reported, chiefly from a historical point of view, but it was a substantial part of our own growth. Without it we could not have been certain of the need of a standardization study of the developmental examination which is the heart of this book, nor could we have foreseen the application of our school-placement findings in our present North Haven study. Now after the first lap of the North Haven study we are able to reinterpret some of our Weston findings and realize what they meant and where they were leading.

The Weston study came about as an outgrowth of a consultation service we performed for the Fund for the Advancement of Education in 1956. The Fund was at that time exploring the use of Teacher Aides. We welcomed this, our first opportunity to go into the schools and to act as consultants. We had previously been in close contact with educational facilities, but chiefly to carry out our own research in defining age levels and in describing behavior characteristics of the several grade levels.

Through our clinical service over the years we have become aware of a serious degree of overplacement in schools. In fact, the majority of the children brought to us because of difficulties in school were found to be overplaced. This was not always their whole problem, but it was usually at least an important part of their problem. We wondered, however, if our impression of the extent of this overplacement might not be exaggerated because of the fact that the children who came to us were children already in trouble. Our experience in Weston soon showed us

19

that the problem of overplacement was even greater than we had supposed.

In our consultation service for the Fund, we were impressed by the Teacher Aide program, especially in that those children who needed extra attention received it by this means, and thus many of the burdens of an overworked teacher were alleviated.

But, over and over again, we questioned the presence of certain children in a group. So many of these children who needed extra attention were obviously too young either in age or behavior or both. So many simply couldn't keep up with the work, let alone understand what was expected of them. These were often the daydreamers, or the ones who busied themselves in odd sorts of ways such as trips to the pencil sharpener, the bathroom, or the nurse's office.

We became so aware of these misfits that we tried to spot them as soon as we began to observe in a new classroom. Very soon we came to realize that the very ones we had spotted were more often than not given over to the Teacher Aide for extra attention or help. This extra help afforded definite relief for the teacher and a better experience for the child—but was this the best way to solve the problem?

Was there a danger that the schools were only patching up a problem rather than solving it? Might not one of the chief difficulties of these children who appeared as misfits be that they were merely too young for the grade? We had seen many children of this variety on our clinical service; they did surprisingly well once they were placed in the grade they should have been in.

We also noted that a number of those who were not catching on, who tended to escape, had already been held back a year or two and still weren't moving with their group. Again we recalled our clinical experience and wondered how many of these children might be what we called "reality-bound." This, as we have previously explained, is a term we use for children who seem to need to be taught with real things, things they can put their hands on. Such children abstract poorly and find it difficult to learn through the more usual methods of teaching. Merely holding such children back doesn't help enough. We had already noted that as soon as these children are two years behind their original class they are completely out of the running, unable to keep up with the group even at this slower pace.

With this initial experience of being able to spot misfits in the classroom relatively quickly, our own past clinical experience began to take on more validity. We soon came to suspect that the problem of overplacement was far more universal than we might originally have predicted. It was then that we approached the Fund for the Advancement of Education for support for the study on school placement which we felt needed to be carried out. It was then that the Weston study came into being.

This study was initially conceived as a one-year pilot study but was later extended to three years. We chose the Hurlbutt school in Weston, Connecticut. Weston was not only a fairly nearby community, but more than that, the principal of its single elementary school, Mr. Edward Summerton, was sympathetic to our work and eager to put our theories to a test. We realized that any study which attempted to examine a large number of children individually would require good cooperation on the part of the school staff.

Weston suited our purposes nicely because it is a community of a fairly broad base even though a fair proportion of its population commutes to New York and may be classed as being in an above average socio-economic group. The majority of the children, too, showed a high average or better level of intelligence.

We picked one kindergarten, one first, and one second grade out of three or four available at each grade level. Each group contained from 20 to 30 children.

We examined the kindergarten group as a starter, evaluating each child first through a developmental examination as described in Chapter 5, secondly through the use of two projective techniques (the Rorschach and the Lowenfeld Mosaic tests), and thirdly through a battery of visual tests plus the Keystone Visual Skills series. The three areas of approach were conducted by three separate examiners—the two authors of this volume and Dr. Richard J. Apell.

It became apparent, very shortly after we began, that at least 40% of the kindergarten group we had chosen were overplaced, by our standards. This finding was so disquieting that we feared we might have inadvertently picked a poor or "low" group. We therefore considered it advisable to include in our study the entire kindergarten population of around 100 children. Fortunately we were able to carry this total kindergarten group, with some inevitable losses to be sure, over the proposed period of 3 years. We restricted the first and second grade coverage to the single classes we had chosen in the beginning, following them longitudinally over the 3-year period, but recognizing the disadvantages of such small groups.

All tests were given annually in the 3 successive school years from the fall of 1957 to the spring of 1959. After each test—developmental, projective, or visual—was given and scored, the examiner giving the test rated each subject as +, ±, or − with regard to readiness for the grade to which the school had assigned him on the basis of his chronological age. (In Weston a child was admitted to kindergarten if he became 5 before December 31.)

A rating of + meant that the child was ready for the grade he was in, and was potentially capable of being promoted to the next grade at the end of the year. The scoring of ± meant that there was a question, both about his being in the grade he was in, and about his being ready to be passed on into the next grade at the end of the year. A − score indicated clearly that a child did not belong in the grade in which he was placed and would not be able to be promoted at the end of the school year.

In weekly meetings the three examiners reported as a group on their +, ±, and − decisions about each child and discussed the child's response in detail. In this way a complete running record was kept not only of objective scorings for each child, but also of qualitative judgments as to each child's performance in each of the three types of test.

Questions to Be Answered[1]

The chief questions to be answered by this investigation, and the answers determined, follow.

1. PERCENTAGE OF READINESS

The first question was: What percentage of a public-school population, on the basis of standard developmental, projective, and visual tests, will be judged ready, questionable, and unready for the school grade in which their chronological age has automatically placed them?

Table 2 gives data in answer to this question. As this table shows, insofar as the developmental test ratings are concerned, in only the first grade, and on the final test for the kindergarten group given at the end of second grade, were as many as 50% of subjects ready for the grade in which their age had placed them. The percentage of children who were ready ranged from 34.5% to 59%. The percentage clearly showing unreadiness ranged from 9% to 31% for the different groups. The number of subjects judged as questionable ranged from 30% to 40%.

Readiness was shown to be only slightly greater according to the visual tests. The percentage of those fully ready, in the different groups, ranged from 44% to 68%. The number who were clearly unready ranged from 9% to 21%. A substantial number, ranging from 23% to 36%, fell in the questionable category.

According to the Rorschach findings, except in the kindergarten group, slightly over 50% were judged ready on each test. The percentage showing readiness ranged from 38% to 59%. The Mosaic findings gave more subjects a + rating than did any of the other tests used. The per-

---

[1] Weston findings are reported in full in Frances L. Ilg, Louise B. Ames, and Richard J. Apell, "School Readiness as Evaluated by Gesell Developmental, Visual and Projective Tests," *Genet. Psychol. Monogr.*, in press.

TABLE 2   *Percentage of All Cases Seen Consistently Which Are Ready,*
Questionable, or Not Ready

Grade	Number of Subjects	Ready		Questionable		Unready	
		Test 1	Test 4[a]	Test 1	Test 4	Test 1	Test 4
Developmental							
Kindergarten	69	46	58	40	30	14	12
First grade	22	55	59	36	32	9	9
Second grade	29[a]	38	34.5	38	34.5	24	31
Visual							
Kindergarten	69	44	54	36	30	20	16
First grade	22	50	68	36	23	14	9
Second grade	29	45	52	34.5	28	21	20
Rorschach							
Kindergarten	69	38	43	40	41	22	16
First grade	22	59	59	27	32	14	9
Second grade	29	59	52	27	20	14	28
Mosaic							
Kindergarten	69	45	51	30	33	25	16
First grade	22	68	73	18	18	14	9
Second grade	29	50	56	34.5	24	14	20

[a] For second grade there are only three, not four, successive tests.

centage of subjects obtaining a + rating on the Mosaic ranged from 45% to 73%, though the number which showed unreadiness was approximately the same as on the other tests, ranging from 9% to 25%.

We may compare this group with a North Haven kindergarten group examined in the spring of 1963 at the end of kindergarten. The North Haven evaluation consisted mainly of a developmental appraisal. Table 3 compares the percentage of North Haven kindergarten subjects

TABLE 3   *Developmental Appraisal of Two Kindergarten Groups*

	Weston (%)	North Haven (%)	Recommendation for North Haven for Following Year
Ready	46	32	Promote to regular first
Questionable	40	50	Promote to preprimary or 5½-year-old group
Not ready	14	18	Repeat kindergarten

ready for the grade in which age had placed them with the Weston kindergarten subjects. These figures show more unready children in the North Haven than in the Weston groups, perhaps largely because North Haven judgments were more seasoned and less tentative. We were more ready to accept the evidences of unreadiness as the tests revealed them.

2. CONSISTENCY OF EXAMINER'S RATINGS

The second question asked about the Weston subjects was: How consistent were the ratings of each examiner from year to year? Consistency was highest for the developmental examination, on which 78% of kindergarten, 95% of first grade, and 79% of second grade subjects rated the same on first and final examinations. Next most consistent were the Rorschach ratings which remained the same, first to final tests, in 70%, 91%, and 76% of the three class groups.

Visual findings came next with 81%, 73%, and 76% of kindergarten, first, and second grade groups consistent throughout the years of the study. Finally, the least consistent were the Mosaic findings—with 65%, 77%, and 79% of the three groups showing consistency.

3. RELATIONSHIP OF INTELLIGENCE AND AGE TO READINESS

We were especially interested in exploring the relationship of intelligence and age to readiness. We had assumed that if the children in any school class were divided into three groups—those who were judged ready for the grade they are in, those questionably ready, and those not ready—it would be reasonable to expect that children in the ready group might be of a somewhat higher intelligence and somewhat older than those in the questionable or unready group.

A check on our Weston subjects based on their readiness or unreadiness for their grade as judged by their developmental response, confirmed this expectation for intelligence, but only partially confirmed it with respect to age.

As to intelligence, with only one exception (median IQ score of questionably ready kindergarten subjects was higher than for ready group) the ready subjects for each of the three class groups had a higher mean and median IQ than the questionably ready subjects. These in turn had higher mean and median IQ's than the unready subjects. However for second grade subjects, the median IQ of the questionable group was nearly as good as that of the ready group (see Table 4).

These exceptions are all the more significant since the IQ ratings are so often used by the educator for grade placement. Thus, though a child may be too young for a grade—e.g., a child of 4^8 entering kindergarten—he is considered ready for the grade in many school systems if he has a superior IQ. These are the very children whom we consider as not ready because of their youth. We even have a name for these children—"superior immatures."

As to age, in each group, ready subjects were slightly older at the time of school entrance than the questionably ready subjects. The ready

TABLE 4   *Age and IQ of Subjects Consistently Ready, Questionable, and Unready on Developmental Examination*

| | IQ | | Age | |
	Mean	Median	Mean	Median
Kindergarten				
Ready	116.5	113	5^5	5^6
Questionable	114.3	115.5	5^2	5^1
Unready	99.3	97	5^3	5^2
First grade				
Ready	113.8	115	6^4	$6^{3 \cdot 5}$
Questionable	101.8	104	6^0	$6^{\cdot 5}$
Unready	88	88	7^0	7^0
Second grade				
Ready	114.3	111	7^1	7^1
Questionable	109.9	109	6^9	7^1
Unready	89	93	7^7	7^9

subjects were also older than the unready subjects in kindergarten. However in the first and second grade groups the unready group were on the average 6 or more months older than the ready and questionable subjects. This older average age was undoubtedly a result of the presence of older repeaters in the unready group. Even with added age some of these children were still failing, indicating they probably fell in the group that we describe as "reality-bound," or were otherwise outside of the main stream of education.

It was especially noted that children not yet 5 at the time of kindergarten entrance were more likely to be judged as unready than ready.

4. CORRELATION WITH TEACHER'S RATINGS

The fourth and final question asked was: To what extent could developmental test findings predict, in the fall of any given school year, what a child's progress and success would be during that year as judged by the teacher's evaluation of his progress made at the end of the year?

Correspondence between predictions based on the developmental examination response and the teachers' ratings at the end of any given school year were reasonably high for kindergarten subjects. With minor exceptions, this agreement decreased with added age and higher grade placement. Thus for comparisons made during the first year of this study there was 83% agreement between results of the developmental examination and the teachers' estimates for kindergarten subjects.

For first grade subjects (that is first graders seen the first year of the study) the agreement was only 68%. For second graders seen during the first year of the study, the agreement was only 59% (see Table 5).

TABLE 5 *Extent to Which Teachers' Judgments Agree with Developmental Ratings*

Class	Number	First Year		Second Year		Third Year	
		Agree (%)	Disagree (%)	Agree (%)	Disagree (%)	Agree (%)	Disagree (%)
Kindergarten	69	83	17	68	32	73	27
First grade	22	68	32	82	18	No discrimination in teachers' ratings	
Second grade	29	59	41	No data		52	48

Our interpretation of this decreasing correspondence is that kindergarten teachers are still looking at the child's performance with relatively fresh and objective eyes. It appears to be quite within the average kindergarten teacher's ability to consider that a child is questionably ready for promotion to first grade, or even that he might need to be retained in kindergarten.

Even by the end of first grade the possibility of retention is less frequently entertained. By second grade and following, it appears to be the exceptional teacher who will recommend that a child repeat a grade.

However, at all grade levels, agreement between the developmental rating and teacher's judgment was very close for the fully ready (+) and the fully unready (−) children. The major area of disagreement was that group of children rated by us as questionable (±).

Even here, agreement was closer than might appear from the table. Though in many instances teachers gave our questionable children a + rating, and thus passed them on to the next grade, they often qualified this + rating with such statements as the following:

> A bit of a puzzle. Tests poorly.
> Have to just get after him and after him.
> Question of his reading, and not ready in arithmetic. Very slow but a good worker. At least he tries. No comprehension.

As this research was set up, we were not to discuss our findings with the teachers until all testing had been completed and all evaluations and predictions as to school progress had been made. However once the work was completed, we were free to discuss our findings with teachers. In all our discussions with the teachers we found that, in general, the kindergarten teacher was the most perceptive, or at least she seemed able to see the child most clearly in his current stage of development. But as soon as a teacher became more involved in and responsible for the child's learning, as happened with the older children, the clarity of her judgment became mixed up with excuses for poor behavior and anticipation of better behavior. It seemed to us that she needed help to see the child more clearly.

An encouraging clue to the fact that teacher ratings and developmental findings were probably closer together than tabular findings might suggest, was thus found when at the end of our 3 years of examining we were free to impart our findings to the teachers. Their interest was intense. They appeared ready for new insights.

One dramatic moment came when a child with a December birth date was revealed by the developmental examination as being extremely immature in spite of her real intellectual capacity. Her teacher was at first shocked by this revelation. She felt that the developmental findings must be very inaccurate. It took her only a week, however, to come to the conclusion that these findings were correct. Her comment then was, "How could I have been so blinded by this child's intellect? I have been teaching her for a whole year and yet I never saw these immaturities, or at least I didn't realize what they meant."

In the spring of 1964, we checked the actual grade and group placement of all those members of the original kindergarten group who were still in the Hurlbutt school. These children (except for two who had been double-promoted into seventh grade and two who had been left behind in the fifth grade) were all in sixth grade. The grade had been divided, on the basis of general ability and school performance, into four groups, with the most excellent students in group one, the least excellent in group four.

Correlation between our original kindergarten predictions, made in the fall of 1957, and the actual school performance of these children as judged by this school placement 6 years later, showed a correlation of .74 between our prediction of readiness and grade placement. Table 6 gives these data.

TABLE 6 *Correlation Between Kindergarten Prediction and Later Sixth Grade Placement of Weston Subjects*

(Percentage)

	Grades 7 and 6–1	Grade 6–2	Grades 6–3A and 6–3B	Grades 6–4 and 5	
9 ready by 3	67	11	22	0	= 100
15 ready by 2	40	47	13	0	= 100
17 questionable	6	47	35	12	= 100
11 unready	0	0	36	64	= 100

CHAPTER 4

SUBJECTS CHOSEN
FOR STANDARDIZATION PROGRAM

‖‖‖

Though we had initially surmised that the Weston study could serve in standardizing the developmental examination, we soon realized that this was not practical. The number of subjects was too small. We needed at least 100 children—50 boys and 50 girls—at each of the seven age levels from 5 to 10 years, including 5½. With the need of much more extensive examining we also wished to cut down our commuting time. It was then that North Haven was chosen as the community that could best satisfy our needs. We were assigned to two school districts (Center and Montowese) each of which had around 100 children at each grade level, thus affording us an ample population to work with. Since each school contained the expanse of grades from kindergarten through fifth grade, the needed years of 5 to 10 for the standardization study were adequately covered.

North Haven has proved to be a most fortunate choice. We have had unfailing cooperation from the two schools involved. Through this cooperation we have each learned to respect the other. It was because of this respect on the part of the schools that we are now launched on our present 3-year Fund project to apply our findings and theories in these very same two schools.

We, on our part, have come to recognize the intricacies of the job of education, and marvel that a school day can be made to run so smoothly. This respect has made us know that we don't want to do anything to upset the forces, multiple in nature as we have discovered, with which school authorities need to work. Our desire is to work with schools rather than to impose a new program upon them. The final decisions must in all cases be theirs.

In our standardization study the age ranges for each age level were as follows: the 5-year-old could be from 4^{11} to 5^4; the 5½-year-old from 5^6 to 5^{10}; the 6-year-old from 6^0 to 6^8, and similarly for ages 7, 8, 9, and 10.

Since we knew that a fair number of children would be lost to the study, especially through moving, we examined 65 boys and 65 girls at each age level. Our goal was to examine as many of the subjects as possible at *successive* age levels. Since, however, the entire examining program was conducted over a period of 4 school years (September, 1958 to May, 1962) not all of the subjects could be followed longitudinally. However we arranged it so that one group of 65 subjects of each sex was seen at 5, 5½, 6, and 7 years; another group of the same size was seen at 6, 7, and 8 years; and still a third group at 8, 9, and 10 years.

To be certain of having 50 cases of each sex at each age level, we added 200 extra cases at the ages 5, 5½, 9, and 10—cases which did not overlap as in our longitudinal planning. These extra cases were examined only once each.

All subjects to be examined were selected at random (other than that age was checked) from class lists. A list of the number of children examined at each age with the dates when they were examined, is given in Table 1, Appendix A. Since most subjects were seen at more than one age, 301 different children gave us the 700 examinations needed.

The final decision of the 100 records at each age level which were to be analyzed was made on the basis of completeness of recording. The examinations had been conducted by a variety of research assistants under a variety of examining conditions. Some records were thus more detailed and some examinations more adequately given than others. Selection was not made on the basis of excellence of performance of the child.

The subjects were above average in intelligence, with a mean IQ of 117.4 (standard deviation 13.3) for both boys and girls on the California Mental Maturity Scale (CMMS), the one used by the schools. However, when this score was corrected for a sample of the children to a score on the Wechsler Intelligence Scale for Children (WISC), the mean IQ for girls was 104.8 and that for boys 106 (see Tables 2 and 3, Appendix A). The California scale is considered by many psychologists to be a less effective measure of intelligence and also gives a less consistent rating from year to year than the Wechsler. It usually scores at least 10 points higher than other tests such as the WISC. The WISC scores here are more in keeping with our own subjective impression of the present subjects.

Socio-Economic Status

The socio-economic status of our subjects has been rated both on the U.S. Government Scale (1961) and the Minnesota Scale of Parental Occupations. We have given both scales since there is considerable difference in classification.

As Table 4, Appendix A shows, according to the U.S. Government Scale the highest percentage of fathers (34%) fall in Class I or within the professional grouping, with 13% in Class II, semiprofessional or managerial. This gives 47% in either Class I or II as opposed to the Minnesota rating of only 27% in Classes I and II. On the Minnesota scale the majority (40%) fall within Class III or the clerical, skilled labor, or retail business grouping.

In our opinion the U.S. Government Scale has some of the same flaws as the California Mental Maturity Scale. The ratings of both are too high. Along with the choice of the WISC we would prefer to use the Minnesota Scale in which the majority (40%) of parents of our present subjects fall chiefly in Class III.

These needed controls have been a necessary part of our study, but as we work with a child in securing a developmental appraisal, neither intelligence nor socio-economic background is uppermost in our minds. Each has its place, but this place is relative to a larger whole. Our interest centers around a child's developmental level and the quality of his behavior. We want to know more about the source of his actions and thus know how we can best serve him in an educational environment.

CHAPTER 5

THE TESTS AND MATERIALS

|||||||||||||||||||||||||||||||||||||||||||||||||||||||||||||||||||||||||||||||||||

How can we best get at this bundle of vitality which is the child?—that is the question. How can we distill the essence of a growing human being at a certain age and as a unique individual who can deflect age and make it into his very own? This is not an easy task. And yet if we but use simple tools the child reveals himself to all those who will stop and listen to what he says, and who will watch what he does with seeing eyes.

We at the Gesell Institute have been working with developmental tools for many years. Dr. Gesell was already thinking of possible tools that would reveal the growth process before he started his magnificent march, in 1911 at Yale, literally chiseling his way bit by bit in the field of child development. It was a long and intricate way, the way of the research scientist who gives his heart and soul as well as his mind to his chosen work. In reverie one can still hear him say, "The mind grows." This short sentence summarizes his whole professional work.

What simple tools he chose to probe the mind's depths—a rattle, a ring on a string, a one-inch cube, a cup and spoon, a tiny sugar pellet, a pencil and paper. The same tools used at succeeding age intervals, he found, could reveal changes so specific and well-patterned that they could be documented as closely as at four-week intervals in the first year of life. That a tiny sugar pellet could tell so much seems unbelievable, but its revelation can be re-enacted over and over again, as we watch the baby grow. We can document the *stages* of the infant's response even to such a simple stimulus.

His first response to the pellet is secured at 4 months when he sits propped in front of a table top and spies it on the table top within his near vision. He pounces on it visually, even though only momentarily.

31

He grasps it, as it were, with his eyes. Within the coming months he will also grasp it with his fingers. Initially his arms activate as he regards the pellet.

By 7 months of age the infant approaches the pellet with his hands, but his raking finger movements do not allow him to successfully secure it. By 9 months, the hand has differentiated so that its radial side (thumb and index finger) has come into priority use. The pellet is approached with extended index finger which is placed on top of it. It is then drawn in toward the thumb. This movement may effect a successful inferior grasp, but more often the index slips over the side of the thumb in scissors fashion, leaving the grasp of the pellet a bit precarious. Soon comes further growth with the crowning ability of the 1-year-old child to pluck the pellet with "precise pincer prehension," an expression coined by Dr. Gesell from his ever-productive verbal mint.

How often the parent has seen this miracle of nature being enacted before his very eyes as the infant sits in his high chair plucking tiny bits of sugar left on his tray. The parent is amused by the child's intentness and by his success. The child smiles back as he successfully places the grain of sugar into his mouth. Each knows in his own way that something wonderful has happened.

If we can capture the wonder of growth in the tiny infant we will never lose it. We will become humble and receptive as we listen and watch. We will become surer in our actions toward the older child, judging what he needs from us, knowing better how to respond to him.

There is something magical about the flow of good energy that can be set up between mother and child, father and child, teacher and child, human being and human being when things are right.

We, alas, too often let things go wrong. We take a wrong turn, we foster a wrong attitude, we impose a wrong will. Then the child withers like a plant or rages like a lion. This interplay between human and human is not easy. It is very intricate, especially in these modern times when the child is stepping out into the arena of life much sooner than he did in the olden days. He is now, indeed, both seen and heard.

Let's consider for a minute the child we wish to know, on the threshold of coming into the world on his own as a kindergartener. What a lovely image this word stimulates—a child's garden. Is it still the same garden it once was or was meant to be? We need to ask ourselves this question when we see the vultures of experimental education poaching on this tender territory, forcing advanced curricula in learning into the young child's receptive but unknowing mind. When and if this happens, the sympathetic flow between adult and child may cease. There is the danger of setting up an unnecessary hierarchy of learning steps through which the child may have to endure.

What is worse, such an educator may be a slave to his own unknowing. He means well, but sometimes he can be misguided. He, like the parent, needs to know more about development.

Any learning needs to become a part of the learner's experience. He can be shown the way, but he must do the learning himself. With an attitude of listening and watching the child, both parent and educator become more perceptive. They start seeing things they have previously missed. Some behaviors, such as the blinking of eyes, are readily seen once you start watching for them. The adult needs to question what he sees, for instance, to ask himself if there are ages when this blinking is more likely to occur and circumstances under which it may be more evident. We have found blinking to occur most commonly in the 4-year-old and more often in the child who needs protection from stimuli he can't absorb. Such a child may need to progress more slowly in school, bright as he may be. He may also adjust better to a smaller group.

Other behaviors are less obviously significant but may still be important and may need to be drawn to the adult's attention, especially when they are behaviors so common that we are apt to disregard them. A good example might be the sweeping tongue movements of the 5½-year-old as he struggles in such fine motor activities as with pencil and paper. This tongue movement is within a normative frame at 5½ years of age. But when it still occurs at 8 years, when the mouth is more often quiet though gaping, a further investigation into the rest of this 8-year-old's behavior is indicated. Are other younger patterns present? Is this child keeping up with his third grade classmates and with his school's demands?

These examples are used to show that behavior is right there before our eyes—special tests or no—and also to emphasize that nothing that the child does or says is inconsequential. Everything has its own significance. It is for us to find out the ways in which each thing is significant.

Over the years of examining many children we have come to know what approaches and tests tell us most about the child. Our final battery of tests chosen for school-placement usage may seem rather a potpourri, a little bit of this, a little bit of that. Actually many similar tests have been devised by other examiners and have been used with good success. We must remember that any test is only as good as the person administering and interpreting it.

Some tests, we have come to realize, have more developmental range, can be used consecutively over more ages, show more significant changes from age to age, than do others. Sometimes the range of a test can be increased by adding more difficult but related items.

Dr. Gesell's original Copy Forms test shows how simple a test can be and still be revealing. He merely seriated six forms in increasing difficulty moving from circle to cross to square to triangle to divided rectangle (the dividing lines being from corner to corner and from mid-side to midside, looking like a British flag), and finally to diamond. We still use this Copy Forms test in its original form, but have since increased its range by adding two three-dimensional forms—a cylinder and a cube.

We have steadily come to realize that the significance of such a test as Copy Forms is not simply in the success of copying. It is the way the child copies, the size form he makes, the place on the paper where he chooses to draw his forms, all these and many more qualifying categories that tell us more fully about the child than do merely his success or failure in copying the forms in question.

This Copy Forms test and a number of our other inclusions undoubtedly tap subverbal levels of the brain. We may be criticized in our choice of tests for an absence of more formal verbal test items. Our observations of verbal behavior in the present test battery may be considered more incidental. We attempt to put down everything the child says in the short interview at the beginning and end of the test, in the naming of parts of the body, in the carrying out of commands on the Right and Left tests, and in the projection of responses to the 16 forms on the 4 cards used for memory of designs (Monroe Visual Three).

Our one, more formal, verbal test is the 1-minute naming of animals from Binet. Binet was criticized for his overemphasis on the verbal aspects of behavior. Though much was learned from his concentration, for the time being we have chosen not to include more verbal items until we have more fully explored the developmental aspects of language tests that would be of use.

Besides our own tests of Copy Forms and the completion of an Incomplete Man figure, we have included in our battery an adaptation of Jacobson's Right and Left test, Visual One and Visual Three from Marion Monroe's Reading Readiness test, and the naming of animals for 1 minute from Binet. These borrowed tests we have adapted to our own use to the extent that we suspect their authors might not entirely recognize them.

The initial and concluding interviews which we give cannot be considered tests, but they tell us a great deal about the child. They suggest his level of intelligence, his powers of organization, his interests. These short interviews also help the child to feel the freedom of easy movement at the beginning and end of the examination and may determine in part his enjoyment of this examination. Part of the enjoyment which many seem to experience may be attributed to the feeling of success they get from being allowed to succeed at whatever level they are functioning. One 6-year-old, when she finally got her turn, summed it up as follows: "Now I'm going to find out how you make the kids so smart." To allow a child to feel successful in himself suggests that an examination may also be successful in itself.

Developmental Examination Tests

The examination as we give it may be considered to fall into seven separate parts:

1. *The initial interview.*   Questions about age, birth date, birthday party including favorite activity and present received; siblings—names and ages; father's occupation.
2. *Pencil and paper tests.*   Writing name or letters and address; numbers 1 to 20; copying six basic forms (circle, cross, square, triangle, divided rectangle, diamond in two orientations), and two three-dimensional forms (cylinder and cube in two orientations); completing Incomplete Man figure and giving his facial expression.
3. *Right and left (adaptation of Jacobson's Right and Left tests).* Naming parts and sides of body, carrying out single and double commands, responding to a series of pictures of a pair of hands in which two fingers are touching. Response is first verbal and then motor.
4. *Form tests.*   Visual One (Monroe)—matching forms; Visual Three (Monroe)—memory for designs; projection into forms.
5. *Naming of animals for 60 seconds.*
6. *Concluding interview.*   Reporting on what child likes to do best in general, at school indoors and outdoors and at home indoors and outdoors.
7. *Examination of teeth.*   Recording of both eruption and decay or fillings.

Supplementary test: the Lowenfeld Mosaic test.

Materials[1]

Copy Forms: White cards $7\frac{1}{2}$ by 5 inches with the following forms outlined in black in the center of each card. *Circle:* diameter 8 cm.; *cross:* lines at right angles, 7.5 cm.; *square:* 7 cm.; *triangle:* equilateral, 9.5 cm.; *divided rectangle:* rectangle 10 × 6.5 cm. with two diagonals and a perpendicular to the center of each side; *diamond:* horizontal: 5.5 cm. each side, top angle 125°.

[1] Test materials and Recording Sheets can be obtained from Programs for Education, Publishers, P.O. Box 85, Lumberville, Pennsylvania, 18933. Test materials are illustrated in the appropriate chapters. Recording Sheets are illustrated in Appendix D.

Three-dimensional forms: Two three-dimensional objects, a 1.5 inch cylinder and a 1.5 inch cube, of red painted wood.

Incomplete Man: Green, letter-size paper with drawing of unfinished man (see Figure 4, page 132).

Right and Left direction cards: Small cards on which are printed commands which examiner gives to subject for (1) naming parts of (examiner's) body; (2) naming right and left, own and examiner's; single commands, double commands.

Right and Left verbal and motor pictures: This part of the test material consists of six pictures. In each of these there are two hands with some fingers touching as follows (see Figures 7 & 8, pages 182, 183):

Verbal: Left index, Right little	*Motor:* Left ring, Right middle
Left middle, Right ring	Left index, Right ring
Left little, Right ring	Left little, Right index

Visual One: Material for this test is in two parts. The first part is a record form sheet, 8½ by 11 inches, marked off into twelve small squares, three across and four down. In each square are two paired but opposed figures (see Figure 10, page 191). (The child has to choose which of these figures matches one shown him on separate card.)

The second part of the test material is a set of twelve cards, each 8½ by 5½ inches in size. On each is printed a figure which resembles one of the two shown on the record sheet.

Visual Three: Material for this test is in two parts. There is a (pink) record sheet, 8½ by 11 inches in size, marked off into four horizontal lines. On each line are to be reproduced as many forms as a subject can remember (see Appendix D). The second part of the material is a set of four cards, 11 by 8½ inches in size. On each are printed, in horizontal alignment, four black geometric forms (see Figure 11, page 197).

Gray Oral Reading Test (Bobbs-Merrill Co., Inc., 4300 West 62nd Street, Indianapolis 6, Indiana): This is a standardized individual reading test consisting of a series of paragraphs of graduated difficulty.

Iota Word List: Three cards, each with a list of single words.

Lowenfeld Mosaic Test: Box of 456 plastic pieces, $\frac{1}{16}$ of an inch thick. Pieces are in 6 colors and 5 shapes. This box can be obtained from Badger Tests Co. Ltd., Liverpool House, 15–18 Eldon Street, London, E.C. 2. (The large box of 456 pieces is $55.00; smaller half-box is $35.00.) The working surface on which patterns are to be made is a sheet of white paper which covers the surface of a rectangular wooden tray having a raised rim on three sides with the side placed nearest the subject being rimless. The standard size of this working surface is 10¼ inches by 12⅜ inches. Tray can be purchased from Badger for $3.00.

Rorschach cards: A set of ten 9½ by 6½ cards on each of which is printed a symmetric inkblot, some in color, some in black and white, available to qualified psychologists through the Psychological Corporation, 304 East 45th Street, New York, New York.

The separate tests which make up this placement examination will be dealt with more fully in the following section. It is an examination that is easier to give than to interpret, which is probably true of examinations in general. At one time we thought it might be possible to put this examination into the hands of the classroom teacher. Now we feel this should be done only under supervision.

We also realize that both training and a wide range of continuing experience with developmental testing is essential. Therefore we are suggesting the possibility of establishing a new kind of examiner, a Developmental Guidance Co-ordinator. This name suggests that the developmental appraisal is only the first step and only one part of such an examiner's place in the school system. A next step, after such an examination has been given, would be to put the findings into operation through various guidance means.

Lastly and most important of all is the co-ordination of what is revealed on the test for all those involved with the child—the parent, the school administrator, the teacher. This is no small task, but the job needs to be done, and there are many individuals capable of doing it.

PART II
THE DEVELOPMENTAL EXAMINATION

THE DEVELOPMENTAL EXAMINATION IS GEARED TO TAKE AROUND a half hour, more or less. However the tempo will vary according to the tempo of the child and also according to the tempo of the age. The examiner will soon discover, for instance, how quickly a 6-year-old can be examined and how laboriously the 7-year-old may extend the time of the examination.

The fairly short length of time which the examination requires (half an hour or less) allows for a substantial number of examinations to be conducted within a reasonably short span of time, and also has the advantage of not removing the child from the classroom for too long.

The developmental examination should allow for easy spontaneous flow between child and examiner even though it is held within the limits and form of an examination. Because it is developmental in outlook, its demands can be shifted to a higher or lower level according to the child's abilities. The child should feel a sense of success at the level at which he is operating, and the examiner should be quick to shift to a level of questions or demands at which the child can respond successfully.

CHAPTER 6

INTERVIEW

‖‖‖

Administration

A short initial interview not only puts the child at his ease, since the questions are within the realm of his immediate knowledge and experience, but also gives the examiner a quick glimpse of the child's level of performance and of his powers of organization. It is often surprising to look back over these short interviews to see how fully the child has revealed himself. Some children have their answers at their tongue's tip, ready to give, whereas with others each item has to be teased out bit by bit.

The examiner's questioning needs to be both deft and fluid. The child is being asked to specify as far as he can without being pressured. If he hits an impasse, it is up to the examiner to shift his questioning or to proceed with the next item. It is important to get down what the child says, exactly as he says it. Even his sentence construction, grammatical errors, pronunciation, all tell a story about this specific child in this specific situation. Thus it is extremely important to record well and accurately.

QUESTIONS ASKED ROUTINELY

1. How old are you? If fingers are shown, child is asked, "How many does that make?" If he still does not answer, he is asked to count his fingers and give the total.

2. When is your birthday? If the child names a season, or mentions proximity to a holiday, this suggests that he is not yet thinking in terms of months. If he gives the month, he should be further asked, "What day of the month?"

41

3. *Did you have a birthday party?* If child says "Yes," examiner can explore further as to who were the guests, whether both boys and girls were invited, etc. (If the party was rather far in the past, examiner can shift questioning to a projected future party.) The child is then asked, "What was the favorite thing you did?" and "What was your favorite present?" and "Who gave it to you?"

4. *How many brothers and sisters do you have?* Regardless of whether the child gives a total number or separates them into boys and girls, or brothers and sisters, he should then be asked "What are their names and how old are they?" If he cannot give ages, he is asked whether they are bigger or smaller than he is. If this proves too difficult, he can be asked whether they stay at home or go to school, or what school they go to.

5. *What does your Daddy do?* If the answer is a simple "He works," a further question such as "Tell me about his work" often elicits further detail.

Each examiner should feel free to build up his own battery of interview questions. However, the examiner needs a sufficient stability of repetitive questions so that he can compare one child with another. This short interview allows him to become acquainted with the child and sets up an ease of relationship for the examination that is to follow.

Findings

1. *How old are you?* This question presents no problem for children of either sex from 5 years on. A few at 5 may gesture by showing their five fingers, but can readily respond verbally when questioned further. Also at 5 there may be a reference to the previous year when they *were* 4 (see Table 7). Reference to half- or quarter-years alerts the examiner to a potentially higher intellect or mathematical interest.

TABLE 7 *Age*
(Percentage of Responses)

	5 years		5½ years		6 years		7 years	
	G	B	G	B	G	B	G	B
No answer, or says doesn't know	4	9	2	4	2	2	0	0
"I was 4," etc.	4	4	0	0	0	0	0	0
Incorrect	4	6	4	2	0	8	4	0
Correct[a]	**88**	**81**	**94**	**94**	**98**	**90**	**96**	**100**

[a]Responses such as 5¼, 6¼ when correct are so recorded, but are so infrequent as not to be shown separately.
NOTE: Boldface figures in tables indicate normative percentages, that is, those over 50%.

2. *When is your birthday?* Seven-year-olds can give both the month and day of their birthday (78% G, 74% B) (see Table 8). Both sexes can give the month alone correctly at 6 years (60% G, 58% B). The 5- or 5½-year-old is more apt to reply that he doesn't know, that he forgot, or that he had it already. A few gaily absorb their unknowing by reporting that their mother didn't tell them.

TABLE 8   *Birthday*
(Percentage of Responses)

	5 years[a]		5½ years		6 years		7 years		8 years		9 years		10 years	
	G	B	G	B	G	B	G	B	G	B	G	B	G	B
Month														
Correct	40	30	46	32	60	58	80	84	96	96	92	98	98	98
Incorrect	0	9	0	0	6	4	4	0	0	0	2	0	0	2
Don't know	44	60	40	58	30	26	16	16	4	4	6	2	0	0
[b]	12	0	14	10	4	12	0	0	0	0	0	0	2	0
Day														
Correct	8	9	26	16	50	38	78	76	92	90	92	94	96	100
Incorrect	8	4	0	0	6	8	2	4	2	2	4	2	2	0
Don't know	72	87	60	74	40	42	20	18	6	8	2	2	0	0
[b]	12	0	14	10	4	12	0	2	0	0	2	2	2	0
General reply, as, "I had it"	12	24	16	18	10	0	4	2	0	0	0	0	0	0
No answer or "I forgot"	32	36	18	34	20	28	14	14	2	4	0	0	0	0
Gives day date, but wrong	0	0	4	8	6	0	16	4	0	0	0	0	0	0
Day and month, both correct	8	9	26	16	43	38	78	74	92	88	89	96	96	98

[a] Given selectively at 5 years.
[b] A correct but general answer such as "Halloween," "First day of summer," etc.

3. *Did you have a birthday party?*   The answers to this group of questions are highly varied and individual and are therefore not presented in tabular form. The examiner will need to tease any information out of most 5-year-olds. By 5½ to 6 years of age, however, children are becoming more knowing about and interested in parties, and actually have had more experience with them. Having the cake and blowing out the candles is often uppermost in their minds. Playing games is also as important as having the cake for many 6-year-olds. The mention of their favorite present can give the examiner some clue as to their level of interest.

4. How many brothers and sisters do you have? Even the 5-year-old reports well on his siblings, both as to names and ages. Some report on the family group more easily than do others. FIVE is so concerned about the family group that he often includes himself, along with his siblings. Others include their parents and even mention household pets. The reference to girls or boys is more common at 5, even though the child has been asked about "brothers" and "sisters." Children in the 5- and 6-year realm often report about the siblings they don't have. "I don't have any brothers, just sisters." It is interesting to note how they organize their siblings in their mind, whether they separate the boys from the girls, seriate them from oldest to youngest or vice versa, name their favorite first, etc. Those who have trouble with age are apt to refer to size, as "big" and "little." When they are beginning to grasp age they will then refer to "older" or "younger."

See Table 9 for level of success in reporting on siblings.

TABLE 9   *Siblings*
(Percentage of Responses)

	5 years		5½ years		6 years		7 years	
	G	B	G	B	G	B	G	B
No answer	4	0	0	0	0	0	0	0
Fails all ages	28	27	12	20	0	8	0	0
Fails some ages	8	13	6	10	2	0	0	0
Ages correct	**60**	**60**	**82**	**70**	**96**	**78**	**97**	**100**
Names correct	**96**	**100**	**100**	**100**	**100**	**100**	**100**	**100**

5. What does your Daddy do? Replies to this question do not lend themselves well to tabular analysis. The important thing is to find out if the child has a concept of his father going out of the home to work. Many 5-year-olds still refer to their immediate knowledge of their father as they see him around the house. "He works down cellar," "He eats dinner," "He digs in the garden."

But a fair number of FIVES know that their father goes to some special place to work such as a farm, a garage, a bank, an office building. By 5½, they are more aware of what he does—"He makes telephones," "He prints," "He makes plans for boats," "He fixes things." Even at 5 a child may be able to report that his father is a dentist, an engineer, or an electrician. And by 5½ one is a bit taken aback by the occasional child who reports such professions as draftsman, police auxiliary, or bank executive. It is the quality of response here which tells us much about the child's concept of his father's work.

PAPER AND PENCIL TESTS

||||||||||||||||||||||||||||||||||||||||||||||||||||||||||||||||||

NAME AND ADDRESS

Administration

When the initial interview has been completed, the examiner directs the child's attention to the paper (green 8½ × 11) and pencil already awaiting him on the table. The 5-year-old is asked if he can print any letters. If he is unable to comply, he is asked if he can print his name. Often he does not realize that printing his name is printing letters.

It might thus be better to ask him initially to print his name. If he cannot, then he can be asked if he can print some letters, or if he can print somebody else's name. Some FIVES have learned to print a sibling's name before their own. If the child cannot respond to either request, the examiner may make one last attempt by dictating a few letters, the first letter of his name, or the letter A. (At 5 years of age the child is also asked to write any numbers he knows at the same time that he is writing letters. At other ages, numbers are delayed until the end of the Paper and Pencil tests. Thus numbers will be discussed under a separate section.)

Before FIVE starts, he often asks where he should place his name or letters. He is told that he may place them wherever he chooses. His spontaneous choice of place is significant, as will be discussed in the analysis of placement on page.

By 5½ years, the child is usually capable of printing his first name or nickname. If he stops with his first name, the examiner then asks, "Can you print your last name too?" This should also be asked of him at older ages if he neglects to write his last name. This encouragement is not usually needed after 7 years of age but any such need should be recorded. The simple notation of "last" in parentheses (last) indicates that the examiner had to ask for the last name.

As the child is writing his name (and address after 8 years), the examiner should record any shift of his paper or his body. Head shifts, arm shifts, torso shifts, any foot and leg activity all are significant. An awareness of shift in body posture comes as the examiner becomes more expert. It will come with refinement of observation. Initially only the grossest items such as shift of paper can be noticed and recorded. With further awareness, however, eye movements, mouth and tongue movements, along with hand postures of both dominant and nondominant hand will be duly noted and recorded.

The posture of the nondominant hand is significant and this might be noted initially along with recording on shift of paper. Analysis of the method of grasping the pencil might better be delayed until a bit later in the examination when more time is allowed as the child is writing his numbers.

When the child has finished writing (FIVE prefers printing) his name with his dominant hand, he is asked to write his first name with his nondominant hand. The examiner requests, "Now write your first name with your other hand." The child may say that he cannot. If so he is asked to write only the first letter of his name.

It is important to record what he says and also any awkwardness he may show as he holds his pencil. Some of course write as well or better with the nondominant hand as with the dominant hand. The fact that a child hasn't established good dominance may be important in any final analysis of his behavior. After 8 years of age the request to try the nondominant hand is delayed until the child has completed both his address and the date.

By 8 years of age the child is asked initially to write his name and address. If he says he can't write his address he is asked to tell it. Then he is asked to write any part of it that he can. Often he stops after writing his street address. He is then asked if there is anything more to his address. This may remind him of the rest, but more often he will need to be asked specifically about the town and state.

Findings

NAME

The printing of letters becomes a passion to many 5 and even some 4-year-olds. FOUR dashes out his strokes, may make his letters lying down, but even so with a little imagination they can be recognized. By 5 years of age, most have grasped the concept of their own name and the majority are at least capable of printing their first name or nickname. Most use capital letters. As one sees the child struggling in his execution of any small letters, making them large as if they were capitals, it becomes evident that small or lower-case letters should wait for both better visual and better manual control. The child has enough troubles with reversals at 5½ without our adding to his burden by requiring that he make small letters, which tend to reverse more than the capital letters do.

Many who have been unable to write their name at 5 years, even though they could print a few letters, are able to write at least their first name by 5½ (see Table 10). A good number at this age (54% G, 52% B) are even making some inroad on their last names either by printing the first letter or so, or by printing their last name fully. However even at 6 years of age when a large proportion can write their last name (70% G, 74% B) many still are apt to stop after writing their first name and need to be prodded into continuing. SEVEN is more congenial with his last name. He may be thinking of the succession of generations, of ancestry which links his interest to last names.

By 7, the child shows that he has come through in all sorts of ways and is now on surer and higher ground. Reversals and substitutions, so common especially at 5½, are no longer a problem to him. If they do occur, he recognizes them, can erase them and make them right.

SEVEN sees the relative values of capital and small letters, even though he may struggle with their various usages until he is 10. But he no longer mixes them at random, or executes the small letters as if they were capitals. He now feels very comfortable with small letters. But the fact that he did make small letters large like capitals when he was 6 suggests that he might have worked better with capitals alone until he was ready at 7 to make the small letters as small letters.

SEVEN's control of his stroke is shown by the fact that his letters are now medium in size in contrast to his tendency to print large letters when he was 5 and 6. He also tended earlier to execute his letters in an uneven fashion. But now that he is 7 he executes his letters more evenly (72% G, 54% B) (see Table 10).

In view of this newly expressed desire and ability to write smaller, a true evidence of advancement, it is odd that many educators persist in their use of widely spaced lined paper which the child happily used at 6 years of age. Now that he is 7 he becomes irritated by this unnatural demand, and figures out ways of circumventing something that is no longer natural to him.

Even without lines, SEVEN is beginning to form a straight base line as he writes, but this does not come into sure form before he is 9 or 10 years of age. The tendency to undulate the base line which was so marked at 5 and 6 years of age steadily reduces, but still holds at the 30th per-

TABLE 10 *Writing Name*
(Percentage of Responses)

	5 years		5½ years		6 years		7 years		8 years		9 years		10 years	
	G	B	G	B	G	B	G	B	G	B	G	B	G	B
Percentage of Success														
No response	4	20	0	0	0	0	0	0	0	0	0	0	0	0
Random letters	26	24	4	2	0	0	0	0	0	0	0	0	0	0
First name only	44	36	42	46	10	10	2	2	0	2	0	0	0	0
First letter or letters last name	10	12	10	30	20	16	0	0	0	0	0	2	0	0
First and last names	16	8	44	22	70	74	98	98	100	98	100	98	100	100
Method of Writing														
No name	28	38	2	4	0	0	0	0	0	0	0	0	0	0
All capitals	26	28	10	2	0	2	0	0	0	0	0	0	0	0
All small letters	2	0	0	0	0	0	0	0	0	0	0	0	0	0
Incorrect use of small and capitals	8	2	12	28	6	6	0	0	0	0	0	0	0	0
Correct use of small and capitals	36	32	76	66	94	92	100	100	100	100	100	100	2	100
Printing	100	100	100	100	98	98	98	98	46	44	30	24	22	14
Cursive writing	0	0	0	0	2	2	2	2	54	56	70	76	78	86
Size of Writing														
Large	88	78	92	86	70	70	16	36	12	22	10	16	16	14
Medium	8	2	8	14	24	26	82	56	74	76	54	60	62	70
Small	0	0	0	0	6	4	2	8	14	2	36	24	22	16

Placement on Page														
Bottom of page	16	6	4	4	0	0	0	0	0	0	0	0	0	0
One-half way down	14	36	16	26	16	20	0	6	0	0	0	0	0	0
One-third way down	30	12	20	22	12	14	6	4	2	8	6	10	0	2
Top right	2	2	0	2	0	2	4	2	2	2	8	4	18	6
Top center	6	4	8	2	8	8	12	18	14	16	8	10	8	6
Top left	**28**	**20**	**52**	**44**	**64**	**56**	**78**	**70**	**82**	**74**	**78**	**76**	**74**	**86**
Size Consistency														
Uneven	80	70	82	86	78	80	28	46	16	32	10	18	4	14
Even	16	10	18	14	22	20	**72**	**54**	**84**	**68**	**90**	**82**	**96**	**86**
Relationship of First and Last Name														
Separate lines	14	14	6	14	14	10	2	4	2	4	2	2	2	0
Too narrow space	10	6	28	30	20	16	6	16	6	10	4	12	6	16
Too wide space	0	0	0	0	26	24	16	10	20	14	4	16	10	8
Good spacing	2	2	18	10	30	42	**76**	**74**	**72**	**70**	**90**	**70**	**82**	**76**
Base Line														
Undulating	**60**	**52**	48[a]	56[a]	58	54	24	44	34	32	26	38	30	28
Falling	14	8	18	18	16	16	10	6	16	22	2	8	2	16
Rising	10	6	24	12	16	18	10	12	2	6	4	2	4	6
Straight	0	4	6	12	10	12	**50**	**38**	**42**	**40**	**68**	**52**	**64**	**50**
Errors														
Reversals	18	0	10	36	6	2	0	0	0	0	0	0	0	0
Substitutions	16	16	20	22	22	22	0	0	0	0	0	0	0	0

[a] Four percent of girls, 2% of boys have no base line.

centile even at 10 years. Consistent rising or falling (instead of undulating) of lines or even of individual words is less common, though both are conspicuous at 5½ and 6 years (18%±) and a falling line persists at this level through 8 years of age. Whether this tendency to make rising or falling lines relates to optimism and pessimism is at least interesting to conjecture.

SEVEN's final conquest in writing his name is to show good spacing between his first and second name (Table 10). There was a time, especially at 5½, when in some there was no separation at all between first and last names. Then with increased awareness of this need at 6 years of age, the child overdid this spacing. At 7 he is recognizing a better relationship, better spacing. He rarely puts his first and last name on separate lines one underneath the other any more. This did occur as often as 14% in the 5- and 6-year-old period.

The placement of name on the page also tells something of age. Nearly a third or more of 5- and 5½-year-olds place their name in the lower half of the sheet of paper. By 6 this number tapers off. SIX tends to place his name in the upper left hand corner of the page and this placement predominates from 6 on. A tendency to place the name at top center of the page, at both 7 and 8 years of age (16%±) may be either an individual or an age response. Any central response in the middle of the page suggests to us a potential restriction.

ADDRESS

SEVEN may be fully capable of writing his whole name, but the addition of his address is definitely beyond him. He may not even know the meaning of the word "address" or he may give his telephone number instead. But as soon as the examiner asks him where he lives he can readily supply the answer. Maybe he will give only his street address initially, but he can usually be prodded to give his city and state. Most, however, are not interested in writing any part of it.

By 8 years of age most are ready to tackle this task even though it is not altogether easy for them, and most would prefer to write only their street address. They do not yet grasp the total concept of a name and address as it would be placed on a letter, but tend to string it out on one or two lines (60%). At 8 years of age, 54% of girls and 46% of boys can give their street and number, city and state, and nearly all can give these four items at 9 and 10 years of age. However, errors especially in punctuation persist through 10 years of age (see Table 11).

NAME AND ADDRESS

It is not until 9 years of age that the child grasps the concept of placing his name and address on three or four lines (72% G, 66% B) as

TABLE 11   *Address*
(Percentage of Responses)

	7 years[a]		8 years		9 years		10 years	
	G	B	G	B	G	B	G	B
Part Correct								
Street number	14	6	86	76	100	100	100	100
Street	12	6	86	82	100	100	100	100
City	6	2	56	48	100	100	100	100
State	6	2	56	40	98	100	98	100
All four	6	2	54	46	98	100	98	100
Errors								
Shift from cursive to printing			14	16	6	12	0	4
Does not capitalize			32	32	14	28	8	8
Extra capitals			6	6	0	0	2	2
Wrong spelling			26	20	12	24	2	6
Wrong punctuation			32	50	74	78	70	60
Number of Lines Used (Name and Address)								
One line			22	30	10	10	4	18
Two lines			38	30	18	24	12	28
Three lines			24	14	58	50	66	42
Four lines			4	6	14	16	18	12
Three or four lines			28	20	72	66	84	54

[a] Given only selectively at 7 years.

one does on an envelope (see Table 11). (It is no wonder that with his new-found ability, the 9-year-old begins to use the United States Postal Service, sending in box tops, asking for information.) Though cursive writing has been introduced in the school curriculum, many shift to printing their address after writing their name in a cursive style. NINE may still have trouble remembering that words should be capitalized. His spelling may not be the best, but he knows how to place his name and address on a sheet of paper or on an envelope and can put it to use.

It is interesting to scrutinize NINE's method of writing because it is a definite mark of his age. First of all it tends to be smaller. He is coming into good precision. Secondly, his letters are well-formed, with a tight but rounded stroke. This is no product of the Palmer method, but rather the product of the intricate organization of NINE's mind.

Nine is the age when the child enjoys the flow of cursive writing, when he wishes to master it. As we see him struggle with cursive writing at 8 years of age, with letters growing larger, lines drooping down, we might question the reason for instituting cursive writing in the third grade. Printing is still more congenial to the 8-year-old, whose desire for speed is hampered by cursive writing.

The practice and perfection of cursive writing at 9 pays off handsomely at 10. TEN tosses off his name and address as easily as he wrote his name alone at 7. This greater ease of execution is already allowing his individuality to show through. Teachers begin to recognize children by their handwriting alone. One child may show a flourish, another a loose structure, and still another a stiff structure. But there is a consistency in each product. We could discover much about TEN in his own right if we allowed his handwriting to speak for him. This is indeed an expressive behavior that has taken him a long time to acquire. He still has a long way to go and his handwriting will evolve through many stages. But the very surety of its 10-year-old form should alert us that TEN is trying to tell us something about himself through the language of handwriting.

DATE

Correctly naming the date (which includes month, day of month, and year) may seem easy to the 8-year-old, but the history of this ability to name a moment in time is long and complicated.

The 2-year-old thinks of the day in its 24-hour span, dividing it into night and day, darkness and light. The 3-year-old gives the day its parts, thinking of it in terms of morning and afternoon. By 4, days are known to have names such as "Saturday when Daddy is home." By 5, the child knows all the days of the week, separately and in order.

The child has already, by 4 years of age, begun to grasp the concept of seasons, especially the extremes of summer and winter. By 5, these seasons can be broken up into months. FIVE begins to learn the names of months as earlier he learned the names of the days of the week, but he still needs to cling to happenings and special occasions, such as Halloween and Christmas. By 6 it is the month of his birthday that has specific meaning for him. It will be another year before he can give the day of his birth.

When a child knows his birthday date, he is ready to start thinking of time in relation to date. The calendar has interested him since he was 5. Initially it was the numbers that interested him most. By 7 most are ready to name though not necessarily to write the day's date.

Administration

As with address, SEVEN may best be asked to give the date without being asked to write it. SEVEN's laborious and time-consuming execution in writing needs to be kept at a minimum during the test situation. He reveals himself in so many other more important ways.

But his knowledge of the date, when he is asked, "What day is it today?" gives a clue as to his orientation to the naming of time. If he gives the name of the day of the week, as Tuesday, he is then asked, "What month is it?"

If he cannot answer this, he may be asked if it is some specific month other than the correct one (such as December, when it is June). He is then asked the day of the month. If he cannot answer this, he may be asked if it is the beginning, middle, or end of the month. Finally he is asked what year it is. If he cannot answer, he is asked if it is some far-fetched year, such as 1492. (This type of questioning may also be needed for an older child in case he cannot give the date.)

By 8 years of age the child is asked to write the date without any preliminary questioning. He may need to be asked specific questions such as the above to encourage his writing. If he omits the year, he should be asked if he has completed the date. If this does not give him a clue, he should be asked what year it is. Any specific clues given should be recorded in parentheses such as (year), indicating that the examiner had to give the child the idea.

Findings

The ability to write the date in its complete three-part form is well established by 8 years of age (82% to 92%). Our figures at 7 (30%± success), show a beginning interest. As with some other behaviors, the half-year period of 7½ may show the beginning of a normative rating.

Most children are highly accurate about day, month, and year at 8 years and following (see Table 12).

TABLE 12   *Writing Date*
(Percentage)

	7 years		8 years		9 years		10 years	
	G	B	G	B	G	B	G	B
Succeeding								
Any date	32	34	92	86	98	98	100	100
Month	32	28	90	86	98	96	100	100
Day	26	20	90	86	98	96	100	100
Year	32	30	92	82	94	96	100	100
Errors in Punctuation								
Omits dot for abbreviation, or comma			6	6	4	16	8	14
Misuse of punctuation			2	0	0	0	2	2
Unnecessary dot where no abbreviation			4	4	6	6	2	14

When the date is asked directly after the writing of name and address, the child usually places it under his name and address if it is organized in three or four lines, or he continues on the same line if name and address are placed on one or two lines. A small number (10%±) separate the date from name and address, especially to the upper right half of the paper or even the upper right corner.

Errors in writing the date are few from 8 years on. Errors in punctuation are also limited but do point up difficulties which some children experience. Punctuation is more often omitted, but it also may be overused as when a dot is unnecessarily placed after the unabbreviated name of the month.

A significant item that is just appearing at 10 years of age is the recording of the month as a number. Though this occurs infrequently (2% G, 8% B) it is interesting that it occurs four times as often in boys as in girls, again bearing out an impression that boys more often than girls think in numbers.

NUMBERS

The writing of numbers is often easier to evaluate than the writing of letters with their upper and lower case forms. Much can be learned from the child's writing of numbers up to 20 or as far toward 20 as he can go.

Administration

At 5 years of age when a child's ability to write numbers is often spotty, he is asked to write what numbers he knows, after he has completed printing the letters he knows. If he asks, as he often does, where he should put them on the paper, he is told to place them wherever he chooses.

After 5½ years, when the ability to write numbers has markedly improved, this task is delayed until after the three-dimensional forms have been copied. The child is then asked to write his numbers from 1 to 20, or as far as he can go. Part of the reason for this delay is to see how he will utilize the space left on the page, or whether he will feel the need for starting a new page.

Writing of numbers is a good opportunity for the examiner to become more aware of the child's pencil grasp and to record any observations about this along with his recording about the writing of numbers. The posture and behavior of the child's nondominant hand is as important as that of the dominant hand. Is it flat on the table top and held close to the dominant hand? Does it move as the dominant hand moves?

Does the child shift the paper instead of moving his hands? Does the nondominant hand stabilize the paper? Is the nondominant hand placed inside the dominant hand and thus crossed over to the right side of the paper (if the child is right-handed)?

Findings

NUMBERS WRITTEN

If FIVE can write no other numbers he may at least be able to write the number 5. Difficult as it may be, this number seems to have meaning to him, since it represents his age. The majority of FIVES can write the first 5 numbers or nearly so. By 5½, knowledge of numbers has greatly expanded with from 36 to 40% of children writing up to 6 to 10 or even beyond. By 6 years, the ability to write to 20 is close to a normative level (42% G, 56% B). Since figures for success are almost at the 100th percentile at 7 years (see Table 13), we may conjecture that a substantial growth must have occurred at 6½ years.

TABLE 13 *Numbers Written from 1 to 20*
(Percentage of Responses)

	5 years		5½ years		6 years		7 years	
	G	B	G	B	G	B	G	B
No record	16	18	2	4	2	2	0	0
1 to 5	38	66	20	24	6	2	0	0
1 to 6 or more (up to 10)	30	6	40	36	14	14	2	0
1 to 11 or more (up to 20)	14	10	38	36	78	82	98	100
1 to 20	2	0	16	8	42	56	96	100
Omits numbers	18	22	6	12	6	2	0	0
Mixes or reverses sequences	4	0	2	4	4	2	0	0
Confuses letters and numbers	0	4	0	0	0	0	0	0
Trouble around 10	6	2	0	0	0	0	0	0
Trouble around 20	2	0	0	0	4	8	0	0
10 for 20	0	2	0	0	8	0	0	0

FIVES, especially, may omit numbers as they write a sequence. There may be some mixing up of order, but on the whole this is negligible. Or numbers may be confused with letters. We had expected that this would continue up into 6 years, but analysis of our findings shows that it occurs only at 5 years and even then minimally.

PLACEMENT ON THE PAPER

The majority of 5-year-olds write numbers on the lower half of the paper. Placement from 5½ years on is difficult to analyze since it is so varied and so dependent on the available space after the three-dimensional forms have been completed. Even when good space is available at the bottom of the page, the child at any of these ages may choose a free area at the top of the page for writing his numbers. Some turn the paper and write on the back. In present subjects this persists in around one-third of the children as late as 6 years of age and continues in a few right through 10 years of age. A few write over existing forms, suggesting a lack of adaptability. Perhaps more significant than place on paper is the way in which the child organizes his numbers in a line.

ORGANIZATION OF LINES

Random placement of numbers occurs mostly at 5 years of age. From 5½ on, the writing of numbers seems to demand, in the majority, a horizontal organization on the page. Vertical organization persists in a few (4–6%) with a slight rise at 8 and 9 years.

To write all 20 numbers on one line or in one column demands planning of space, and also an ability to write small enough so that all the numbers from 1 to 20 will fit on one line. This ability shows a peak at 8 years of age (38% G, 36% B) (see Table 14). If a second line or more is needed, the succeeding numbers are usually placed under the original line in a L to R direction. However, especially at 6 and 7 years, the second line may be placed above the first one or the numbers may be placed from R to L or up or down, thus maintaining a linked continuity. Or the paper may be shifted to a horizontal position perhaps to secure a better expanse of space for writing the numbers horizontally.

SIGNIFICANT BREAKING POINTS IN GROUPING OF NUMBERS

On the whole the breaking points in writing a series of numbers are determined by the space available. Thus a child will break his line either if he runs into an existing form on the paper or if he reaches the edge of the paper. However there appear to be special favored stopping points which suggest numerical grouping, even though enough space is available to continue. The most common of these points is the number 10 (see Table 14). As many as 12–14% of girls, 16–20% of boys at 9 and 10 years break their first line at the number 10.

SIZE

The size of numbers made gives a very good clue to age. At 5 and 5½ years the predominant size is large (½ to 1 inch). Even very large numbers 1 to 2 inches in height show up in sizable percentages (22–32%) at these same ages. This very large size does not occur after 6 years of age (see Table 15).

TABLE 14 *Organization of Lines of Numbers*
(Percentage of Responses)

	5 years		5½ years		6 years		7 years		8 years		9 years		10 years	
	G	B	G	B	G	B	G	B	G	B	G	B	G	B
Organization in General														
No record	16	18	2	4	2	2	0	0	0	0	0	0	0	0
At random	?	?	0	4	0	2	2	0	0	0	0	0	0	0
Writes on extra side of paper	34	38	14	32	36	36	12	6	8	16	14	14	10	28
H-line or lines	?	?	92	78	86	74	84	88	96	84	88	92	92	98
V-line or lines	4	4	4	6	4	6	6	6	4	16	10	6	6	2
1 to 20 on one line	0	0	0	0	10	20	22	28	38	36	26	30	14	24
Second line above	0	0	2	4	0	6	6	6	0	0	2	0	0	0
Paper shifted to horizontal	0	0	0	2	2	12	2	6	6	0	2	6	0	6
Writes over forms	0	0	2	0	4	4	0	8	0	0	2	0	0	2
Line continues back, up, or down	0	0	0	4	8	10	2	0	0	0	0	2	2	0
Numbers at Which Lines Break and New Lines Start														
Five					0	0	0	0	0	0	0	2	0	0
Seven					0	0	0	0	0	0	2	0	0	0
Nine					0	0	0	2	0	2	0	0	0	0
Ten					14	14	4	10	2	8	14	20	12	16
Twelve					12	0	2	4	0	0	2	2	2	0
Thirteen					12	0	0	2	2	0	4	4	2	2

Six appears to be a transition age so far as size of numbers goes. By 7 and after, medium-sized numbers (¼ inch ±) predominate. The large-sized numbers are almost nonexistent from 8 years on, but small numbers (⅛ inch ±) increase at 8 and reach their high point at 9 years (36% G, 46% B). (Letters, too, tend to be small at 9 years of age. It will be interesting eventually to correlate this tendency to write small at 9 with the level of a child's achievement. It may be that the good achievers are also the children who write small at this age.)

The relative size of numbers is also significant (see Table 15). In the early ages—5 and 6 years—before a greater stabilization of evenness has occurred, one can almost feel the dynamics of energy exchange as one views the shifting size of a child's numbers. Some get larger as the child proceeds, others get smaller, or they may fluctuate. By 7 years of age numbers are executed more evenly (68% G, 50% B) and this evenness steadily increases into 10 years of age.

TABLE 15   *Size, Base Line, and Spacing in Writing Numbers*
(Percentage of Responses)

	5 years		5½ years		6 years		7 years		8 years		9 years		10 years	
	G	B	G	B	G	B	G	B	G	B	G	B	G	B
Actual Size														
No record	16	18	2	4	2	2	0	0	0	0	0	0	0	0
Small (⅛ inch)	0	0	0	0	2	4	4	2	24	18	36	46	30	26
Medium (¼ inch)	12	10	18	18	38	40	76	74	74	82	62	54	70	72
Large (½ inch)	48	42	58	46	46	36	20	24	2	0	2	0	0	2
Very large (1 inch±)	24	30	22	32	12	18	0	0	0	0	0	0	0	0
Relative Size														
Uneven	38	22	22	30	32	46	8	10	16	12	0	2	0	2
Getting larger	22	14	20	28	12	28	16	20	14	6	10	2	0	10
Larger, then smaller	8	10	32	26	20	2	0	4	2	0	0	0	0	0
Getting smaller	2	0	8	2	4	6	8	16	4	2	8	0	0	6
About even	2	8	12	8	28	16	68	50	64	80	82	96	100	82
Base Line														
Uneven	70	66	78	84	74	84	26	32	24	22	12	10	0	6
Even	0	2	16	10	22	12	74	68	72	78	88	90	100	94
Spacing														
Inadequate record	44	56	8	6	4	2	0	0	0	0	0	0	0	0
Poor spacing	18	30	12	34	4	8	2	0	0	0	0	0	0	0
Fair spacing	38	14	70	58	78	84	58	68	46	58	24	44	26	42
Good spacing	0	0	0	2	14	6	40	32	48	42	76	56	74	58

BASE LINE AND SPACING

Along with an evaluation of size it is important to evaluate the base line and also the spacing of the digits, especially digits in the teens. An uneven, often undulating base line persists through 6 years of age. At 7 years, there is a sharp switch over into a predominantly even base line, and this predominates thereafter (see Table 15). This again suggests that a marked area of growth has occurred at 6½ years.

Correct spacing is more difficult to achieve. Spacing may well have something to do with rhythm. Jangly poor spacing, especially in boys, shows up very clearly at 5 and 5½ years. Good spacing does not become normative till 9 years of age (Table 15).

A rhythmic shift in spacing is often noted in the teens. A fairly typical example of this shift is a short interval between one number and the next in the early double numbers (10 to 12), followed by a widening of the spacing in the mid-teens, and again a narrowing of the spacing at the end of the series (18 to 20). When an examiner has once noted this type of spacing he can easily recognize it thereafter. This rhythmic spacing shows a marked increase in girls at 7 years (30%) and persists from 8 to 10 years at a fairly high level (14–22%).

The good spacing which began at 6 years steadily increases until it reaches normative levels at 9 years of age (76% G, 56% B). It is interesting to note that the manual execution of numbers is better in girls, but the concept of numbers as shown by the breaking points is higher in boys.

YOUNG METHODS OF EXECUTION

Often the child, especially the 5- to 6-year-old, cannot execute a number as he has been instructed to do. Each has his own special way of writing numbers, but there is similarity from child to child, even in errors (see Table 16). Thus a child may still place his numbers horizontally as if they were lying down, very much as a 4-year-old may do. This occurs infrequently and occurs only at 5 and 5½ years.

Another pattern at these early ages is to use only vertical strokes: one for 1 (|), two for 2 (||), three for 3 (|||), etc. Children who write in this way seem to be pleasantly delaying the agony of making real numbers. This agony is very real for some, especially in the 5- to 6-year period.

Some numbers are best executed in two parts.

$$7_{(7)} \quad 8_{(8)} \quad 9_{(9)}$$

Others are best executed in a continual stroke.

$$3 \quad 4 \quad 5 \quad 9_{(9)}$$

These productions are mainly the mark of the young child of 5 to 6 years of age with the exception of the two-piece 9

$$9|$$

which is still quite strong as late as 7 years. When these younger forms do persist after 6 years of age they help us to be alert for other immaturities.

REVERSALS

Reversals may be considered along with other younger patterns (see Table 16), as they show up in the same age realm (5–6 years). The numbers 1 and 8 cannot be reversed from R to L or vice versa, but they can

TABLE 16 *Numbers: Younger Patterns and Reversals*
(Percentage of Responses)

Young Methods of Execution

	5 years G	5 years B	5½ years G	5½ years B	6 years G	6 years B	7 years G	7 years B	8 years G	8 years B	9 years G	9 years B	10 years G	10 years B
Horizontal — = ≡	2	6	0	2	0	0	0	0	0	0	0	0	0	0
3	6	2	2	0	0	0	0	0	0	0	0	0	0	0
5	2	4	6	4	4	0	0	0	0	0	0	0	0	0
⌐	2	0	0	4	0	6	0	10	0	2	2	2	0	2
00	4	10	10	10	4	4	2	2	0	0	0	0	0	0
8	12	8	6	10	6	6	0	0	0	0	0	0	0	0
8	2	2	10	12	14	14	8	2	0	4	2	0	2	2
6	0	0	0	0	4	2	0	0	2	0	0	4	0	0
9	4	6	8	8	6	12	2	0	0	0	0	0	0	0
0	2	6	28	28	36	**52**	16	32	0	8	2	0	0	6

Reversals of Individual Figures—Quality

S	26	8	14	20	10	0	0	0	0	0	0	0	0	0
3	16	10	24	8	14	0	0	0	0	0	0	0	0	0
4	14	10	12	8	4	2	0	0	0	0	0	0	0	0
25	8	12	6	14	6	6	2	2	0	2	0	0	0	0
b	8	4	6	10	6	6	0	0	0	0	0	0	0	0
J	10	2	12	14	14	12	2	2	0	0	0	0	0	0
p	12	2	8	10	12	10	0	2	0	2	0	0	0	0

Reversals of Individual Figures—Quantity

Stumbles on numbers	0	0	6	3	9	11	24	24	16	28	8	20	4	16
01 for 10	0	0	8	4	4	4	0	0	0	0	0	0	0	0
02 for 20	2	4	6	6	10	16	10	4	0	0	0	0	0	0
Other teens backward	0	2	2	10	12	6	0	4	0	0	0	0	0	0
Writes teens, second digit first	0	0	4	4	26	30	10	26	10	12	0	8	2	8

Reversal of Order

Once only	20	12	34	28	20	22	8	10	0	4	0	0	0	0
More than once	24	8	28	32	26	12	4	2	0	0	0	0	0	0
None	26	48	32	34	52	64	88	88	100	96	100	100	100	100
Once	2	4	0	6	4	0	0	0	0	0	0	0	0	0
More than once	4	0	2	0	2	0	0	0	0	0	0	0	0	0
None	64	64	92	88	90	100	100	100	100	100	100	100	100	100

be executed in reverse (from the bottom up). Similarly the zero is often reversed by being drawn CW from the bottom up. We lack figures, but our impression is that this shift in direction occurs more often in boys and mostly from 5 to 6 years of age.

The position of the parts of a double number may be reversed without reversing the numbers themselves. Thus 10 becomes 01, 20 becomes 02, and 14 becomes 41, though they may be formed correctly and, as in 14, the 1 is written before the 4. It is interesting to note that reversals of 10 and 20 are likely to occur as isolated reversals, suggesting that the strain of these transition points may have produced the reversal. (The strain of the transitional points is also evident when a child is counting. He may be going along splendidly and then get stuck at 29 or 99.)

Rather than reversing the actual position of the double number digits, the child may reverse them merely by writing the second digit first. Thus a 16 may be made by first writing the 6 and then placing the one in front of it. This occurs especially at 6 years of age (26% G, 30% B) and continues minimally through 8 years of age. It is still present in a few boys at 9 and 10 years (8%). It can readily be understood that a boy who continues to execute his double numbers in this way cannot build up the rhythmic flow of spacing that one anticipates by 9 and 10 years.

This flow can also be broken into when the child stumbles on a number, even though he may then be able to correct himself. This stumbling occurs especially at 7 and 8 years (24%, 16% G; 24%, 28% B). A few boys still stumble on numbers as late as 9 and 10 years (20%, 16%).

The number of reversals made is sizable, especially at 5½ years (62% G, 60% B) (see Table 16). There is a definite reduction at 6 years when the normative subject does not reverse (52% G, 64% B). This absence of reversals increases definitely at 7 years (88%) and reversals are not expected to occur from then on.

CHAPTER 8

COPY FORMS

||||||||||||||||||||||||||||||||||||||||||||||||||||||||||||||||||||||||

Introduction

All too often we miss the simple or reject it, and embrace the difficult, only to find that we have made life unnecessarily difficult. Failure to use any one of the six seemingly simple forms

$$\bigcirc \quad + \quad \square \quad \triangle \quad \boxtimes \quad \diamondsuit$$

in the testing of the growing child seems to us like throwing away part of his birthright. In his response to these forms the child seems to give evidence of recapitulating the history of the race. As we see him struggling from one stage to the next, we somehow come to know what the race must have struggled through from its primitive beginnings to its modern stance of civilization, precarious as it sometimes appears.

How does the child begin to show us his own experiencing of these forms? Is it not from this matrix of his own inner experiences that he is finally capable of projecting into them, first with the visual recognition of his eyes and then with the capacity to reproduce them with the movements of his hands?

The very experience of rolling over at 3 months of age is a circular movement. Also, the infant's first locomotion, pivoting, which occurs around 29 weeks of age as he lies in a horizontal position on the floor, is actually in a circular direction.

Earliest vigorous arm movement, banging, seen also around 7 months, is clearly vertical in nature. It is followed, at around 9 months, with plainly horizontal arm movements as the child plays pat-a-cake or claps together objects held in either hand.

By 1 year of age the infant is stretching his arms upward above his head as he is triggered by the delightful nursery game of "so big." This is no mere nursery trick. It is a new penetration in space, soon to be followed by the supreme vertical penetration in space when he rises to his feet and walks the earth, *Homo erectus.* This posture has become such an important part of anthropological thinking that it has attracted much study. Arriving at the upright posture required eons of growth.

Might the child not feel the sense of a square as he rises from the floor to all fours and for a short time even prefer this seemingly animal method of locomotion? Certainly the oblique aspect of the triangle is soon his as he begins to walk and thrusts his legs obliquely forward from the fixed point of his pelvis.

The above analogies may seem a little farfetched, but they do point out that experiencing occurs at different levels. Growth in its orderly way, if we but know this order, demands that one stage follow another. If internal or external influences cause the child to skip stages or to mix them up, the smooth flow of growth may be disrupted. The variables may be too extreme for the good of the growing organism. It is for us to try to find out more about the grand design so that we can relate the variables, and either control them or release them as needed by our knowledge and our use of this knowledge.

Over the years, in our own study of infant and preschool behavior we have been fascinated by the child's response to pencil and paper. At first it is the paper itself that intrigues the infant of, say, 7 months. He wants to get it in his hands and to crumple it. He likes the sound it makes and he loves to tear the paper and bring it to his mouth. A big red crayon, which is presented in place of a pencil up to 3 or 4 years of age, is an interesting object to this same 7- to 10-month-old or slightly older infant, but nothing more. He will pick it up in one hand, transfer it to the other, bring it to his mouth, chew on it, and bang it until it finally breaks.

It is not until around a year of age that the infant bangs the crayon against the paper, making marks of which he is aware. By 15 months, his own back and forth arm movements against the table top suggest that he is getting ready to make a *horizontal scribble.* He can, in fact, imitate a horizontal scribble and shows his awareness of what he has done by the look of pride in his eyes and by his obvious enjoyment as the crayon makes a mark back and forth on the paper.

Within a few months he will be able to make a more selective, isolated stroke. At 18–21 months he shows this new readiness as he goes on his daily walk. He selects any stick he can find, squats down, and strokes with it on sidewalk or earth. It is a vertical stroke that he makes, more often drawn toward him.

When confronted with a paper and crayon at this age he will obligingly imitate a *vertical stroke,* but a *horizontal stroke* is beyond him until he is 27 months of age. To combine these two strokes takes considerably more time. By 30 months he will make two parallel strokes in imitation, but they do not cross. It is not until 3 years that the average child can successfully *imitate a cross.*

At the same time that the child is mastering the control of the vertical and horizontal stroke he is also struggling with the circular movement. The 15-monther can scribble back and forth in a continuous stroke, but to bend this stroke into a *circular scribble* will take another 6 to 9 months. This circular scribble may reverse itself at 2½ years. Finally by 3 years of age or younger the child is able to stop on the first circle around, making *a single circle,* but this does not complete the ability to make an effective and usable circle. Many stages will need to be traversed before this form becomes an integral and very important part of his handwriting.

The next stage after the cross in the use of vertical and horizontal is to put two of each of these strokes together in a square formation. At first the child sees the square more as a circle, or at least he draws it as such. His eyes have been aware of corners from the time he was 30 months old, following his marked awareness of walls at 2 years. In these years that precede the time when he can *imitate a square,* at 4 years of age, he has been preparing to take this step of expressing a square space in miniature. At first it is the sides of the square which he sees, wherefore he often makes two vertical lines and crosses them with two horizontal lines with very sloppy corners. He will gradually become better able to turn the corner with his pencil, as he makes a square. The multiple ways in which children copy the square formation will be discussed late on.

Following the mastery of the square comes the conquest of the *triangle.* It is only as we see a child of 6 or 7 years still having difficulty in executing an oblique stroke that we realize what an accomplishment the ability to copy a recognizable triangle at 5 really is. What is this oblique, other than a modification of both horizontal and vertical lines? This is a more complicated stroke, but like all complicated processes, once they are mastered they simplify further development. Note how often the child who has trouble in the early school years and who has trouble in grasping reading, may also have had trouble in mastering the use of the oblique stroke earlier.

The fifth form, *the divided rectangle* as it is called, is a unique form in that it combines the preceding three forms in some way or other. From the vantage point of the study of development, this Copy Forms test is a gold mine. Even now after years of experience with this test we have in no way mined all of its secrets. However, much has been revealed even though there is still much to come.

Last but not least of the six forms to be copied is the *diamond,* in both horizontal and vertical orientation. How it captures the imagination of the child when he finally experiences it so that it is within his grasp! He practices and practices so that he can reverse the oblique lines—so like a triangle and yet so different. Further discussion of behavior stages in response to this form will reveal how different!

The use of these six forms, seriated as they are, is the expression of the genius of Arnold Gesell. He did not live to see the full impact of these forms in their revelation of growth, but he firmly established the ground work for this test.

Administration

The presentation of the six Copy Forms cards in a pile is made after the child has written some letters, or his name and address, and numbers, according to his age capability, on an $8 \times 11\frac{1}{2}$ inch sheet of paper, preferably green in color.

Often the 5-year-old and the $5\frac{1}{2}$-year-old has worked in the center of the page as he wrote the letters and numbers he knows. In such cases, when the Copy Forms cards are presented, it is wise to turn the page over so that the child may have a fresh start and can give a better idea as to how he will handle the clear expanse of a page without the interference of his earlier markings.

By 6, if he has confined the writing of his name to the top quarter of the page there will be no need to turn the page. Actually it is useful to use the same side, in order to relate the child's printing or writing ability to his Copy Forms performance. Therefore it is best if they can be seen together on the same page.

The pile of forms is presented by placing it beyond the upper edge of the paper. The examiner indicates the top card which bears the circle, and asks the child to "Make one like this on the paper."

FIVE may be slow to start. He may not quite understand what is asked of him. He may pick up the pile of forms and move them closer to him. He should be allowed to handle the cards in this way much as a 4-year-old might do. As soon as he has made his start, the examiner can replace the pile just above the upper edge of his paper, removing the top form from the pile as he completes each one.

The sixth form, or diamond, is presented initially in a horizontal position as it is presented on the card, and is then shifted to a vertical position.

Rarely does the examiner need to present one card at a time as with the preschooler. Nor does he need to increase his tempo as with a 4-year-old to prevent the child from taking over. FIVE can wait, and shows a certain deliberateness. He often asks orienting questions before he starts. He wants to know where the forms should be drawn on the page, how big they should be. He is told he may place them where he wishes and may make them as big as he chooses.

He may name the forms as he draws them, calling the circle a "round circle," etc. These verbalizations should be recorded on the Copy Forms recording sheet along with the direction and sequence of lines. If he shifts his paper to a horizontal position this, too, should be recorded. Also if he shifts the paper in his execution of single lines, the notation on the recording sheet of top (T) at the top of the line drawn, will indicate how the paper was shifted, and the arrow on the line will indicate the direction of the line.

Following the copying of the six forms, two three-dimensional objects, a 1.5-inch cylinder and cube are presented, and the child is asked to draw a picture of each on the paper. The cylinder alone is presented at 5 and 5½ years. By 6, the cube can be presented, first in a face-on and then in a point-on position.

In the early stage of copying, at 5–6 years, when it is difficult to know what part of the three-dimensional form the child is drawing, since he usually draws but one surface, it is wise to ask him, "What part did you draw?" He may be able to respond with "top," "bottom," or "whole thing." But if he cannot respond he may be asked, "Did you draw the top, bottom, or the whole thing?"

Recording of Direction of Child's Copy of Forms

Since the child's method of copying is fully as important as his finished product, the examiner should, after the examination, transfer his recording of direction onto the child's product, as he is analyzing and summarizing the response. A small arrow of direction should be made near the start of a line. If the line turns a corner, this may be indicated by an inconspicuous outer line.

These markings of direction are placed on the child's forms so that the examiner may reconstruct in his mind just how the lines were executed. These arrow marks and numbers should be drawn with pencil, as small and inconspicuously as possible. When they are drawn big and bold, they interfere with one's appraisal of the child's drawing.

At times a form may not be recognizable, especially the products of the 5- to 6-year-olds. These forms should be labeled with a miniature reproduction of the form attempted.

Analysis of Responses to the Individual Forms

Each of the Copy Forms will be dealt with both as to outstanding trends in the method of execution and also as to the success of the final product so far as its quality is concerned. The latter appraisal is more subjective, but we use it to point out significant items that tell us about the process of growth.

CIRCLE

Method of Drawing

The successful copying of a circle has been normative since 3 years of age. Thus in the present age range we are more interested in noting the way in which the child makes the circle than merely in whether or not he can copy it.

The salient feature of the 5-year-old circle is that it is copied from the top down in a CCW[1] direction. This, however, is true of girls only, at 5 years of age (66%) and does not reach a normative level in boys until 5½ years (56%) (see Table 17). Five-year-old boys still execute the circle from the bottom up in a CW direction in the manner characteristic of the 4-year-old. From 5½ years on, the circle becomes well established in both sexes in a top-down CCW direction. There is, however, an exception with the left-handed child who from the age of 7 tends to make his circles in a CW direction from the top down.

Some few start from either side of the circle, but this is more common in the 5- to 6-year age range and does not exceed 16% for either side for either sex at any one age. Another variable is the execution of the circle using two lines, either continuous or in opposite directions, with one side CCW and the other side CW. This occurs quite infrequently, though it rises in boys to 16% at 8 years and to 12% at 10 years. It is interesting to note with such boys whether any other splits or shifts of pencil or paper occur.

[1] Throughout, counterclockwise is abbreviated CCW and clockwise is abbreviated CW.

TABLE 11 Copy Circle
(Percentage of Occurrence)

	4½ years G	B	5 years G	B	5½ years G	B	6 years G	B	7 years G	B	8 years G	B	9 years G	B	10 years G	B	Adult
Starting point																	
Bottom	40	72	18	48	14	26	4	20	0	4	0	2	0	4	0	0	
Top	40	18	66	28	82	56	90	66	100	94	98	96	92	94	96	98	100
Right side	4	4	4	8	2	8	6	10	0	2	2	0	6	2	4	2	
Left side	14	6	12	16	2	10	0	4	0	0	0	2	2	0	0	0	
Number of lines																	
1	96	96	98	100	96	98	98	96	92	100	98	84	92	100	94	88	100
2	2	2	2	0	4	2	2	4	8	0	2	14	8	0	6	10	
3	0	2	0	0	0	0	0	0	0	0	0	2	0	0	0	2	
Direction																	
CW	52	70	40	60	24	40	16	36	6	18	8	10	8	6	12	6	
CCW	46	30	58	40	72	58	82	60	86	82	90	74	84	92	82	82	100
2 lines: CCW and CW or CW and CCW	0	0	2	0	4	0	2	4	6	0	2	14	6	0	4	12	
2 lines: CCW and CCW	0	0	0	0	0	2	0	0	2	0	0	2	2	0	2	0	
Qualitative Aspects																	
Well-proportioned	10	10	44	44	52	30	56	58	84	76	82	64	94	84	90	92	
Oval	20	20	16	30	16	42	18	14	4	12	8	14	0	10	2	6	
Lopsided	36	44	26	14	20	10	8	14	6	2	0	4	0	2	0	0	
Open space at closure point	10	4	8	6	8	6	6	8	0	4	0	8	0	2	4	0	
Overlapping	6	12	4	0	4	8	2	2	0	2	0	4	0	0	2	2	
Wobbly	10	6	2	6	0	4	0	0	0	0	0	0	0	0	0	0	
Apple-shaped	6	4	0	0	0	0	10	4	6	4	10	6	6	2	2	0	

Quality of Product

A more or less perfectly proportioned circle has been achieved by 56% G, 58% B in the normative group by 6 years of age. This is confirmed by the actual measurement of the relationship of the horizontal to the vertical diameter. By this age, there is a definite reduction in the oval circle (flat, vertical, or oblique), the wobbly circle, the lopsided circle, and the circle with overlapping or open closure point.

These last four are all reminiscent of the preschool years when the stroke is wobbly in character and there is real difficulty in closure points either in missing the mark or overemphasizing the closure point. The lopsided circle is of special interest since it suggests the 3½-year-old's difficulty in the last half journey of his circle. He starts out so well with a nicely formed half-circle, only to wobble back to the beginning point by truncating the form. The 5- to 6-year-old's lopsided circle does not show this extreme, but the return path of the last half is difficult and often produces a wobbly and short-cut path.

An interesting variation that occurs to only a small degree from 6 years on is what may be called the apple-shaped circle. This is a circle whose closure point resembles the stem-end of an apple. In the process of drawing, the originally planned circle has enlarged so that its course has to be cut back in order for the beginning point to be met. This phenomenon of enlarging the form as it is drawn and needing to fill in the resulting gap is also seen in the other forms of square, triangle, and diamond, but it is often covered up unless the perceptive examiner is on the alert. What this means is hard to conjecture, but it involves a repeated pattern of enlarging and the need to adjust.

By 7 years of age the circle has achieved a beauty of perfection in its form especially with girls. This quality is delayed until 9 with many boys.

CROSS

$$+$$

Method of Copying

The execution of the cross has not proved too difficult for the child from 4 years of age on, but making a more or less perfect cross with good proportions of length of line and crossing of lines at midpoint of the two lines is something else again. It is not until 9 years of age that this achieves normative rating in both sexes (54% G, 56% B).

To the adult eye it is surprising that the crossing of a vertical line with a horizontal line could pose such problems for the preschool child. To the 3½-year-old especially it is as if the vertical line had bisected the horizontal line into two parts, one to the right and one to the left of the vertical line. (A similar but less common response is when the horizontal stroke is left intact and the vertical stroke is bisected.)

When the horizontal line is made in two parts at 3½ years, each of the two horizontal parts is usually drawn out from the center or vertical stroke. The 3½-year-old who shifts his pencil readily from one hand to another solves his problem readily by drawing the right-sided line from L to R with his right hand, and the left-sided line from R to L with his left hand. This phenomenon of split horizontal stroke occurs infrequently after 3½ years and shows up only at the 5th percentile by 5 years. From then on it is very uncommon. Its presence, as with all other splits which we have mentioned or will mention along the way, alerts us to a two-sidedness that has not yet taken the next integrative step.

The most common method used in copying the cross, established by 5 years, is the making of two lines, vertical down (100% G, 82% B) and the horizontal from L to R (80% G, 72% B). The vertical stroke up is made infrequently (its high point is 18% in boys at 5 years), but the R to L direction of the horizontal line occurs conspicuously and persists around a 14%± level throughout this 5 to 10 age range (see Table 18). Though this may be a reversal phenomenon at 5 and 6 years, it becomes the preferred method of drawing for the left-handed child from 7 years on.

Quality of Performance

The rather elaborate list of the qualifying descriptions of the cross (Table 18) suggests why it takes so long before a perfectly proportioned cross is finally produced by 9 years of age. There is the vertical cross, quite conspicuous at 7 years of age (28%), the horizontal cross lingering in the 4th to 8th percentile throughout, and the Latin cross with the long vertical stem and a shorter horizontal stroke across the upper part of the stem. The latter reaches a peak at 6 years of age (16% G, 12% B). The lines may be wavy (this drops out after 5½ years), the horizontal line may be executed at an oblique angle or in a curved fashion with the total form appearing tipped or lopsided. The lopsided cross, often with one side of the horizontal stroke larger than the other, occurs conspicuously through 7 years, especially when forms which have had an additional third line added are included. The addition of an extra line, usually horizontal, to a lopsided cross suggests an effort to restabilize and make the two sides equal. This tends to decrease at 6 years of age but

TABLE 18 *Copy Cross*
(Percentage of Occurrence)

	4½ years		5 years		5½ years		6 years		7 years		8 years		9 years		10 years	
	G	B	G	B	G	B	G	B	G	B	G	B	G	B	G	B
Direction of V line																
Down	94	76	100	82	100	94	98	98	98	98	100	100	100	100	100	100
Up	4	24	0	18	0	6	2	2	2	2	0	0	0	0	0	0
Direction of H line																
L–R	78	58	80	72	84	80	80	82	86	84	86	82	86	90	86	86
R–L	12	24	14	20	14	20	18	16	14	16	14	18	14	10	14	14
Other	10	18	6	8	2	0	2	2	0	0	0	0	0	0	0	0
Number of lines																
2	84	78	84	84	94	96	100	94	100	100	100	100	98	100	94	96
3	16	22	16	16	5	4	0	6	0	0	0	0	2	0	6	4
Order of lines																
VH	74	70	70	72	92	92	94	88	98	96	100	100	98	92	94	96
HV	8	14	10	6	0	4	2	2	2	4	0	0	0	4	0	0
V–H–H	12	14	16	16	6	4	0	6	0	0	0	0	0	2	6	4
Other	6	2	4	6	2	0	4	4	0	0	0	0	2	2	0	0

Qualitative Aspects

Perfectly pro-portioned cross	+	12	10	22	18	34	24	34	32	24	24	56	40	54	56	62	74
Vertical	+	40	22	4	10	6	12	10	16	8	24	18	20	14	20	4	0
Latin	+	8	12	16	6	6	4	16	12	8	4	0	16	0	0	6	2
Horizontal	+	6	20	0	4	6	10	4	10	2	6	8	4	4	6	8	8
St. Andrew's	X	0	0	2	4	2	0	2	2	0	0	0	0	0	2	0	0
Lopsided	+	26	32	14	18	20	20	18	10	18	18	6	12	16	6	8	6
Tipped	X	4	2	6	2	4	2	10	6	12	8	8	8	8	8	6	2
H-oblique	+	0	0	8	8	8	8	4	4	2	10	2	0	2	2	0	0
Curved	+	0	0	2	4	8	4	2	2	2	2	0	0	0	0	0	0
Wavy lines	+	0	0	4	6	0	12	0	0	0	2	0	0	0	0	0	0
Split lines: Middle		0	0	6	4	0	0	0	0	0	0	2	0	0	0	0	0
H sides		2	0	10	12	6	4	0	6	0	0	0	0	2	0	6	4
Other		2	0	6	4	0	0	0	0	0	2	0	0	0	0	0	4

then shows a rise, though small, at 10 years of age (5%). The cross of St. Andrew's

occurs very infrequently and suggests a younger preschool pattern.

SQUARE

The square is recognized, named, and drawn successfully by 4 to 5½ years of age. A method common at 4 (drawing the square with two parallel vertical strokes which are then crossed top and bottom by two horizontal strokes) drops out mostly after that age. Already by 5, children show a variety of ways of copying the square. With four sides to cope with, considerable variability is possible.

Method of Copying

The outstanding method of copying the square at all ages from 5 to 10 years is in a CCW direction (see Table 19), most often with one continuous line, and most often starting with the left side down.

This method or some near variation reaches normative proportions in both sexes by 5½ and 6 years (54% G, 50% B at 5½ years; 66% G, 64% B at 6 years), and gradually reduces in percentage from then on, though it is still the most common method of copying even at 10 years of age (40% G, 30% B).

The CW method of drawing is much less common, and most often starts with the right side down

and reaches a peak at 5½ years of age (24% G, 32% B). This method is seldom used after 7 years of age.

A method conspicuous at most ages may be described as a D formation.

With its variables it ranges between 8% and 36%, showing a low point at 5½ and 6 years and a peak at 5 years (28%), and also at 8 and 9 years (29%, 25%). A form closely allied to the D form and called a broken D

shows a definite rise from 8 years (up to around 18% at 9 and 10 years). Both the D and the broken D are among the more common adult methods of copying.

Another method which shows some increase by 9 and 10 years is what may be called the "corner" method of drawing the square. The more common corner method is left side down, then top from L to R, followed by bottom from L to R, then right side down.

Or the child may draw the corners in two strokes.

Both of these methods have their own variables. This method appears to be used more often by girls than boys. By 10 years of age 24% of girls and only 10% of boys draw in this way.

Two less frequent methods, but ones which show an increase by 9 and 10 years are classified as a double-start method

and a parallel line method suggestive of the 4-year-old's method of drawing.

Both of these methods are used increasingly in the 11- to 16-year-old period.

It is interesting to note to what an extent the starting stroke of left side down predominates and maintains high normative values throughout these years from 5 to 10. Starting the square in this fashion may be compared with drawing the circle CCW and from the top down.

TABLE 19 *Square: Number and Direction of Lines and Type*
(Percentage)

	4½ years G	B	5 years G	B	5½ years G	B	6 years G	B	7 years G	B	8 years G	B	9 years G	B	10 years G	B
Number of Lines Used																
1	24	32	56	44	70	72	80	68	58	64	52	40	28	32	44	30
2	16	18	34	30	18	20	14	22	22	28	26	42	26	32	18	32
3	12	8	2	4	6	6	2	4	18	6	16	8	26	12	18	8
4	38	32	6	20	4	2	4	6	2	2	6	10	20	24	20	30
Other	8	10	2	2	2	2	0	0	0	0	0	0	0	0	0	0
Type of Structure																
CCW																
⬜	8	4	42	20	48	40	58	58	38	46	42	32	26	26	36	26
⬜	0	2	4	6	4	6	8	4	8	4	4	4	2	6	4	4
⬜	0	4	4	0	2	2	0	2	0	4	0	0	0	0	0	0
⬜	0	2	0	2	0	2	0	0	0	0	0	0	0	0	0	0
All CCW	8	12	50	28	54	50	66	64	46	54	46	36	28	32	40	30
CW																
⬜	2	12	6	16	12	10	10	4	4	8	2	0	2	0	4	2
⬜	8	2	4	6	2	10	0	2	2	2	2	0	0	0	0	2
⬜	2	6	0	2	10	12	4	2	6	2	0	4	0	0	0	2
All CW	16	20	10	24	24	32	14	8	12	12	4	4	2	0	4	6

All continuous	24	32	**60**	**52**	**78**	**82**	**80**	**72**	**58**	**66**	**50**	40	30	32	44	36
D and variables																
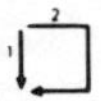	12	8	24	22	8	12	8	14	18	22	22	28	22	16	4	20
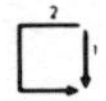	0	6	0	4	0	0	0	2	2	0	0	8	0	0	2	0
	4	0	2	4	0	0	0	2	2	0	0	0	4	8	6	4
All D	16	14	26	30	8	12	8	18	22	22	22	36	26	24	12	24
Broken D and variables																
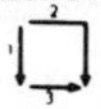	12	2	2	6	6	0	8	2	8	6	14	14	16	20	16	18
Corners																
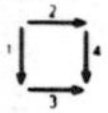	8	0	8	2	0	0	0	4	0	0	6	6	8	6	10	6
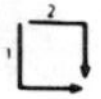	2	0	0	2	4	0	2	2	2	0	0	0	4	0	0	2
Variables	28	40	4	2	4	4	0	0	6	4	4	2	12	4	12	2
All	44	42	12	12	8	4	2	6	8	4	6	8	24	10	24	10
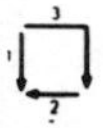	0	0	0	2	0	2	0	2	4	2	4	2	4	6	4	6
Parallel lines																
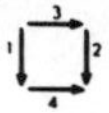	8	12	0	4	0	0	2	0	0	0	0	0	0	8	0	6
Total	96	100	100	100	100	100	100	100	100	100	100	100	100	100	100	100

Another significant trend is that the continuous one-line stroke, which reaches a peak at 6 years (80% G, 72% B) and is still normative at 7 years (58% G, 66% B), breaks up into two, three, or even four strokes (see Table 18). This breakup is still seen in the adult in whom the D and the broken D forms are common. The shift of the bottom stroke of the broken D form to L to R suggests the strength of the drive to stroke from L to R.

Qualitative Aspects

Though the method of copying the square in this 5- to 10-year-old period shows real differentiation and clear age trends, actual success in copying a really well-proportioned square is not conspicuous. As we judge performance, a well-proportioned square has reached only around 40% incidence even by 10 years of age (Table 20). The too-vertically shaped square so common at 4 years is still conspicuous at 5–6 years of age, but steadily decreases thereafter until it is negligible by 8 years and following. The horizontally shaped square, on the other hand, is minimal at 5 years of age and steadily increases until it predominates at 8 and 9 years, especially with girls (38%, 42%).

One of the main difficulties in copying the square is to make good vertical and horizontal lines. One or more lines are often made at an oblique angle. This finding is quite persistent throughout, with a peak at 6 years (38% G, 36% B). Another error is the execution of lines with a wavy or circular stroke, but this does not assume any high proportions (10%±) at 5 years of age, and reduces to around 4% by 8 years of age. A single rounded corner, especially the last one drawn, occurs at 5 and 5½ years, but only occasionally thereafter.

Closure points pose a problem, especially at 5–6 years. A line is apt to lap over or two lines may cross (25%±). Leaving an open space is less common (14%±) and is not much of a problem after 5½ years. Some correct an open space by adding an extra separate line, and others adjust by turning an extra corner so they can contact the beginning line.

TRIANGLE

The triangle presents a whole new problem to the 5-year-old in both the angled control of a line and the conquest of the oblique stroke.

TABLE 20 *Square: Qualitative Aspects*
(Percentage)

	5 years G	B	5½ years G	B	6 years G	B	7 years G	B	8 years G	B	9 years G	B	10 years G	B
Vertical square	32	22	22	36	22	30	6	24	4	16	2	0	0	2
Horizontal square	2	8	8	6	14	16	18	20	38	30	42	38	40	30
A well-proportioned square	12	6	28	16	20	10	34	32	26	32	34	44	42	40
Some oblique side	30	26	22	22	38	36	28	32	24	18	18	14	14	28
Wavy or circular side	4	16	6	10	4	6	12	12	6	4	4	4	4	0
Rounded corner	10	22	12	8	0	2	2	0	0	0	0	0	0	0
Closure points														
Overlapping lines	28	28	22	26	28	24	12	18	8	6	12	2	4	2
Space between lines	12	14	14	16	4	4	8	2	4	4	2	3	0	0
Extra line added	4	6	0	4	0	4	0	4	2	0	0	0	0	0
Adjusts line back	4	2	4	6	6	4	4	4	0	0	6	2	0	0
Starting point														
Left side down	72	50	66	56	76	82	72	78	86	78	86	92	78	88
Left side up	2	12	2	10	0	2	2	2	4	0	0	0	0	2
Right side down	6	24	12	12	12	6	8	10	6	10	2	0	10	2
Top L to R	2	2	14	12	4	4	10	2	0	4	8	2	8	2
Top R to L	6	6	2	8	8	4	8	4	4	8	4	6	4	4
Other	12	6	4	4	0	2	0	4	0	0	0	0	0	2

Though FIVE may not be totally successful in reproducing the triangular form (17% at 5 make a well-proportioned triangle which becomes normative at 7 years and following), he is still not a complete failure. Only 15% of children (20% G, 10% B) fall down entirely at this task even at 5. Failures include the making of either a circle or square form and even then most show awareness that something should be different. A square executed from the bottom up may be left without its top.

Or the two sides may be bridged with a rounded point.

A circular form may have a point, or the addition of a vertical line at the top of the attempted form may be an effort at making a point.

Method of Drawing

No single method of copying the triangle reaches normative proportions, but a starting stroke of left side down, as with the square, maintains a high normative rating throughout.

The various methods of execution may be compared with the square, though the patterns are simpler since there are only three lines to contend with. A continuous CCW line, especially starting left side down, reaches its high point at 6 years of age (26% G, 28% B) and stays close to this figure through 7 years (see Table 21). The CW method, either a continuous or broken line, especially with the left side drawn upward, occurs about the same as in the square at the early ages of 5 and 5½ (18%±). Both the CCW and the CW methods persist, but settle down to a 6 to 16% level by 9 and 10 years.

More frequent are triangles in which lines are not drawn in a single continuous direction. A form that is similar to the D form of the square is made with a single line in one direction plus the two further sides in the reverse direction. Its most common form is left side down, then right side down, plus bottom line drawn R to L, the two latter lines in one continuous stroke.

This form shows a high point from 5 to 7 years (girls, 22%–34%; boys, 22%–30%) and maintains a fairly high level throughout though slightly lowering by 10 years to 24% G, 20% B (see Table 20).

An opposite of this form, occurring minimally, is a triangle starting with the first two sides in the same direction followed by the third side in reverse. The more common structure of this form is the continuous stroke of left side down and bottom from L to R, followed by right side down.

This form reaches its high point at 7 years of age (16% G, 14% B).

An increasing method executed with three separate lines is similar to the broken D form of the square. Its initial stroke is left side down, followed by right side down and concluded by the bottom stroke L to R.

This form reaches normative proportions by 9 years in girls (50% G, 42% B). This is one of the more common methods of execution in the adult.

As with the square, the starting point of left side down predominates increasingly (see Table 22) with high normative values. Also there is a shift (though not as striking as with the square) toward an execution of the triangle with two, and finally with three strokes. Three strokes become normative by 8 years in girls, 9 years in boys (see Table 22).

Qualitative Aspects

The quality of the final product (see Table 22) gives a better clue to age than does the method of execution. Though the majority of children from 5 years following can make some sort of acceptable triangle, a successful, well-proportioned product is not normative in both sexes until 7 years of age (56% G, 68% B). Fortunately, its execution seems to lack some of the pitfalls of the square with its four-sided form. Even a too-vertical execution is not too common, its high points being 14% in girls at 5 and 12% in girls at 7 years. A too broad horizontal form is seldom drawn.

It is the angle of positioning and the difficulty of success with closure points that tell us most about the quality of the triangle. One side only, especially the initial left side, may be drawn vertically downward.

TABLE 21 *Triangle: Number, Direction, and Order of Lines*
(Percentage of Responses)

	5 years G	5 years B	5½ years G	5½ years B	6 years G	6 years B	7 years G	7 years B	8 years G	8 years B	9 years G	9 years B	10 years G	10 years B
CCW														
△	6	6	12	12	18	24	16	22	8	22	6	10	6	8
△	4	2	2	6	4	4	2	4	0	2	0	2	0	0
△	0	0	4	2	4	0	6	0	2	0	0	0	0	0
All CCW	10	8	18	20	26	28	24	26	10	24	6	12	6	8
CW														
△	10	8	14	12	12	8	6	4	6	8	6	6	8	16
△	4	6	4	4	4	2	0	0	2	0	0	0	0	0
△ (2)	6	0	0	0	0	0	0	0	0	0	0	2	0	0
All CW	20	14	18	16	16	10	6	4	8	8	6	8	8	16
One side plus 2 continuous sides in reverse, and variables														
△ (2)	34	26	22	22	26	26	34	30	26	22	18	22	24	20
△ (2)	4	14	2	20	4	4	0	2	2	4	0	2	0	2
△ (2)	0	2	4	2	0	2	0	2	0	0	0	4	0	2
All	38	42	28	44	30	32	34	34	28	26	18	28	24	24

Two continuous sides plus 1 side in
reverse, and variables

△	6	10	6	12	12	6	14	16	2	8	8	4	6	2
△	0	2	0	0	2	2	0	2	2	0	2	4	4	0
△	2	6	2	8	0	2	2	0	0	2	0	2	0	2
△	0	0	0	0	0	2	2	0	0	0	0	2	2	0
	0	0	0	0	0	0	0	0	0	0	2	2	2	2
All	8	18	8	20	14	12	18	18	4	10	12	14	14	6
Three lines														
△	42	42	42	50	28	40	24	16	26	16	6	18	14	14
△	2	2	2	0	0	2	4	2	0	2	2	4	2	0
All	44	44	44	50	28	42	28	18	26	18	8	22	16	14
Other	0	0	0	0	0	0	0	0	0	0	0	0	6	12

TABLE 22 *Triangle: Number of Lines, Starting Point, and Qualitative Evaluation*
(Percentage of Responses)

	4½ years G	4½ years B	5 years G	5 years B	5½ years G	5½ years B	6 years G	6 years B	7 years G	7 years B	8 years G	8 years B	9 years G	9 years B	10 years G	10 years B
Number of lines																
1	8	14	26	20	36	30	40	38	30	30	20	32	12	18	12	22
2	26	26	46	36	34	**52**	40	32	**52**	48	30	26	26	26	36	18
3	**50**	40	28	44	30	18	20	30	18	22	**50**	42	**62**	**56**	**52**	**60**
Fails entirely	28	**56**	20	10	2	0	0	0	0	0	0	0	0	0	0	0
Some success	**72**	44	**80**	**90**	**98**	**100**	**100**	**100**	**100**	**100**	**100**	**100**	**100**	**100**	**100**	**100**
Well proportioned triangle	18	14	14	20	38	42	36	50	56	**68**	**78**	**62**	**66**	**64**	**82**	**70**
Variations																
Too vertical	△		14	2	4	2	6	8	12	2	8	8	2	4	0	4
Too horizontal	◁		2	2	0	4	4	2	0	0	0	2	0	0	0	0
One vertical side	△		16	6	18	8	8	6	0	0	0	2	2	0	0	0
One curved side	△		6	26	16	16	2	2	2	6	0	4	0	2	0	0

84

Oblique base line	14	28	22	18	20	18	10	8	8	8	6	8	10	8
Lopsided	4	2	2	0	14	18	16	14	2	2	16	14	8	14
Extra line for closure	8	4	2	2	0	2	2	0	2	2	4	2	6	0
Upside down	2	0	2	0	0	4	0	0	2	2	0	0	0	0
Space at closure	6	8	10	2	4	4	8	4	10	10	2	2	2	4
Overlapping line or lines	16	12	20	20	20	10	8	10	10	10	4	4	0	10
Line extended to fill gap	8	4	4	0	0	4	2	2	0	0	0	6	6	0
Starting point														
Left side down	62	40	60	46	78	68	82	80	78	80	84	80	82	76
Left side up	14	16	14	10	8	14	6	6	8	8	14	12	14	20
Right side down	10	28	12	28	8	8	4	6	8	6	2	2	4	2
Right side up	2	4	4	4	0	4	6	2	4	2	0	0	0	0
Bottom L to R	6	8	10	12	6	6	2	6	2	2	0	6	0	2
Bottom R to L	6	4	0	0	0	0	0	0	0	2	0	0	0	0

This is most common at 5 and 5½ years when the ability to make two oblique lines, one to the right as well as one to the left, has not yet been mastered. A curved line may be used instead of an oblique line. This is more commonly noted at 5 and 5½ years when the final side may be curved down from the point.

Placing the triangle flat on its base does not occur substantially before 7 and 8 years of age. Rather the base line is more often tilted at an oblique (14–28% at the 5- to 6-year level). From 7 on this tilting occurs only from 6 to 10%. Though the triangle may be well placed on its base, it may still appear lopsided, which indicates that one side is more oblique or less oblique than the other. This remains within a 15%± range right through from 6 to 10 years.

The difficulty of effecting good closure points may either produce a space or an extension of line or lines which suggests that either the form has increased in proportion as it is being drawn,

or that it has decreased in proportion, thus leaving a part of the original starting line jutting out.

In the case of the increase in proportion the child may leave the space as it is, may add a line to close the gap, or may continue his stroke, turning a corner and returning to the point of origin.

In the case of a decrease in proportion the child often has trouble in stopping. Thus his stroke may go beyond the starting line forming an X-formation.

Closure difficulty ranges anywhere from 14% to 30% in the ages from 5 to 8 years. This difficulty is more extreme at 5 and 5½ years. If it persists after 8 years of age it may indicate a lower quality response.

DIVIDED RECTANGLE

The divided rectangle is often viewed by the 4- or 5-year-old as "too hard" or "tough," and yet most are able at least to tackle it. Four gets the general idea and often makes what we call a "ladder" formation. He makes a vertical square, bisects it with a vertical line, and then makes many horizontal lines in ladder formation on either side of this vertical line. Leftovers of this method are occasionally seen at 5 years of age.

Outside

Five has a closer approach than four to accuracy in copying the divided rectangle both as to inner and outer structure. He may still make a circular framework (8% G, 2% B), but most are coming into some idea of a rectangular shape (38% G, 40% B) (see Table 23). This rectangular shape is coming into surer form by 5½ years (56% G, 62% B) and is well established by 7 years (86% G, 78% B). The too-vertical shape is still produced to some extent at 5 and 5½ years, suggesting a leftover 4-year-old method, but this occurs infrequently thereafter.

As Table 23 shows, production of some kind of successful rectangular outside shape for the divided rectangle is normative at 5½ years and following. The method of making this rectangle varies widely. A continuous line, in either CW or CCW direction, is normative in both sexes at 5½, 6, and 7 years. A continuous CCW line is the leading single method through 7 years of age. Some variation of a two- to four-line product leads at 9 and 10 years.

Since the method of execution of the rectangular outside form follows much the method used in copying the square, even though there are some clear differences, we shall compare methods of making both of these forms in Table 24. There is in general less of a tendency to use continuous strokes with the divided rectangle than with the square. This use of a continuous line is strong for both forms through 7 years, but occurs slightly less for the outside of the divided rectangle than for the square, thereafter. Also the divided rectangle is less likely to start with the left side down.

There is at most ages slightly more drawing in a continuous CW direction for the rectangle than for the square. Another method which is used quite a bit more in the divided rectangle than in the square is the method of making two solid corners.

TABLE 23   Divided Rectangle: Pattern of Outside
(Percentage)

	4½ years G	B	5 years G	B	5½ years G	B	6 years G	B	7 years G	B	8 years G	B	9 years G	B	10 years G	B	Adult
Shape of outside																	
No trial	8	8	0	0	0	0	0	0	0	0	0	0	0	0	0	0	0
No outside	8	18	0	2	0	0	0	0	0	0	0	0	0	0	0	0	0
Circular	18	18	8	2	0	0	0	0	0	0	0	0	0	0	0	0	0
Square	32	32	38	42	40	18	28	34	12	18	4	6	0	0	0	0	0
Rectangle	14	20	38	40	56	62	64	62	86	78	96	92	100	98	100	100	100
Vertical rectangle	20	14	16	14	4	20	8	4	2	4	0	2	0	2	0	0	0
Continuous CW																	
⬜			4	4	10	16	10	12	12	4	4	8	4	2	8	8	0
⬜			8	12	4	14	6	8	10	6	2	0	2	0	0	0	0
⬜			2	2	2	4	0	4	2	2	0	0	0	0	0	2	7
Other			2	—	2	—	2	—	0	—	4	—	0	—	0	—	0
All continuous CW			16	20	18	36	18	26	24	12	10	8	6	2	8	6	7

Continuous CCW

The age-column headings (across the top of the full table) are not captured in this crop; the 15 data columns are shown below as C1–C15. Bold values mark the leading behavior at each age, per the note.

Behavior	C1	C2	C3	C4	C5	C6	C7	C8	C9	C10	C11	C12	C13	C14	C15
[□ symbol]	14	16	20	18	10	24	24	48	32	38	46	28	36	14	22
[□ symbol]	0	0	0	0	0	0	0	2	0	0	2	6	0	4	2
[□ symbol]	0	6	4	4	0	8	4	4	4	6	4	4	6	0	6
Other	0	2	2	2	2	2	0	2	0	0	4	6	2	0	0
All continuous CCW	14	24	26	24	12	34	28	56	36	44	56	44	44	18	30
All continuous	21	30	**34**	**42**	18	**42**	**38**	**68**	**60**	**70**	**74**	**80**	**62**	38	**46**
Two solid corners	0	6	10	**14**	**12**	4	10	8	2	4	4	6	8	4	20
Variations															
[□ symbol 1→]	21	18	10	22	12	26	26	18	18	10	4	4	4	4	10
[□ symbol 1→ 2,3]	36	12	2	4	10	2	4	0	2	2	4	0	2	4	8
[□ symbol 2,1]	0	2	10	4	8	4	0	0	4	4	2	2	0	0	0
[□ symbol 1→ 2,3]	0	4	4	4	6	6	4	0	4	4	2	2	0	2	0
All these variations	**57**	**36**	26	34	**36**	38	34	18	28	20	12	6	16	10	18
All other	21	28	30	26	34	16	18	8	10	6	10	8	14	**48**	16

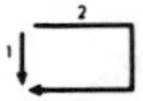

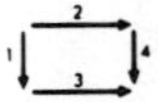

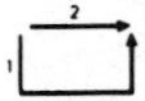

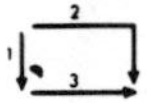

NOTE: Since so few types of response reach normative values, boldface items in this table indicate merely leading behaviors at each age.

TABLE 24   *Comparison of Methods of Reproducing Outside of Divided Rectangle and Square*
(Percentage of Each Type of Drawing)

	5 years		5½ years		6 years		7 years		8 years		9 years		10 years	
	G	B	G	B	G	B	G	B	G	B	G	B	G	B
Continuous line														
Square	**56**	**58**	**78**	**80**	**80**	**72**	**58**	**66**	**56**	40	28	32	44	36
Rectangle	46	38	**62**	**80**	**74**	**70**	**60**	**68**	38	42	18	26	34	30
Starting point, left side down														
Square	**72**	**50**	**66**	**54**	**76**	**82**	**72**	**78**	**86**	**78**	**86**	**92**	**78**	**88**
Rectangle	36	22	40	**54**	**54**	**54**	**66**	**56**	**58**	**58**	34	48	36	46
Continuous CCW														
Square	48	26	**54**	48	**66**	**64**	46	**54**	48	36	26	32	40	28
Rectangle	30	18	44	44	**56**	44	36	**56**	28	34	12	24	26	24
Continuous CW														
Square	8	32	24	32	14	8	12	12	8	4	2	0	4	8
Rectangle	16	20	18	36	18	26	24	12	10	8	6	2	8	6
Two solid corners														
Square	0	0	4	0	2	2	2	0	0	0	4	0	0	2
Rectangle	20	4	8	6	4	4	2	8	10	4	12	14	10	6

Some of the highlights of both are: (1) there is a rising predominance of drawing in a CCW direction with the starting point left side down, with peaks from 5½ to 7 for the square, from 6 to 7 with the rectangle; (2) the D formation (left side down, rest of square in a continuous CW direction starting with the top line) shows a similar peak for both square and divided rectangle at 8 years of age (22% for square, 26% for divided rectangle).

Inside

The inside of the divided rectangle poses a much more complicated problem of analysis than does the outside as well as being more difficult for the child at the earlier ages to reproduce correctly.

In spite of its complexity there are three predominant patterns which can be observed (Table 25). They are discussed in the following sections.

CENTRAL STAR PATTERN

The first is a central star pattern with lines radiating either out of or into a central area.

TABLE 25 *Divided Rectangle: All Inside Patterns*
(Percentage of Responses)

	4½ years		5 years		5½ years		6 years		7 years		8 years		9 years		10 years	
	G	B	G	B	G	B	G	B	G	B	G	B	G	B	G	B
Vague inside markings or H line or lines	38	48	4	12	0	0	0	0	0	0	0	0	0	0	0	0
Central star patterns	14	16	12	6	8	6	4	8	0	4	2	0	0	0	0	0
Vertical cleavage patterns	34	10	38	32	36	28	22	24	20	26	6	20	8	4	2	2
Cross-over patterns	6	18	46	50	56	66	74	68	80	70	92	80	92	96	98	98
Central Star Pattern, Lines Meeting at Center																
All central star patterns	14	8	12	6	8	6	4	8	0	4	2	0				
Accurate 8 lines	6	2	6	0	4	0	2	4	0	4	2	0				
Inaccurate lines	8	6	6	0	4	6	2	4	0	0	0	0				
Poor center	8	8	12	6	6	4	2	6	0	2	2	0				
Good center	6	2	0	0	2	2	2	2	0	2	0	0				
Dot center	6	2	4	0	2	2	2	6	0	0	0	0				

This is an immature pattern which does not occur much beyond 6 years of age and even in the 5- to 6-year period it occurs only between 4 and 12 percent (see Table 25). This response suggests that the individual who uses this form is working from a focal point. The accuracy of the number of lines is no better than 50%. However, when this pattern occurs after 6 years, the eight half-lines are drawn so carefully that unless the examiner has observed the method of production he would judge the final product to be highly successful.

The eight half-lines may all be drawn in or out from the center, or some may be drawn in and some out. Lines are most accurate at their point of origin. Thus the center point will be the more accurate if the lines start there; the corners and sides will be the more accurate if the lines start there.

CLEAVAGE PATTERNS

The cleavage pattern, chiefly made with a vertical central line separating the several shorter horizontal or oblique lines on each side which do not cross the central vertical line, is especially common at 5 and 5½ years (30%±), though it persists at only a slightly lower level (24%±) through 7 years and reduces fairly steadily from then on (see Table 26). At 5 years of age the expected three lines on either side of the vertical line tend to be inaccurate. However from 6 years on the accuracy is very high.

The problem of pulling the six half-lines into a central point is especially difficult for the 5-year-old. He still tends to draw the lines horizontally, parallel to each other as he did when he was 4. He is, however, beginning to make the outer top and bottom side lines slope obliquely inward toward a center.

By 5½ years, he becomes more concerned with the central area and may affix a dot from which he may draw the lines in or out.

He may thus secure a good central meeting area, but this success is not sizable.

Most draw the six lines out from the central vertical line or from some central point on this line, rather than in. Initially lines are drawn in order (usually from top to bottom), but when the child selects to make the obliques first, followed by the horizontal stroke, he is showing a reorganization.

TABLE 26 *Divided Rectangle: Vertical Cleavage Patterns*
(Percentage of Responses)

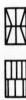

	5 years		5½ years		6 years		7 years		8 years		9 years		10 years	
	G	B	G	B	G	B	G	B	G	B	G	B	G	B
All with central V-line	38	32	36	28	22	24	20	26	6	20	8	4	2	2
Short H- or oblique-lines on each side of central V-line:														
3 on each side	14	20	26	20	18	24	18	26	6	18	8	4	2	2
More than 3	14	12	6	6	2	0	0	0	0	0	0	0	0	0
Less than 3	6	0	2	2	2	0	2	0	0	2	0	0	0	0
Centering														
Poor	18	8	22	10	12	18	16	20	2	12	2	0	2	2
Good	2	2	6	14	4	6	2	6	4	8	6	4	2	0
Dot	0	0	6	4	0	0	0	2	0	0	0	0	0	0
Beginning oblique	8	10	4	0	4	0	0	0	0	0	0	0	0	0
Parallel lines	6	14	4	4	2	0	2	0	0	0	0	0	0	0
Direction of lines related to center														
Out	24	20	22	12	12	18	10	16	4	0	6	2	0	0
In	6	8	6	14	4	4	2	2	0	2	0	0	0	0
In and out	4	4	8	2	6	2	8	8	2	18	2	2	2	2
Obliques first, then H-line	0	0	0	8	2	6	0	0	0	0	0	0	0	0
Pairing both sides	4	8	12	12	2	2	2	0	0	4	0	0	0	0
H, same direction	0	0	0	2	2	2	2	10	0	8	2	2	2	2
Obliques, same direction	0	0	0	0	0	0	2	18	0	18	2	2	2	2

Further evidences of change occur when the child pairs two lines as he draws, as for instance the upper two obliques followed by the two horizontal lines. This suggests an approach to the crossing over of the vertical line which will come later. This pairing of lines occurs especially at 5½ years (12%). The final step before the cleavage pattern is broken into and lines are drawn straight through or across the central vertical line is shown by the two parts of a line on either side of the vertical line being executed in the same direction. Thus a horizontal line might be drawn in toward the center on one side and then out from the center on the other side, though still in two parts.

One might predict from this that within a short time the child who made such a pattern would make a continuous horizontal line.

CROSS-OVER PATTERN

The cleavage pattern is broken into when any one of the three horizontal or oblique lines crosses over the vertical line. The remaining one or two lines may at first remain split in various ways. The variety of patterns is so multiple especially when the shifts in direction of stroke are noted that it seems best in this analysis mainly to consider the form and sequence of stroke without including the direction, other than in a general way.

The four-line cross-over pattern executed in many different ways makes up a majority of the inside patterns from 5 years on and steadily increases (see Table 27). Even by 6 years of age it shows a normative rating (66% G, 58% B). The most prominent sequential patterns are as follows:

$$+ \times \; ; \; \times + \; ; \; | \times -$$

The most common directions in which these three combinations are drawn are

A R to L stroke or bottom-up stroke is infrequent, but when these do occur they are significant in that they suggest, as do other similar patterns, a backtracking or reversal of stroke which may be linked with other reversal patterns.

The pattern,

takes the lead as the most common four-line cross-over pattern at 6 and especially at 7 years (42% G, 26% B). However, the

pattern takes the lead at 9 and 10 years, reaching close to normative values by 10 years (46% G, 40% B) (see Table 27). This is also probably the most common adult pattern.

Two line cross-over patterns persist throughout this whole period, slowly decreasing from a 16% level at 5 years to a 6% level at 10 years. The commonest of these is

$$+ \ \times$$

The oblique lines may radiate out from or in to the center, but the more common pattern is out from the center. It is interesting to note the continued presence even in low percentages (4–8%) of the splitting of oblique lines from 5 to 10 years. The H- and V-line splits,

$$\times \ -\!\!\mid\!\!-$$

on the other hand, are very infrequent and occur only at 5 years of age.

Qualitative Aspects

The quality of the final product is always significant. The demands of the divided rectangle are far greater than those of any other form. There are many line contact points that demand a mastery of spatial relationships. The vertical and horizontal lines need to be placed at half-way points. The obliques need to originate or end in corners. The fact that the four lines need to cross at a central point, in addition to fulfilling all the other demands of this form, makes one aware of why a fully correct performance, at least from a qualitative point of view, has not yet reached normative levels even by 10 years of age.

Table 28 presents data on contact points between inner lines and frame, on corner contacts, and on central crossing of lines.

TABLE 27 *Divided Rectangle: Cross-Over Patterns*
(Percentage of Responses)

	5 years G	5 years B	5½ years G	5½ years B	6 years G	6 years B	7 years G	7 years B	8 years G	8 years B	9 years G	9 years B	10 years G	10 years B
					Younger Patterns									
Omission of H-line	10	6	4	0	4	4	2	0	2	2	0	0	0	0
Omission of V-line	4	2	0	0	0	0	0	2	0	2	0	0	0	0
Omission (+ ; X)	2	4	0	0	0	0	0	0	0	0	0	0	0	0
Extra line (+)	4	2	6	0	0	2	0	2	0	0	0	0	0	0
Central dot	2	2	0	4	0	2	0	2	0	0	0	0	0	0
			Total of Two Lines Including Broken Lines											
≻<	4	10	8	8	2	2	4	4	8	4	4	4	4	8
⊹	2	0	0	0	0	0	0	0	0	0	0	0	0	0
Variables (X)	8	2	6	8	6	8	6	8	4	4	2	6	0	0
X ; + alone	2	4	2	2	0	0	0	0	0	0	0	0	0	0
Total	16	16	16	18	8	10	10	12	12	8	6	10	4	8

Three Lines														
`| X ⋮ X |`	4	6	4	0	0	0	0	0	0	0	0	0	0	0
`X ╱`	4	0	0	0	0	0	0	0	0	0	0	0	0	0
Total	8	6	4	0	0	0	0	0	0	0	0	0	0	0
Four Lines														
`╱ +`	2	4	0	2	4	0	2	0	0	0	0	4	0	0
`╲ ╱⋰`	2	0	4	4	4	4	8	10	4	2	0	2	2	8
`⎯ |`	0	2	0	0	0	0	0	0	0	0	0	0	0	0
`| ╳`	12	10	8	14	22	18	42	26	32	18	36	30	22	12
`╳ +`	10	10	6	18	20	18	10	12	20	26	14	16	24	30
`+ ╳`	6	2	8	10	16	18	8	10	24	26	36	34	46	40
Total	32	28	26	48	66	58	70	58	80	72	86	86	94	90
All cross-over patterns	56	50	46	66	74	68	80	70	92	80	92	96	98	98

TABLE 28   *Inside Pattern Divided Rectangle: Qualitative Aspects*
(Percentage of Responses)

	5 years G	B	5½ years G	B	6 years G	B	7 years G	B	8 years G	B	9 years G	B	10 years G	B
Contact Points Between Lines and Frame														
Line overlaps frame	**64**	**42**	**58**	**58**	**74**	**74**	**64**	**68**	42	32	40	26	12	18
Line misses frame:														
Wide space	26	16	14	4	8	4	4	4	0	0	0	0	2	0
Small space	10	6	30	30	46	**52**	46	44	34	22	18	22	18	12
Corner Contacts														
0 corners good	46	**50**	18	16	22	28	22	18	4	4	0	6	2	2
1 corner good	22	20	26	18	40	30	34	24	12	6	16	2	4	12
2 corners good	22	20	32	26	30	26	28	26	34	36	28	40	34	36
3 corners good	6	10	18	20	6	12	10	24	34	36	28	40	34	36
4 corners good	4	0	6	20	2	4	6	8	16	18	18	26	40	32
Crossing of Four Lines														
2 lines cross	18	18	24	24	32	32	42	24	30	34	20	24	26	20
3 lines cross at one point	2	8	16	10	20	24	16	28	34	28	40	32	22	26
4 lines cross at one point	6	0	0	0	14	2	14	12	24	14	28	34	44	42

CONTACT POINTS BETWEEN INNER LINES AND FRAME

The spaces left between contact points in the divided rectangle are wider, the overlapping lines are longer, than in any other forms. Even so, it seems almost unbelievable that the contact with the frame could be missed by such a wide space as is left by many, especially at 5 and 5½ years of age.

It seems as though, as the child concentrates on one aspect of the form, he cannot include all other aspects. Very wide spaces are uncommon after 5½ years of age. Missing the frame by a small space, however, is still strongly evident even at 7 years and though it definitely decreases, it is still present in a few children as late as 10 years.

The overlapping of inside lines over outside frame is even more in evidence and reaches a peak at 6 years of age (74%). The control of stroke slowly improves but is still a problem with a few as late as 10 years of age.

CORNER CONTACTS

The success of corner contacts of the diagonals with the frame is in large part dependent upon whether the diagonal is started or ended at the corner in question. The chances of success are far greater for the start of a line than for the ending. The 5- or 6-year-old line may wobble into a corner, but on the whole it has only reached this corner by great restabilizing efforts, or by chance. At 5 years the item "no correct corners" is so high that it is at near normative levels (46% G, 50% B).

A 5-year-old may have the full four lines crossing each other, but he has great trouble in controlling their angle. They may even land up on top of each other.

Corner contacts steadily improve with age. One or two are usually correct at 5½, 6, and 7 years, two or three at 8 and 9 years, and three or four at 10 years (see Table 28). When a child at 10 is still unable to contact one single corner, something is seriously wrong with him.

CENTRAL CROSSING OF FOUR LINES

Centering patterns have already been discussed under cleavage patterns. It was noted how poor the centering patterns were with the cleavage pattern until 9 years of age. The success of these centering patterns was largely dependent upon whether the lateral lines radiated out from the central point or not. With the starting points from the center the success is more assured. This same situation arises with the cross-over pattern when the obliques are split.

$$+ \quad \times$$

If the obliques radiate out from the center of the cross the success of the center is more assured.

Table 28 also considers the four-line crossing patterns. A fully successful pattern is achieved when all four lines cross at a single central point.

Other less successful productions involve any three lines crossing at the same point; or any two lines crossing. This latter type of two-line crossing is especially evident up to 8 years. By 6 years of age there is fair success in the crossing of three lines. This rises steadily from 7 to 9 years and is superseded at 10 years by the correct crossing of all four lines at a central point. Even at 10, this correct crossing does not reach normative proportions (44% G, 42% B). It will still take the draftsman potentials of the 13-year-old to pull this pattern up into normative levels.

DIAMOND

The diamond, the sixth and last of the Copy Forms, was an essential item included by Binet. He considered it to be a 7-year-old item, which it still turns out to be with 76% G, 60% B making it correctly at that age (see Table 29), but it has a long developmental history both before and after this 7-year critical stage. Although Binet presented this form only in a vertical position, a true diamond position, we had it printed on our cards in a horizontal position since it fitted better in this orientation.

TABLE 29   *Success in Copying the Diamond in Its Two Positions*
(Percentage of Responses)

	$4\frac{1}{2}$ years		5 years		$5\frac{1}{2}$ years		6 years	
	G	B	G	B	G	B	G	B
Neither correct	98	98	94	82	74	62	60	46
V alone correct	2	0	4	8	14	14	18	36
H alone correct	2	2	2	10	10	16	4	12
Both correct	0	0	0	0	2	8	18	6
Shifts and Reversals								
Paper shifted to H, child draws V	2	0	0	0	0	2	0	0
H and V reversed	0	0	0	0	2	4	2	0
V drawn for both H and V	2	0	4	8	6	8	6	4
Refusals	22	8	2	6	0	0	2	0

	7 years		8 years		9 years		10 years	
	G	B	G	B	G	B	G	B
Neither correct	0	4	0	4	4	0	0	0
V alone correct	20	28	20	28	12	20	4	12
H alone correct	4	8	4	8	2	0	6	0
Both correct	76	60	76	60	82	80	90	88
Shifts and Reversals								
Paper shifted to H, child draws V	8	4	2	10	10	4	8	4
H and V reversed	0	0	4	2	4	0	0	0
V drawn for both H and V	2	6	4	4	2	0	0	0
Refusals	0	0	0	0	0	0	0	0

Originally we shifted the card so that the diamond would be presented to the child in a vertical position. Almost by accident we stumbled onto letting the card remain in its original position with the diamond oriented horizontally. We then presented it a second time in a vertical position. We frequently noted that a child could copy the diamond in one position, but not in the other. We also noted that often his method of copying varied, undoubtedly stimulated by his own shift in orientation to the two different positions of the stimulus.

Responses to the horizontally and vertically presented diamond as shown in the accompanying tables actually are very comparable, but the differences are also sizable.

The need of the child to shift the horizontal diamond to a vertical position in order to draw it is four times as common as the opposite of needing to shift a vertical diamond to a horizontal position. Younger patterns are more persistent in response to the horizontal diamond, and when one form only is copied successfully it is more often (three to four times) the vertical diamond in the period from 6 to 8 years when there is a differential response to the two positions (see Table 29).

The 4-year-old initially views the diamond as being "hard," but still he is willing to tackle it. Even the younger, unsuccessful patterns do show some patterning and reveal an edge of comprehending the form. These young patterns are seen most often at 5 and 5½ years (Table 30). They vary from a primitive irregular blob, to a single line in either a vertical or horizontal direction, to two lines, to a single open point, a point coming out of a shapeless mass, two points, three points and finally a shape in which two side points jut out like ears. When closure is difficult the form may even end with five sides. Another variable may be a horizontal or vertical rectangle suggesting that the child recognizes the relative shape, but cannot execute an oblique stroke. An interesting but infrequent pattern is one in which one of the points is reversed in on itself.

On the whole the three-sided form and the forms with ears are the most common of the younger patterns. They persist through 6 and even into 7 years of age (see Table 30). No younger patterns are used in reproducing the V-diamond and virtually none in reproducing the H-diamond after 7 years.

Though the younger patterns predominate at 5 years of age they rapidly reduce thereafter. Even by 5½ years the more patterned forms have reached a normative level. But the successful reproduction of both forms is not normative before 7 years of age (see Table 29).

The patterns of reproduction fall chiefly into the CCW and CW continuous forms, D and broken D patterns, and vertical and horizontal

TABLE 30   *Diamond: Younger Patterns*
(Percentage of Occurrence)

		5 years G	5 years B	5½ years G	5½ years B	6 years G	6 years B	7 years G	7 years B
	◇								
Blob		2	2	0	0	0	0	0	0
Line or lines		2	2	2	0	2	0	0	0
2 lines		6	6	8	2	0	0	0	0
Open point		0	0	2	2	0	0	0	0
1 point		16	12	0	2	0	0	0	0
2 points		4	2	2	4	0	4	0	0
2 triangles		0	2	0	0	0	0	2	0
Triangle of 3 points		16	18	10	6	4	6	0	0
Ears		12	4	10	12	16	8	14	2
5 sides		2	0	2	2	4	4	2	0
Rectangle		14	6	2	0	2	0	0	0
Inverted point		2	0	0	0	2	2	0	0
		76	54	38	30	30	24	18	2
	◇								
Blob		4	0	0	0	0	0	0	0
Line or lines		6	0	0	0	2	0	0	0
2 lines		6	6	4	2	0	0	0	0
Open point		2	6	0	2	0	0	0	0
1 point		6	12	0	0	0	0	0	0
2 points		2	0	4	0	0	0	2	0
Triangle of 3 points		14	16	10	12	2	4	0	0
Ears		12	6	14	12	14	8	6	0
Rectangle		4	6	0	0	2	0	0	0
5 sides		4	4	4	0	2	2	2	0
Inverted point		2	0	0	0	0	0	0	0
		62	56	36	28	22	14	10	0

cleavage patterns (see Table 31). Less frequent are mixed patterns which may be described variously. The characteristic aspects of so-called "mixed" forms might be, for example, a two-line start followed by an opposite parallel line with the final line then executed in a reverse direction

or another example might be

Another mixed pattern includes two starting points.

The frequency of occurrence of all these different patterns for horizontal and vertical diamonds is shown in Table 31.

All continuous patterns combined reach normative values for the horizontal diamond at 7 years of age (54% G, 66% B) and for boys only (54%) for the vertical diamond at this same age. On the whole the CCW direction, mostly starting with left side down, definitely leads. The continuous method of drawing, however, decreases slowly from 7 years on (see Table 31).

The D pattern occurs much more frequently for the horizontal than for the vertical diamond, reaching a peak at 8 years of age in the horizontal diamond (24% G, 20% B). The broken D on the other hand is more common with the vertical diamond, reaching its high point at 7 years (8% G, 10% B), though even these figures are, obviously, low.

Vertical cleavage patterns are, as might be expected, twice as common with the vertical diamond as with the horizontal, showing a sizable peak at both 8 and 9 years (40%). The most common vertical cleavage pattern is made with two single side strokes.

The horizontal cleavage patterns are more alike for the two positions of the diamond than are vertical cleavage patterns. The most common horizontal cleavage pattern is a four-stroke pattern.

TABLE 31 *Diamond: Different Patterns of Response*
(Percentage of Responses)

	5 years		5½ years		6 years		7 years		8 years		9 years		10 years	
	G	B	G	B	G	B	G	B	G	B	G	B	G	B
No trial	2	6	0	0	2	0	0	0	0	0	0	0	0	0
All younger patterns	76	54	38	30	30	24	18	2	2	0	2	0	0	0
Continuous CCW	0	0	12	6	16	22	20	30	14	24	10	8	12	10
Variables	2	2	8	14	6	4	4	10	6	10	8	8	0	4
All CCW	2	2	20	20	22	26	24	40	20	34	18	16	12	14
CW	2	12	6	4	10	10	22	22	8	10	4	18	10	18
Variables	4	8	8	4	2	6	8	4	0	2	0	4	0	6
All CW	6	20	14	8	12	16	30	26	8	12	4	22	10	24
All continuous	8	22	34	28	34	42	54	66	28	46	22	38	22	38
D and broken D	2	2	14	14	18	8	6	12	26	20	12	18	18	12
V-cleavage and variables	8	6	8	6	12	14	8	12	18	6	22	10	30	12
H-cleavage and variables	4	10	4	16	4	10	10	8	18	22	30	30	22	34
Mixed patterns	0	0	2	6	0	2	4	0	8	6	12	4	8	4

No trial	4	6	0	0	0	0	0	0	0	0	0	0	0	0
All younger patterns	**62**	**56**	36	28	22	14	10	0	0	0	0	0	0	0
Continuous CCW	2	0	10	16	16	18	18	36	18	28	12	18	14	16
Variables	2	6	10	8	10	2	2	4	4	0	4	2	2	2
All CCW	4	6	20	24	26	20	20	40	22	28	16	20	16	18
CW	2	6	4	4	10	14	8	6	4	8	2	8	4	14
Variables	6	0	6	2	4	4	2	8	2	2	2	0	0	4
All CW	8	6	10	6	14	18	10	14	6	10	4	8	4	18
All continuous	12	12	30	30	40	38	30	**54**	28	38	20	28	20	36
D, broken D, and variables	4	4	6	10	8	18	14	14	12	6	8	4	8	12
V-cleavage and variables	10	10	12	14	16	22	22	24	44	34	36	40	28	14
H-cleavage and variables	8	12	12	14	14	6	22	4	10	18	30	24	38	34
Mixed patterns	0	0	4	4	0	2	2	4	6	4	6	4	6	4

It is steadily rising for both positions of the diamond, showing higher figures with the vertical diamond. The two-line horizontal pattern

is fairly common in response to the horizontal diamond, but occurs infrequently with the vertical diamond. This two-line horizontal pattern for the horizontal diamond occurs fairly frequently with the adult.

"Mixed" patterns occur throughout but at a low level (2 to 10%). In general they occur more often at 8 to 10 years.

The quality appraisal of the copy diamond can be very demanding (see Table 32). There is the obvious poor quality of a wide space between contact points which actually demands extra lines to close up the gap, or these spaces may be left gapping especially at 5 and 5½ years. A small space is evident in some at these younger ages and persists at the older ages especially with the vertical diamond, (6% at 7–8 years). The opposite of an open space also occurs—an overlapping of line or lines. The overlapping line is most common at 5–6 years. On the whole, however, from 7 years of age on, contact points are usually good.

The rounded or curved line is especially conspicuous at 5 and 5½ years. Its occurrence after this age, which can be as high as 10%, suggests that the individual does not have good control of his line.

The final product, especially of the horizontal diamond, may appear more like a square or a rectangle on its point. This occurs especially in the male from 5½ to 8 years of age (35%±).

Either the top or bottom half of the diamond, especially of the vertical diamond, may be the longer. Or the diamond may appear lopsided, with one side more prominent than the other. The side points of the vertical diamond may be at different levels, or the figure may be placed at an oblique angle.

The diamond may still be relatively successful even with some of these quality flaws. The quality, however, becomes an important part of the final appraisal. Probably one of the evidences of superiority is a relatively good diamond at 5 or 6 years of age.

Sex differences come out rather strikingly with the diamond, especially in relation to younger patterns. Girls have more difficulty with this form than do boys and these difficulties persist into 7 years and beyond. Boys on the whole show more continuous patterns.

THREE-DIMENSIONAL FORMS

The Cylinder

The 5-year-old is most likely to merely draw a circle in response to the request that he draw the cylinder (52% G, 60% B) and to report that he has drawn the bottom of the form, or that he has drawn the whole thing. A circle remains the preferred, though decreasing, method of copying through 6 years of age. However, at 6 years most say that they have drawn the top of the cylinder. This single circle method of copying is strong through 6 years and also in boys at 7, but uncommon after that.

Another fairly common method of copying, right through 8 years of age, is a front view drawn as a square or triangle. As a child begins to recognize surfaces he may draw a square formation and then cut into it with a curved line at top and bottom (see Table 33, line 6). This response occurs, minimally, throughout the entire age range.

Another expression of the recognition of surfaces, which occurs in a few children, is to draw two circles—one for the top and one for the bottom either in vertical formation or one inside the other. A next step is to combine the two separate circles with vertical lines.

This response is coming in at 5½ and 6 years, is quite sizable by 7 years of age (22% G, 20% B), and still occurs conspicuously in boys at 9 years (24%). Children who make this response know the bottom of the cube exists and can't seem to eliminate it in their drawings even though they don't see it.

By 7 years of age many make a fair semblance of a cylinder, but the base line is flat (24% G, 32% B). However at 7 years most use more or fewer than the expected four lines, suggesting a real struggle in the child's mind with surfaces and lines and their combination.

By 8 years of age a curved base line is coming in (22% G, 28% B). This curved base line has come into normative value for boys by 10 years of age (40% G, 64% B). It is interesting that this is one area where the behavior of boys is advanced over that of girls.

Table 33 gives age changes in the response to copy cylinder.

Face-on Cube

Although the face-on cube is easier to copy as a single square surface through 7 years of age, the symmetry of the point-on cube becomes

TABLE 32 *Diamond: Qualitative Aspects*
(Percentage of Responses)

	5 years		5½ years		6 years		7 years		8 years		9 years		10 years	
	G	B	G	B	G	B	G	B	G	B	G	B	G	B
Contact points														
Wide space	4	8	8	4	2	2	2	4	0	2	2	2	2	2
Small space	18	6	10	6	2	0	0	2	2	0	2	4	0	0
Extra line or lines	4	10	6	6	2	2	2	2	0	0	0	0	0	0
Overlap	18	20	8	2	8	10	2	0	0	4	0	2	0	4
Cross-over	6	0	6	4	4	0	2	0	2	0	0	0	0	2
Shape in general														
Rounded or wobbly side	2	14	14	14	6	8	4	6	6	6	8	0	4	10
Angled rectangle	0	6	10	22	14	16	10	18	2	2	0	8	2	0
Angled square	0	6	10	10	14	18	10	18	14	32	0	12	4	0
Longer top	0	0	8	2	8	0	4	0	4	4	0	0	0	4
Longer bottom	0	0	2	2	6	0	0	2	0	0	6	2	4	4
Lopsided	6	0	14	18	8	24	22	12	10	16	14	8	4	6
Top points off	0	10	2	4	10	6	14	4	16	20	12	14	8	12
Oblique angle	0	2	8	12	14	6	16	30	20	22	20	18	12	14
One side flattened	0	0	0	6	6	8	4	8	4	0	2	0	0	0

108

Contact points														
Wide space	12	16	10	8	0	2	0	0	0	0	2	0	0	0
Small space	18	2	14	8	4	4	6	6	6	6	2	6	0	2
Extra line or lines	12	6	18	4	4	2	0	0	0	0	0	0	0	0
Overlap	18	12	8	0	2	10	4	2	2	2	2	0	0	0
Cross-over	6	2	2	2	2	6	0	0	0	4	2	0	0	0
Shape in general														
Rounded or wobbly side	6	10	24	8	4	10	0	8	2	6	4	2	4	4
Angled rectangle	4	2	2	2	8	2	4	0	0	4	0	0	0	0
Angled square	2	6	6	12	4	10	0	2	0	4	0	0	2	2
Longer top	2	2	12	10	10	2	6	4	2	4	14	8	8	2
Longer bottom	6	0	4	4	6	2	8	2	8	12	8	8	10	2
Lopsided	0	6	12	12	14	16	16	10	22	4	8	8	10	10
Side points off	10	8	12	12	20	18	18	26	26	20	12	18	6	8
Vertical	0	2	2	2	2	2	6	8	2	0	20	8	0	2
Oblique angle	0	2	6	6	10	4	8	18	20	10	20	23	10	6
One side flattened	0	0	2	18	4	2	6	2	0	0	0	0	2	2

TABLE 33 *Copy Cylinder*
(Percentage of Responses)

	5 years G	5 years B	5½ years G	5½ years B	6 years G	6 years B	7 years G	7 years B	8 years G	8 years B	9 years G	9 years B	10 years G	10 years B
No response	20	34	12	26	2	4	0	0	0	2	0	0	0	0
○	52	60	44	48	34	46	12	26	8	0	4	2	0	2
◁	6	4	4	0	2	0	4	0	4	0	0	0	2	0
□	10	2	22	10	12	8	12	6	10	10	0	0	2	0
◎	4	0	6	2	2	0	0	2	0	0	0	0	0	0
00	0	0	4	0	8	0	8	6	2	8	8	4	2	0
▭	4	0	0	2	8	0	0	6	0	6	0	0	0	0
⊐	0	0	6	4	20	12	22	20	14	8	6	24	10	8
⊐⊏	0	0	0	2	6	4	6	0	6	0	10	0	18	2
cylinder (4 lines) ±	0	0	0	2	0	12	22	32	14	20	20	20	10	10
cylinder (4 lines)	0	0	2	0	6	2	2	0	12	4	14	12	16	8
cylinder (4 lines) ±	0	0	0	0	0	0	8	0	18	26	30	26	28	28
cylinder (4 lines)	0	0	0	0	0	0	0	0	4	2	6	12	12	36
Other	4	0	0	4	0	12	4	2	8	14	2	0	2	6
Any shading	2	0	0	6	2	0	0	0	0	8	8	2	0	0
Double lines	0	2	2	0	2	0	2	0	2	0	4	0	4	0

easier to master from 8 years on when the child has gone beyond the single-surface response.

With the face-on cube the single square surface, which may relate to the bottom, the top or the front surface, is normative from 5½ through 7 years (see Table 34). The next step is a response to the awareness of two surfaces, usually the top and the front. These two surfaces may be drawn either in horizontal or vertical alignment. An awareness of and need to draw the bottom as with the cylinder, occurs with some children.

An awareness of the side of the cube is beginning to come in at 7 years, but doesn't come in strongly before 10 years of age (see Table 34). It becomes evident in looking over the table that it is difficult for the child to put the surfaces together. At times he draws both sides. A certain number at 9 years have learned the trick of a transparent drawing. Only a few, mainly boys, copy this form correctly even by 10 years of age (2% G, 20% B), though a few others are close to success as they make a good face-on cube but with a flat base line (6% G, 10% B).

Point-on Cube

The point-on cube may not be attempted much before 7 years of age. SEVEN's capacity to draw a diamond shows up very nicely as he draws only the top surface of the point-on cube as a diamond shape (34% G, 44% B). This response remains fairly high at 8 years (22% G, 34% B) (see Table 35). At the same time a fair number are making a rather good reproduction of the cube, showing the two sides, but with a flat base line to the figure. This type of response reaches a peak at 9 years of age (36% G, 32% B), but is superseded by a correct copy with angled base lines at 10 years of age in 34% of girls, 46% of boys. The success of the copy of this form is in marked contrast with that for the face-on cube, but for both forms the boys are definitely ahead of the girls.

Organization of Forms on Page

After the individual forms are analyzed, it is wise for the examiner to secure an overall impression of the way the child organizes the forms on the sheet of paper, the size of the forms, their place on the paper, the quality of strokes, and other factors. Whatever a child does is an expression of himself, though some of his actions are more revealing than others. This Copy Forms test, with its very definite longitudinal potentials, gives us almost a capsule picture of both age and individuality.

As an examiner slowly learns to read the records, he will be struck with the almost portrait-like quality of a child's Copy Forms product. Some products have a stronger impact than others. A messy page is very evident especially when the forms are drawn large with heavy stroke

TABLE 34 *Copy Face-on Cube*
(Percentage of Responses)

	5 years		5½ years		6 years		7 years		8 years		9 years		10 years	
	G	B	G	B	G	B	G	B	G	B	G	B	G	B
None	78	72	16	26	34	32	0	0	0	0	0	0	0	0
	22	24	74	72	54	56	60	54	40	28	16	8	0	2
	0	0	8	0	2	4	18	2	12	10	8	10	4	6
	0	0	0	0	6	0	6	16	0	16	20	22	20	26
	0	0	0	0	0	2	0	6	10	6	10	0	10	4
	0	0	0	0	0	0	0	2	10	6	0	4	0	10
	0	0	0	0	0	0	2	0	0	4	10	4	14	2
	0	0	0	0	0	0	2	2	4	10	4	8	0	0
	0	0	0	0	0	0	2	2	0	0	0	0	0	0
Transparent	0	0	0	0	0	4	0	0	4	2	10	10	10	4
	0	0	0	0	0	0	4	10	16	4	12	12	32	6
	0	0	0	0	0	0	0	0	0	6	2	4	6	10
	0	0	0	0	0	2	0	2	2	2	2	8	2	20
Other	0	4	2	2	0	4	6	4	2	6	6	10	2	10

NOTE: Since so few types of response reach normative values, boldface items in this table indicate merely leading behaviors at each age.

TABLE 35 *Copy Point-on Cube*
(Percentage of Responses)

	5 years		5½ years		6 years		7 years		8 years		9 years		10 years	
	G	B	G	B	G	B	G	B	G	B	G	B	G	B
None	**82**	**74**	**84**	**66**	**44**	**62**	12	0	4	0	0	0	2	0
□	12	10	6	8	14	8	8	10	2	2	2	2	2	0
⊟	0	0	0	0	4	4	2	2	2	6	0	2	0	0
⊞	0	0	0	0	0	0	6	10	8	4	6	8	8	4
⊟⊟	0	0	0	0	4	0	6	0	4	2	6	0	6	0
△	2	4	2	6	4	2	0	0	0	2	0	2	0	0
◇	0	4	8	18	**22**	18	**34**	**44**	**22**	**34**	6	10	2	2
✛	0	0	0	0	0	0	8	8	8	4	8	4	4	8
⊠	0	0	0	0	0	0	0	2	6	4	4	2	4	4
Transparent	0	0	0	0	0	0	0	0	4	2	0	0	0	0
⬦ (point)	0	0	0	0	8	2	20	12	**26**	18	**36**	**32**	**32**	**30**
⬡ (point-on)	0	0	0	0	0	0	0	6	8	12	16	**30**	**34**	**46**
Other	4	8	0	2	4	4	4	6	6	10	16	8	6	6

NOTE: Since so few types of response reach normative values, boldface items in this table indicate merely leading behaviors at each age.

and piled at random on top of each other. In marked contrast is an orderly page with the forms drawn neatly and small in a horizontal row.

There are many variables between these two extremes in the way a child organizes his forms on the page. Age is in part a determinant, but the child's individuality is also made evident along with his age. Figures 1–3 give examples of more or less typical organization of forms (and name and numbers) on the page, at each age level from 5 through 10 years of age. Examples given are not strictly normative, but each is characteristic of the response which may be expected at the age in question. In series they give a clear impression of the changes that may be expected with age.

SPACE USED

For the majority of subjects in this age range, one page or less is sufficient space to contain all ten forms. (Two positions of the diamond and two of the cube are counted as four.) Varying from 2% to 12% (see Table 36), a relatively small proportion of children from 5 years on need more than one page. At 4 years this demand for an extra page or extra pages may be very strong even to the point of the child's needing a new sheet for each form, with forms usually drawn large and centrally placed. In marked contrast, less than half a page is needed by many at older ages when the forms are smaller and better organized. The use of less than one-half page does not become consistently normative in this age range, though a sizable number of children use this smaller amount of space from 5½ years on.

PLACE ON PAPER

The overall age trend is that figures become increasingly small and less and less of the page is used with increasing age. As Table 36 shows, 5-year-olds tend to use the whole page, more or less. From 5½ years following, the largest number of subjects place forms in horizontal rows, though this does not become normative in girls until 7 years, in boys until 10 years.

From 5 through 7 years substantial numbers of children place forms in more or less shapeless bunches (14% to 30%). An increasing number arrange figures in neatly boxed squares in one of the four quadrants of the page, though percentages for this are always small.

FIVES, when not using the whole page, may work initially in the lower half of the page. By 6, most are able to orient more toward the top of the page, more often to the left. When this orientation occurs it means that the child is establishing a L to R direction.

If he orients initially in the center of the top of the page, he may work either from L to R or R to L, indicating that a single direction has not been established. Some who work in one quadrant of the page only, can nevertheless maintain their L to R direction. When a shift in direction occurs as the child works, this suggests that other reversal patterns may also be present, as with reversal of letters or numbers.

There are some children who need to make multiple starts. This is more common at 5 years. And there is the child who shifts his paper repeatedly so that he may execute each stroke as a vertical stroke toward himself, or away from himself. This need to shift the paper suggests difficulty in orienting to a given position. The only way such a child can solve this problem is to shift the environment, in this case the paper. These children often need an environment which will adjust to them until they have acquired the ability to adjust to their environment.

ARRANGEMENT OF FORMS ON PAGE

Table 36 gives a comprehensive idea of how organization becomes manifest in the years from 5 to 10. At 5 years of age there is great variation in performance from child to child. The largest number arrange forms in some sort of crude circular formation, either in or out of order. Conspicuous numbers, however (nearly one-fourth of subjects), still have merely random placement, and almost an equal number are already placing forms horizontally, in correct order.

By 5½ years, the largest number of subjects, though still only about one-third, have horizontal placement. However, horizontal placement predominates from here on, and becomes normative in girls at 7 years following, in boys not till 10 years of age.

RELATIVE SIZE OF INDIVIDUAL FORMS

The individual forms are quite variable in size, especially at 5 and 5½ years. There is a slight tendency for succeeding forms to get larger, especially at 6 and 7 years and especially when the execution of a certain form is difficult for the child. (The opposite trend of forms getting smaller is sometimes seen.) By 7 and 8 years, the girls are showing a marked tendency to draw their forms more even in size. This steadily increases until even size is normative in girls at both 9 and 10 years, though in boys only 46% make even forms as late as 10 years (see Table 36).

When a marked and irregular shift in size from a very small form to a very large one in the several forms made by any one child occurs after 7 years, the presence of an unstable mechanism should be suspected. However, when the shift is orderly and well-patterned, as with a sudden shift with the three-dimensional forms to very small or very large forms in contrast to an even size of the Copy Forms, it may be considered that it is merely the harder demands of the more difficult task which have brought about this shift in size.

Figure 1. Sample Copy Forms pages at 5 and 5½ years.

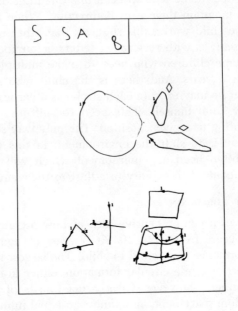

GIRL 5³

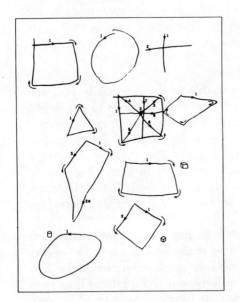

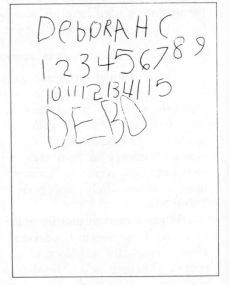

GIRL 5¹⁰

116

One look at this record reveals a 5-year-old of good ability. The forms are distinct; all can be easily recognized.

5-YEAR HALLMARKS

1. Circle is placed quite centrally on page; executed top down CCW, with some difficulty on last lap.
2. Cross has extra line added to equalize sides of H-line on either side of V-line.
3. One side of triangle is extended to match other side; base line is at oblique angle.
4. Divided rectangle shows attempt to angle 2 lines from a central point; other 2 oblique lines are drawn H.
5. V- and H-diamonds show their position and general outline.
6. Forms vary in size, lines are at times wobbly, and organization is spotty.

GOOD QUALITY

1. Square is drawn CCW with continuous stroke.
2. Triangle has 2 good obliques.
3. Rectangle has 1 cross-over line (H); 2 upper obliques are paired and lower ones are drawn in same direction.
4. Careful closure points.

LETTERS AND NUMBERS

At Age

Child writes only a few letters and numbers, placed in middle of page.

Quality

Execution is excellent. Figures are of relatively small size, and there is an excellent attempt to make an "8" in advanced pattern.

GIRL 5[10]

5½-YEAR HALLMARKS

1. Surety of stroke.
2. Beginning of organization with many shifts—circle is placed at top of page, cross and square on either side of it; H-organization L to R on next line, then V-organization.
3. One form runs into another.
4. Good centralizing of divided rectangle with a dot; central H-line is from R to L.
5. Trouble with closure points—either has wide space, as with circle; or overshoots, as with square.

GOOD QUALITY

1. Fair consistency in size.
2. Good obliques in triangle.
3. Excellent H-diamond.
4. Child is able to tackle point-on cube; draws top in diamond shape.
5. Closure points steadily improve.

LETTERS (WITH RIGHT AND LEFT HAND) AND NUMBERS

At Age

1. Child is able to write whole first name.
2. Small letters size of capitals—child prefers capitals; wavy base line.
3. Child writes to 15; reverses 14 to 41; numbers vary in size; wavy base line.

GOOD QUALITY

1. No individual letter or number reversals.
2. Organizes well on a line.

Figure 2. Sample Copy Forms pages at 6 and 7 years.

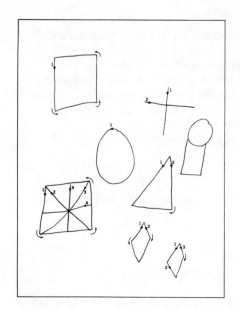
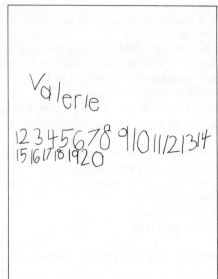

GIRL 6⁰

BOY 7⁸

GIRL 6[0]

6-YEAR HALLMARKS
1. Divided rectangle drawn with cross-over pattern; outside is a square; H central line from R to L.
2. V- but not H-diamond is correct.

GOOD QUALITY
1. Divided rectangle nicely executed, with central meeting point of all 4 lines.
2. Cylinder shows 2 parts.
3. Good closure points.

QUESTIONABLE QUALITY
1. Only 1 oblique to triangle.
2. Organization of forms around a central circle.

NUMBERS
At Age
1. Child writes numbers to 20.
2. Numbers are of variable size but tend to be big; no spacing; wavy base line.
3. Child executes "9" in 2 parts.

LETTERS
At Age
1. Child writes full name (last name written but not shown).
2. Letters are medium to large.
3. Base line tends to go down.
Quality
1. Child handles small letters well but still uses them as capitals (not shown).
2. Name placed third of way down paper (5½ years).

BOY 7[8]

AT AGE
1. Forms are relatively small, fairly even in size.
2. H-organization is consistent.
3. Divided rectangle has rectangular shape, cross-over pattern; central H-line is from L to R.
4. Child draws relatively good V-diamond; fair H-diamond.
5. Child draws base of cylinder, but then erases.

QUALITY
1. Good placement on the page.
2. Good cross-over pattern on divided rectangle.
3. Good point-on cube.

NAME AND NUMBERS
1. Excellent small printing of name (last name not shown), placed high in L corner.
2. Numbers nicely formed with spacing of teens (8 years), but large size (6–6½ years).

Figure 3. Sample Copy Forms pages at 8, 9, and 10 years.

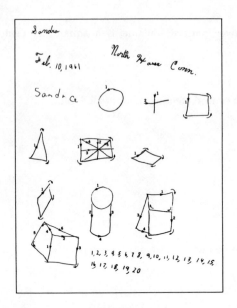
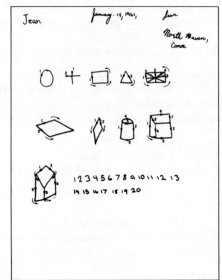

GIRL 8[4]   GIRL 9[8]

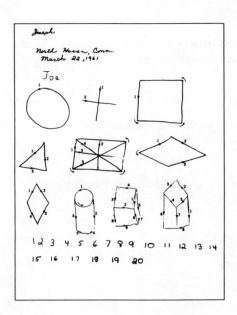

BOY 10[4]

120

1. Child writes cursively.
2. Child writes address on same line with name, plus second line.
3. Good date, with abbreviation and correct punctuation.

COPY FORMS
1. Organized horizontally, three on a line.
2. Fair size consistency.
3. Good quality: Central crossing of divided rectangle; rounded base line of cylinder; good attempts at 2 cube positions.
4. Less good quality: Child uses continuous stroke for square, triangle, and diamonds. Triangle is vertical with oblique base. H-diamond has a curved line and points are off-center.

NUMBERS
Small and moderately well executed. Separation of teens by spacing but child still uses commas to separate numbers.

GIRL 9[8]

NAME (WITH LEFT AND RIGHT HAND), ADDRESS, AND DATE
1. Child organizes name and address nicely on 4 lines (4th line not shown).
2. Typical, carefully formed 9-year-old cursive handwriting.
3. Date shows overuse of punctuation, with period after month.

COPY FORMS
1. Small, 4 or 5 on a H-line.
2. Nice breakup of lines of triangle and diamonds.
3. Oval top to cylinder, rounded base line.
4. Partial angulation of lines of cubes—good quality.

NUMBERS
1. Adequately formed.
2. Some irregularity in size, spacing, and angle of stroke.

BOY 10[4]

NAME (WITH RIGHT AND LEFT HAND), ADDRESS, AND DATE
1. Good placement.
2. Nice flow to handwriting.

COPY FORMS
1. Fair size consistency.
2. Child organizes forms horizontally, with 3 to 4 on a line.
3. Square is drawn in continuous CCW line, but triangle and diamonds are broken up.
4. Divided rectangle forms show good attack; cylinder has rounded base line, but top still circular. Face-on cube has fair side with base angled, but top still square. Point-on cube has flat base.

NUMBERS
1. Nicely shaped, medium in size; good separation between numbers, especially teens.
2. Good base line.

TABLE 36 Copy Forms: Organization on Page
(Percentage)

	4½ years G	4½ years B	5 years G	5 years B	5½ years G	5½ years B	6 years G	6 years B	7 years G	7 years B	8 years G	8 years B	9 years G	9 years B	10 years G	10 years B	Adult
Place on Paper[a]																	
Whole page ±	62	96	44	54	34	28	24	26	18	24	26	24	34	24	14	26	7
Bunches	18	0	24	20	20	30	22	26	14	20	4	14	0	12	0	0	0
Quadrants	2	4	0	0	2	0	2	2	4	4	10	6	2	4	8	6	7
Vertical	4	0	2	4	2	2	6	10	10	10	8	12	16	14	12	14	50
Horizontal	14	0	30	22	42	40	46	36	54	42	52	44	48	46	66	54	36
Arrangement on Paper[a]																	
Random																	
Superimposed	0	0	6	8	6	8	0	0	0	0	0	0	0	2	0	0	0
Other	52	32	20	24	20	22	22	18	16	18	12	18	10	18	4	18	0
All random	52	32	26	32	26	30	22	18	16	18	12	18	10	20	4	18	0
Crude circular																	
Out of order	16	28	26	16	24	12	20	12	10	8	6	8	6	4	0	4	0
In order	4	18	16	26	4	4	6	4	8	8	16	16	6	8	6	4	0
All circular	20	46	42	42	28	16	26	16	18	16	22	24	12	12	6	4	0

	1	2	3	4	5	6	7	8	9	10	11	12	13	14	15	16	17
Vertical																	
Out of order	6	2	0	0	0	0	4	2	0	0	0	0	0	4	4	0	0
In order	4	8	2	12	8	6	6	12	10	14	16	8	24	14	30	20	50
All vertical	10	10	2	12	8	6	10	14	10	14	16	8	24	18	34	20	50
Horizontal																	
Out of order	8	2	0	0	4	0	8	4	0	0	0	0	8	2	2	6	0
In order	6	10	28	12	28	38	28	40	52	48	50	42	44	40	54	52	50
All horizontal	14	12	28	12	32	38	36	44	52	48	50	42	52	42	56	58	50
H and V mixed	4	0	2	2	6	10	6	8	4	4	0	8	2	8	0	0	0
Relative Size of Individual Forms																	
Variable	70	56	42	54	40	46	38	30	24	34	32	32	30	34	16	24	14
Getting larger	8	16	6	14	14	24	20	30	22	18	10	20	14	14	10	28	7
Getting smaller	20	28	24	20	20	8	12	22	6	20	10	20	6	16	4	2	7
Even	2	0	28	12	26	22	30	18	48	28	48	28	50	36	70	46	72
Amount of Space Used																	
More than 1 page	28	48	6	10	8	4	4	2	2	4	2	6	12	4	4	0	0
½ to 1 page	58	48	72	68	50	56	60	60	60	40	50	60	74	60	36	66	7
Less than ½ page	14	4	22	22	42	36	36	38	38	56	48	34	14	36	60	34	93

[a]Figures for these two do not always agree since a "whole page" or quadrant might be made horizontally or vertically, or two horizontal lines might be made vertically: 1 3 5 7 / 2 4 6 8

There is also marked variability in performance from child to child. The circle, which shows the greatest variation of all forms, especially at 5 years, may range from .6 cm. to 10 cm. with considerable difference in the vertical and horizontal diameters. But by 10 years the variation from child to child stabilizes to between 1.5 and 4.5 cm. with only around 3% of children above or below these limits. Furthermore, the circle, by 10 years of age, has really become a circle, with a good proportion of children showing equal vertical and horizontal diameters.

Special attention should be given to the somewhat complicated methods of organization used especially by the 5- to 7-year-olds. Thus the immature methods of placing one form on top of another, or placing forms around a central circle are conspicuous at 5 and 5½ years. Placing forms inside other forms or arranging them in a circle like a necklace also occur minimally in the 5- to 7-year-old age period.

Some young patterns are fairly easily seen. Others may be more difficult to unravel. The examiner needs to pick his way, locating one form after another in sequence, to see if even in the midst of apparent confusion the child may have had at least an initial sense of organization with the first three or four forms. Often this initial organization is broken into by the intrusion of later forms copied in the in-between spaces. As organization begins to take place, the size of the forms becomes more consistent, and thus the pattern is more readily seen.

Thus an infrequent but interesting pattern of working on both sides of center, either horizontally or vertically, occurs through 8 years at an 8 to 12% level. In about half the cases, only three forms are involved, the central

is flanked by the

and

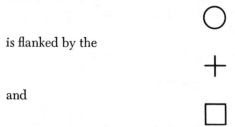

either to R and L or up and down (see Table 37); or four forms may be included in the initial grouping, with more variation in pattern.

Another early grouping is a circle of the first three forms, which occurs most often at 5½ years (8%) and at 9 years (13%).

A conspicuous pattern (30% at 5 years and around 20% at each age thereafter) is the organization of the first four forms into a square formation. This pattern may be executed in a circular direction CW or CCW, or it may be executed as two lines, drawn horizontally usually from L to R.

TABLE 37 *Patterns of Partial Arrangement*
(Percentage of Occurrence)

	5 years	5½ years	6 years	7 years	8 years	9 years	10 years
Circle centered ☐ ◯ + ◯ + ☐, etc. △	12	8	12	7	8	4	3
Group of first three forms ☐ + ◯	4	8	1	2	6	13	3
Group of first four forms + △ ◯ ☐	30	23	17	26	17	23	21

The actual patterning of the remaining forms after the first three or four, except when they are in clear horizontal arrangement, is so varied and multiple that it is difficult to summarize. What we now classify as random may not be random if we knew more about the underlying pattern. Thus the circular pattern of the first four forms either CW or CCW may set a further circular pattern in operation, with the rest of the forms often being arranged circularly around these first four forms. The organization on either side of a central form produces other oppositional placement. In the following example the triangle, like the circle, becomes the center of opposed placement.

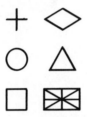

QUALITY OF STROKE

The quality of the stroke is one further aspect of the response which should be considered. There is the querulous stroke, the heavy stroke, the slashing stroke, the faint stroke—all possibly telling something of the personality of their maker. At times the type of stroke seems to have an age relationship. The 3½-year-old makes the querulous, wobbly, light stroke. He is anxious and unsure of himself. But not so 6 months later, when as a 4-year-old he becomes forthright, ready to step out into the world and to make dashing, gross motor strokes as he copies the Copy Forms.

The stroke may have heavy pressure in this 4- to 6-year-old period, but by 7 modulation and inhibition are coming in along with a lighter stroke on the paper, which goes along with SEVEN's new found capacity to whisper.

LONGITUDINAL AGE CHANGES

The shifts from age to age can be so significant and revealing that it is fortunate when yearly records for any one child can be taken so that he can be seen in movement, revealing increment from age to age.

But there is much more than just a growth increment to be looked for. The manner in which a child grows from one age to another must also be watched for. Some will leap ahead and then later fall back. Some gain in one area and lose in another. Good organization at one age may break up into relative disorganization at a succeeding age. At one age the forms may be very small, as at 9 years, only to be followed in the same child by very large forms at 10 years, or vice versa.

In general, there is fairly steady improvement in that children, with increasing age, use less of the page in copying forms, and improve from random order to the use of three horizontal rows, and from large uneven figures to medium-sized even figures.

Handedness

A question arises whether it is always a sign of immaturity when children, in copying forms, draw lines opposite to the expected direction. Could it sometimes merely be a matter of handedness?

Responses to Copy Circle give at least a partial answer to this question. Preschoolers tend to copy a circle in a CW direction, but copying in a CCW direction becomes normative at 5½ years and following. However, at all ages some children continue to draw CW.

Table 38 (line A) shows what percentage of the children who draw CW are left-handers. As this table shows, through 5½ years in girls and through 6 years in boys, only a small percentage of those drawing the circle CW are left-handed. However, from 7 years on, with some exceptions, most children who draw a circle CW are left-handed.

Thus we may fairly consider any drawing of a circle in a CW direction by a right-handed child beyond the age of 6 years an immaturity.

Next, the question arises, do the majority of left-handed children continue to draw a circle CW up into the older ages? Table 38 (line B) answers this question by giving the percentage of left-handers who draw CW, that is counter to the usual manner. As this table shows, in the age range from 5 to 10 years, at two of the ages in girls and at five in boys, drawing CW is normative in left-handed children.

Table 38 also presents figures for drawing the horizontal line of the cross from R to L, the first line of the square down the right side or across the bottom, the first line of the triangle up or down the right side, the outside of the divided rectangle starting down the right side and continuing CW, or the inside lines of the divided rectangle mostly from R to L.

Nearly all of these patterns of drawing, which are contrary to the normative methods, occur mostly in left-handed children, and the percentage of left-handers so drawing tends to increase with age.

In spite of this, many left-handed subjects do draw in the generally normative direction and manner for nearly all of the different forms.

Thus, for most forms used in the Copy Forms test we can expect children, both right- and left-handed, to follow the usual normative progressions with age. But when a child does draw in a direction opposite to that which is usually chosen, chances are high, as Table 38 shows, that he will be a left-hander.

Therefore, with left-handed children, care should be taken in adversely judging a reversal in the usual direction of drawing.

TABLE 38 *Extent to Which Directionality Contrary to the Usual Is the Work of Left-Handed Subjects*
(Percentage)

A = Percentage of this kind of response made by left-handers
B = Percentage of left-handers who respond otherwise, i.e., more conventionally

		5 years		5½ years		6 years		7 years		8 years		9 years		10 years	
		G	B	G	B	G	B	G	B	G	B	G	B	G	B
CW (○)	A	30	7	33	30	63	22	100	55	100	100	75	25	100	100
	B	25	80	43	33	44	55	63	29	43	57	50	83	14	66
R to L	A	55	50	85	60	55	62	100	87	100	100	71	80	85	100
	B	50	50	14	33	55	55	12	33	0	30	11	83	14	66
CW	A	69	17	100	16	100	100	100	80	100	100	100	0	80	100
	B	75	80	14	77	33	66	50	43	57	30	83	100	43	77
CCW	A	69	66	100	50	50	50	75	50	50	75	100	77	50	100
	B	75	80	86	77	77	88	62	86	86	70	66	66	86	77

	CCW △											
A	100	100	50	50	100	100	100	100	100	100	100	100
B	87	80	85	88	77	100	57	73	71	86	71	88

	CW △											
A	80	14	83	36	100	100	75	66	100	100	100	0
B	50	80	28	44	55	66	62	70	71	70	83	100

	CW ⊠											
A	25	16	100	28	100	50	100	100	100	0	100	0
B	87	90	71	77	55	77	75	57	43	100	83	100

R to L ⊠

Inside Lines Mostly from R to L

A	33	11	50	28	71	50	66	33	71	77
B	66	88	50	71	28	50	33	44	28	22

CHAPTER 9

INCOMPLETE MAN

||||||||||||||||||||||||||||||||||||||||||||||||||||||||||||||||||||||||||

Introduction

Of all parts of the examination, this is often the child's favorite. It intrigues him. It stirs him. He remembers it if he is re-examined, and tackles it with renewed pleasure.

It is indeed a fortunate juxtaposition of forces when a test both pleases the examined and reveals much to the examiner. The simplicity of the formula of this test is part of its charm. The missing parts are fairly obvious and stimulate the child to get right down to work to make things right, to complete this unfinished figure. Each of the missing parts, with the exception of the eyes, has a model already drawn to guide the child.

The line, angle, and length of each part, especially the arm, leg, and tie, allow for many stages of perception and therefore of execution. Thus, the fact that a part is added is only the beginning of an evaluation of the child's response. It is the way the child completes, the quality of his performance, that is especially significant.

The examiner will become increasingly aware of the quality of the child's additions as he himself gains more experience with this test. In time, he will become aware of the length of line—the longer, sometimes wildly uncontrolled lines being reminiscent of the 4- and 4½-year-old. He will also note the wobbly line or the curved line more noticeable in the 5- to 6-year-old. With increased control, a line or form may be cut down in size, showing for a while the opposite trend of the wild stroke —that is, a too-short length. This reduction of size may occur especially in the 5- to 7-year-old age range. Increased modulation, which produces lines of the "correct" length, takes place sometime around 9 years of age, or in some instances not until 10.

Similar extremes are evident in the contact points of the added missing parts to the figure. FOUR slashes the stroke of an arm or leg well into the body area, right through the outlined circle. On the other hand, he may miss contacting the body by a wide margin. He may then link the space with an added line, since he likes to tie things together, or he may be content to leave an arm or a leg dangling in space.

This over- or under-control is especially evident as the child adds hair. The 5- to 6-year old is still likely either to cross over the head line as he draws the hair, or to fail to contact it. By 7, the child shows better control of his stroke, a greater awareness of detail and of his own performance, and a desire to improve things by erasing if they are not quite to his liking, but the process is still laborious. It is not until 9 that the stroke is under fluid and sure control.

The quality and type of stroke is determined both by the child's ability to maneuver his pencil in his hand as he executes, and also by the way he sees what he is to do. What he sees or does not see is especially evident with the neck area. Some see only the missing body line at 5–6 years. Others see only the missing neckline at the same age. It may take until 7 years before they see the tie area. As for the ability to make an oblique stroke for hair, arm, or leg, this may well tax many 5- and 6-year-olds.

Fortunately perhaps, the eyes have no model. Therefore the child fashions them spontaneously. It is indeed a far cry from the wide open circles of the 5-year-old to the oval, seeing eyes of the 9- and 10-year-old.

Administration of the Test

The material and procedure for this test are simple. The test consists of a letter-sized sheet of green paper on which is stamped (in black ink) the outline of a man having half his hair, one ear, nose and mouth but no eyes, and half a bow tie with its central knot and one side of his neck, one arm and hand and opposite leg and foot (see Figure 4). There are nine parts in all to be completed, ten including the body line. The eye itself may have several parts: outline of eye, eyebrow, eyelashes, pupil. Belly button, buttons, clothes, and marks on nose, mouth, and ear as well as cheeks, teeth, and extra arm, leg, fingers, and so on are counted as extras and scored as such.

As the examiner presents the sheet of paper stamped with the form of the Incomplete Man, and a pencil, he asks, "What does this look like to you?" If the child cannot respond, it is wise not to press this question until he has completed the figure.

The examiner may then proceed by saying to the young child of 5, "Somebody made him and forgot to finish him. You finish him." With the

Figure 4. Incomplete Man.

older child the examiner can be more forthright and simply say, "You finish him."

As the child adds parts, the examiner should record the order and method of drawing, plus any verbalization. The preschooler (3- to 4-year-old) often talks out loud as he is finishing the man, naming the parts as he completes them, and delightedly reporting new powers he has given the man as he completes the parts—"Now he can walk," when the second leg is added, or "Now he can see," when the eyes are added. The preschooler deals with this task as he deals with other aspects of his life. Things come alive. He thinks of inanimate things as real.

If the child lags in his completions, the examiner will encourage him with "What else?" This is recorded as a broken line - - - - - - - - - - to indicate that a stimulus was given. If any parts are omitted after this suggestive urging, the examiner points to the region of the unfinished part and asks, "What did they forget to draw here?" or "What does he need here?" This is recorded by a solid line _____ indicating that a definite clue was given.

The 4-year-old is seldom budged by this additional help. He has given what he can, and wishes to give no more. FIVE may be responsive. At one time we were interested chiefly in the number of parts a child added to the man, but now we consider that it is the way the child completes the part that is more important than the numerical fact that the part is added. But the record should show whenever a specific clue has been given.

FOUR may interrupt his completions to ask, "Who made him?" He is usually satisfied with the information that the man was printed. He is also aware, as is the 5-year-old, of the black ink with which the form was printed, and some request a black pen so that their lines will be the same as those on the paper.

(If the child has not named the Incomplete Man before he completes him, he is asked what it is after he has finished. Most name easily after the man is completed. Difficulty with naming is not usually present after 5 years.)

When the man has been completed, the examiner holds the paper up for the child to see and asks the 5- to 6-year-old, "How does he look?" This question is difficult for some 5- to 6-year-olds. Whether they answer or not, they are then asked, "How does he feel inside?" This may be even more difficult than the first question of "How does he look?" but it often induces more revealing responses.

At times, neither of these questions is responded to more than superficially with a bland positive response of "good" or "fine."

Then the third question which is more specific and directive is asked, "Is he happy or sad?" It is at times surprising to see a switch in opinion from an earlier response such as "good" to "sad" just because the child had not considered the possibilities suggested by the question about happy or sad. Such a switch is most common at 5½ years (40% G, 18% B). After the child has responded he is asked, "How could you tell?" or "How do you know?"

From 7 years on, the child is initially asked, "What is his facial expression?" It is not until 8 years that most girls understand this question (56% G), though boys are still lagging (only 36% B). When children are able to respond to this query the two questions of "How does he look?" or "How does he feel inside?" can be omitted, since the child no longer needs this step-by-step type of encouragement.

If he responds to the question about facial expression, then he is asked, "How do you know?" At 7–8 years when a child may not know the meaning of, or cannot respond to, the question about facial expression, he is asked the subsequent query of "How does he look?" (He often responds to this as though he were thinking of facial expression.) Then he can be asked directly, "How do you know?" or "How could you tell?"

Findings[1]

NAMING

The majority of children from 5 years on refer to this figure as a "man." This response is increasingly qualified as the child grows older, with such remarks as "part of a man" or "half of a man," or the child may describe the figure as "a man with . . ." or "a man without . . ." certain parts. By 7 or 8 years of age, children are more concerned over the fact that the man is not completed, and may refer to him as half-drawn, unfinished, or not completed.

The second most common name given is "boy." This is especially high at 5½ years (38% G, 30% B). From then on the response "boy" steadily declines until it is only 14% at 10 years. The third most common naming is "person" which is minimal at 5–6 years, but steadily rises to its peak at 9 years (26% G, 34% B). Both the responses of "boy" and "person" are qualified in the same ways that the response "man" is qualified.

There are still a few responses, especially at 5–6 years, which are reminiscent of the preschool responses: monkey, doll, snowman, humpty-dumpty, scarecrow, girl, or lady. Some children shift back and forth as

[1] Responses of the 2- to 6-year-old to the Incomplete Man test are reported in Louise B. Ames, "The Gesell Incomplete Man test as a differential indicator of average and superior behavior in preschool children." *J. Genet. Psychol.*, 1943, **62**, 217–274. Weston findings are described fully in Louise B. Ames, Frances L. Ilg, "The Gesell Incomplete Man Test as a measure of developmental status." *Genet. Psychol. Monogr.*, 1963, **68**, 247–307.

they name the figure alternately girl or boy. Table 39 gives figures for naming.

FACIAL EXPRESSION

"How does he look?" (*5–7 years*). The 5- and 5½-year-old, especially initially (apart from a small percentage who find it difficult to respond), answer in a forthright and positive way. "Good" is a common and typical 5-year-old response. "Funny" is still fairly common though more typical of the 4-year-old. "Fine," "happy," "OK," "all right" have their smattering of occurrence and further emphasize FIVE's positive approach. A very common response is to reiterate the initial naming, i.e., "He looks like a boy," or "He looks like a man." The 6- and 7-year-old, however, is more likely to express some negative emotion such as "sad" or "unhappy."

"How does he feel inside?" (*5–7 years*). This query of how he feels inside more often brings forth some positive response, especially from the 5-year-old. He often persists in his use of "good," but he also projects into "happy" and "sad." A few, from 5 to 6, report that the man (or boy) feels "sick," "awful," or "bad." This response of "sick" is quite common with the 4-year-old.

A certain number of the more literal-minded refer to the paper the Incomplete Man has been printed on as "soft" or "hard." Some have considerable difficulty in projecting an answer to this query as to how the man feels, but find no difficulty with the more specific question which follows.

"Is he happy or sad?" (*5–7 years*). It is surprising to see how often this query stimulates the response of "sad" even though the initial response may have indicated a positive emotion. FIVE-AND-A-HALF may even change to "mad."

"How can you tell?" (*5–7 years*). The cocksure 5-year-old, sounding almost more like a 4-year-old, may respond with "cause" or "I can tell." Or he will report that he made the man that way, or that he looked and could see. On the positive side he refers to the fact that the man now has everything he wants or is finished, or he may refer to the parts of the body he has given the man.

"What is his facial expression?" (*7–10 years*). Though the majority cannot respond to "facial expression" before 8 years of age (56% G, 36% B)—and even then the boys are lagging—the 7-year-old should be asked this question initially. Even though the child may not be able to respond, the added question of "How does he look?" usually produces a response relating to facial expression.

Some response implying a negative emotion is most common at 7 and 8 years, and in girls as early as 6 years (60% G). This is most com-

TABLE 39 *Naming the Incomplete Man*
(Percentage of Responses)

	4½ years		5 years		5½ years		6 years		7 years		8 years		9 years		10 years		Adult
	G	B	G	B	G	B	G	B	G	B	G	B	G	B	G	B	
Some naming	84	76	98	92	98	98	98	96	98	100	90	92	100	100	100	100	100
No naming	16	24	2	8	2	2	2	4	2	0	10	8	0	0	0	0	0
All kinds of "man" combined	36	34	48	62	50	64	68	56	64	58	50	54	62	56	60	66	77
All kinds of "boy" combined	22	10	24	16	38	30	20	24	22	18	18	14	12	10	14	14	7
All kinds of "person" combined	0	4	4	0	6	2	6	10	8	20	14	24	26	34	22	18	7
Man	34	32	44	54	42	52	58	38	42	44	34	32	42	24	30	36	69
Part (or ½) of man	2	2	4	4	4	10	8	16	24	14	16	18	18	32	30	30	7
Little boy	6	0	10	2	2	2	0	0	0	0	0	0	2	2	2	0	7
Boy	14	10	14	14	28	20	16	22	20	10	6	8	6	6	2	8	0
Part (or ½) of boy	2	0	0	0	10	8	4	2	2	8	12	6	4	2	10	6	0
"Boy or man"	0	0	0	0	0	0	0	2	0	0	4	0	0	0	0	0	0
Person	0	4	4	6	6	2	4	6	2	14	10	14	16	12	16	12	7
Part of person	2	0	0	0	0	0	2	4	6	6	4	10	10	22	6	6	0
Monkey	2	0	4	0	0	0	0	0	0	0	2	0	0	0	0	0	0
Skeleton	0	0	0	0	0	0	0	0	0	0	2	2	0	0	0	0	0
Snowman	12	4	2	4	2	2	2	2	0	0	0	2	2	0	0	0	0
Scarecrow or dummy	8	8	2	0	0	0	0	0	0	0	0	2	0	0	0	0	0
Doll or baby	2	2	4	0	2	0	0	0	0	0	0	0	0	0	2	0	0
Girl	0	4	8	0	2	0	0	0	0	0	0	0	0	0	0	0	0
Lady	0	0	4	2	0	2	0	0	2	0	0	0	0	0	0	0	0

monly expressed as "sad," "unhappy," or "not happy." A few children, especially at 8 years, refer to the man as "crazy," "horrible," or "scared."

These projections should not be taken lightly, especially at 8 years. Or when a 9- or 10-year-old reports, "He looks worried because he's afraid he's not going to pass," this should be investigated.

The positive "happy" or "smiling," predominant at 5 years of age, remains close to the 25% level from 7 to 10 years. A few NINES sharpen their perception of a smile to a "grin," and one 9-year-old boy of high intellectual status though immature in his emotional responses, referred to the smile as a "dull smile."

Some children have trouble in deciding whether the emotion expressed is positive or negative. A few at every age (most at 10 years—14% G, 12% B) settle for both, giving a double answer, "fine/sad," or "happy/sad." The 5½-year-old mentions both kinds of emotion, but makes the distinction that the man "Looks good, but feels sad" (40% G, 18% B). The 7-year-old may deny both emotions, "Not happy and not sad."

Others do not have to weigh the opposites, but come straight to the point and speak of the facial expression as "normal," "regular," "plain," or "natural." This class of responses shows a steady rise from 8 years on, reaching its highest point at 10 years of age (18% G, 22% B).

The responses of "thoughtful," "serious," or "bored" are infrequent with the exception of boys at 9 years of age (12% B). In contrast to this more inward response, the outward response of "excited," "surprised," or "startled" is strongest at 8 and 9 years.

"How do you know?" (7–10 years). By 7 years of age, most children can substantiate their answer with real thought. Sometimes their answer has a relationship to how the figure looks, or it may be related more to the child's own inner state of mind. But by 9 years of age, there is an accurate perception and reporting about facial expression.

At times the child will actually control the expression by adding a mark to the mouth (either up or down), but often it is the expression of the eyes that seems to determine the interpretation of the expression of the mouth.

The less perceptive child will refer in general to the face, or will say that the man "looks it" (i.e., happy, sad, etc.). A more perceptive child will refer to the presence or absence of a smile. A certain group will refer to an opposite emotion: "He is sad because he is not smiling," "He is happy because he is not crying," "He is calm because he is not excited." A small proportion refer to the rest of the body besides the face, especially the arms and the legs. Thus the man may be described as jumping for joy, arms stretched out because of fright, so happy that he is waiting to embrace someone.

The hair has a definite relationship to fright or being scared because it is standing up straight. To determine whether this is reported by the truly frightened child or by the one who enjoys the symbolization of fright would need further study.

The majority of responses to the query of "How do you know?" are related to the facial features and especially to the mouth. It is indeed quite fascinating to see how many different emotions can be projected into the mouth. Many refer to it as straight, but others refer to it as up or down according to the projection of positive or negative emotions. The mouth alone is most often referred to. At times, however, both eyes and mouth are mentioned and in some, the eyes alone. The inclusion of nose is more common at 5 and 7 years and suggests that the child is just naming parts of the face.

The inclusion of extraneous remarks, such as at 6 years of age, "He's happy because he wants flowers" is suggestive of a younger response, more common at 4 years when the child might report, "He feels awful because his Mommy spanked him." But when the 8- or 9-year-old refers to some negative emotion and supports it with the explanation, "He's just seen a ghost" or "a horror movie" one needs to judge this response according to the content and the possible meaning to the child, as well as for its indication of possible immaturity.

Table 40 gives figures for "What is his facial expression?" and "How do you know?"

COMPLETION OF PARTS

It is interesting to watch the attack of different children at different ages on this incompleted figure. Some children may give the clue to their thinking in their original naming of the figure as they list the missing parts: "Man with one arm, one leg . . ." and so on. The preschooler's initial attack is usually on the leg. This omission he recognizes most clearly. The majority also recognize the need of another arm. It is difficult for most children under 4 to see the missing parts of the upper portion of the figure. Often these areas need to be pointed out and even then are not responded to. Because of the absence of any eye model, eyes are often omitted entirely by the very young child. Also the neck region eludes the 4-year-old, even though he may complete the body line.

A few recognize the need of another ear even as early as $3\frac{1}{2}$ years, but how to execute it remains a problem for some years to come. If the young child is right-handed, he may find it difficult to place the ear on the left side of the figure as it faces him. He may solve this problem by shifting his pencil to his left hand and by this shift find it easier to execute the needed ear.

TABLE 40 *Facial Expression*
(Percentage of Responses)

	5 years		5½ years		6 years		7 years		8 years		9 years		10 years		Adult
	G	B	G	B	G	B	G	B	G	B	G	B	G	B	
Some answer about emotion	94	86	92	84	98	76	96	98	94	90	98	94	94	96	100
Facial Expression															
Answers	4	0	6	0	14	0	18	18	56	36	80	86	94	90	100
Fails to answer	96	100	94	100	86	100	82	82	44	64	20	14	6	10	0
How looks	2	6	0	12	2	0	8	8	14	14	2	0	0	2	0
How feels	48	46	18	36	68	48	26	10	22	38	4	4	0	4	0
Happy or sad	36	34	78	36	14	28	44	62	2	4	12	4	0	0	0
Smiling, happy, OK	28	28	18	8	18	20	22	32	20	20	28	18	14	22	31
Fine, good, nice	22	20	4	20	8	12	6	4	0	2	0	2	0	0	0
Sad, unhappy, not happy	22	26	22	30	52	36	56	50	36	36	32	28	30	26	7
Plain, normal, in between	0	0	0	0	0	2	2	4	12	4	10	18	18	22	0
Mad	0	0	0	0	2	0	4	2	4	0	4	6	6	8	7
Thoughtful, serious, bored	0	0	0	0	0	0	0	0	6	2	2	12	6	8	0
Fine/sad or happy/sad, a double answer	2	0	4	6	6	2	0	6	6	6	8	6	16	12	7
Looks good, feels sad, not a double answer	18	6	40	18	0	4	0	0	0	0	0	0	0	0	7
Sick, crazy, horrible, scared	2	6	4	2	6	0	4	0	4	8	0	0	2	2	0
Excited, staring, surprised, startled	0	0	0	0	0	0	0	0	6	12	10	4	8	4	15
Other	0	0	0	0	6	0	2	0	0	0	4	0	0	0	23
Some positive emotion only	50	48	22	28	26	34	30	40	32	26	28	38	30	44	31
Some negative emotion only	24	32	26	32	60	36	60	52	50	58	38	50	34	34	7
Both in some way	20	6	44	24	6	6	0	6	6	0	8	6	14	12	7
How tell															
Some answer	32	26	46	56	52	50	74	72	40	64	68	66	72	68	68
Mouth or smile	20	14	30	42	42	34	62	62	36	46	54	50	42	54	54
Face	8	6	8	4	12	6	10	4	4	6	12	10	12	8	8
Eyes	4	2	8	6	4	2	6	2	8	12	8	4	14	6	6
Hand, Arm	0	0	0	0	2	8	2	2	2	6	6	10	4	0	0
Other	0	4	0	4	0	0	0	2	0	0	0	0	2	0	0

The preschool stroke is often wobbly and uncertain, though by 4 years of age it often assumes the dashing, out-of-bounds character so typical of FOUR and FOUR-AND-A-HALF. Thus the Incomplete Man may take on a wild look at 4½, with long hair, long arm and leg, long fingers and long foot.

The imaginative child of this age is likely to supply a belly button, though by 5 years of age only 6% of girls and only 2% of boys add this item. A very few preschoolers may also add genitals and breasts. (Older children may clothe the man with hat, guns, pockets, belt, and any other equipment their minds may dictate.) Others at 4, with less imagination, draw over the lines already there, or reproduce the figure as it stands, at one side of the paper.

Coming up into the 5- to 10-year-old range, less help is needed either to get the child started or to help him in completing all of the parts. Boys may attack the arm and leg region first, girls the head region. Some proceed in a very orderly fashion from hair to ear, to eyes, neck, arm, and leg. Others start with the area of greatest interest to them. Age may determine this response in part. SEVEN's interest in the tie area may be so strong that he will attack this first. The part most frequently omitted is the body line, especially after the tie has been added.

Table 41 indicates the age at which each part is first added by 50% or more of subjects.

Hair. FIVE has some trouble in seeing the need of hair. Even at this age, 14% of girls and 24% of boys omit it entirely. It may have to be pointed out to them. Hair is often drawn too long both at 5 and 5½ years, and is likely to extend too far down the side of the cheek, but even this is a definite inhibition of FOUR-AND-A-HALF's tendency to make the hair all the way around the head or way under the chin.

The opposite, that is, too little hair, is also a possibility occurring in some throughout the 5- to 10-year-old period. The marked reduction of hair to only three or four hairs suggests a much younger pattern.

It takes an extremely precise child to count the exact number of hairs on the printed figure and to reproduce them accurately. Even by 10 years of age, only 6% of girls, 12% of boys, reproduce this number correctly.

In the child's attempt to control the length of his stroke, he is also trying to hit the head line precisely. In the early period of 5 to 6 years he is more likely to overshoot and cross this line than to contact it accurately. Failure to reach the line is less common.

With the better control of stroke by 7, the majority achieve good length of hair (56% G, 60% B), but it is not until the precision of NINE that the majority place the hair accurately (58% G, 52% B). See Table 42 for details of hair production.

Eyes. The eyes, probably more than any other part, provide the

TABLE 41 *Incomplete Man: Age in Years at Which Parts Are Added by 50% or More of Subjects*

	Girls	Boys
Hair		
Adds	4	4
Good placement	9	9
Good length	7	7
Eyes		
Adds	4	4
Good placement	6	6
Matching types	5	5
Any pupil	10	9
Ear		
Adds	4	4
Good placement	9	8
Good size	9	9
Neck Treatment		
Body line	4	5
Neck	$5\frac{1}{2}$	6
Bow	$5\frac{1}{2}$	6
All 3 parts	7	7
Neck and bow only	10	
Arm (and Fingers)		
Adds	4	4
Upper third	$5\frac{1}{2}$	5
Good direction	5	5
Good length	10	10
Fingers good	8	8
Leg (and Foot)		
Adds	4	4
Placed correctly	7	8
Good direction	10	10
Good length	9	10
Foot good length	10	10
Naming		
Some naming	5	5
Names some kind of man	$5\frac{1}{2}$	5
Facial Expression		
Answers	8	9
"Happy or sad?"	$5\frac{1}{2}$	7
How feels	6	
Tells because of mouth	7	7
Positive emotion only	5	5
Negative emotion only	6	7

TABLE 42 *Hair*
(Percentage at Each Age)

	4½ years G	B	5 years G	B	5½ years G	B	6 years G	B	7 years G	B	8 years G	B	9 years G	B	10 years G	B	Adult
Makes any	88	76	86	76	98	90	96	96	100	100	98	92	100	98	100	100	100
Number																	
Too few	62	60	62	56	70	74	80	88	72	84	76	82	86	80	90	82	43
Too many	18	10	22	12	18	12	12	0	20	10	12	4	4	6	4	6	0
Looks correct, but isn't	0	0	0	2	0	0	0	0	0	0	0	0	0	2	0	4	57
Correct	8	6	2	6	10	4	4	8	8	6	10	6	10	10	6	12	0
Place																	
None	12	24	14	24	2	10	4	4	0	0	2	8	0	2	0	0	0
Too far around	38	30	48	26	48	38	54	38	46	34	46	26	30	30	18	18	14
Too little space	30	22	20	34	22	26	10	20	14	22	8	20	12	16	20	32	43
Correct	20	24	18	16	28	26	32	38	40	44	44	46	58	52	62	50	43
Length																	
Too long	40	54	50	42	60	52	30	46	30	16	6	24	10	6	2	2	0
Too short	30	4	26	20	6	18	26	4	12	24	32	26	28	30	26	20	57
± correct	18	18	10	14	32	20	40	46	56	60	60	42	62	62	72	78	43
Good	0	0	2	0	2	2	0	0	0	0	0	0	2	2	0	4	0

potential drama of this test. Because the eyes have no model, the child is able to express himself spontaneously. He can, at least at older ages, determine the inner character of the figure by the look he gives the eyes.

The bare execution of eyes is usually all the younger child can manage. However, eyes are added by the majority of children at 4 years and thereafter, and even as early as 5 years of age 96% of girls, 90% of boys, do add some kind of eyes.

The placement of the eyes may be too high or too low, but on the whole they are fairly well placed by 6 years (52% G, 66% B) and this placement steadily improves. For the most part eyes are quite even in size and level of placement. But when they are both different in size and in level, especially at 5 and 5½ years, it does suggest instability and an erratic nature on the part of the maker. However this type of unevenness is not too unusual at these early ages and subsequent tests should determine whether this finding is a quality of the age or of the child's personality.

A fairly infrequent (2–8%) type of eye is the horizontal or vertical line eye. Such a response is undoubtedly stimulated by the line models of nose and mouth.

The type of eye changes with age in an interesting sequence from the scribble or large, loose, or open circles of the 3-year-old to the large, dark, colored-in circles of the 4- and 4½-year-old, to the more controlled, open circles of FIVE, and finally to the small, closed, or filled-in circle eyes of the 5½- to 7-year-old, whose size may be so small that they are closer to a dot. The small, closed circle or dot is at its height at 7 years of age (16% G, 10% B).

The small, open eye reaches its high point at 8 years of age (26% G, 26% B), and continues at about that level at 9 and 10 years of age. However by 9, the oval eye is becoming more prominent, especially in girls (38% G, 28% B). These oval eyes tend to be slanted upward and outward at 9 years of age.[2]

The presence of pupils in eyes begins as early as 4½ years of age (26% G, 12% B) and steadily increases until it nears the 50% mark at 9 and 10 years. Pupils are of various sizes and may be filled in or open. As a rule they are centrally placed when the eyes are round, though they may be placed at the top or bottom, suggesting that the eyes are looking either up or down. By 8–9 years of age the pupils take on a more active role. They look to one side or the other, or they may be drawn as to give a cross-eyed or wall-eyed expression.

The addition of eyebrows becomes especially marked at 8 years

[2] If we follow the age-by-age products of some one child, we often see the eye first as a large, open circle, which becomes smaller and filled in, then a dot, then opening out round and small but with a pupil, and finally taking on the more mature oval shape.

(34% G, 20% B) and steadily but slowly increases thereafter, especially with girls. Eyelashes are less frequent, not much above a 6% level at any age for either boys or girls (see Table 43).

Ear. The ear is sometimes omitted at 5 years of age (12% G, 14% B), perhaps in part due to FIVE's tendency to concentrate on one thing at a time. If he concentrates on the hair he seems apt to forget the ear, and vice versa.

It is not easy, especially for the 5- and 5½-year-old, to execute even a fair semblance of an ear. Five-year-old ears may be classified as "poor," within the realm of the 75th percentile. They are often placed too low or even too high and are usually too small or too large. The shape may vary from a circular ear plastered on or near the headline but without becoming a part of the head to a horizontal or vertical ear (which may also take on an oblique position), or an ear in the shape of a cup handle.

There is a steady improvement in both placement and size of the ear until by 9 years good placement is normative (58% G, 54% B), as is also good size (60% G, 58% B). The shaping of the ear, however, remains a difficult problem. An early awareness of line and an attempt to give the ear correct shape may well indicate an advanced intellectual perception. As early as 5½ years of age, 28% of girls and 14% of boys make some effort to give a correct shape to the ear, but a correctly shaped ear does not even appear until 7 years of age (12% G, 12% B), an age when we expect to find finer awareness of both shape and detail. Even by 9 and 10 years a correct shape remains below a normative level (40% G, 30% B at 10 years).

Thus, after a slow start at 5 years of age when not all children add the ear, and only 28% place it correctly, only 18% make it of an accurate size, and none reproduce the shape correctly, there is slow but steady improvement with age. Gradually the ear is placed higher, becomes smaller and of better shape. The average child achieves both correct size and correct placement by 9 years of age, though correct shape remains beyond the average child in this age range. (See Table 44 for details of ear production.)

Neck and tie. This part of the test demands most of the child. In the first place what is it that is to be copied? Many children don't seem to know. To be sure it is an old-fashioned tie, which adds to the difficulty. Thus, it can be mistaken for an arm, and it *is* shaped rather like the sole of a shoe. Then there is the middle knotted area which may be ignored, or duplicated either to the right or left. These special difficulties are on the whole quite infrequent, but they give some idea of the difficulties the child encounters in completing this area. A few 4-year-olds have even been known to interpret the tie area as the arm of somebody behind the man's back. Since they duplicate the tie as the other arm, they may describe the person behind the man as hugging or choking him.

TABLE 43 *Eyes*
(Percentage at Each Age)

	4½ years G	B	5 years G	B	5½ years G	B	6 years G	B	7 years G	B	8 years G	B	9 years G	B	10 years G	B	Adult
Makes any	98	84	96	90	98	98	98	100	100	100	100	100	100	100	100	100	100
Placement																	
None	2	16	4	10	2	2	2	0	0	0	0	0	0	0	0	0	0
Too low	44	62	48	62	34	32	14	18	24	14	6	24	32	24	14	10	21
Too high	22	6	34	12	32	26	32	16	24	18	12	18	10	16	6	4	0
Correct	32	16	14	16	32	40	52	66	52	68	82	58	58	60	80	86	79
One only	0	2	4	0	0	0	0	0	0	0	0	2	0	0	0	0	0
Uneven	48	48	26	34	28	30	22	14	18	14	8	10	8	10	4	4	21
Even	50	34	70	56	70	68	76	86	82	86	92	88	92	90	96	96	79
Different types or sizes	48	70	26	0	26	22	16	20	16	22	12	8	10	18	8	12	0
Matches	50	14	66	90	72	76	82	80	84	78	88	92	90	82	92	88	100
Types																	
Knot or scribble	6	2	2	2	0	0	0	0	0	0	0	0	0	0	0	0	0
H- or V-line	2	6	4	2	0	2	8	6	0	0	6	0	2	4	4	6	0
Large open	56	64	26	28	8	22	10	22	4	4	4	2	0	4	2	2	0
Small open	12	6	6	18	14	12	14	22	20	20	26	26	22	26	24	34	7
Large filled circles	2	4	8	4	12	14	8	0	2	4	0	4	0	6	0	0	0
Small filled circles	8	2	26	10	32	24	26	24	24	16	16	12	8	6	0	6	0
Dot	12	0	12	6	6	4	6	10	16	10	6	8	10	4	4	4	0
Pupils in round	26	12	10	24	20	22	20	16	22	22	18	28	22	28	22	30	28
Oval, no pupil	0	0	0	0	0	0	2	0	2	2	2	4	12	6	12	6	14
Oval, with pupil	0	0	0	0	6	0	4	0	10	12	22	16	26	22	32	12	21
Any pupils	26	12	10	24	20	22	24	16	30	34	40	42	48	50	54	42	50
Eyebrows	12	10	2	6	8	6	16	18	12	10	34	20	36	28	42	14	71
Eyelashes	2	4	2	2	4	0	6	4	2	2	6	4	8	6	6	6	0
Pupils, brows, lashes	2	0	0	0	0	0	2	0	2	2	6	2	6	6	2	0	0

TABLE 44 Ear
(Percentage at Each Age)

	4½ years		5 years		5½ years		6 years		7 years		8 years		9 years		10 years		Adult
	G	B	G	B	G	B	G	B	G	B	G	B	G	B	G	B	
Makes any	70	78	88	86	96	92	92	96	100	100	94	96	100	100	100	100	100
None	30	22	12	14	4	8	8	4	0	0	6	4	0	0	0	0	0
Placement																	
Too low	34	46	42	40	52	44	58	30	52	38	44	32	32	36	32	24	21
Too high	10	18	18	18	18	16	8	18	8	16	6	14	10	10	16	20	0
Correct	26	14	28	28	26	32	26	48	40	46	44	50	58	54	52	56	79
Size																	
Too big	42	24	28	38	34	24	24	42	32	32	14	34	16	20	12	20	7
Too small	18	38	42	30	32	50	34	24	28	24	36	30	24	22	28	22	28
Correct	10	16	18	18	30	18	34	30	40	44	44	32	60	58	60	58	64
Shape																	
Poor	44	58	84	74	68	74	48	40	38	52	26	28	10	20	6	12	28
Separate from head	8	8	0	2	2	0	4	0	0	0	0	0	0	0	0	0	0
Correct except no indent	8	4	2	4	10	4	10	12	22	16	28	18	22	18	28	16	0
Some indent though not correct	8	8	4	6	28	14	24	44	28	20	20	36	32	38	26	42	28
Correct	2	0	0	0	0	0	0	0	12	12	20	14	36	24	40	30	43
Good ear	0	0	0	0	0	0	0	0	0	0	4	2	10	8	6	8	28

The tie as such may not even be noted by the 5-year-old. It is the completion of the body by adding the body line that interests FIVE most (72% G, 76 % B). He makes this body line in various ways, all of which reveal his relative immaturity. It is more often than not wobbly and shows his difficulty in achieving good contact points. He is apt either to overshoot or undershoot. The direction of his line is variable, but it often contacts either the middle or top region of the central tie area, or may be drawn under the tie area in an effort to join it with the rest of the body.

The need of a second side to the neck is recognized at 5 years (38% G, 34% B) and is well established by 6 (80% G, 70% B). This neckline is executed in various ways. When drawn alone (that is without the body line and tie), it is apt to be executed as an oblique, from the chin line down to the beginning of the printed body line, giving the impression of a bull neck. This oblique bull neckline may be supplanted at $5\frac{1}{2}$ to 6 years and following by an L-shaped line which includes both neck and part of the body line in one line.

More often, however, neckline and body line are two separate lines. At earliest ages the neckline may be centered. As the child grows older, the neckline gradually moves to the right, providing a wider neck.

The next step is to include the bow or tie. (The final step is to drop out the unnecessary body line.) The bow is rarely drawn alone without neck or body line, or both. Its presence is recognized by a few children even at 5 years of age (20% G, 10% B), and it is well established by 6 years (74% G, 62% B). Within this period from 5 to 6 years the child really struggles with the bow. He may add only a small loop well within the neckline. He may reproduce the bow quite accurately, placing it within the expected area but leaving it unattached to the existing bow. It may be executed either horizontally or vertically.

The central area of the bow may be reproduced on the outer or left side of the existing bow. The big loop of the bow may be attached to the inside or outside of the neckline. A more advanced bow, still incorrect, is one which reproduces the existing bow in opposition, with two—instead of the desired one—central knots. We are always on the alert when this happens, as it suggests that the child may have difficulty in visual centering.

By 7, the tie area is coming under good control with an awareness of all three parts: the body line, neck, and tie (54% G, 50% B). But the bow still tends to be drawn right over the neckline or the neckline over the bow, and it will still be some time before it is properly shaped and placed in a three-dimensional setting with no body line, and with the neckline and bow not crossing each other.

Even at 10 years, though 58% of girls and 28% of boys make bow and neck only, only 42% of girls and 12% of boys make these two parts in really good form. A good many still add one part after the other.

Thus the body line may be drawn first, then the neckline may be drawn to meet the body line, and the tie drawn over these two. If the tie is drawn first there is more chance of inhibiting the neckline as it meets the tie area, and of omitting the unnecessary body line.

Table 45 gives in detail age changes in the reproduction of the three neck area parts, singly and in combination.

Arm. The need of an arm is quite easily seen from 4 years on, and no more than 2–4% at any age omit the arm through the years from 5 to 10. The tie, as described above, may be considered as an arm, and fingers may be added to the central knot area of the tie as if it were a hand, but this occurs very infrequently, and seldom beyond 5 or 6 years of age.

Some FIVES still persist (16% G, 14% B) in drawing the arm downward as does the 4- and 4½-year-old. This downward direction gives the impression that the arm is drawn as if it were a continuation of the printed arm line. This may in part be why many still place it low on the body as well as pointing it downward. Such an arm also tends to be longer than the model arm, suggesting a 4-year-old pattern.

On the whole, however, the 5-year-old arm tends to point straight out horizontally from the body (52% G, 34% B, and much reduced thereafter), or to point upward, if even only slightly (normative at 5½ years and following, and close to the 90th percentile from 7 years on), even though it only slightly matches the given arm.

In the preschool years the arm may be placed midway on the body or below. Even as late as 5 years the place of attachment is variable. It may be either in the upper third of the body line, near the middle, or still in the lower third (36% G, 12% B). By 5½ years of age, however, it is well established within the upper third (66% G, 60% B).

To place the arm just right is not yet normative for girls even at 10 years of age (38% G, 58% B). Awareness of correct placement is especially evident at 9 years when some children are seen to make an imaginary line from the attachment of the printed arm across the body to where they wish to start the arm they are adding.

The arm tends to be too long through 6 years of age in many, although it may be too short or just right. Even by 7, the honors are pretty equally divided between the three possibilities of just right, too short, and too long. From then on the trend is toward a proper length arm, though correct length does not become normative until 10 years (50% G, 70% B).

The addition of fingers poses its own special problems. If the 3-year-old adds an arm it is usually just a horizontal line without any attempt to make fingers. By 3½, an awareness of a hand is often evident with a crude extension of the arm line. But by 4 and 4½ years an awareness of the fingers is very apparent, though fingers often turn out to be what

TABLE 45 *Neck Area*
(Percentage at Each Age)

	4½ years G	4½ years B	5 years G	5 years B	5½ years G	5½ years B	6 years G	6 years B	7 years G	7 years B	8 years G	8 years B	9 years G	9 years B	10 years G	10 years B	Adult
Makes any	94	82	92	90	98	98	100	100	100	100	100	100	100	100	100	100	100
None	6	18	8	10	2	2	0	0	0	0	0	0	0	0	0	0	0
Body line	82	75	72	76	76	84	84	76	78	82	72	84	62	38	42	72	21
Neck	36	28	38	34	64	44	80	70	80	76	98	88	92	88	98	98	86
Bow	28	14	20	10	52	38	74	62	92	86	98	78	100	94	98	96	93
Scribble only	0	4	2	0	0	0	0	0	0	0	0	0	0	0	0	0	0
Body line only	48	38	44	50	18	32	6	10	0	4	0	2	0	2	0	0	0
Neck only	0	0	12	6	6	4	2	2	0	0	0	0	0	0	0	0	0
Bow only	4	4	0	4	2	0	0	0	2	2	0	0	4	2	0	0	14
Body line and neck only	18	24	14	24	22	22	18	28	8	10	2	20	4	6	2	4	7
Body line and bow only	6	6	6	2	14	14	14	6	12	18	2	10	4	8	2	2	0
Body line, neck, and bow	10	2	8	0	24	16	46	32	54	50	68	52	58	60	38	66	14
Bow and neck only	8	2	2	4	10	2	14	8	26	16	28	16	34	22	58	28	57
Inadequate center treatment	14	2	7	8	12	10	16	12	4	12	12	12	4	2	6	4	7
Neck crosses bow	0	0	2	8	8	2	10	16	18	20	8	26	12	20	6	18	0
Good 3	0	0	0	2	0	0	0	0	6	2	8	8	6	4	26	14	14
Good 2	0	0	0	0	0	0	0	0	4	0	10	8	12	4	42	12	57

we call "rake" fingers, since the oblique stroke is not yet at the child's command.

The fingers may be in the form of a simple vertical line which crosses the arm in this 4–6 year period. The ability to make three fingers with the two side fingers angled obliquely improves steadily, however. A further refinement is to place the fingers just as they have been placed on the model hand with side fingers a little curved. The more perceptive child even at 5 years may try to reproduce these fingers accurately. A stumbling block is that he may reproduce them as given, without making the shift needed for the opposite side of the body. Thus the curve of the fingers may come out more in cup-formation.

Some see neither the shape nor the number of fingers. They simply add the kind of hand they most usually make when drawing. Thus it may have a round part suggesting the palm with the fingers (usually five in number) radiating out from this part. Fingers are conspicuously too long even through 6 years of age (48% G, 38% B).

Number of fingers may range from two to six. FOUR often makes four fingers; possibly he is enamored of his age. FIVE often prefers five, being literal-minded. In fact, this number may persist in the more literal individual even into adulthood, with some even adding two extra fingers to the three given on the model hand. Two fingers can persist even up to 8 years of age, but six are very infrequent and rare beyond 5 years. By 8 years of age well-drawn fingers are normative (62% G, 62% B). When it comes to a well-reproduced arm and fingers which are accurately placed and just right in length, the expectation is not very high even by 10 years of age (28% G, 32% B).

Thus the overall trend is that with increased age the arm moves upward on the body line, shifts from pointing downward to straight out to upward, and becomes gradually shorter in length. It is placed in the upper third of the body line at 5½ years by girls, at 5 years by boys. Direction is upward by 5½ years. Length is accurate by 10 years. Fingers are correctly reproduced from 8 years on (see Table 46).

Leg. The leg, although here discussed last, is more often than not the first part to be completed. It is the part closest to the child, and most easily seen by him. Its placement presents the same general range of possibilities as that for the arm. It can be placed just right or too far in or too far out on the body line. Likewise its direction can be just right or too straight down or too obliquely outward. The length also has its threesome possibilities of just right, too short, or too long.

Legs made by preschoolers tend to be either an overly long slash, slanting outward and crossing the body line, or a too long stroke placed too near the given leg, directed straight downward and often completed with a too long foot pointing in the same direction as the given foot. Gradually the leg shortens in length, moves outward to a more or less

TABLE 46 *Arm*
(Percentage at Each Age)

	4½ years G	B	5 years G	B	5½ years G	B	6 years G	B	7 years G	B	8 years G	B	9 years G	B	10 years G	B	Adult
Any arm	96	96	96	98	98	100	100	100	98	100	98	100	100	96	100	100	92
Placement																	
None	4	4	4	2	2	0	0	0	2	0	2	0	0	4	0	0	7
Lower third	18	8	36	12	10	10	6	4	0	2	8	4	2	0	2	8	0
Middle	36	50	22	22	22	30	22	12	10	20	10	16	14	10	4	8	7
Upper third	42	38	38	64	66	60	72	82	88	78	80	80	84	86	94	92	86
Just right			6	10	22	12	20	12	20	22	24	38	36	46	38	58	28
Direction																	
Down	22	16	16	14	2	8	10	0	2	2	4	4	4	2	2	0	0
Straight	40	44	52	34	30	16	16	8	2	12	6	4	2	2	2	6	0
Up	34	36	28	50	66	76	74	92	94	86	88	92	94	92	96	94	92
Length																	
Double	0	6	0	2	0	0	0	0	0	0	0	0	2	0	0	0	7
Long	54	54	36	64	34	46	38	54	32	38	2	26	22	24	12	14	7
Short	28	14	34	16	44	28	26	22	36	34	50	32	32	34	38	16	21
Correct	14	28	26	18	20	26	36	24	30	28	46	42	46	38	50	70	63
Fingers																	
None	2	10	8	4	2	2	0	0	2	0	0	0	0	0	0	0	7
☼	4	4	8	6	0	0	0	0	0	0	0	0	0	0	0	0	7
2 fingers	4	10	8	32	4	10	4	4	6	0	4	2	2	0	0	0	0
More than 3	8	12	8	18	8	4	8	8	2	4	4	4	2	8	0	0	7
┼	4	4	20	16	16	4	4	16	10	12	0	0	0	2	2	10	0
Varied	44	34	30	4	8	8	4	12	12	18	0	0	2	0	4	2	0
± correct but too long	14	18	8	18	50	42	48	38	36	34	28	32	22	22	10	6	0
Correct	16	8	6	2	12	30	32	22	32	32	62	62	72	64	84	82	79
All OK	0	0	0	0	0	0	0	2	2	2	8	10	10	12	28	32	50

correct position and direction, and the foot itself turns to the right and becomes shorter.

Boys especially, through 7 years, tend to place the leg too far out on the body line. It is not until 8 years that it is fairly well placed by a slim majority (50% G, 54% B), and this does not hold up too well at 9 and 10 years. Even the proper direction is not strongly normative by 10 years (46% G, 54% B). The majority at most ages tend to make the leg too straight. The too widespread leg is most conspicuous from 5 through 6 years. (What are known as parallel or railroad tie legs do not occur often, but do maintain a 2–4% level of occurrence even through 9 years of age.) The length is either too short or too long at 5–5½ years, too short at 6 and 7 years. But by 8 years a good length is coming into the ascendancy, though it is not established until 10 years of age (54% G, 60% B).

The foot shows some of the same difficulties as do the fingers, but to a lesser degree since it is but a single stroke. The leg and foot are most often executed as a single continuous line after 5 years with a well-defined shift in angle from leg to foot. FOUR may make the foot as a separate stroke which is likely to over- or under-contact the leg. By 5, this contact of foot with leg (if they are made as separate strokes), is quite secure.

It is the length and position of the foot that need chiefly to be considered. The foot is mostly too long at 5 years, as at earlier ages. The findings are actually very similar to those for the leg, with the too long losing ground, the too short increasing through 8, and the just right not coming through at a majority level before 10 years (54% G, 62% B).

The position of the foot is quite good even as early as 5 years. A fair proportion still point it in the wrong direction or to the left as earlier —actually a reproduction of the model foot and more characteristic of the preschool response. This persists at around a 25% level up through 6 years, and largely drops out thereafter. The foot is frequently drawn horizontally in a flat position, especially when the leg is more vertical, or too straight to match the leg in the model.

Or the oblique angle of the foot may exceed that of the model. Occasionally with the subtended angle more than the expected right angle, the foot gives the appearance of a dropped foot. A good leg and foot do not come through as well as a good arm and hand even by 10 years (only 14% G, 14% B). This figure appears very low, but even with the adult, only 28% make a "good" foot and leg which accurately match the model. In fact in following longitudinally the products of any one child from year to year, we note that the drawing of leg and foot often does not show the steady improvement seen in other parts of the man. Sometimes it almost seems as if a child at an older age, possibly trying too hard, makes a less accurate leg and foot than he may have produced earlier.

Table 47 gives details of age changes in the drawing of leg and foot.

Extra parts and extra marks. The addition of extra parts and marks occurs less in the standardization group than we would have anticipated from our clinical experience and from other studies. Genitals, belly button, and nipples are at a minimum even at 5–6 years, even though the belly button is a very common addition at 4½ years. Buttons, however, are added throughout at an 8–12% level and clothes are added, especially by boys, at a 2–6% level throughout. The coloring in of parts, so common at 4 years, occurs minimally at 5 and 5½ years, very little thereafter.

The nose and mouth are the parts most often added to or marked over. The mouth is often completed by adding extra upward lines at the ends, thus shifting the man's expression to a happy one. This desire for a smiling face at 5 and 5½ may be so strong that a child of this age may disregard the drawn mouth entirely and make a new smiling mouth. Teeth are rarely added even though our clinical impression has been that they were quite common at 5 and 5½ years, the time when children are so aware of their own teething.

Table 48 gives age trends for the addition of extra parts and extra marks, and Table 49 shows the extent to which arm and leg either meet, cross, or fall short of the body line.

Illustrations

Figure 5 shows plainly outstanding and characteristic age changes which take place in response to the Incomplete Man figure from ages 2 through 9. As this figure shows, an initial mere scribble response is followed, by 2½ to 3 years of age, with a long slash of arm and leg. As the child grows older it will be seen that the arm in general tends to move upward on the body line, turn upward and become shorter with fingers coming into increasingly good form.

Leg becomes shorter and is increasingly well placed and angled. Hair varies from too much and too far around at some ages to too little at others, but finally settles down. Ear becomes increasingly well placed and of increasingly good shape.

Eyes which are at first large open circles gradually acquire pupils and finally take on an oval shape. Neckline is most difficult for many children. Around 4 years of age many add a simple body line. Neckline is added by 5, tie comes in around 6–7. By 9 or 10, many are able to add just the neckline and bow without the body line.

Figure 6 shows characteristic age changes which take place in the Incomplete Man completions of four individual children at three successive age levels each.

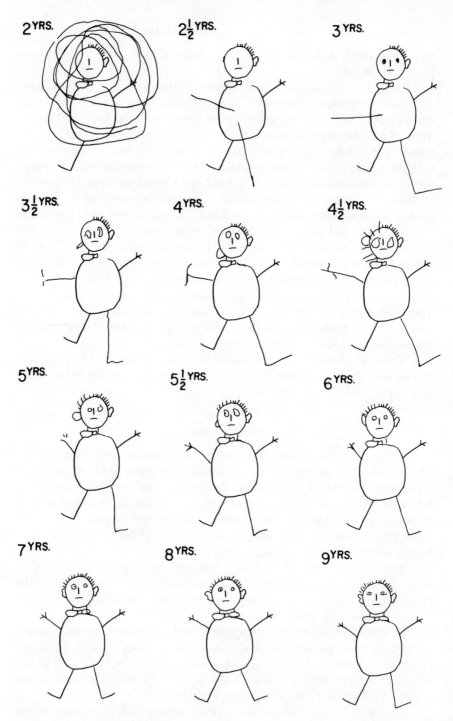

Figure 5. Typical responses, at successive age levels, shown to the Incomplete Man test.

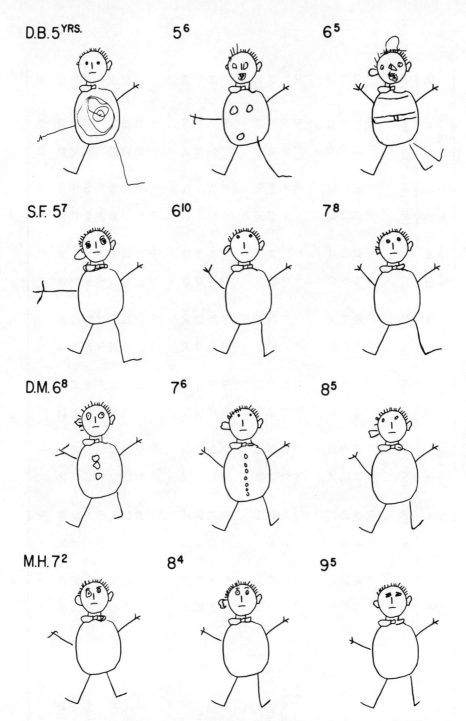

Figure 6. Samples from among selected individual cases showing characteristic age changes as they take place from one year to the next.

155

TABLE 47 Leg
(Percentage at Each Age)

	4½ years G	4½ years B	5 years G	5 years B	5½ years G	5½ years B	6 years G	6 years B	7 years G	7 years B	8 years G	8 years B	9 years G	9 years B	10 years G	10 years B	Adult
Makes any	100	96	96	100	100	100	100	100	100	100	100	100	100	100	100	100	100
Placement																	
None	0	4	4	0	0	0	0	0	0	0	0	0	0	0	0	0	0
Too far	54	54	40	64	48	70	42	52	28	50	44	32	36	40	44	32	0
Too near	16	12	30	14	26	8	16	8	14	14	6	14	12	18	10	6	28
Correct	30	30	26	22	26	22	42	40	58	36	50	54	52	42	46	62	71
Direction																	
± parallel other	6	2	8	0	4	4	0	0	2	0	4	2	2	4	2	0	0
Too widespread	14	6	20	34	22	48	8	36	10	2	4	8	4	6	6	0	7
Too straight	62	58	56	52	52	32	62	30	46	64	58	54	64	50	46	46	64
Correct	18	30	12	14	22	16	30	34	42	34	34	36	30	40	46	54	28
Length																	
Double	0	2	0	0	0	0	0	0	0	0	0	0	0	0	2	0	7
Too long	54	66	42	24	32	40	26	20	24	28	16	24	32	28	30	24	28
Too short	28	10	44	50	32	38	52	42	40	42	42	28	14	36	16	16	7
Correct	18	20	10	26	36	22	22	38	36	30	42	48	54	36	54	60	64
Foot																	
None	0	10	4	0	0	0	0	0	0	0	0	0	0	0	2	0	0
Too long	48	42	44	50	42	32	32	36	24	32	14	22	22	18	18	22	36
Too short	32	20	34	34	16	28	28	34	48	24	48	34	32	36	26	16	28
Good length	20	28	18	16	42	40	40	30	28	44	38	44	46	46	54	62	36
Double	4	0	10	0	0	0	0	0	0	2	0	4	4	0	2	2	7
Up too much	10	6	2	16	16	32	12	46	28	32	60	26	50	46	20	42	0
Pointed wrong	24	38	26	32	26	26	28	16	12	10	2	4	4	4	2	2	7
Pointed right	76	52	70	68	74	74	72	84	88	90	98	96	96	96	98	98	93
Good leg and foot	0	0	0	0	2	0	2	2	6	2	6	6	6	6	14	14	28

156

TABLE 48 *Extra Parts and Extra Marks*

	4½ years		5 years		5½ years		6 years		7 years		8 years		9 years		10 years		Adults
	G	B	G	B	G	B	G	B	G	B	G	B	G	B	G	B	
Mean number	8	7	10	8	9	9	10	10	10	10	11	10	11	11	10	10	10
Median number	9	8	8	8	9	9	10	10	10	10	10	10	10	10	10	10	10
						Percentage at Each Age											
Subjects adding extras	**56**	**50**	34	32	18	26	24	20	12	24	16	22	30	30	20	32	**64**
Belly button	8	16	6	2	2	8	2	0	0	0	0	0	0	0	0	0	0
Buttons	6	6	8	8	8	8	10	10	2	8	6	2	10	8	2	12	28
Clothes	10	2	2	6	0	4	2	0	4	2	2	2	0	4	0	4	36
Filling in	10	6	4	2	0	2	0	2	0	0	0	0	0	0	0	0	0
Nipples	0	0	0	4	0	2	0	0	0	0	0	0	0	0	0	0	0
Genitals	0	0	0	4	0	0	0	0	0	0	0	0	0	0	0	0	0
Marks on																	
Nose	14	4	10	2	2	4	8	0	2	6	4	4	8	4	6	10	21
Mouth	14	10	10	4	6	10	8	2	4	12	4	12	16	14	14	12	28
Ear	2	0	4	2	2	0	0	0	0	0	0	0	0	0	0	0	0
Foot	2	4	6	0	0	2	0	0	0	2	0	4	0	2	0	0	0
Finger	0	6	0	0	0	0	0	0	0	0	0	4	0	0	0	0	7
Cheeks	2	2	0	0	0	0	0	2	0	0	0	0	0	0	0	0	0
Teeth	2	0	0	0	0	0	0	2	0	0	0	0	0	4	0	0	0
Extra arm	0	2	0	2	0	0	0	0	0	0	0	0	0	0	0	0	0
Extra leg	0	4	2	2	0	0	0	0	2	0	0	0	0	0	0	0	0
Extra fingers	8	12	0	0	0	0	0	0	2	0	4	0	2	0	0	0	14
Double arm	2	4	0	0	0	0	0	0	0	0	0	0	2	0	2	2	7
Double leg	0	4	0	0	0	0	0	0	0	0	0	0	4	0	2	2	7

TABLE 49 *Extent to Which Arm and Leg Meet, Cross, or Fall Short of Body Line*
(Percentage)

							Years							
	2	2½	3	3½	4	4½	5	5½	6	7	8	9	10
Arm (girls)													
None	100	57	25	9	8	0	4	2	0	2	2	0	0
Crosses	0	31	31	33	64	26	16	14	10	24	8	8	6
Falls short	0	6	17	14	7	12	24	16	24	8	12	14	12
Correct	0	6	27	44	21	62	56	68	66	66	78	78	82
Arm (boys)													
None	100	77	38	24	10	6	2	0	0	0	0	4	0
Crosses	0	12	37	48	25	31	20	12	14	10	10	12	6
Falls short	0	0	15	14	20	19	14	22	26	6	10	8	4
Correct	0	11	10	14	45	44	64	66	60	84	80	76	90
Leg (girls)													
None	100	44	10	12	0	0	4	0	0	0	0	0	0
Crosses	0	31	52	38	65	37	26	14	22	12	4	6	4
Falls short	0	19	21	12	7	12	14	20	16	4	8	4	6
Correct	0	6	17	38	28	50	56	66	62	84	88	90	90
Leg (boys)													
None	66	12	13	14	0	0	0	0	0	0	0	0	0
Crosses	4	44	32	55	25	50	26	24	14	8	6	6	6
Falls short	0	0	30	14	15	6	22	10	12	12	8	2	6
Correct	33	44	25	17	60	44	52	66	74	80	86	92	88

CHAPTER *10*

RIGHT AND LEFT

||||||||||||||||||||||||||||||||||||||||||||||||||||||||||||||||||||||||||||

Introduction

In examining children over the years, we have been especially interested in their orientation to right and left, not only as related to their own bodies, but also to the bodies of others. We have observed a great deal of confusion about sidedness especially in children between the ages of 4 and 7 years.

The more confused children seemed to have other confusion patterns as well, especially as to the orientation of letters. Even single letters posed a problem for them, for they knew not which way these letters were supposed to go. No sooner had they worked out a correct orientation than flip-flop the letter turned in their minds in the opposite direction. Sometimes, as at $5\frac{1}{2}$ years, we found that some children even became fixed in an inaccurate direction and named right as left and left as right with utter certainty and consistency.

This orientation difficulty in some children extended considerably beyond the mere naming of right and left. Thus a child might be able to name his right hand and left hand but when asked to name his left ear, would become bewildered. A request might have to be spelled out: "If this is your left hand" (pointing to left hand), "then what is this ear?" (pointing to left ear). Usually this clue was enough, but this did not necessarily mean that over a period of six alternating requests the child could maintain an accurate orientation.

Some years ago we came upon the work of Dr. J. Robert Jacobson in relation to an adult test of right and left orientation.[1] We were intrigued by the comprehensiveness of his testing, his use of many parts of

[1] J. Robert Jacobson and Helen Gay Pratt, "Psychobiologic disfunction in children." *J. nerv. and ment. Dis.*, 1949, **109**, 4.

the body, his idea of timing of the individual's ability to carry out certain commands including orientation to pictures of opposing hands in which certain fingers were touching each other. These pictured hand postures were to be reproduced by the subject being examined, either verbally or motorwise.

We first tried these tests on adult friends, recognizing the unique potentials of such a testing series for a longitudinal study of behavior. Many people even as adults were still confused, and showed real orientation difficulties.

By degrees, we sorted out the tests, choosing the ones we considered most pertinent to the young child, cutting down the number from the point of view of time, as well as limiting the selection to orientations that would tell us the most about a child.

We soon discovered that the 5-year-old could not take the whole battery we had chosen both because of his lack of sustaining power and because of the complexity of the tests. He could name his thumb, little and middle fingers, giving them his own special names, but the index and ring fingers were not only difficult to name but also hard to find after they had been named. Any requests involving index and ring finger were therefore omitted in testing the 5-year-old.

The concept of right and left begins to intrigue, and confuse, a child of 3 or 4 years. At 3 or even younger the child has grasped the concept of top and bottom, right side up or upside down (even though he may still look at his books upside down). By 4, he is grappling with front and back and may still put his shirt on backward.

The step of mastering sidedness and of distinguishing right from left is a far harder step to take. At one point a child may seem to have figured it out, has supposedly learned it, and suddenly a switch around occurs and one side becomes its opposite in his mind. Right becomes left and left becomes right. This confusion may continue in some all through life.

With many 4-year-olds the subject of right or left becomes a reality as they put on shoes all by themselves. (Some may think first of right and wrong, but soon the idea of right and *left* takes over.) One session of teaching may bring results, but as a rule the lesson needs to be repeated over and over again. It may be learned for a while and later lost. This whole question of sidedness and right-left reversals is not a simple, but rather a very complicated matter, with many steps toward its final mastery.

The ten single and ten double commands in the third and fourth sections of this test appear fairly simple at first glance, but the task of recording stop watch readings in seconds and simultaneously fathoming and ironing out the child's misconceptions and errors, presents the examiner with many hazards.

If the examiner himself has trouble with concepts of right and left, he may be ready to give up this test before he has had enough practice with it to become proficient. A beginning examiner should not become discouraged; he needs time to become more comfortable with the test. He will develop skill in orienting the child, in manipulating the stop watch, and in recording his timing and his observations of the child's process of carrying out the commands. Initially, if he is unsure of his timing and recording, he may rely most heavily on his general impression of the child's response. This test is not so important in the final analysis of an individual's record as to demand great precision. It is a test that can tell us much, but at the same time it is difficult to know with what the findings can be most closely and usefully correlated.

When a child, especially one of 5 or 6 years, orients easily and well and scores well on this test, the evidence points to a well-integrated and effectively operating organism. At one time we thought there might be a close correlation between good response on this test and good reading, but this is not necessarily true, although a facility in right and left orientation is a part of good reading. We are now more concerned with the relationship between these test findings and achievement. A well-oriented child does not have to fight with confusion, loss of orientation, fatigue, and other factors.

After the examiner has mastered the easy manipulation and reading of a good stop watch with a quiet mechanism (nothing can be more disturbing than a noisy stop watch that startles the child every time it is clicked on or off), he is well advised to learn by doing. If he learns on the 5-year-old, he will have mastered the most difficult task first, because the 5-year-old needs expert handling and many allowances.

Because the right–left examination is more difficult with a 5-year-old than with an older child, the demands of the test are clipped down to what the child should be able to do. Any questioning or directions about index or ring fingers, as mentioned above, are omitted. Also the time demanded for sustaining is clipped down to what the 5-year-old can manage. Thus the ten single commands are cut down to six, and the ten double commands are cut down to two at 5 years of age.

Materials and Parts of Test

Materials for this test include a set of cards with directions and a scoring sheet on which directions for the various parts of the test are printed, with adequate space to record the timing and behavior. The chief material is a set of six $8\frac{1}{2} \times 5\frac{1}{2}$ inch cards on each of which is drawn in outline a pair of hands with some fingers touching (see pages 182, 183).

A fourth and most important item is a stop watch; the scoring is determined by averaging the time it takes for carrying out the various commands. As suggested above, both for the examiner's convenience and in an effort not to disturb the child, a silent, easily manipulated stop watch should be chosen.

The different parts of the test as we use it are as follows.

1. Naming parts of (examiner's) body.
2. Naming Right and Left, own and examiners.
3. Single commands.
4. Double commands.
5. Right and left Pictures, verbal response (see Figure 7, page 182).
6. Right and left Pictures, motor response (see Figure 8, page 183).

Detailed instructions for the separate parts of the test as we use it are given in the text which follows. All of these are given from 5 to 10 years except the pictures which are given only from 8 to 10 years.

Administration and Findings

1. NAMING PARTS OF THE BODY (5–10 YEARS)[2]

First we wanted to see if and how the child named parts of the body. We also wanted to make sure that he knew the names of the parts of the body that he would be asked to orient to in later sections of the test.

In administering this section, the examiner points to parts of his own body, telling the child, "I'm going to point to some parts of my body and I want you to tell me what I am pointing to."

He then points, in turn, to his own eye, eyebrow, palm, elbow, thumb, index finger, middle finger, ring finger, and little finger.

"Heel" and "cheek" which are used later were inadvertently not included. It soon became evident that the preschooler frequently confused heel and toe, and cheek and chin. We decided not to teach "heel" and "cheek" ahead of time, just to see whether this confusion was still present after 5 years.

Eye. The naming of the eye poses no problems even for the 4-year-old or younger child (see Table 50). A certain number, around 10% from 6 years on, may refer to the eye in the plural as "eyes." On the other hand, the child with the almost too precise mind may respond with "corner of the eye," "the upper (or lower) eyelid," or he may refer to the right or left eye, whichever the examiner is pointing to, naming it correctly or otherwise.

Eyebrow. Eyebrow is not quite so easy, though even by 5, 50% of subjects were able to name it (see Table 50). A few, thinking in more

[2] For the 5-year-old omit index and ring finger.

general terms, may call it "head." Others restrict their scope slightly and call it "forehead." With this type of naming, the examiner usually needs to give the clue, "What is this hair up here called?" This usually enables the child to name correctly.

There are still a few, however, who may need to be further helped with the name itself: "Point to your eyebrow." When they have done this, then the examiner again points to his own eyebrow and asks, "Then what is this?" "Eyelash" is a fairly common substitute for eyebrow. If this is given, the examiner will point to his own eyelashes, saying, "This is the eyelash, but this (again pointing to the eyebrow) is the eye—?" Usually the child is then able to respond correctly.

Palm. The palm is more usually named "hand" by the 5- and 5½-year-old. If pressed for a more specific name ("What else do they call it?"), a child in the 5½- to 6-year-old age range may say "middle." If pressed still further he may say "skin," "wrist," "vein," "wrinkles," "fist," or "bottom."

At an earlier age, at 4 years, he may refer to the palm as the "place where you hold things," or "place where you carry things."

If it becomes obvious that the child cannot give the name "palm," the examiner, as with eyebrow, asks the child to point to his own palm. If this is successful, as it usually is by 5 years, the child is then asked, "If that is *your* palm, what is this on me?"

If with all this coaching the child still returns to his former response, persisting with "middle" or whatever he has first called it, then there is very real evidence of a stuck mechanism which may impede learning. "Palm" however, is a difficult word and is not usually mastered before 7 or 8 years[3] (see Table 50).

Elbow. As a rule elbow is as easy or easier to name than eye. Most 5-year-olds (91%) can name it (see Table 51). A few persist in the more global or general response "arm" or "bone." Some have trouble in saying the word clearly or understandably. A very few confuse elbow with knee.

Thumb. Some form of the word thumb is well known to the 4-year-old (80%). He is perhaps more apt to give the response "thumkin" which he has been taught in finger-play songs, especially if he has attended nursery school. By 5, the child is moving out of this younger realm. "Thumb" then becomes the name of choice (see Table 51).

Index. Though the index finger is included in finger-play exercises in nursery school and is often called pointer, it is neither easily named

[3] When the news got around in the North Haven schools about our testing program, many 6-year-olds (or younger children) were apparently taught at home to name palm correctly. But even though a 6-year-old was able to name his palm, he still showed his true 6-year-old quality as he responded to further commands.

TABLE 50   *Naming Parts of the Body (Eye, Eyebrow, Palm)*
(Percentage of Responses)

			Years			
	5	5½	6	7	8	9	10

	5	5½	6	7	8	9	10
Naming Eye							
Fails	5	0	0	0	0	1	2
Eyes or the eyes	4	3	10	11	9	5	11
Some other, with help	10	9	0	0	3	4	0
Eye	**81**	**88**	**90**	**89**	**88**	**90**	**87**
Naming Eyebrow							
Eyebrow	**50**		46	**71**	**82**	**91**	**82**
Eyebrows	18		34	11	4	4	13
Success, second trial	10		4	5	10	2	0
+variations							
Eyelash	4		8	0	2	1	1
Eyelashes	2		8	12	0	2	0
Eyelid	0		0	0	0	0	0
Forehead	4		0	1	2	0	2
Other	12		0	0	0	0	2
Naming Palm							
"I don't know"	0	14	14	0	0	1	0
Hand	74	62	42	**52**	20	10	0
Middle	15	0	14	0	3	0	0
Other	0	4	1	0	0	2	1
Palm	11	20	29	48	**77**	**87**	**99**
Palm (Weston)			17	43	**75**		
+ palm on second trial	7	4	9	0	3	10	2
+ learns palm	**65**	17	33	40	18	2	1
+ can't learn palm	8	0	0	8	0	0	0

NOTE: Other names given for palm:
5 years: center, inside, skin, wrist, arm bones (1 each); fingers (2).
5½ years: skin, veins (1 each).
6 years: inside, skin, fingers, wrist, veins, wrinkles, fist, bottom (1 each).
7 years: skin, veins, wrinkles, fist, bottom (1 each).
8 years: wrist, pocket (1 each).

nor located by the young child (apart from the finger-play songs with demonstration) before the child is 5½ or 6 years of age (82% at 5½ years).

The index may be called simply "finger." To give it a more specific name is not easy for the 5- or 6-year-old. If the examiner helps by pointing and asking the child what he (the examiner) is doing (at 5½–6 years), the child may quickly be able to answer "pointing" (82% at 5½ years to 92% at 6 years). (See Table 51.) Or he may say "tapping." The examiner can then translate this into calling the finger "pointer finger."

TABLE 51 *Naming Parts of the Body (Elbow, Thumb, Index Finger)*
(Percentage of Responses)

				Years			
	5	5½	6	7	8	9	10
Naming Elbow							
"I don't know"	5	10	14	1	0	1	0
Incorrect	4	2	0	5	1	1	0
Correct	**91**	**88**	**86**	**94**	**99**	**98**	**100**
Naming Thumb							
"I don't know" or other failure	3	8	6	0	0	0	0
Variations on thumb							
Thumkin	3	2	1	0	0	0	0
Your thumb	0	8	6	6	6	4	7
The thumb	1	2	0	2	2	1	0
Thumb	**93**	**92**	**94**	**98**	**100**	**97**	**100**
Thumb, second trial	3	0	0	2	0	3	0
Naming Index Finger							
"I don't know"		10	8	3	0	0	0
First finger		0	0	0	9	9	3
Pointer finger							
After demonstration		**82**	**92**	50	37	31	18
Without demonstration		0	0	32	28	35	**64**
Forefinger		0	0	0	0	0	2
Other		8	0	8	0	1	0
Index		0	0	7	26	24	13

Because of the difficulty both of naming and locating the index finger, it is best not to include it in the test battery before 5½ years of age.

Middle finger. The middle finger (often called "big finger" or "tall man" by the young child) can be picked out readily because of its size. The child also feels comfortable in moving it separately from the other fingers. As a matter of fact, this middle finger was often used as a pointing finger from 3½ years on and may be preferred in this use to the pointer or index finger. The 4- or 5-year-old locates this finger readily and is apt to call it "big finger" or "tall man" according to how he has been taught.

A fair proportion (29%) refer to it as second or third finger, at 5 years, when number interests rank high. Others may refer to it simply as "finger" (10% at 5½ years).

Some will name it spontaneously with one of its possible names or when given the clue, "What size is it?" If the child of 5 or 5½ cannot name it, he may be given a choice as to whether he wishes to call it "big finger" or "tall man." His choice is important, since his own naming is later used when specific commands are given.

By 6 years, 50% still call the middle finger "tall man," but an increasing number have given up this preschool naming. They are often at a loss, however, because they have not yet learned the more advanced name of "middle." As soon as they are helped by the examiner's demonstrating on his own hand with "Two on this side and two on this side, and it's in the _____," they are usually able to respond with "middle."

By 6 years of age even though they have named this finger "tall man" or "big finger," they are told that it also has a different name. Then they are taught "middle" by means of the above demonstration. The name "middle" is purposely used from 6 years on, both because they are ready for it and also to contrast the sound of "middle" to the sound of "little" (see Table 52).

TABLE 52   *Naming Parts of the Body (Middle Finger)*
(Percentage of Responses)

				Years			
	5	5½	6	7	8	9	10
Naming Middle Finger							
"I don't know"	5	0	0	0	0	0	0
Thumb, or pinkie	1	1	0	0	0	0	0
Ring man	3	1	0	2	0	0	0
Finger	0	10	0	0	0	0	0
Pointer	3	4	0	0	0	0	0
Index	0	0	0	0	0	2	8
Second	7	8	0	0	0	0	0
Second or third	29	5	0	0	0	0	0
Third one	0	0	0	2	1	1	0
Big	13	9	0	4	0	1	2
Tall man or tall finger	14	27	**50**	18	8	8	1
Middle	15	18	14	30	37	37	**59**
Second trial	10	5	0	0	0	0	9
Examiner demonstrates (2–2)	0	12	36	44	**54**	**51**	21

Ring finger. The ring finger, even though it may be used in preschool finger play, when it is usually called "ring man," is as difficult to remember or to locate as is the index finger. Therefore it, too, is omitted from the battery of tests before 5½ years of age. It is not named spontaneously before 7 years (see Table 53). Prior to this age, the help of "What do you wear on it?" (examiner pointing to a ring on his own finger or to the area where it would be worn), usually brings forth the correct answer.

TABLE 53   *Naming Parts of the Body (Ring Finger, Little Finger)*
(Percentage of Responses)

	5	5½	6	Years 7	8	9	10
				Naming Ring Finger			
"I don't know" or other failure		13	30	1	0	0	0
(Wear?) Ring		40	24	20	16	18	0
Ring man		30	6	8	1	3	0
Fourth		0	0	4	0	0	0
Second to last		0	2	2	2	2	0
Some other		2	8	2	0	0	0
Ring		14	30	63	81	77	100
				Naming Little Finger			
"I don't know"	6	8	0	0	0	0	0
Pinkie	17	25	44	32	21	12	16
Ring, or fifth	0	1	0	1	0	0	0
Tiny, small, smallest	7	0	10	8	8	12	13
End man, last one	6	6	10	0	1	3	0
Baby	23	20	6	31	25	32	33
Other	4	7	10	8	4	1	2
Little, first trial	37	33	20	20	41	40	36
Little, second trial	3	0	8	8	4	0	0

Little finger. The little finger is as well known to the preschooler as is his thumb. Both are on the outside of the hand and thus are easily located. They may even be confused with each other at 4 years of age. The very young child does not refer to this finger as "little," but more often calls it "pinkie," "baby finger," or "small finger." "Little" is actually not normative even through 10 years of age. "Baby finger" (33%) is almost as frequently used as "little" (36%) at 10 years. "Pinkie" steadily drops from a high of 44% at 6 years to a low of 16% by 10 years (see Table 53).

Though the little finger may be named variously (pinkie, small, baby), the examiner steers the child into the use of the name "little" after 6 years of age. If the child has not called it this, the examiner will suggest "another name for this finger is 'little.' I'm going to call it 'little' when I ask you to do various things." The sound of "little" is used to contrast with "middle" to determine whether or not there is difficulty in auditory discrimination.

2. NAMING RIGHT AND LEFT (5–10 YEARS)

In this part of the test the examiner asks as he points to the child's right hand, "What is the name of this hand on you?" (Or, "Show me your right hand.") He then asks about the following parts of the body: left hand, left ear, right eye, right ear, left eye, and then about his own right hand.

Naming right hand. As suggested above, the examiner points to the child's right hand and asks, "What's the name of this hand on you?" FIVE is likely to name some specific part that the examiner is pointing to (back of hand, knuckle, thumb, little finger), having just been naming parts of his body—or he may not understand what the examiner means.

The next step is to help him by saying, "Show me your right hand." With this much help a bare majority of 5-year-olds know their right hand (60% of girls, 48% of boys). It is not until 7 years (or possibly 6½) that the child can correctly name his hand without this help (82% of girls, 68% of boys at 7 years). (See Table 54.)

Telling how he knows which hand. Once the child has responded, he is then asked how he knows. Answers are highly variable. Some come

TABLE 54 *Shows or Names Right Hand*
(Percentage of Responses)

	5 years		5½ years		6 years		7 years	
	G	B	G	B	G	B	G	B
Names								
Fails	74	66	78	76	62	56	14	16
Correct	18	20	12	22	34	34	82	68
Opposite	8	14	10	2	4	10	4	8
Shows								
Fails	8	4	2	0	2	2	0	0
Correct	42	28	66	60	36[a]	34[a]	10[a]	10[a]
Opposite	22	34	10	16	24	20	4	6
Shows or names correctly	60	48	78	88	70	68	92	78
Reasons Why Child Knows Right and Left								
No answer	6	10	2	4	14	12	6	2
I don't know	24	2	16	16	6	10	4	14
Mummy (or someone) told me	26	18	18	14	20	12	12	12
Just know, thought, or guessed, or because	20	34	26	36	10	22	18	4
Confused, or some other answer not listed	10	8	10	2	12	14	0	12
Facing this way or on this side	6	0	10	8	8	6	14	16
Physical clue	0	6	2	2	0	6	0	2
Write, eat, pledge allegiance	8	12	16	18	30	18	26	18

[a] These numbers are smaller at older ages since if subject succeeds in *naming*, he is not asked to *show*.

right out and confess that they don't know. Others give a cocky or cock-sure response in a 4-year-old manner: "Just knew," "'cause," or "Just thought," or "Just guessed."

Those who give the source of their knowledge as "Mummy showed me," are responding in a characteristic 5- or 6-year-old way, relating themselves both to an experience and to a person. Their knowledge of right and left does not yet stand on its own.

Their own action may also be the basis of their knowledge, as when they report that they eat with, write with, or pledge allegiance with the hand in question. The experience at school as reflected in the pledge of allegiance is indeed becoming a part of the process of learning. A few will relate a side to some physical clue, such as a scratch or a wart. This is helpful as long as these clues last.

Some have a vivid memory of being taught at the piano or the table, or as they were putting on their shoes. At the opposite extreme, an 8-year-old who says "Right because it's on the right side" is thinking like an adult and gives a suggestion of having built up a fluid use of right and left in his thinking process.

Naming left hand. When the right hand has been named correctly or incorrectly and the reason given, the left hand is then pointed to, as the question is asked, "And what is the name of this hand?"

Most FIVES, just after having had the experience of naming their right hand will be able to name the left hand correctly. A few who still respond more like 4-year-olds may call the left hand the "wrong" hand. Some FIVE-AND-A-HALFS are so obliging, as well as possibly thinking of both sides together, that as soon as they have named the right hand they will immediately refer to the left, saying, "And this is my left hand."

If the child has named his right hand as its opposite (left), or has shown his left hand as his right and is consistent in naming the right hand as left, the examiner will need to decide as to whether he will allow the child to settle for the opposite. The consistent use of the opposite is most characteristic of FIVE-AND-A-HALF.

Table 54 gives data for telling how they know right and left.

Right and left eye, right and left ear. At the ages of 5, 5½, and possibly 6, the child's orientation to sidedness is further tested by point-ing to each eye and each ear, right and left alternately. That is, examiner first points to the child's left ear and asks, "What's the name of this?" (The same for right eye, right ear, and left eye.)

The transition of relating these parts of the body to sides, rather than just naming them, is difficult for many 5- and 5½-year-olds. When the examiner points to the child's left ear and asks, "What's the name of this?" the child may simply respond with "ear." Then the examiner needs to point first to the child's left hand, saying, "If this is your left hand,

TABLE 55   *Shows or Names Six Parts of Body: Right and Left Hand, Eye, Ear*
(Percentage of Responses)

	5 years G	5 years B	5½ years G	5½ years B	6 years G	6 years B
All correct	36	34	74	82	50	62
All opposite	14	24	18	6	18	20
All correct or all opposite	50	58	92	88	68	82

then this is your _____ ear" (pointing to the child's left ear).
With this help the child of 5 can usually respond correctly. If he doesn't,
it indicates that his processes of response are below the expected 5-year-
old level.

By 5 years of age a slim majority will either name all correctly
(36% G, 34% B) or all opposite (14% G, 24% B). By 5½ or 6, they will
name all correctly, in a majority of cases, but an established conception
of right and left on ones's own body is not secure before 7 years of age.
(This is the age of being well grounded, of knowing in which direction
you are going. This is the age when, in our opinion, more formal learning can and should be given.)

Table 55 gives data for showing or naming the six parts of the body.

Identifying examiner's right hand. Having established his knowledge of his own right and left sides at 6 years, it is next important for

TABLE 56   *Naming Right and Left: Identifying Examiner's Right Hand*
(Percentage of Responses)

	Years 6	7	8	9	10
No response	0	0	3	2	0
Opposite	36	26	2	2	0
Correct	64	74	95	96	100
Reasons for Giving Answer					
No answer	14	0	4	2	0
"I don't know"	12	6	8	1	1
Some individual response	32	16	15	4	1
Response related to fact that they write with right hand	0	10	10	0	0
"I just know"	2	0	3	1	0
"Opposite my left hand"	2	6	5	5	8
"Facing different way" or "My right opposite yours"	24	38	31	72	62
"Because if I turned around ..." and those who turn around	14	24	24	15	28

the child to adjust to an opposing person face on, a situation in which the sides are reversed. This takes a new capacity of adaptation, a new ability to manipulate sides in space.

The examiner, facing the child, holds up his right hand and asks, "What's the name of this hand on me?"

Sixty-four percent of subjects named this hand correctly at 6 years of age, and a correct response was established in nearly all subjects by 8 years (95%).

Reasons for knowing examiner's right hand are given in Table 56.

3. SINGLE COMMANDS (TIMED IN SECONDS)

The ten single commands are as follows (only six of these commands are given at 5 years):

1. Touch your eye.
2. Show me your pointer finger. (Not asked at 5 years.)
3. Show me your ring finger. (Not asked at 5 years.)
4. Show me your middle finger. (Not asked at 5 years.)
5. Close your eyes and bend your head.
6. Bend your head and tap the floor with your heel.
7. Raise your head and open your mouth. (Not asked at 5 years.)
8. Touch your right ear.
9. Show me your right thumb.
10. Show me your left index finger. (Left middle substituted at 5, using the child's own naming of "big finger" or "tallman.")

(The recording of timing, demanded in the last four parts of the test, may seem very difficult to a beginning examiner. The timing is taken from the moment the examiner has completed his command to the moment that the child finally carries out the instructions. The word "finally" is used since there may be many steps in the child's process of carrying out a command. As the examiner becomes more proficient, timing a child's response is like second nature to him. It becomes automatic.)

As we analyze responses to these commands, we find that the request to "show" is easily understood by the child. "Touch" is equally understood, though the very literal child may actually touch his eyeball when asked to touch his eye. Closing the eyes is understood, though a few 5-year-olds and a fair proportion of 4-year-olds may refuse to obey this command. "Bending," however, can pose a very real problem. The child may ask "Which way?" referring to back, forward, or to one side or the other. If he does ask, he is told he may choose whichever way he wishes.

"Raise your head" poses the problem of not knowing what "raise" means. That is why this command is omitted at 5. Even at 6 and 7, some children do not know what "raise" means, or they are unsure as to whether they should bend their head back or stretch it straight up. They can be told to lift it up, or the examiner can demonstrate for them. "Tap" poses a problem for the 5-year-old because he usually relates tapping to a hand movement. Thus he often brings his hand to the floor in carrying out the command in which the heel is supposed to tap.

The only part of the body referred to here that has not up till now been named or pointed to in the initial requests is the heel. The child may need to be taught "heel" before he can carry out the command. Often the clue, "the heel of your shoe" is all that he needs to locate it quickly.

For this part of the test the scoring results (Table 57) show that FIVE is responding nicely to the single commands within the two-second (2.1″–2.5″) realm, with the exception of "Bend your head and tap the floor with your heel" (5.4″) and "Show me your big finger" (3.7″).

TABLE 57   *Right and Left Single Commands*
(Average Time in Seconds)

	5	5½	6	Years 7	8	9	10	Adult
Touch your eye	2.1	1.8	1.1	1.2	1.2	1.0	.8	.9
Show index		1.9	3.5	2.4	2.0	1.0	1.1	.6
Show ring		6.2	3.3	2.8	2.4	1.6	1.5	1.1
Show middle		2.0	1.7	1.6	1.1	.6	.7	.7
Close eyes, bend head	2.2	1.2	.9	1.4	2.4	1.1	1.0	.5
Bend head, tap floor with heel	5.4	5.8	3.4	3.8	3.3	1.8	1.8	2.1
Raise head, open mouth		3.0	2.4	2.0	1.4	1.2	1.0	.6
Touch right ear	2.5	2.6	1.9	1.7	1.8	1.3	1.2	.7
Show right thumb	2.4	2.0	1.8	1.5	1.3	.9	.8	.7
Show left index	3.7	3.6	2.8	2.5	2.1	1.2	1.1	.6
Average in seconds per command	3.0	2.8	2.3	2.1	1.8	1.2	1.1	.85
Range, time in seconds	.4–30.0	.3–25.0	.3–20.0	.2–15.0	.2–10.0	.2–7.0	.2–6.0	

FIVE reveals himself most clearly by the way he responds to "Bend your head and tap the floor with your heel." To begin with, his whole body is involved. If he doesn't know "heel," this has to be taught. Though he has just responded to "Close your eyes and bend your head," this command was confined to the head region. Now bending the head becomes to him something different. He tends to bend his head way over onto the table if he remains seated, or into his lap if he pushes his chair back, or even down to the floor, especially if he chooses to stand. Along with this excessive bending, he is apt to bring his hand to his foot, to his heel or to the floor. The examiner may have to repeat the command emphasizing, "Tap the floor with your *heel*." No wonder it can take him as long as 20″–25″ to carry out this command.

The next single command that the 5-year-old has some trouble with is to locate the middle or big finger on his left hand. To locate it in the first place is difficult. He is most likely to look at all of his fingers held tightly together and to chose the biggest one. Choosing the correct left hand is still a fair matter of chance, which makes the scoring difficult in this 5- to 6-year-old period.

The examiner needs to record not only the time it takes to respond to the command (and by this is meant the time it takes to respond correctly even though with help), but also to record as far as possible the way the child carried out the request. If he responds to the command of "Touch your eye" with right hand to right eye, "R to R" should record this move. If, however, he points to his right eye with his left hand, the recording should show "L to R." This is a significant pattern which we designate as a cross-over pattern and relate to a younger age. Other younger patterns may also be present in the child who shows a cross-over pattern.

If the child bends his head back or to the side, these movements should be recorded. Bending the head back is an extensor pattern more expected of a 4-year-old. If this occurs, other extensor patterns are watched for, such as a sharp extensor release of the pencil. Along with extension or quick release patterns, the sustaining capacity of the child is often found to be below par.

Bending the head to the side doesn't occur very often and may be thought of as possibly atypical. However it occurs frequently enough at 9 years of age (15%) to make us wonder whether it is not an expression of some age pattern at 9.

FIVE is known to have "stuck" patterns. Part of this is related to the fact that he so often completes himself through another person. This is why he often cannot act until he is given permission, as when his teacher replies to his request, "Yes, you may go and get some paper." In a similar way, after he has responded to "Close your eyes and bend your head," he may remain stuck in this position until the examiner releases him either with the next command or by telling him, "You may come up now." (50–60% at 5–6 years). Even this may not be enough because the examiner only told him to "Come up" but did not mention opening his eyes. Therefore the examiner may need to add, "And you may open your eyes." If a child tends to overhold, this can be recorded with the letters O.H.

By 5½, most children can take the full battery of Right and Left tests, both single and double commands. If it becomes apparent that the full set of commands is beyond a child, the examiner should restrict the test to the 5-year-old battery.

The greater fluidity of FIVE-AND-A-HALF's characteristic response is soon apparent. He studies his fingers as he chooses them. They pop up as he locates them. He may talk to his fingers, saying, "Hey you," when they don't do quite what he wants them to. He may still confuse thumb and little finger or toe and heel (15% at 5 years, 9% at 5½).

By 6 (or even 5½) there is no question but that the child is ready for the full battery of commands. He often starts at once before the examiner has completed his request, or he may repeat the command out loud before he executes it. Sometimes the child repeats the request as a question, thus needing further help from the examiner. Often his response to a command is very rapid. SIX, by nature, responds with speed and completes with speed.

By 7, though the child may still repeat some of the commands, he is more likely to repeat them in a whisper. He often reveals his process of thought as he inhibits an initial response such as the choice of the opposite hand, or of a wrong adjacent finger before he responds correctly. This inhibited response should be recorded if possible (e.g., inh. opp; inh. adj. ring).

Single command scoring shows, on the whole, a steady improvement from age to age (see Table 57). The request of "Bend your head and tap the floor with your heel" remains the hardest of the ten single commands throughout these years from 5 to 10 and even into adult life. (It is interesting to note that the 10-year-old on the average is faster to execute this command than the adult—2.1″ for the adult in contrast to 1.8″ for the 10-year-old.) The average time it takes to respond to these ten single commands shows a steady decrease from 3.0″ at 5 years to 1.1″ at 10 years. These figures undoubtedly show that there are definite growth patterns that have occurred in these years. The growth of more advanced neurological contacts has undoubtedly enabled the organism to respond with increasing speed.

It is also interesting to consider the *range* of time of the responses which can occur in a standardization group of 100 subjects. As shown in Table 57, range is fairly wide at 5 years but decreases from an outer limit of 30″ at 5 years to 6″ at 10 years. The very fast responses of .2–.4″ are found in some from an early age.

There can be a markedly fluctuating timing for a single child in the 5- to 7-year realm especially, as sample time records for a selected 6-year-old and a selected 9-year-old show (see Table 58), but on the whole the timing tends to settle down by 9 years of age and no longer shows wide variation from one command to another.

TABLE 58 *Sample Time in Seconds for Two Individual Children Aged 6 and 9 Years on the Ten Single Commands*

Number of Command	6 years	9 years
1	.6″	1.1″
2	16.4	.3
3	7.6	1.0
4	2.0	.3
5	.6	1.1
6	2.1	2.0
7	1.7	1.0
8	.8	2.1
9	2.0	2.0
10	11.2	.2
Average	4.5	1.1

4. DOUBLE COMMANDS (5–10 YEARS) (TIMED IN SECONDS)

The ten double commands are as follows:[4]

1. Touch your right thumb with your right little finger.
2. Place your left hand on your left knee.
3. Put your left ring finger to your right eyebrow.
4. Put your right elbow in the palm of your left hand.
5. Put your right middle finger on your left cheek.
6. Place your left thumb against your right thumb.
7. Place your right middle finger against your left little finger.
8. Place your right little finger against your left ring finger.
9. Place your left middle finger against your right index finger.
10. Place your left thumb against your right ring finger.

These are all straightforward requests. The one stumbling block may be "cheek" since the child has not been checked on this. A few confuse cheek and chin. The examiner needs to be careful to give the word used by the child for his index finger. Very few use "index" or "forefinger." The majority speak of the index as "pointer" and respond best to its being called this.

Though the requests may be straightforward, the responses, especially in the 5-year-olds take a varied and multiple-step process to reach the goal of the initial request. The examiner needs to sharpen both his pencil and his wits to record what the child does and says. He needs to simplify the process by formalizing his recording. An example sheet (Figure 9) will be given at the end of this chapter to familiarize the examiner with abbreviations and ways and means of recording responses.

[4] Only Numbers 1 and 7 are given at 5 years.

1. Touch your right thumb with your right little finger. This first double command is one of the two exacted of the 5-year-old. It usually taxes his ability to its limit, but at the same time reveals much about him. We can trace the origins of his difficulties as we examine the 4-year-old's response. To begin, FOUR needs to locate his right hand, then the thumb and little finger of that hand. As he looks at his outspread hand, he often says, "I can't."

When urged to try, he will try to push the thumb and little finger together just above the knuckle area. This is almost impossible to do without breaking a finger. The examiner, sensing his dilemma, then demonstrates that fingers can come together over the palm area rather than over the back of the hand. Even such a gesture may be difficult for the 4-year-old since his fingers tend to remain in extension, or one finger may flex, but the other extend. The child will then need to push them together with his free hand.

There is one delightful response of the superior ingenious 4-year-old who, sensing his dilemma with his extended thumb and little finger on his right hand, closes the gap by placing his left thumb and little finger against his right thumb and little finger. You can't argue with him for he has by this circuitous route touched his right thumb with his right little finger.

Both 5- and 6-year-old still tend to flex thumb and little finger over the back of the other fingers, but they effect closure just above the nail area or first joint. On occasion the fingers are physically not long enough to be able to touch each other.[5] (This reminds us of a European method once in use to determine a child's readiness for kindergarten. If he could flex his arm over his head and grasp the lobe of his opposite ear this indicated that his body was advanced enough for him to start kindergarten. We admit that this is a rather crude test, but it does show respect for physical as well as mental growth.)

This first double command persists in being one of the most difficult commands to carry out even at later ages. It is not until 7 years that the majority (63%) are able to execute it correctly on first trial (see Table 59).

Besides the above-described difficulties, a good proportion at 5½–6 years (60% at 5½, 54% at 6 years) cross over to the other hand, placing their right thumb against their left little finger or vice versa.

The examiner repeats the request as often as an error persists. If repetition is not enough, the examiner will need to give help in a step-by-

[5] It is interesting to note that the 3 kindergarteners in the North Haven group of 200 children who showed this inability were not only too young, but also not ready for kindergarten according to our tests.

TABLE 59 *Double Commands: Percentage of Children Responding Correctly on First Trial*

	5	5½	6	Years 7	8	9	10
Right thumb, right little	60	42	46	63	69	91	91
Left hand to left knee		51	72	76	83	86	83
Left ring, right eyebrow		24	44	44	58	78	80
Right elbow, palm left hand		60	64	75	92	98	96
Right middle, left cheek		38	24	54	64	87	78
Left thumb to right thumb		95	100	100	100	100	100
Right middle to left little	45	58	58	52	76	92	89
Right little to left ring		45	54	54	71	96	87
Left middle to right index		30	36	61	73	92	87
Right thumb to left ring		35	28	79	78	98	98

step fashion (21% at 5½, 24% at 6 years). He will say, "Show me your right thumb." When this is located, examiner holds the child's right thumb so he won't lose his choice. Then examiner continues, "Now show me your right little finger." When this is finally located the child is told, "Now put them together." This need to be helped in a one-by-one fashion indicates a lack of good combining ability. It is as if the child can handle only one request at a time. This is an example of the focalization on a single idea or item so characteristic of FIVE.

2. *Place your left hand on your left knee.* The majority of subjects at 5½ (51%) can respond correctly to this request on first trial. Enacting the opposite of the command (that is, right hand on right knee) is the most common error (46% at 5½), but this decreases rapidly from then on. A probably significant error is a cross-over pattern of placing the left hand on the right knee. The very literal child will need to expose the knee. Another variable is to lift the knee to the hand, a move which may demand swinging the knee out from under the table and thus consuming more time.

3. *Put your left ring finger to your right eyebrow.* This is a surprisingly difficult command to execute. It is consistently one of the commands taking the most time throughout the years it is given (from 5½ to 10), though the average time scores show steady and significant improvement (see Table 60).

Not only is finding the ring finger difficult, but also finding specifically the left ring finger. Added to these difficulties is the universal difficulty of isolating and extending the ring finger by itself so that it can be used to touch the right eyebrow.

The commonest error in finding the ring finger is to choose an adjacent finger, usually the middle finger, or to confuse ring and index fin-

TABLE 60 *Right and Left Double Commands*
(Average Time in Seconds)

	5	5½	6	7	8	9	10	Adult
				Years				
Right thumb, right little	14.6	12.1	11.6	6.8	6.0	4.3	3.3	2.2
Left hand, left knee		3.8	4.1	3.8	2.3	1.6	1.7	1.3
Left ring, right eyebrow		11.8	10.0	9.2	7.3	4.2	3.6	1.3
Right elbow, palm left hand		4.6	4.0	4.3	2.5	1.1	1.1	.6
Right middle, left cheek		9.1	7.6	6.9	4.9	3.1	1.6	.9
Left thumb, right thumb		2.7	2.3	2.1	1.5	1.2	.8	.7
Right middle, left little	12.1	9.6	6.3	8.2	4.8	3.0	2.9	1.4
Right little, left ring		8.0	8.0	6.8	5.2	2.0	2.5	1.2
Left middle, right index		12.6	9.8	9.7	6.0	3.0	2.9	2.3
Left thumb, right ring		9.8	7.2	5.7	4.2	2.3	2.4	1.5
Average time per command	13.3	8.4	7.1	6.4	4.5	2.6	2.3	1.3
Range	1.2–55.0	.6–40.0	.3–40.0	.3–40.0	.3–35.0	.2–20.0	.2–15.0	

ger. Another common error is to choose the same side eyebrow rather than the requested opposite eyebrow. The confusion this command produces is often expressed by the child who says, "I'm all confused." Some need to be helped out of their confusion, especially at 5½–6 years, with step-by-step help.

4. *Put your right elbow in the palm of your left hand.* This is a relatively easy command even for the 5½-year-old (60%). There is the usual error of choosing the opposite. Occasionally a 5½- to 6-year-old will think he has been asked to place his right elbow in his right hand and flatly and correctly denies that this is possible.

5. *Put your right middle finger on your left cheek.* It is 7 years of age before the average subject can comply correctly with this command on first trial. There is a slight tendency to choose an adjacent finger in error; a greater tendency, especially at 6 years, to choose the little finger for the middle finger. Some children become quite indignant saying, "But you said 'little,' " or "I thought you said 'little.' " The choice of the wrong hand is fairly common through 6 years. Chin is confused with cheek especially at 6 years (18%). And the choice of the same side or right cheek is quite common (36% at 6 years). Errors persist fairly strongly with this command through 8 years of age. There may be need for step-by-step help at 5½ and 6 years.

6. *Place your left thumb against your right thumb.* This becomes a delightful moment of relaxation for the child after some of the harder commands. Ninety-five percent of subjects can obey this command correctly on first trial at 5½ years of age. In some, however, there is an unusually long delay in touching the two thumbs. This may be due to a literal interpretation that the left thumb must be sought first, so that it can touch the right thumb.

7. *Place your right middle finger against your left little finger.* The four double commands (#7 to #10) should be considered together since they all involve a finger of one hand touching a finger of the other hand. The sequence of timing (Table 60) shows the clearly increased speed of response which comes with increased age.

This is the second of the two double commands asked of the 5-year-old, and may not be easy for him (6% refuse). One of the commonest errors is to choose both fingers on the same hand (22%). This may be influenced by the previous double command (#1) given the 5-year-old. This error persists through 9 years. Quite often (17%) the child needs to be helped out of his difficulties by a step-by-step process.

By 5½ years the majority (58%) can execute this command on the first trial, but there is not a good margin before 8 years of age (see Table 59). There are the usual opposite and adjacent errors. Thumb may be confused with little finger through 5½ years. A common response which may show later significance is to match either both little fingers or both middle fingers.

8. *Place your right little finger against your left ring finger.* By 6 years, the majority (54%) are able to carry out this command on the first trial (see Table 59). There are the usual errors of opposite side, adjacent finger, middle for little, index for ring, choice of same side, or a tendency to match the same finger of the opposite hand. The thumb may still be chosen in place of the little finger through 6 years of age (4%). Step-by-step help may still be needed through 6 years of age (6%). It may be difficult to pry the ring finger up so that it can be used to point to the little finger.

9. *Place your left middle finger against your right index finger.* This command doesn't achieve majority rating of success on the first trial until 7 years of age (61%). (See Table 59.) The choice of opposite (incorrect) fingers is still quite marked at $5\frac{1}{2}$–6 years (40–50%). This may partially be due to fatigue. As with the above two commands (#7 and #8), the errors include an adjacent choice, mixing little for middle or ring for index, and matching the same finger on the opposite hand. Considerable confusion is engendered during the carrying out of this command and also considerable help through a step-by-step method (10% at $5\frac{1}{2}$ and 6 years) may be needed.

10. *Place your left thumb against your right ring finger.* As with the above command (#9), the majority do not succeed on first trial before 7 years of age (79%). (See Table 59.) As above, the choice of opposite fingers is strong at $5\frac{1}{2}$ and 6 years (50%). The confusion of ring and index, considerable at $5\frac{1}{2}$–6 years (23% at $5\frac{1}{2}$, 20% at 6 years), as well as adjacent errors (10% at $5\frac{1}{2}$ years, 16% at 6 years) indicate that it is difficult to localize an individual finger, especially if it is the ring finger. Only a few match with the same finger on the opposite hand or choose both fingers on the same hand. Some step-by-step help may be needed.

As with the single commands, very definite improvement with age is apparent in the double commands in relation to the scoring time (see Table 60). The harder commands persist in their higher time scoring and the easier commands persist in their lower time scoring. Steady but real improvement is evident from year to year. Substantial gains are evident at 8 years, with definite consolidation of these gains by 9 years.

Comparison of individual records of two different subjects at 6 and 9 years shows that the fluctuating timing—much longer for some commands than for others—is even more marked at 6 years on the double commands than it was on the single commands (Table 61).

In analyzing these two records it becomes apparent that commands #4 and #6, usually the easier commands, are easiest also for these two children. The 6-year-old shows difficulty with commands #1, #3, #9, and

TABLE 61 *Sample Time in Seconds for Two Individual Children Aged 6 and 9 Years on the Ten Double Commands*

Number of Command	Selected Records at 6 years	9 years
1	11.8	1.0
2	8.0	1.2
3	13.8	1.3
4	1.4	.4
5	8.9	3.0
6	1.2	.4
7	3.4	2.3
8	5.1	.4
9	14.3	3.0
10	14.8	1.0
Average	8.3	1.4

#10. In the 6-year-old record there is a range from 1.2″ to 14.8″ (range of 13.6″), whereas on the 9-year-old record there is only a range from .4″ to 3.0″ (range of 2.6″). (See Table 61.) This indicates the greater stability of the 9-year-old, as well as his greater speed.

RIGHT AND LEFT PICTURES

By 8 years of age the child is increasing his speed and his ease in carrying out the single and double Right and Left commands. He is ready for a new challenge. The examiner may also feel that the range of this test needs to be increased. The most effective area is in the child's adaptation to an opposing figure. By 8 years of age he has shown that he is well established in his ability to name an opposing person's hand (95%) so that it is reasonable to ask him to put this ability to use.

Jacobson devised a very clever method of testing this ability by showing pictures of hands with fingers touching each other for the individual to describe verbally or to reproduce with his own hands. We have chosen six of these single pictures—three verbal and three motor as they are called. The fingers touching in the pictures (see Figs. 7 and 8) are as follows:

Single verbal	*Single motor*
1. left index—right little	1. left ring—right middle
2. left middle—right ring	2. left index—right ring
3. left little—right ring	3. left little—right index

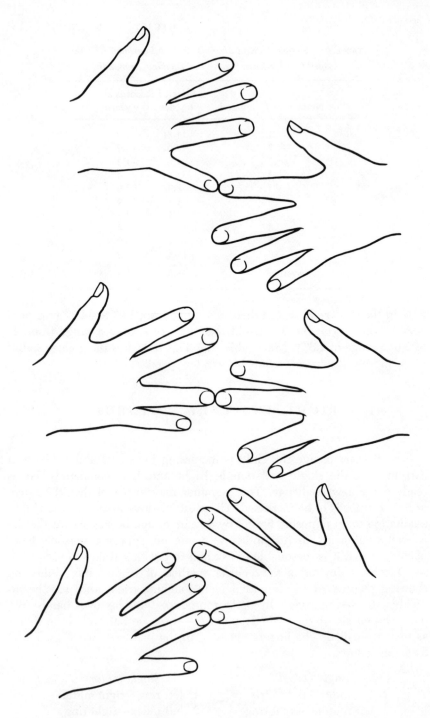

Figure 7. Verbal pictures.

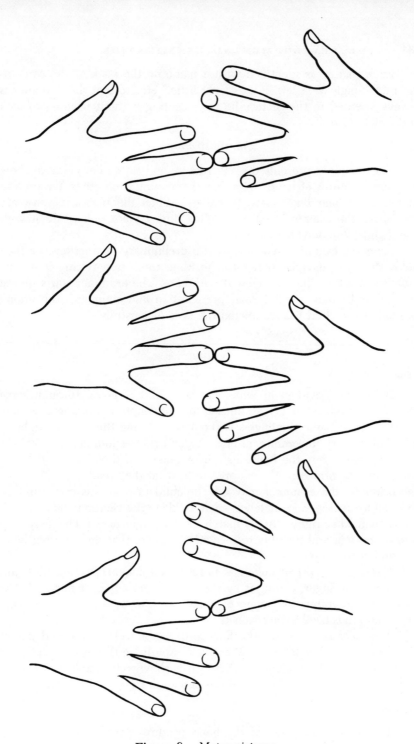

Figure 8. Motor pictures.

Each picture is identified with a name on the back of the card indicating "Single V-1: left index—right little," etc., so that the examiner is always oriented to the picture he is presenting without needing to look at the picture itself.

Administration

The examiner presents the first picture and says, "I'm going to show you some pictures of hands with fingers touching each other. I want you to tell me which fingers are touching." When the motor pictures are presented, the examiner will say, "This time I want you to do it with *your* hands. You don't have to tell me."

After the examiner has given these preliminary instructions, he then holds the card at right angles to the table top, often resting it on the table so that the child can view it with ease. The examiner starts timing as soon as he makes this formal presentation and completes the timing as soon as the child has completed the task successfully.

Findings

VERBAL PICTURES

It becomes evident at once that the child is going through some mental gymnastics to orient himself to the opposing pictures. A few EIGHTS (10%) name the fingers without considering the sides as right or left. This is very uncommon after 8. A good proportion, close to 50% at 8 and 9 years, view the hands as mirror images of their own and therefore name them incorrectly as opposite to what they really are. To check the response, the examiner may ask the child to place his own hand on the picture to see if it matches—that is, does the pictured hand which he has named as right actually match his own right hand? This may help him to reorient and possibly to recognize the fact that an opposing hand is different from his own.

Naming the correct fingers is fairly easy for EIGHT though he is apt to misname a finger, calling it by the name of an adjacent finger. A few may have forgotten the name of some one finger, especially the ring finger, and thus need to be coached.

A correct response on the first card is not well established before 10 years (70%) but learning takes place rapidly on the second and third cards. By 8 and 9 years both of these cards show well-established, correct initial responses in the 70th and 80th percentiles (see Table 62).

MOTOR PICTURES

The motor enactment of the hand postures poses a far more complicated problem, especially for the 8-year-old. It is too difficult for 25% of our normative group. This is why the findings in Table 63 for the

TABLE 62 *Right and Left Pictures: Quality of Responses*
(Percentage of Each Type of Response)

	First Picture			Second Picture			Third Picture		
	8 years	9 years	10 years	8 years	9 years	10 years	8 years	9 years	10 years
		Verbal							
Correct first trial	54	40	70	71	89	76	67	88	89
Mirror image	33	46	19	12	10	10	3	6	0
Names fingers without indicating right or left	10	6	4	1	0	0	1	0	0
Turns body around	0	2	3	0	0	2	0	0	2
Matches pictures with own hands	25	14	4	4	1	2	2	1	1
Adjacent finger errors	6	7	5	10	4	10	2	6	5
Matches fingers	2	0	0	2	0	0	1	0	0
Forgets name of finger	0	0	0	3	0	0	2	0	0
		Motor							
Not given, too difficult	22	0	0	26	0	0	26	0	0
Correct first trial	32	31	47	46	45	64	53	50	63
Mirror image	31	32	34	11	29	26	9	33	25
Turns body to match picture	5	4	3	3	4	2	2	4	1
Matches picture with own hands	5	13	5	1	8	2	1	7	2
Crosses over arms to match picture	9	4	8	5	7	2	4	4	2
Needs to match body and hands with picture	19	21	16	9	19	6	7	19	13
Adjacent finger error	1	7	4	1	7	5	3	8	10
Matches fingers	11	21	10	3	7	3	0	0	0

8-year-old present some problems in interpretation. (That is, since only the more capable EIGHTS undertook to solve this test, mean figures for EIGHT suggest a quicker performance than do the figures for NINE when all attempted the test.)

An opposite response, similar to that expressed to the verbal pictures when the child treated the picture as a mirror image of his hands, is also evident as the child tries to reproduce the picture with his own hands. This opposite or mirror image response persists in motor enactment through 10 years of age and does not clear up to any marked degree on the second and third trials on the second and third pictures. To respond correctly to the pictured hands of another person is not an easy readjustment for a child to make (see Table 62).

TABLE 63   *Right and Left Pictures*
(Average Time in Seconds)

	8 years		9 years		10 years	
	G	B	G	B	G	B
			Verbal			
Card 1	40.5	32.4	23.7	23.0	15.9	19.1
Card 2	25.0	22.9	13.8	11.3	10.7	11.6
Card 3	15.0	13.6	9.2	8.4	8.7	7.1
Cards 1–3	80.5	68.9	46.7	42.7	35.3	37.8
			Motor			
Card 1	26.3	25.4	23.7	28.6[a]	14.9	18.8
Card 2	16.4	22.2	18.6	20.9	10.1	12.4
Card 3	15.3	14.5	10.8	16.1	7.4	10.6
Cards 1–3	58.0	62.1	53.1	65.6	32.4	41.8

		Sexes Combined		
	8 years	9 years	10 years	Adult
		Verbal		
Card 1	36.4	23.4	17.5	12.3
Card 2	24.0	12.5	11.1	8.7
Card 3	14.3	8.8	7.9	6.3
Mean 1–3	74.7	44.7	36.5	27.3
Median 1–3	56.9	38.5	31.0	26.0
		Motor		
Card 1	25.8	26.2	16.9	10.2
Card 2	19.3	19.7	11.2	6.3
Card 3	14.9	13.5	9.0	3.4
Mean 1–3	60.0	59.4	37.1	19.9
Median	49.3	40.9	27.4	18.0

[a]Figures for Motor 1, boys at 9, are higher than for 8, because some 8-year-olds do not attempt these pictures.

Those who can make an inner readjustment to an opposing figure reproduce the hands with ease. A few who have initial difficulty receive a sharp insight when the examiner has them place their hands correctly on the pictures. A fair proportion, however, need to use some sort of matching device such as turning their own body (either sitting or standing), so that they are in the same position as the person in the picture, or they may spontaneously place their hands on the pictures, crossing their arms and turning their hands so that their hands match the hands in the picture.

With some the act of placing their hand on the picture in response to just the first card may be enough to orient them to the fact that their own hands are opposite from a pair of opposing hands. But others cannot make this inner adaptive switch even with this help. They need to place their hands over each picture in turn, matching right hand over right hand, having to cross their arms as they do so. (This does, of course, also help them to get the right fingers.) As soon as the child has given a correct response, even though the arms may be crossed and hands oddly positioned, the timing should be concluded.

The examiner may attempt to untie this awkward posture by holding the two fingers that are touching together, and then uncrossing the child's arms so that the backs of his hands are facing the backs of the model hands in the picture. This demonstration of showing the child how he might reproduce the hand postures more easily may carry over to the next two pictures.

However, often the child who initially orients in this seemingly backhanded way by having to match his hands on the hands of the pictures will continue to need to go through this process for all three cards. This persistence tells a great deal about such a child's mechanism. He will quite likely be found to be restricted in other ways. This type of child seems to need to move from reality, the reality of the hand in the picture that he can match with his own hand. Because these children often lack a more advanced method of behavior, they are apt to learn by rote if they learn at all. But rote memory becomes inadequate when the load of learning becomes too heavy and there is no inner processing of learning. Rote learning does not give a child the support he needs, nor does it help him to move through a process of growth within himself. Thus such a child is better off working through his own laborious methods which at least have meaning for him and afford support.

Selecting the correct fingers during the motor enactment is not too difficult for most. However adjacent errors are evident as with the verbal pictures and within a similar range (under 10%). A tendency to match fingers (middle to middle, or ring to ring) is especially evident on the first motor card, due in part to the closeness of the middle and ring fingers, but it may also be related to the newness of this experience.

The scoring in seconds shows some very positive trends. The average time per card (three cards combined) for the ages from 8 to 10 years, plus an adult sampling, is shown in Table 64.

TABLE 64   *Average Time in Seconds of Response Per Card*

Age in Years	Verbal		Motor	
	Mean	Median	Mean	Median
8	24.9	19.0	20.0	16.9
9	14.9	12.8	19.3	14.6
10	12.2	10.5	12.4	9.6
Adult	9.5	8.7	6.6	5.6

From these figures it is evident that the 10-year-old is well on his way toward the adult norm. His motor response is still no faster than his verbal response, but both are poised at the same threshold ($V = 12.2''$; $M = 12.4''$). One would have expected that enacting the pictures would take less time than describing them, but this is not consistently true of child subjects, though it is shown to be true with the adult ($V = 9.5''$; $M = 6.6''$). The median figures are also included in Table 64 since there is often considerable difference between them and the means. The scoring of the majority of children falls closest to the median figures.

Details of timing for each of the three motor and verbal pictures separately at ages 8 to 10 are given in Table 63, showing sex differences in performance.

Though the enactment of the postures should, in general, become easier than the verbal naming, some children move best through the verbal sphere of naming first before they enact the postures, even though they have been told that they don't need to "say it." Thus after an initial attempt to have them enact the pictures without naming, they may be allowed to name first if this desire persists and shows itself to be an orientation method a special child needs to use.

The opposite may also be true. Some children may wish to enact the postures shown in the pictures first, before verbalizing what fingers are touching. Again the child is first urged to carry out the instructions as given, but he is eventually allowed to use the method by which he seems to move best and which helps him to carry out the request—in this case enacting which fingers are touching each other before he verbalizes.

Table 62 summarizes major behavior trends and shows quality of responses which occur in the response to the verbal and motor pictures.

Figure 9 illustrates a typical response of a 6^{11} boy as it is recorded on the Right and Left record form.

Name Boy

Age 6^{11}

Naming parts of body

1. Eye
2. Eyebrow
3. Palm hand (what else) (show)
4. Elbow

Summary Comments:

Scoring better than quality shows. Bends head back; confuses thumb and little; adj. errors. Deficit on double commands 7 to 10.

Naming fingers () 5 yr. items

(1) Thumb
2 Index (pter)
(3) Middle (2-2) ring, tallman
 (2-2) center (or)
4 Ring (wear)
(5) Little pinkie

Naming R & L

R hand _____the_____ (Show me your R hand)

How do you know? Idk

L hand   R eye   L eye

L ear   R ear

Ex-er's R hand (How do you know?) If I turned over that way it would be my R. hd.

Single Commands () 5 yr. items

(1) Eye	1.4	R to R
2 Index	10.1	mid(r) ring(r) L to R
3 Ring	2.9	R to L
4 Middle	1.0	R to L
(5) Cl. eyes, bend head	1.4	c.u.
(6) Bend head, tap fl. with heel	3.9	b.back
7 Raise head, open mouth	5.4	
(8) R ear	2.4	
(9) R thumb	1.4	L to R
(10) L index (5 yrs-L big)	2.1	inh. mid, R to L
Total	32.0	Av. 3.2 (7 years 2.1)

Double Command () 5 yr. items

(1) R thumb-R little	3.1	on top
2 L hand-L knee	1.6	
3 L ring-R eyebrow	7.2	L e.b. (r)
4 R elbow-palm L hand	5.4	L fist (r)
5 R middle-L cheek	3.0	
6 L thumb-R thumb	4.0	inh. R lit.
(7) R middle-L little	1.8	
8 R little-L ring	4.8	ring pulled up
9 L middle-R index	17.2	R ring(r) R mid(r)
10 L thumb-R ring	18.1	R index(r); L hand on top of R hand
Total 66.2	Av. 6.6 (7 yrs 6.4)	

Suggested abbreviations:

O.H.	overholds
(r)	examiner repeats
s by s	step by step
adj.	adjacent
inh.	inhibits
c.u.	come up

Form No. 104

Figure 9. Sample record, Boy 6^{11}, of Right and Left tests.

CHAPTER 11

MONROE VISUAL TESTS

|||||||||||||||||||||||||||||||||||||||||||||||||||||||||||||||||||||||

VISUAL ONE

In our early exploration of ways and means to test the young child's mind in its readiness for school, we glimpsed his pleasure in matching forms. Visual One, a matching test from Marion Monroe's Reading Readiness Test, suited our purposes ideally. We found it to be a task that demanded understanding of direction, carrying out of orders, and the ability to sustain and to find one's place repeatedly. This was no small demand of the 5-year-old, yet this is what he needs to have at his command before he can accept the demands and enjoy the delights of a kindergarten situation. Visual One, we soon came to realize, had only a short longitudinal life of usefulness as a test—the three age periods of 5, 5½, and 6 years—but what it tells us makes it well worth including in our test battery.

Material

The Visual One work sheet (see Figure 10) neatly assembles twelve double forms (one of each pair being the same as the model presented on the test card) in twelve squares, three across and four down, thus nicely orienting the child to the vertical page. In each square the correct form which matches the one on the card may be either at the top or at the bottom. (The correct forms are checked in Figure 10.) Its counterpart may be a right or left reversal, only two forms showing a vertical reversal:

$$\begin{array}{cc} \triangle & \underset{\bullet}{\overset{\bigcirc}{}} \\ \triangledown & \bigcirc \end{array}$$

190

GROUP TESTS

Visual Test 1

Memory of Orientation of Forms

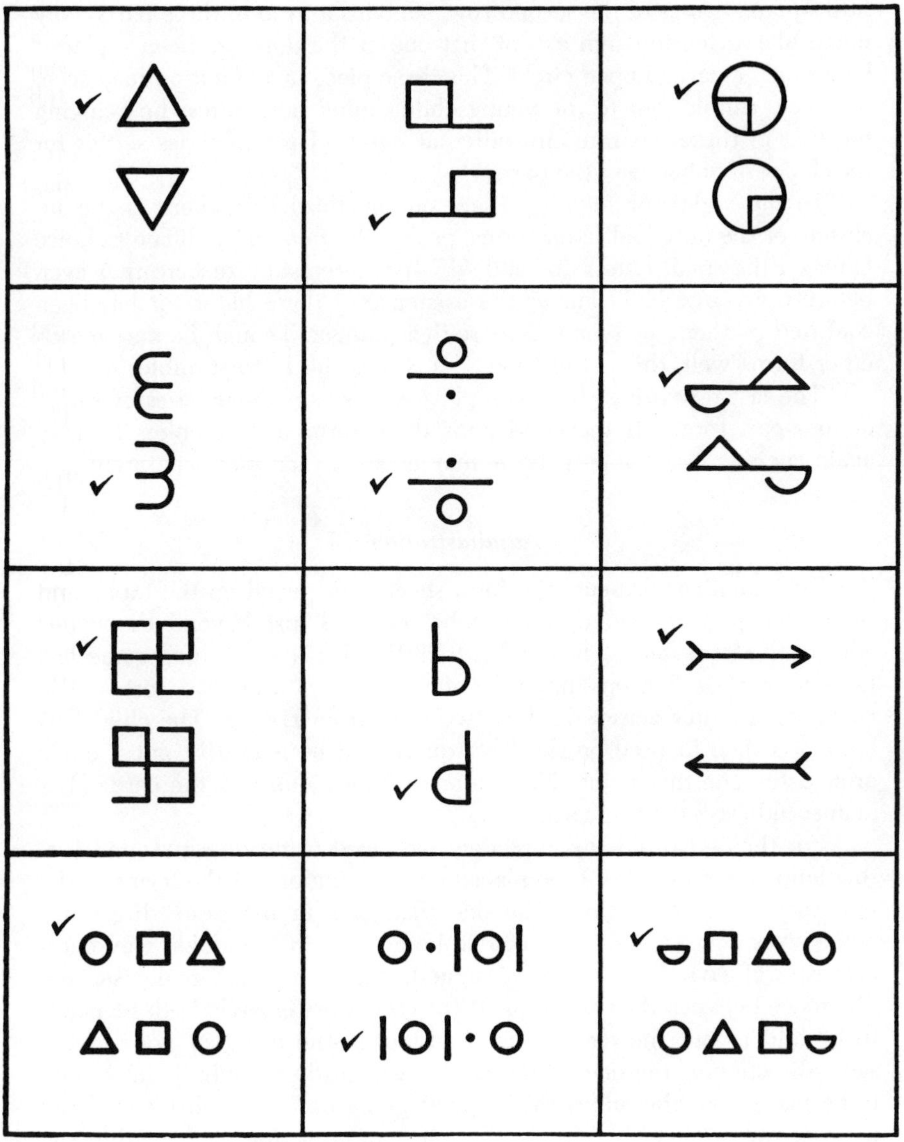

Score............

Figure 10. Visual One form sheet.

The author of this test must have had a good feeling for the 5-year-old to have started with a triangle, for which FIVE shows such an intense interest. The sequence of forms is arresting as one analyzes them. The fifth square, center of the second row, contains a form of three parts, very much like a division sign except that one of the dots has been replaced by a much enlarged open circle. This three-piece configuration may seem relatively simple, but to the young child's mind it requires the bringing together of three separate and different parts. (He sometimes settles for the choice of only one of the parts.)

In the eighth or middle square on the third line, there is the inclusion of the only real letter forms, posing the frequently difficult choice between the small letters "b" and "d." It is interesting to note that even before the young child knows the existence of these letters or has been confused by them, he seems to sense their danger. Though he may match other forms well, this is the choice he is most likely to stumble over.

The last row brings back complexity, in a horizontal series of three- or four-part forms. If the child finds these forms too complex, he may again encircle just one part, or he may encircle each part separately.

Administration

The examiner presents the form sheet with pencil on the table, and places the pile of twelve cards to be matched just beyond the upper edge of the form sheet. The child is told that this is a matching game and he is to start at the top (upper left-hand square) and read across. The examiner gestures across the first two rows from L to R. The child's attention is then focused on the first square and he is told to put a circle around the one that is just like the one in the picture on the card. (Examiner indicates the first card.)

For the 5-year-old this directive may need to be repeated, and further emphasis may need to be placed on choosing one of the forms as the examiner points to them: "The one that goes in the same direction." Some FIVES (8% G; 18% B) encircle both forms in the global way characteristic of FIVE. This response suggests that they don't really see the difference between the two forms. If the child does encircle both he needs to be told to put the circle around just one—the one that goes in the same direction as the one on the card. Even further emphasis may need to be placed on "the one with the point going up." Still other FIVES may indicate the correct choice, but they may draw a tiny circle within the form, trace the triangle with their pencil, or reproduce it to one side. Then further clarification as to how it is to be encircled is given. Rarely does the examiner need to demonstrate by encircling the chosen form.

Another complication may occur when the child picks up the top card or the pile of cards to bring them closer to him, often placing them to one side of the work sheet, thus tending to destroy the orientation of the form, especially if he turns the card sideways. If this happens, the examiner can replace the card in the correct position and allow the child to match the first form with the card close by.

After this initial adaptation, the examiner should return the cards to their original position *above* the test sheet. As each square is completed, the examiner removes the top card. Some all-too-helpful children wish to take the top card off themselves. This should be initially allowed and they should be duly thanked, but then it is time for the examiner to get there first so that further complications won't occur.

The demands of the test may still have to be further clarified on the second square. The child may persist in choosing the top form, since the first correct choice was a top form. Then the examiner needs to reiterate by gesturing over the horizontal base line of the form on the card from R to L and asking, "Which one goes this way?"

From then on the child is on his own except as he needs help in locating the square he is to work on.

By 6 years of age the test is almost too easy for many. If they finish the first row with extreme ease, the number of exposures of the last nine cards can be reduced to the fifth, eighth, and tenth cards. These provide an adequate test of the child's ability. If he falters and shows difficulties, the other cards can be added either in sequence or by backtracking.

Findings

Visual One is FIVE and FIVE-AND-A-HALF's test. Children of these ages enjoy it so much that later in the examination, when asked what he likes to do best, FIVE often refers back to this test. He is so related to the immediate and the now, that he construes the question, "What do you like to do best?" as relating to the time at hand. FIVE-AND-A-HALF often prefaces his attack on the test with "Oh boy!" showing his obvious delight. SIX may still enjoy it, but his ease and nonchalance suggest that he thinks the examiner hasn't chosen too well.

The actual scoring results show how well this test is suited to both FIVE and FIVE-AND-A-HALF. FIVES are just over the 50% hump of getting ten or more out of the twelve correct, whereas FIVE-AND-A-HALF's fall in the 90th percentile (see Table 65). A marked improvement has occurred from 14% of the girls and 8% of the boys giving all correct at 5 years of age, to 76% of the girls and 66% of the boys at 5½. Six- and seven-year-olds are secure with the number giving all correctly in the 80th and 90th percentiles.

Even though a test, so far as actual scoring goes, becomes too easy, the quality of the response can still reveal much. The quality is especially important at 5 and 5½ years. In the first place, FIVE often has difficulty

TABLE 65   *Visual One*
(Percentage)

| | 5 years | | 5½ years | | 6 years | | 7 years | |
	G	B	G	B	G	B	G	B
			Number Correct					
10 correct	26	14	4	10	6	2	0	4
11 correct	18	30	12	20	6	6	16	0
12 correct	14	8	76	66	86	90	84	96
10 or more	58	52	92	96	98	98	100	100
Tracing	4	4	2	0	0	0	0	0
			Closure					
No record	4	4	0	0	0	0	0	0
Poor	30	34	42	44	6	30	4	0
Fair	50	46	52	46	68	56	56	60
Good	16	16	6	10	26	14	40	40
			Starting Point					
Bottom, all forms	8	18	12	18	16	16	0	8
Top, all forms	8	8	22	16	38	34	48	32
Bottom, more than ½	46	60	32	48	26	26	32	44
Top, more than ½	36	22	42	36	60	64	68	54
			Direction					
CW, all	8	42	14	26	22	18	28	12
CCW, all	24	6	32	30	42	46	36	48
CW, more than ½	56	78	30	46	34	38	36	28
CCW, more than ½	40	22	66	50	66	62	64	72

in understanding what he is to do. He usually can be made to understand and can carry out the instructions, even though he is apt to lose his discriminative powers on the last half of the test and is likely to encircle each top form, without matching. The child is thus becoming perseverative in his 5-year-old way, but he is still complying, for he wishes most to do what is right, and to please.

Often he has trouble in locating the next square, especially when he has to shift to a new line. Each transition becomes a new task not related to the last task. So having finished one task his eyes dart over the page trying to locate the next square, seemingly so easily in his reach. Over and over again the examiner may need to help locate him in the right square. Then he happily goes about the business of matching, but orienting him once does not necessarily help him to locate the succeeding square, even though he has been told he is to move across the page from L to R.

Achieving the ability to locate the next square occurs so strikingly at 5½ that one comes to know that a real growth step has been taken when the child can go easily from one point to the next in an orderly fashion. It is the 5½- and especially the 6-year-old who is heard to say, "Don't tell me," as he searches for his place. FIVE-AND-A-HALF's main difficulty is shifting to the next line.

The quality of the child's method of encircling with respect to the starting point, direction, and closure also tell us something about his sustained functioning. Though girls can copy a single circle from the top CCW at 5 years of age, the method of starting at the top is not likely to be sustained for the majority of the Visual One forms before 6 years of age (60% G; 64% B). (See Table 65.) The CCW direction, however, tends to be established by 5½ years, when 66% G, 50% B draw over half the forms CCW.

FIVE is most likely to start from the bottom in this test. He may maintain a CW direction. As he comes into 5½, however, he tends to shift a good deal, starting at top, bottom, or at either side—going CW at one time, CCW the next. (This variability characterizes much behavior at 5½.) Closure is hard to judge, but it is at least *fairly* well accomplished by 6 years (68% G; 56% B).

Table 65 gives data on Visual One for the number of responses made correctly, type of closure, starting point, and direction of drawing.

Apart from his scoring, the individual child tells a good deal about himself by the way he encircles. There is the child who encircles the forms with a rapid, heavy, sloppy, gross motor stroke. These are the active, gross motor children. Or, there are those who can't stop and who keep encircling with a circular scribble. This is the type of child who needs limits or he becomes disruptive in the classroom. In the early grades such a child may need to be put on reduced attendance. Then there are those who produce wobbly circles with very poor closure points suggesting that their fine motor control hasn't as yet come into good form. Some of these children need extra stimulation and help in the fine motor field. When a child produces clean-cut, well-formed, well-closed-in circles, consistently starting from the top in a CCW direction, there is every evidence that his is a well-constituted organism.

VISUAL THREE

Along with Visual One from Marion Monroe's Reading Readiness Test, we include Visual Three, a memory-for-designs test which tells us much about the growing child's power of recall. This test, unlike Visual One, has a longitudinal potential. We have found that it still has something to tell us even in the teens. We have even used it in judging secretarial staff and nursery school personnel applying for work. Finally we have used it most effectively in old-age research.[1] It was one of the most discerning tests to help determine whether an older person still held on to those threads of learning-potential that were in the equipment of a 5-year-old or an older child. Alas, many older persons, though in no way obviously senile, had lost this power of recall.

Here, again, as with Visual One, Monroe showed a unique capacity to assemble a variety of shapes and forms without inherent meaning, that demand great accuracy of perception as the subject responds. The

and the

are the only obvious letters, and these can readily be seen as other than letters because of the addition of the dots.

One of the forms

which is often seen as an eleven is for many transformed into something quite different by the presence of the dot. The apparent difficulty of all these forms made it of interest to explore the way in which children saw the forms and the way they would project into them and name them after they had been tested for recall.

Material and Comment

On each of four cards (11 × 8½ inches in size) there are four figures placed in horizontal alignment (see Figure 11). The forms are in black and lines are ⅛ inch wide. It may be because the line is this wide that some children draw it as a double line and may even blacken in the space between these double lines. One form on each of the first three cards is half-blacked in. On each of the first three cards there is also a form with a separate but related dot. On the fourth card there is a form in which the dot is an integral part of the pattern.

[1] Kurt Pelz, Frances Pike, and Louise B. Ames, "A proposed battery of childhood tests for discriminating between different levels of intactness of function in elderly subjects." *J. genet. Psychol.*, 1962, **100**, 23–40.

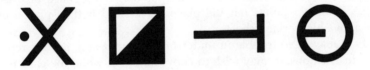

Figure 11.   Visual Three forms.

How the child reproduces these forms gives us an idea as to how he is seeing them. The examiner will find it helpful to know the forms so well that he can readily produce them from memory. Then as the child is being tested he can more readily judge what has meaning to this special child. Does the child choose all the filled-in forms, or all the dot forms? Does he select the first forms, or the last forms? Does he select the first and last forms, that is, the outside forms, in the way in which a 7-year-old often sees only the first and last letters of a word. SEVEN knows how a word begins and how it ends, but he has trouble in the middle.

The examiner soon comes to realize that a child's scoring is only one way in which he should be judged. The how and why of the response to the material is quite as important as the ability to recall.

In addition to the four white cards with their black figures, there is a pink working sheet (pink only for convenience in locating the sheet in a child's record) on which is a boxed-in form with four horizontal spaces —one space for the response to each card (see Appendix D).

Administration and Scoring

The pink working sheet and a pencil are placed before the child. The examiner exposes the first card momentarily, telling the child that he will be allowed to look at this card for a while (actual exposure 10″ by stop watch) and then it will be taken away.

The child is then told that he is to write down as many of the designs or forms as he can remember in the first horizontal space on the pink sheet. (Examiner points out the place.) The card is then placed on the table above his working sheet.

FIVE may have trouble in understanding, and may need a repetition of the instructions, or may wish to copy the forms while the card is being exposed. He is then told that he is to wait until the card is removed. If this is still hard for him to understand, the examiner says he will help him to remember by holding his pencil until it is time.

(With some FIVES and even with some SIXES the method of administration may have to be altered slightly. Many FIVES either want to start drawing at once, or after only a 2″ or 3″ exposure. The examiner then shifts the procedure by asking the child to tell when he is ready. Examiner then records the length of time the card was exposed. If the child seems bewildered by the multiplicity of the forms on the card, examiner may suggest that he choose just one form to look at and to remember.)

After these initial instructions with the first card, no further suggestion is made as to where on the paper the child should place his forms. He may wish to place the forms outside the lined-in area. He may place them all from all four cards in the top space. He is allowed to place them where he chooses.

There is one special exception, most often necessary at 6 years. The child may reproduce the first card by placing the forms vertically, one in each space (or as many as he remembers). This is allowed, but then the examiner gives him a second pink work sheet and asks him to place the forms horizontally in the spaces, for the other cards. The child usually accepts this directive with ease, but at the same time he has revealed a choice of vertical orientation, which may have significance in that his method of organization is quite different from the model.

One other variable is allowed when a child wants more than the allotted 10″ before he is ready to start drawing. This demand is most frequent with the 7-year-old who characteristically has trouble both in letting go and in finishing. He often wishes to take as much as 15–20″ before he is ready. Unfortunately, the longer he takes, seemingly the less he recalls. If this exception is permitted, it must of course be recorded.

The score for this test is determined by giving each correctly reproduced form a score of one point. If the form reproduced is recognizable but partially incorrect, it is given half a point. At times one may need to stretch one's imagination to classify the reproduction as recognizable. In such a case it might best be scored as questionable (?), without giving any point score. This difficulty is rare after 5 years of age.

A second type of score which should be obtained is the percentage of figures tried which are reproduced absolutely correctly. Thus if eight figures are tried but four are completely incorrect or only half-correct, that leaves four or 50% of all tried which are reproduced correctly.

Findings

In Table 66, below, the scores of boys and girls were averaged together, since differences were very slight. The progression from age to age is clear. Since there was such a gap (almost two points) from 6 to 7 years, the Weston figure of 6.8 correct at 6½ years has been inserted.

TABLE 66   *Mean Number Correct on Visual Three*

Age	Score	Deviation of Score from Age	Percentage of Tried Figures Made Correctly
5 years	3.5	−1.5	37
5½ years	4.5	−1.0	54
6 years	5.7	− .3	52
6½ years	6.8 (Weston)	+ .2	
7 years	7.6	+ .6	60
8 years	8.8	+ .8	68
9 years	10.4	+1.4	73
10 years	11.2	+1.2	74

It is interesting to note that this figure (6.8) is closest to the age it is scoring. At one time we thought there was a convenient relationship between the age of the child and the expected score, but this turns out to penalize the child below 6½ and to favor him after 6½. However, though slightly inaccurate, this notion may help some examiners to remember expected scores without consulting their scoring tables. The examiner needs to remember that these scoring figures indicate that 50% or more of the children examined received the score reported.

Table 66 also includes figures for percentage of all tried which are completely correct. As this table shows, by 5½ years we expect half the figures tried to be reproduced correctly.

Table 67 indicates the age at which each form is mastered by 50% or more of subjects. It will be seen that, in general, subjects do better on the first card than for subsequent cards, and that the first form of any given card is the one that is most likely to be correctly reproduced.

The fluctuation of the scoring from card to card reveals as much as the actual final numerical score itself. At 5, children score approximately the same on each card (.5 to 1.0 on each). By 6 years there is a fuller grasp of the forms on a card, which may yield a 3 to 3.5 score on the first card, especially since SIX is good at beginnings. But the scores on subsequent cards may steadily decline to 2, 1, and finally .5. This we call a deficit pattern, so characteristic of SIX, who needs either to be given a change, or to be picked up or salvaged.

The more up and down scoring by SEVEN (2.5, 1.5, 2.0, 1.5, for example) suggests that he is not at the mercy of loss, and can pick himself up in part at least. EIGHT not only picks himself up but may even improve as he proceeds. This may be classed as a "bounce back" (2.5, 1.0, 2.0, 3.0 on successive cards).

An interesting kind of response, more related to personality than to age, is a very high score on the first two cards (2.0, 3.5) followed by a marked slump on the last two cards (1.0, .5). Thus, the scores of the first two cards together might be 5.5 and the last two only 1.5. Children who respond in this way, we feel, can't hold up on a full assignment (the four cards), but they do quite nicely on half of an assignment (two cards). (Teachers should be willing to recognize this inability. If a child like this is pushed in school to do the whole assignment, he's likely to end in doing nothing.)

Sometimes a child can't remember a single thing on some one card. It seems as though everything has flown right out of his mind. This phenomenon we call a blackout. This occurs most in the early years, to the following extent: at 5 years of age, 31% of children experience this blackout on some one card; at 5½ years, 17%; at 6 years, 15%; at 7 years,

TABLE 67 *Visual Three: Age at Which 50% or More Respond Correctly (Sexes Combined)*

		Years
Card I		
Form One	△	$5\frac{1}{2}$
Form Two	◑	7
Form Three	⌐.	9
Form Four	⋁	9
Card II		
Form One	⌔	7
Form Two	|•|	7
Form Three	◧	10
Form Four	⟁	9
Card III		
Form One	•✕	6
Form Two	◿	
Form Three	⊣	10
Form Four	⊖	10
Card IV		
Form One	⋀	8
Form Two	⊔⊓	
Form Three	⟙	
Form Four	⊓⊔	

1%; at 8 years, 5%; at 9 and 10 years, none. Though this occurs most at 5 years, awareness of such a blackout may be more marked at 6 years when the child may say, "I don't know where they all went."

NUMBER OF FORMS ATTEMPTED, AND NUMBER REPRODUCED CORRECTLY AND INCORRECTLY

Tables 68–70 indicate, for each of the four cards separately, how many children at each age attempt or do not attempt each form; and for those who do attempt the forms, how many make the forms correctly and how many incorrectly.

TABLE 68   *Visual Three: Responses to Card I*
(Percentage)

	5 years		5½ years		6 years		7 years		8 years		9 years		10 years	
	G	B	G	B	G	B	G	B	G	B	G	B	G	B
Form One														
Not attempted	28	38	28	26	16	10	8	8	12	8	8	10	4	0
Attempted	**66**	**54**	**80**	**74**	**84**	**90**	**92**	**92**	**88**	**92**	**92**	**90**	**96**	**100**
Correct	28	30	50	60	62	64	82	76	78	80	84	82	88	94
Incorrect	38	24	30	14	22	26	10	16	10	12	8	8	8	6
Unscorable	6	8	2	0	0	0	0	0	0	0	0	0	0	0
Form Two														
Not attempted	44	56	40	60	36	36	16	14	10	16	4	10	2	0
Attempted	**50**	**36**	**58**	**40**	**64**	**64**	**84**	**86**	**90**	**84**	**96**	**90**	**98**	**100**
Correct	16	8	36	16	24	20	52	60	70	74	88	86	82	96
Incorrect	34	28	22	24	40	44	32	26	20	10	8	4	16	4
Unscorable	6	8	2	0	0	0	0	0	0	0	0	0	0	0
Form Three														
Not attempted	**74**	**64**	**74**	**80**	**60**	**62**	34	26	28	14	18	6	6	12
Attempted	20	28	24	20	40	38	**66**	**74**	**72**	**86**	**82**	**94**	**94**	**88**
Correct	2	4	8	6	12	16	30	40	34	48	48	60	48	60
Incorrect	18	24	16	14	28	22	36	34	38	38	34	34	46	28
Unscorable	6	8	2	0	0	0	0	0	0	0	0	0	0	0
Form Four														
Not attempted	**68**	**72**	**76**	**80**	**54**	**62**	44	42	30	38	24	16	16	12
Attempted	26	20	22	20	46	38	**56**	**58**	**70**	**62**	**76**	**84**	**84**	**88**
Correct	8	4	16	12	20	34	34	38	50	48	58	52	58	62
Incorrect	18	16	6	8	26	4	22	20	20	14	18	32	26	26
Unscorable	6	8	2	0	0	0	0	0	0	0	0	0	0	0

TABLE 69 *Visual Three: Responses to Card II*
(Percentage)

	5 years		5½ years		6 years		7 years		8 years		9 years		10 years	
	G	B	G	B	G	B	G	B	G	B	G	B	G	B
Form One														
Not attempted	38	54	22	42	26	16	18	12	16	12	4	8	2	6
Attempted	56	38	76	58	74	84	82	88	84	88	96	92	98	94
Correct	24	10	46	22	40	50	58	64	62	60	70	68	72	76
Incorrect	32	28	30	36	34	34	24	24	22	28	26	24	26	18
Unscorable	6	8	2	0	0	0	0	0	0	0	0	0	0	0
Form Two														
Not attempted	52	58	42	46	42	40	24	14	22	12	8	12	10	16
Attempted	42	34	56	54	58	60	76	86	78	88	92	88	90	84
Correct	28	22	38	40	38	42	54	64	58	82	80	78	76	72
Incorrect	14	12	18	14	20	18	22	22	20	6	12	10	14	12
Unscorable	6	8	2	0	0	0	0	0	0	0	0	0	0	0
Form Three														
Not attempted	80	78	70	78	66	56	34	50	38	32	24	16	6	20
Attempted	14	14	28	22	34	44	66	50	62	68	76	84	94	80
Correct	4	0	10	4	10	12	16	20	24	38	48	46	60	56
Incorrect	10	14	18	18	24	32	50	30	38	30	28	38	34	24
Unscorable	6	8	2	0	0	0	0	0	0	0	0	0	0	0
Form Four														
Not attempted	76	76	72	82	54	86	60	58	42	38	22	44	20	28
Attempted	18	16	26	18	46	14	40	42	58	62	78	56	80	72
Correct	4	6	12	14	22	6	34	32	48	46	60	50	68	54
Incorrect	14	10	14	4	24	8	6	10	10	16	18	6	12	18
Unscorable	6	8	2	0	0	0	0	0	0	0	0	0	0	0

Number attempted. As these tables show, the majority of 5-year-olds attempt Form One on Cards I, II, and III, with decreasing numbers trying the remaining forms. FIVE-AND-A-HALFS do little more.

Six-year-olds try the first two forms on the first two cards, and Form One on Cards III and IV. Seven-year-olds try all forms on Card I, the first three on II, and the first one on III and IV.

Eight-year-olds try all forms on the first two cards, Forms One and Four on Card III, and Forms One and Four on Card IV. Nine-year-olds try all on I and II, Forms One and Four on Card III, and all except Form Three on Card IV. Ten-year-olds at least try all forms.

TABLE 70 *Visual Three: Responses to Card III*
(Percentage)

	5 years		5½ years		6 years		7 years		8 years		9 years		10 years	
	G	B	G	B	G	B	G	B	G	B	G	B	G	B
Form One •✕														
Not attempted	34	26	16	22	6	6	12	6	8	12	8	4	2	0
Attempted	60	66	82	78	94	94	88	94	92	88	92	96	98	100
Correct	16	18	42	30	56	60	46	78	66	70	82	88	84	88
Incorrect	44	48	40	48	38	34	42	16	26	18	10	8	14	12
Form Two ◪														
Not attempted	76	70	68	70	62	56	78	54	56	62	52	46	36	42
Attempted	18	22	30	30	38	44	22	46	44	38	48	54	64	58
Correct	0	8	6	10	6	2	0	12	20	18	28	32	30	40
Incorrect	18	14	24	20	32	42	22	34	24	20	20	22	34	18
Form Three ⊐														
Not attempted	80	80	80	88	74	88	60	80	50	64	48	64	42	40
Attempted	14	12	18	12	26	12	40	20	50	36	52	36	58	60
Correct	8	10	10	10	18	10	32	18	46	28	46	32	52	52
Incorrect	6	2	8	2	8	2	8	2	4	8	6	4	6	8
Form Four ⊖														
Not attempted	74	72	74	84	76	68	64	62	44	44	34	40	38	24
Attempted	20	20	24	16	24	32	36	38	56	56	66	60	62	76
Correct	8	8	18	14	8	16	16	18	32	30	48	36	42	62
Incorrect	12	12	6	2	16	16	20	20	24	26	18	24	20	14

Number responding correctly. No form is reproduced correctly by as many as 50% of 5-year-olds. However, 5½-year-olds succeed (50% or more of children) on Form One, Card I. By 6 years of age, the normative child can reproduce correctly Form One, Card I and Form One, Card III. The 7- and 8-year-old reproduces correctly Forms One and Two, Cards I and II, and Form One, Card III. The 8-year-old also reproduces Form One, Card IV.

The 9-year-old succeeds on all forms, Card I; Forms One, Two, and Four, Card II; Form One, Cards III and IV. The 10-year-old succeeds on all forms Cards I and II; Forms One and Three, Card III; and Form One, Card IV.

Thus it is not until 9 years that the majority of children can reproduce all the four forms of Card I correctly. At 10 years, both Cards I

TABLE 71   *Visual Three: Responses to Card IV*
(Percentage)

	5 years G	B	5½ years G	B	6 years G	B	7 years G	B	8 years G	B	9 years G	B	10 years G	B
Form One														
Not attempted	52	48	34	50	26	32	32	30	36	32	24	18	22	10
Attempted	42	44	64	50	74	68	68	70	64	68	76	82	78	90
Correct	22	24	36	26	44	54	44	42	52	52	70	68	70	82
Incorrect	20	20	28	24	30	14	24	28	12	16	6	14	8	8
Form Two														
Not attempted	68	68	76	78	66	76	66	66	58	46	42	44	34	46
Attempted	26	24	22	22	34	24	34	34	42	54	58	56	66	54
Correct	12	6	14	10	24	16	24	24	34	36	44	52	50	26
Incorrect	14	18	8	12	10	8	10	10	8	18	14	4	16	28
Form Three														
Not attempted	78	70	68	80	76	88	68	74	48	60	58	64	42	48
Attempted	26	22	30	20	24	12	32	26	52	40	42	36	58	52
Correct	22	6	20	16	10	4	24	18	30	34	40	32	50	46
Incorrect	4	16	10	4	14	8	8	8	22	6	2	4	8	6
Form Four														
Not attempted	90	92	92	90	80	82	48	52	50	34	30	20	6	24
Attempted	4	0	6	10	20	18	52	48	50	66	70	80	94	76
Correct	0	0	2	2	2	4	4	8	12	4	8	18	20	12
Incorrect	4	0	4	8	18	14	48	40	38	62	62	62	74	64

and II are reproduced correctly, but only one to three forms on Cards III and IV. It is not until the teens that the majority can master Card IV.

PLACEMENT OF FORMS AND NUMBER OF LINES USED

In the instructions, the child is told to write down as many forms as he can remember from the first card on to the first line or space on the pink sheet. The examiner indicates the place so that there will be no doubt. The majority of 5-year-olds (51%) place forms from one card after another all on the top line, never questioning that it should be otherwise. If the child runs out of space on the top line, especially at 5½ or 6 years, he may backtrack on the second line from R to L. It is not before 6 or 6½ that the child asks where he shall place responses to the second card, as he points to the first space or the second one. He is told to choose whichever one he wishes. He tends to choose the second line for the second card and the third and fourth lines for the third and fourth cards.

There are a number of variables. Some use only two or three lines in all. Sometimes, wide spaces may be left between forms on the top line which are filled in later with forms from subsequent cards. This is more commonly seen at 5½.

The vertical placement of the forms on the first card has already been mentioned. This is more likely to occur at 5½ years (5%). Another variable is placing the forms outside the allotted lined-in space. This is more apt to occur with a 4-year-old who doesn't accept rules or confinement, or with older children who are responding in a similar way.

Though SEVEN is able to take in the whole range of the four forms, he may still respond only to the first and fourth forms on a card. Then he is likely to place his reproduction of the fourth form directly after the first form without leaving a space for the missing second and third forms. He becomes more aware of the way in which he places forms at 7–8 years and may query, "Do they have to be in order?" He is told, "No, it doesn't matter." Even if told it did matter, he might well misplace a number of forms at this age. Placement becomes more accurate from 8 years on. On the whole, direction is from L to R, but a fair proportion (11%) progress from R to L at 5 years of age.

As to number of lines used, as Table 72 shows, 5-year-olds as a rule use only one line. Response at 5½ and 6 years is highly variable. At 7 years and following, however, the majority of children use all four lines on the form sheet. (Clinical experience suggests that this comes in at 6½ years.)

ERRORS

There are many examiners, particularly beginning examiners, who are not going to be too much intrigued by the subject of errors. In fact it is perhaps best for the beginning examiner not to be too much concerned with this aspect of testing. However, an experienced clinician sometimes learns as much about a child's level of performance from the errors he makes, as from the test items which he passes with a correct score.

The variety of errors in reproduction which these relatively simple forms stimulate is rather surprising. Within the gamut of the 5-year span from 5 to 10 years, in our research population of 700 children, the greatest number of different errors was found to occur on the last form.

TABLE 72   *Visual Three: Number of Lines Used*
(Percentage)

	5 years		5½ years		6 years		7 years	
	G	B	G	B	G	B	G	B
No response	6	0	0	0	0	0	0	0
1	54	54	26	38	18	8	2	0
1+	8	6	10	12	2	10	2	2
2	14	12	8	4	10	14	8	2
3	4	14	10	12	28	18	8	14
4	6	8	32	28	42	44	80	78
In space below	2	4	2	0	0	0	0	0
Anywhere else outside lines	6	2	12	6	0	6	0	2
V-orientation of lines	0	0	0	0	0	0	0	2
Average number of forms correct	3.6	3.3	4.9	4.2	5.7	5.7	7.5	7.8

	8 years		9 years		10 years	
	G	B	G	B	G	B
No response	0	0	0	0	0	0
1	0	0	0	0	0	0
1+	2	2	0	0	0	0
2	2	2	0	0	0	2
3	4	6	2	0	0	2
4	90	88	98	98	96	96
In space below	0	0	0	0	0	0
Anywhere else outside lines	2	2	0	0	0	0
V-orientation of lines	0	0	0	2	4	0
Average number of forms correct	8.8	8.9	10.5	10.3	11.2	11.2

There were 132 different kinds of error in reproducing just this one form. Most forms, however, produced no more than from 20 to 35 variables with an increase to 44 on the first form,

a further increase to 54 on the quite difficult obliquely half-filled-in square,

and a decrease to 12 on the simplest form of all, the T on its side.

Eventually a fuller correlation of the child's errors with the rest of his behavior may tell us a great deal about him. For the present we can only describe and conjecture.

The 5-year-old is apt to separate a form into parts if it doesn't seem to him to go together as a whole. Thus the first form of Card I

is often broken up into pieces.

Another form that is often fragmented or separated anywhere from 6 to 10 years is the third form of the last card.

The dot may move into many different relationships:

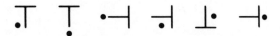

A fairly common error at 5 and 6 years is to shift a horizontal or oblique form to a vertical position. Thus we have the following:

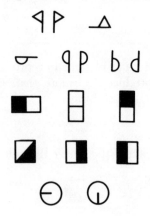

There is also a tendency, at the same ages of 5 and 6, to produce a vertical reversal:

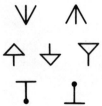

In these same earlier years from 5 to 7, forms are apt to shift. Thus a triangle may be reproduced as a square or a circle; or a triangle, especially at 7 years, may be reproduced as a diamond, the form of greatest interest to SEVEN.

In the 5½- to 6-year realm the desire for symmetry may be so strong that the form is changed to become more symmetric.

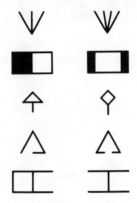

Control of stroke is not well mastered before 7 years. Thus forms may appear at odd angles.

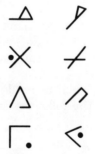

An interesting phenomenon, most likely to occur at 7 years, is the child's pleasure in making a continuous or continuing stroke. This is especially evident on the first and last forms of the fourth card. Thus the first form

becomes

and the last form

becomes

The three filled-in forms

pose many problems and stimulate interesting conjectures. Why do some children see these forms first, and others avoid them? And why are some of the other forms

seen as partially black?

Or the black may be avoided by making an outline form such as

This outline form may be more common at 5 and again at 9 and 10 years, but it also may occur when the child is getting tired. There are many unanswered questions which can only be answered after more research.

The more usual and common reversals include horizontal reversals either to the R or to the L. The following are orderly, and easily understood patterns of error.

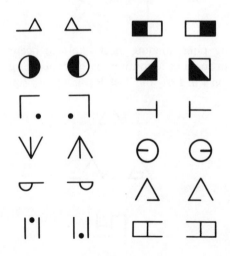

Besides the reversals and errors, the size of the forms and their position within the space allotted may tell much about age and individuality. FIVE's forms may be small and cramped or very irregular in size. SIX's forms tend to be large, filling the whole space of the line. If smaller, they tend to rise to the top of the space. This is not so at 7 and 8 years when a firm footing in reality, a sure grounding, is desired. SEVENS and EIGHTS tend to place their forms surely on the line, giving them a good base on which to stand.

Figures 12 and 13 which follow give sample responses to the Visual Three test at approximately yearly intervals from 5 through 10 years of age.

VISUAL THREE PROJECTIONS

Introduction

It was the child himself who gave us the idea of using Visual Three as a projective test. Often as he responded to this test, we wondered how he remembered the forms. We watched him trace them at 5 with his finger (a method congenial to the 4- and 5-year-old whose kinesthetic touch may have more holding power for learning than his eyes). At 6 years, however, we heard him talk out loud and at 7 years, whisper to himself, naming the forms as he saw them, thus supporting his memory by verbal or auditory means. As he grew silent at 8 and 9 years, we wondered what he was seeing and how he might be supporting his memory.

We fully realized when we started to record the child's projections of how he saw the forms that this was at best a limited projective technique. The forms were, if anything, highly structured in contrast to the unstructured forms of the Rorschach, being more akin to the structured forms of the Mosaic test.

Though offering less potential than the Rorschach, this technique seemed both more usable and possibly more meaningful to the teacher and to the beginning examiner. It appears not to need the training that is required to administer and analyze the Rorschach response. We also discovered that the children enjoyed the exercise of projecting their ideas onto the forms. When they had trouble and did not enjoy the test, that in itself was suggestive and often supported findings of other trouble spots in the individual child's response.

Besides being easy to administer and record, this part of the test gives the examiner many clues about the child, both as to the age of response and his way of seeing. It helps him to feel the child in his inner workings. Also since our developmental battery is short on language items, since we have not yet discovered the language tests which would best provide a developmental appraisal of language, examiners find this

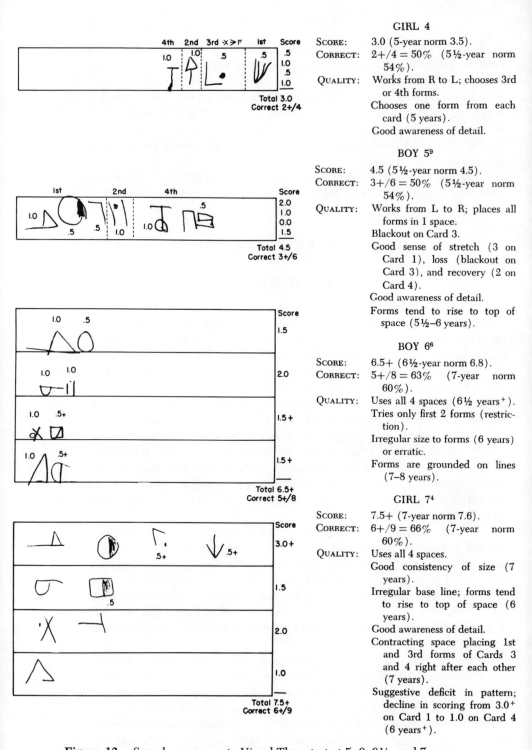

GIRL 4

SCORE: 3.0 (5-year norm 3.5).

CORRECT: 2+/4 = 50% (5½-year norm 54%).

QUALITY: Works from R to L; chooses 3rd or 4th forms.

Chooses one form from each card (5 years).

Good awareness of detail.

BOY 5⁹

SCORE: 4.5 (5½-year norm 4.5).

CORRECT: 3+/6 = 50% (5½-year norm 54%).

QUALITY: Works from L to R; places all forms in 1 space.

Blackout on Card 3.

Good sense of stretch (3 on Card 1), loss (blackout on Card 3), and recovery (2 on Card 4).

Good awareness of detail.

Forms tend to rise to top of space (5½–6 years).

BOY 6⁶

SCORE: 6.5+ (6½-year norm 6.8).

CORRECT: 5+/8 = 63% (7-year norm 60%).

QUALITY: Uses all 4 spaces (6½ years⁺).

Tries only first 2 forms (restriction).

Irregular size to forms (6 years) or erratic.

Forms are grounded on lines (7–8 years).

GIRL 7⁴

SCORE: 7.5+ (7-year norm 7.6).

CORRECT: 6+/9 = 66% (7-year norm 60%).

QUALITY: Uses all 4 spaces.

Good consistency of size (7 years).

Irregular base line; forms tend to rise to top of space (6 years).

Good awareness of detail.

Contracting space placing 1st and 3rd forms of Cards 3 and 4 right after each other (7 years).

Suggestive deficit in pattern; decline in scoring from 3.0⁺ on Card 1 to 1.0 on Card 4 (6 years⁺).

Figure 12. Sample responses to Visual Three test at 5, 6, 6½, and 7 years.

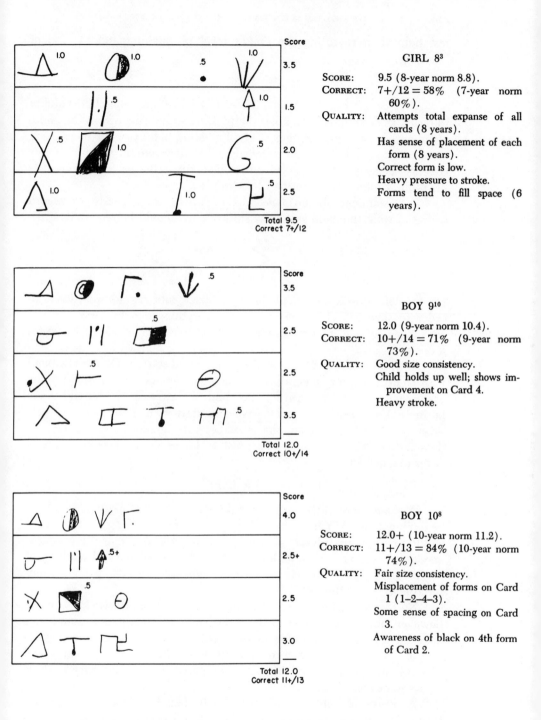

GIRL 8[3]

SCORE: 9.5 (8-year norm 8.8).
CORRECT: 7+/12 = 58% (7-year norm 60%).
QUALITY: Attempts total expanse of all cards (8 years).
Has sense of placement of each form (8 years).
Correct form is low.
Heavy pressure to stroke.
Forms tend to fill space (6 years).

BOY 9[10]

SCORE: 12.0 (9-year norm 10.4).
CORRECT: 10+/14 = 71% (9-year norm 73%).
QUALITY: Good size consistency.
Child holds up well; shows improvement on Card 4.
Heavy stroke.

BOY 10[8]

SCORE: 12.0+ (10-year norm 11.2).
CORRECT: 11+/13 = 84% (10-year norm 74%).
QUALITY: Fair size consistency.
Misplacement of forms on Card 1 (1–2–4–3).
Some sense of spacing on Card 3.
Awareness of black on 4th form of Card 2.

Figure 13. Sample responses to Visual Three test at 8, 9, and 10 years.

test helpful in revealing the child's level of thinking and his use of language.

Administration

After completing the Visual Three test which taps the child's ability to recall, the examiner then takes the pink recording sheet from the child, along with his pencil, and says, "Now I'm going to let you see these cards again. This time I want you to tell me what they remind you of." If this concept seems a little difficult for the child, the examiner further clarifies his request with, "How do they look to you?"

The examiner should have his recording sheet ready to record verbatim what the child says. Any shift of card should be recorded

(to the left, upside down, to the right, back into regular position). In order to slow the child down so that everything can be recorded, the examiner may find it useful to repeat what the child has said as he writes it down.

At times it is difficult to get the young child started. He may respond with some sweeping generalization such as, "letters." Then it is for the examiner to select one form for the child to start with, or the child may be invited to select the one he wishes to start with. If he becomes perseverative in his responses, the examiner may suggest, "And what else does it look like?" But this is no test to linger over when the child is eager to move on.

Findings

We must note at this point that this projective technique is in a bare beginning stage. Much further analysis is needed. In fact, this test needs still to prove its usefulness. However, we ourselves feel that it is valuable enough to present here in its infancy. We shall not give a full work-up of our material, but shall give enough to help the examiner become comfortable in giving the test.

No formal analysis or scoring system has yet been devised. We have, however, utilized a number of the Rorschach content categories and thus have been able to determine percentages of occurrence in this population of 700 children from 5 to 10 years, with 100 children (50 girls and 50 boys) at each age level including 5½ years. Our preliminary analysis shows some very definite age trends.

A perusal of Table 73 indicates clearly that the majority of responses to the 15 different categories we have chosen occur within the 3 categories of letters, objects, and geometric forms (30%, 30%, 17%).

TABLE 73 *Visual Three Projections:*
Total Number of Responses in Fifteen Content Categories

Category	5	5½	6	Years 7	8	9	10	Total	Percentage of All
Letters	325	397	504	**593**	584	512	509	3424	30
Objects	494	499	443	441	451	524	**532**	3384	30
Geometric forms	**341**	301	326	275	218	212	190	1803	17
Numbers	80	**127**	60	66	59	42	36	470	4
Plant	43	46	62	76	66	77	**90**	460	4
Symbols and signs	19	26	21	29	50	72	**111**	328	3
I don't know, or no response	**121**	83	55	19	26	11	13	328	3
Description	**87**	37	49	22	21	10	11	237	2
Human and animal	33	37	27	9	35	29	**39**	209	2
Aerial	29	16	19	14	21	42	**66**	207	2
Nature	11	12	6	16	17	26	**30**	118	1
Food	4	5	13	22	**45**	11	15	115	1
Design	15	10	20	**25**	13	6	4	93	.8
Explosion, fire	**11**	4	6	4	7	3	3	38	.3
Black and white	4	4	3	0	0	1	0	12	.1
Multiple responses	41	15	27	22	24	36	**54**	219	2
Differential responses, giving either detail or position	10%	25%	46%	**58%**	62%	74%	69%		

NOTE: Except in bottom row, boldface figures indicate at what age each item occurs most.

The table tells its own story. Generally figures are in **boldface** at the ages when an item occurs most. In analyzing these peak figures it is interesting to consider them age by age. Four items reach their high point at 5.

FIVE shows inability to respond to certain forms, uses simple descriptions, projects into geometric forms, into explosions and into fire or black and white. The last two are insignificant as far as numbers go, but their occurrence may be significant as related to the individual child.

The inability to respond to certain forms at 5 years (there is no response to 7% of the forms) is fairly conspicuous, but the indications are that this 5-year-old response is still much fuller than that of the typical 4- and 4½-year-old child. The small group of 4- and 4½-year-olds whom we examined showed a tendency to refuse the last two cards (50% of the forms) or to respond with perseverative remarks on these last two cards. The following forms give most difficulty at 5 and later.

We consider a descriptive response to be one step above a refusal to respond. Such a form as

might be described as "a line going this way, and a line going up this way, and a line going up that way." Such a description does tell in simple language what the form is made up of. As a method of response it decreases rapidly after 5 years.

A geometric-form response is at its highest at 5 years. It remains sizable, though steadily decreasing, throughout the total period from 5 to 10. FIVE is in the midst of learning the name of "triangle." He learned "square" at 4, "cross" at 3. He sees shapes in these forms and likes to name them as such.

At 5½ years comes the high point for number responses. The child is interested in numbers. He is recognizing them. He is making them himself. FIVE-AND-A-HALF is actually even more concerned with letters than numbers, as the table shows, but a letter-response does not reach its peak until 7 years of age when it tops all others. This is indeed the age when readiness to read shows itself unmistakably in the majority of children. If only we could accept this clue to delay more formal reading until this age when the readiness to read is so clearly defined!

Another response which reaches its high point at 7, though figures are very small, is "design." SEVEN likes form. This is a part of his rising intellectual growth. He doesn't like to be stumped. He wants to try. It is the last form that most frequently puzzled the younger child.

SEVEN now sees it as "design." The 8-year-old has only one outstanding peak and that is down at a 1% level. It is a food response, predominantly "pie."

Several responses reach their high point at 10 years: objects, plant, symbols and signs, human and animal, aerial and nature. TEN is moving in many different directions. He is sloughing off less mature responses. He is making ready, through putting his abilities to use, for the push that will come at 11 and 12 years.

Though no responses reach their high point at either 6 or 9 years of age, both ages show many interesting trends. At 6, letters, plant, food, and design are all increasing in number. Obviously, the child now projects with greater ease. The 9-year-old gives significantly fewer responses in a number of areas (letters, geometric forms, inability to respond, description, food, design, and explosion), whereas he is giving more in the areas of objects, plants, symbols, aerial, and nature. Nine is indeed an age of much activity, an age of independence, and of the discovery of the joy of learning. NINE's job is to put his house in order, to integrate his forces so that they will become more readily usable at 10, preparatory to the push into 11 and 12.

Two items have been added to Table 73 to help the examiner in his appraisal. Multiple answers do occur although they are fairly infrequent. The peak ages, interestingly enough, are 5 and 10 years, ages which are so alike in other ways.

The final category covers responses which differentiate either detail or position of the form. This shows a steady rise with age and this kind of response becomes normative by 7 years of age. Seven is an age when one would anticipate more awareness of detail and also a sense of position. Even FIVE might infer detail, as in calling the first form

"a train," and by 5½ the child is beginning to differentiate when he refers to this form as "the front of a car." By 6 he might call it "half a swing." But by 7 he might refer to the triangular form of this same first figure as "a tent" and the bottom extended line as "ground under it and beside it."

Similarly, the sense of position shifts from the ease of the 4-year-old who sees things any which way without having to turn them right-side-up, to an awareness of upside down as a general, catch-all phrase at 5½ to 6 for objects which aren't right-side-up, to a more accurate positional sense from 7 on as expressed, for instance, in a "flag sideways."

Some children are very precise both in detail—"a pointed hat,"

and in position—"a patio to the left,"

though this comes with age and is more common at 9 years.

It is interesting actually to feel the changes that occur from age to age in a form such as this first one.

Table 74 suggests changes that can and do occur from age to age in any one kind of projection such as house, hat, and flag.

TABLE 74   *Visual Three Projections: Age Changes in Response to*

Age in Years	House	Hat	Flag
5	House		Flag
5½	Part of a house	Hat	Flag this way
6	Top of a house	Witch's hat	Flag on its back
7	Teepee with grass	Fire hat	Flag fell down
8	Part of a house, wasn't finished	Pointed cap	Flag sideways
9	Desert with a pyramid in it	A boy's cap	Flag on a mailbox
10	Tent on a log	Marionette hat	Football field flag

These responses were not given by any one child, but rather this table is constructed from responses of many different children, and is used more to give an idea of possible change with age rather than the actual movement of response in any one child. The projections speak for themselves. The 9- and 10-year-old projections especially tell of new spheres of interest and items that are meaningful to the child. The resolution of position with such responses as "flag on a mail box" and "football field flag" suggest adept minds.

Tables 75–78 show age changes in the major classes of response given to each of the 16 forms. Out of the 15 possible content categories considered here, anywhere from 2 to 7 are presented for each form, with the percentage of occurrence at each age level. All items that attain a 50% occurrence or better are shown in bold face as are figures which indicate the high points for items which do not reach normative size.

We hope later to correlate the child's projections more closely with his individuality. This may be possible as we put this technique to use in the schools. Another area that is not explored here is the difference of the projections of the two sexes. We attempted this but found the figures not significant. This was also the case with Rorschach responses in the first 10 years. We are, however, aware of certain sex-linked projections. Axe, hatchet, and spear

seem to be exclusively male. Fan and flower

are chiefly female responses, though a male might give such a response his own twist, as when a 9-year-old boy names it "tulip made of sticks."

TABLE 75 *Visual Three Projections: Card I*
(Percentage of Responses)

					Years			
		5	5½	6	7	8	9	10
△	Objects	28	35	43	49	47	**57**	**68**
	Geometric forms	40	36	**45**	38	32	24	20
	Numbers	6	10	4	4	12	9	5
◐	Letters	16	15	9	9	8	6	9
	Objects	27	32	37	32	19	29	26
	Geometric forms	**45**	40	37	35	33	32	27
	Symbol	0	0	0	0	0	2	6
	Human and animal	7	9	6	2	8	5	3
	Nature	2	1	2	8	13	14	20
	Food	0	1	7	16	18	5	7
⌐•	Letters	30	29	41	**56**	**67**	43	**51**
	Objects	23	15	14	16	19	36	19
	Geometric forms	15	10	23	15	4	10	4
	Numbers	16	30	10	4	2	0	1
∨	Letters	9	3	11	15	14	10	12
	Objects	**54**	**66**	60	**69**	**61**	**68**	62
	Plant	5	5	4	4	6	6	7
	Human and animal	6	9	10	2	7	8	7
	Explosion and fire	4	2	3	3	4	2	2

NOTE: Boldface figures here are the leading items at each age, rather than strictly normative items.

TABLE 76 *Visual Three Projections: Card II*
(Percentage of Responses)

					Years			
		5	5½	6	7	8	9	10
⌒	Letters	38	**54**	**62**	**62**	56	50	48
	Objects	23	16	20	24	33	38	**44**
	Geometric forms	12	5	10	5	8	8	5
	Numbers	1	6	3	8	6	1	1
|•|	Letters	18	15	32	**34**	29	28	24
	Objects	17	10	9	4	14	21	20
	Description (lines, etc.)	**24**	12	15	12	9	7	7
	Numbers	29	**52**	40	48	39	26	27
	Aerial	3	1	2	1	1	9	18
■□	Objects	**58**	**68**	**73**	**74**	**79**	**77**	**88**
	Geometric forms	30	26	20	21	19	20	12
⌂	Objects	40	**51**	32	28	34	27	22
	Geometric forms	12	8	11	1	4	2	1
	Plant	32	38	**54**	**68**	59	70	78
	Symbols and signs	4	3	3	2	3	1	5

NOTE: Boldface figures here are the leading items at each age, rather than strictly normative items.

TABLE 77 *Visual Three Projections: Card III*
(Percentage of Responses)

				Years			
		5	5½	6	7	8	9	10

Symbol	Response	5	5½	6	7	8	9	10
·✕	Letters	45	**73**	**89**	**98**	**82**	**80**	**62**
	Geometric forms	**24**	13	6	1	1		
	Symbols and signs	6	6	3		8	9	**15**
	Human and animal	2	1	1		1	3	8
	Aerial	0	0	0	1	3	4	7
◪	Object	29	34	30	38	39	**46**	43
	Geometric forms	**59**	**57**	**64**	**59**	46	43	48
	Food	0	2	4	2	10	4	4
⊣	Letters	48	**61**	**82**	**94**	**93**	**86**	**87**
	Object	17	22	8	4	5	6	14
	Aerial	**5**	1	1	0	2	3	1
⊖	Letters	25	26	35	48	**48**	40	40
	Objects	26	25	16	19	16	20	23
	Geometric forms	**40**	**41**	**39**	29	15	25	26
	Human and animal	1	2	2	3	4	2	4
	Aerial	4	3	3	1	0	5	3
	Food	1	2	0	2	13	2	3

NOTE: Boldface figures are the leading items at each age, rather than strictly normative items.

TABLE 78 *Visual Three Projections: Card IV*
(Percentage of Responses)

				Years			
		5	5½	6	7	8	9	10

Symbol	Response	5	5½	6	7	8	9	10
△	Letters	3	1	2	3	8	5	1
	Objects	21	21	13	18	23	29	**34**
	Geometric forms	**52**	**66**	**73**	**73**	**60**	**53**	**51**
	Aerial	2	0	1	0	1	4	3
⊏⊤	Letters	30	**55**	**60**	**77**	**88**	**86**	**90**
	Objects	**43**	31	28	20	7	11	10
⊤	Letters	37	45	**65**	**80**	**74**	**58**	**60**
	Objects	27	27	23	17	25	36	34
	Description	**10**	9	8		1	1	1
⌐⊢	Letters	10	13	11	11	10	15	12
	Objects	**52**	**44**	**37**	29	26	20	18
	Symbols, signs	0	2	10	16	28	**46**	**56**
	Human and animal	1	4	3	1	4	2	5
	Aerial	5	7	8	6	7	7	6
	Design	5	8	12	**22**	7	4	3

NOTE: Boldface figures are the leading items at each age, rather than strictly normative items.

CHAPTER *12*

NAMING ANIMALS

||||||||||||||||||||||||||||||||||||||||||||||||||||||||||||||||||||||||||||||||||

The naming of animals for 60 seconds is an old Binet item. In our use of it over the years we have noted how often the children enjoyed this test. They seemed to take it as a mental exercise. Further, this naming gave us clues about the child's tempo, the organization of his thinking, his capacity to range. The very demands of a task that asked the child to sustain for 60 seconds gave us some idea of this important capacity. Since we were also short on language items, we included this one which we believe to have developmental value.

Administration

The examiner has his recording sheet ready, and with stop watch in hand he instructs the child: "Name all the animals you can think of until I tell you to stop." The examiner then begins to time.

If the child has difficulty in starting, the examiner may ask, "What is your favorite animal?" Rarely or never does he need to suggest a specific animal. If this should prove necessary, the child is not ready for this test.

The examiner records on his recording sheet all animals named. The 5- or 5½-year-old may stop abruptly after 15″ to 30″ saying, "That's all I can think of." It is not useful to urge him to continue, since he usually will not, even if urged. The number of seconds he did sustain should be recorded.

If, however, at 6 years or later the child stops before the minute is up, he should be encouraged to continue for the full time, with such supportive phrases as "Can you think of any more animals?" or "You still have some time."

Findings

TIME

By 6 years of age, as Table 79 indicates, the majority of children can sustain for the full 60 seconds. This percentage increases until it is well in the 90s by 8 years of age. The 5-year-old has trouble in sustaining, though most can sustain for at least 15 seconds, and by 5½ there is a sizable increase in length of sustaining.

Besides the actual time factor, it is also important to note the tempo of the child's naming. Some name so rapidly initially that the examiner can barely keep up with them. But this is often initial speed followed by being bogged down before the minute is up and being unable to name any more even with extra time. Other children have a nice, steady pace. By 9 some are aware of the examiner's recording and politely ask, "Am I going too fast?"

NUMBER NAMED

The mean number (see also Table 79) shows a steady and almost continual gain from age to age (mean of 7 animals at 5 years increasing to a mean of 15.5 by 10 years). However the range at any given age for individual children is large. Thus, some 5-year-olds can name 15 animals, half as many as the largest number (30) named by any 10-year-old. On the other hand a 10-year-old may name as few as 6 or 7.

TABLE 79   *Percentage Who Can Name Animals for 60 Seconds, and Number Named*

	5 years		5½ years		6 years		7 years		8 years		9 years		10 years	
	G	B	G	B	G	B	G	B	G	B	G	B	G	B
Time: 60″	29	28	43	36	64	74	80	88	92	96	90	92	96	98
Mean number named	7	7	8	8	8	9	11	12	12	14	15	14	15	16
Range girls	0–15		2–19		0–13		7–19		7–21		9–24		6–30	
Range boys	0–12		4–14		3–16		6–19		6–25		9–22		7–30	

TYPE OF NAMING

The continued naming of animals in the plural, which occurs in a few subjects throughout this age range, reminds us of the 4-year-old who enjoys not only plurals in general but also such collective plurals as "people" and "family." FIVE, on the other hand, characteristically prefers to single things out. The use of the article "a" is clearly congenial to FIVE, but the use of such terms as "horse" or "lion" suggests a higher mental process.

Plurals are used infrequently, and more often by girls than by boys. The use of the article "a" persists at a fairly high level through 7 years, especially in girls, and continues, though at a much lower level, through 10 years of age (see Table 80).

The use of the singular is normative at 5 years, with a steady but slow increase thereafter. Boys exceed girls in the use of this form.

TABLE 80   *Naming Animals*

	5 years		5½ years[a]		6 years		7 years		8 years		9 years		10 years	
	G	B	G	B	G	B	G	B	G	B	G	B	G	B
"a . . ."	40	30	20	16	40	26	36	26	14	14	18	10	18	12
Singular	**56**	**66**	**70**	**80**	**58**	**74**	**62**	**68**	**74**	**84**	**80**	**86**	**72**	**82**
Plural	4	4	10	4	2	0	2	6	12	2	2	4	10	6

[a]This falling off of "a" and the sharp increase of the simple singular term at 5½ years is probably a matter of recording, since one whole group of girls and also one of boys has not a single recorded "a."

CLASS OF ANIMAL NAMED

To simplify analysis we have grouped the animals in five different categories: domestic, zoo, intermediate (squirrel, bear, fox, etc.), birds, and fish.

As Table 81 indicates, domestic and zoo animals are clearly the leading classes at every age, though the domestic animals predominate at most ages with girls, and the zoo animals at all ages with boys.

TABLE 81   *Naming Animals*
(Percentage of Responses in Each Class)

	5 years		5½ years		6 years		7 years	
	G	B	G	B	G	B	G	B
Domestic	**39.0**	24.2	35.4	27.4	37.2	28.8	**35.5**	27.4
Zoo	35.5	**45.9**	**44.6**	**47.0**	**41.6**	36.9	34.4	**39.7**
Intermediate[a]	9.0	11.8	5.8	9.9	7.9	8.6	8.8	10.2
Bird	11.0	9.8	7.3	7.8	6.8	11.4	11.6	11.3
Fish	5.0	8.2	6.8	7.8	6.6	14.3	9.8	13.5

	8 years		9 years		10 years	
	G	B	G	B	G	B
Domestic	**40.3**	24.6	**35.6**	24.6	**34.2**	29.4
Zoo	26.7	**35.3**	26.5	**30.8**	29.2	**30.5**
Intermediate[a]	12.9	13.8	11.4	17.2	13.3	15.3
Bird	13.3	11.6	13.2	12.2	12.5	11.0
Fish	6.5	14.0	13.0	15.0	10.8	13.4

[a]Squirrel, bear, fox, etc.
NOTE: Boldface figures here are leading, not normative items.

In considering the number of different animals named in each class (Table 82) a few significant findings emerge. Both boys and girls give the greatest variety of zoo animals at 5½ and 6 years. Fish and related vertebrates are most highly varied at 7 years. Boys name a greater variety of animals than do girls.

TABLE 82   *Variability in Naming Animals*
(Number of Different Kinds of Animals in Each Class)

	5 years		5½ years		6 years		7 years		8 years		9 years		10 years	
	G	B	G	B	G	B	G	B	G	B	G	B	G	B
Domestic	**16**	14	14	16	16	18	18	**21**	18	20	**23**	17	22	21
Zoo	15	14	**19**	**20**	17	**20**	19	20	21	**29**	**23**	25	22	**33**
Intermediate	12	**17**	12	19	**17**	16	15	**21**	**22**	28	22	**30**	**25**	30
Bird	7	5	6	6	7	7	7	7	7	8	8	7	9	10
Fish	9	10	12	10	11	19	**22**	**21**	16	27	20	28	20	28
All	59	60	63	71	68	80	81	90	84	112	96	107	98	122

NOTE: Boldface figures here are leading, not normative items.

NUMBER OF OCCURRENCES OF MOST COMMONLY NAMED ANIMALS

As Table 83 shows, among the domestic animals, dog, cat, and horse lead in that order. Both cat and dog are more commonly named by girls than by boys. In fact all of the domestic animals are much oftener named by girls than by boys.

The most common zoo animals to be named are lion, tiger, and elephant. Boys give the more lions and tigers, but girls name the more elephants.

The intermediate animals do not show any strong trends other than that they tend to increase with increasing age. This is also true of birds and fish. With both birds and snakes, boys show a lead over the girls.

In addition to noting timing and the kinds of animals named, the examiner should be aware of the number of categories used and the sequence of naming. When, for example, a child of 7 names only domestic animals, or only barnyard animals, he gives the impression of being close to home, restricted in his behavior. The opposite may be true when only wild, far-off animals are named, with never a cat or a dog mentioned.

Usually at least three animals in a single class, as, for instance, cat, dog, horse, or lion, tiger, elephant, are named. This is normative from 5 years on to the following extent: at 5 years, 50% G, 58% B name at least three or more in some one class in series. At 5½ years, 74% G, 84% B; at 6 years, 76% G, 78%B; at 7 years, 88% G, 88% B; at 9 years, 88% G, 82% B; at 10 years, 86% G, 88% B.

TABLE 83 *Naming Animals*
(Number of Occurrences)

	5 years		5½ years		6 years		7 years		8 years		9 years		10 years		All	
	G	B	G	B	G	B	G	B	G	B	G	B	G	B	G	B
Dog	**28**	**14**	21	19	**34**	**23**	**42**	**34**	**49**	**38**	**48**	**34**	**46**	40	268	202
Cat	21	9	**22**	13	30	22	37	28	44	34	46	29	**46**	**45**	246	180
Horse	20	12	18	20	22	23	28	23	37	26	37	28	35	35	197	167
Cow	18	12	16	13	14	17	22	22	28	21	31	21	31	30	160	136
Rabbit	10	6	15	10	13	11	13	19	12	15	25	15	23	26	111	102
Lion	**20**	**30**	**26**	**36**	**27**	33	30	**38**	22	**36**	**28**	**30**	25	**35**	178	238
Elephant	17	20	19	17	24	22	**34**	28	**24**	27	25	25	**28**	26	171	165
Tiger	17	29	25	30	26	27	26	31	17	30	25	28	24	26	160	201
Giraffe	13	17	22	25	19	19	16	17	15	23	22	16	20	16	127	133
Bear	16	10	14	15	12	14	14	20	21	16	15	20	14	16	106	111
Zebra	9	8	13	12	15	10	19	12	9	14	12	8	20	18	97	82
Mouse	3	1	**5**	2	3	3	7	7	**12**	**12**	**12**	**15**	12	**21**	54	61
Deer	6	2	3	3	2	5	5	7	7	**12**	11	8	9	7	43	44
Fox	4	5	0	2	4	2	6	**9**	6	4	8	12	**15**	8	43	42
Squirrel	6	6	1	7	3	**10**	5	**9**	8	11	7	10	12	12	42	65
Some Bird	16	16	18	16	9	21	20	31	31	52	44	44	41	14	179	194
Chicken	5	3	4	5	7	13	17	12	18	11	20	13	16	16	87	73
Some Fish	2	4	7	2	8	12	9	15	7	24	21	13	20	14	74	84
Snake	5	6	4	9	6	14	13	23	8	20	16	24	18	16	70	112
Total	236	210	253	256	278	301	373	385	375	426	453	393	445	421	2413	2392

NOTE: Boldface figures here are the leading items at each age, rather than normative items, since no naming here reaches normative proportions.

When clear-cut classification is evident as early as 7 years of age, there is good indication of a high intellect. Boys are especially capable in this regard. They may, for instance, name various members of the cat family, various birds, or various snakes.

As far as separating the mammals from the amphibia, invertebrates, and so on, this is not very much in evidence. A few children from 8 years on might catch themselves as they are naming bird or fish and might say, "Oh, that isn't an animal."

There are certain qualitative items of which the examiner should be aware. The 5- to 6-year-old might name such things as giant, devil, dragon, or witch. But rarely does he get entirely off the track as in the following instance in which a child named "horse, cow, barn, farm."

The naming of young animals (pony, puppy, lamb, colt, calf) shows no clear-cut age trend, though it continues longer in girls than in boys, with 10% of girls giving some diminutive responses as late as 10 years of age. This type of naming suggests a nice differentiation. Naming the male or female animals is less common. The more frequent male animals named are rooster and bull.

The naming of tiny animals such as insects is especially conspicuous at 6 and 7 years. The common fear of bees, wasps, and hornets at 6 years may be the basis of this naming, but at 7 there seems to be a relationship to the smallness. Thus, bug, ant, and even germ may be named.

Any naming of unusual animals should be noted. A 6-year-old who names armadillo or cougar, a 7-year-old who names vulture or octopus, an 8-year-old who names tapir or okapi, all give evidence of a certain erudition that cannot be equated in averages. The naming of "person" or "people" is most probably an individual response, but it can occur at any age, with a slight increase from 8 years on when it is often named in a humorous way, such as "us."

The naming of any animal as wild, i.e., wild cat, or wild boar, always alerts us to the child's possible inner feelings of wildness. This projection is more common in the out-of-bounds 4-year-old who not only behaves wildly, but probably also feels wild. Whether or not a valid relationship exists between the use of the adjective "wild" and a feeling of wildness is hard to say, but the examiner should at least be alert to the possibility.

CHAPTER 13

HOME AND SCHOOL PREFERENCES

‖‖‖

The demands of the examination are coming to a close. They have simmered down through the naming of animals and are now ending on a personal note having to do with the child's preferences in activities.

Administration

The child is asked, "What do you like to do best?" This question is followed, in order, by the following questions:

> What do you like to do best indoors at school?
> What do you like to do best outdoors at school?
> What do you like to do best indoors at home?
> What do you like to do best outdoors at home?

Answers are highly individual and varied. Some children find it difficult to give even a single response to each of these questions; others reply at length. The initial general question is hardest for most. As the questions become more specific as to place, it is easier for most children to respond.

The more structured situation provided at school, especially indoors, and the fact that this is a common experience which all children share, give answers to this part of the questioning more similarity from child to child than do the remaining questions in this group.

On the other hand the home responses, though extremely varied, tell much about an individual child.

Tables 84 to 88 show how many times each kind of behavior was mentioned. Thus, under indoor school preferences at 5 years, 19 girls but only 2 boys mentioned doll play. But since any one child may have men-

227

tioned three different indoor play interests such as dolls, playing house, and toys, the 5-year-old totals of 42 and 55 for girls and boys respectively refer to the number of times these activities were mentioned and not to the number of different children mentioning them.

By grouping general kinds of activities, as for instance play and work activities indoors at school, we obtained fairly substantial numbers which in relation to a certain category give us some idea of the interest level at different ages.

Figures which indicate the number of children who reported on a certain item give clues of interests though most figures are not large enough to be of conclusive use. However, some behaviors such as reading, swinging, and ball play do show up with substantial figures.

Findings

LIKES TO DO BEST

This question should be considered more as a take-off, than as providing an effective evaluation of a child's interests. It is hard for many children to express this kind of a choice. FIVE may not even understand what is being asked of him. Often he is so immediately oriented that he thinks he is being asked what he liked to do best of the different test situations. The Incomplete Man and Visual One are revealed to be his favorites.

Those children who have strong interests or hobbies speak right up. The 6-year-old needs to be checked on the validity of his reporting. A 6-year-old girl may report horseback riding even though she may never have been on a horse.

TABLE 84 *Likes To Do Best*
(Number of Subjects Mentioning Each Class of Activity)

	5 years		5½ years		6 years		7 years		8 years		9 years		10 years	
	G	B	G	B	G	B	G	B	G	B	G	B	G	B
Number of subjects	50	50	50	50	50	50	50	50	50	50	50	50	50	50
Gross motor, mostly ball	11	**13**	**13**	**17**	**17**	**18**	12	**24**	2	**36**	16	**34**	**28**	**47**
Winter or summer sports	3	1	0	1	0	4	2	1	**21**	13	**22**	11	20	12
Play games	7	1	7	1	11	7	7	3	7	4	9	1	13	4
Color, draw, other creative	**18**	12	7	4	12	4	6	8	4	5	2	2	5	2
Do something with parent, sibling, friend	5	5	2	9	9	6	9	5	14	6	7	5	14	2
Play with toys	5	12	5	7	9	8	7	4	3	2	3	4	8	3

NOTE: Boldface figures are the leading items at each age, rather than normative items.

TABLE 85 *School Preferences: Indoors*

	5 years G	5 years B	5½ years G	5½ years B	6 years G	6 years B	7 years G	7 years B	8 years G	8 years B	9 years G	9 years B	10 years G	10 years B
Play														
Play	0	11	10	9	5	3	0	1	1	1	0	0	0	0
Doll corner, dolls	19	2	11	0	2	0	1	0	0	0	0	0	0	0
Play house, store	6	3	0	0	0	0	0	0	0	0	0	0	1	0
Toys[a]	5	24	5	10	7	7	2	4	0	0	0	0	0	0
Blocks	5	12	3	20	3	4	1	1	0	0	0	0	0	0
Puzzles	7	3	4	8	7	6	3	5	1	0	0	0	0	0
Total play	42	55	33	47	24	20	7	11	2	0	0	0	1	0
Play Games	1	2	4	8	9	15	6	10	6	7	6	6	8	5
Work														
Work	0	1	6	4	9	15	22	12	13	6	3	2	1	1
Work sheets	0	0	0	0	9	5	1	5	1	0	0	0	0	0
Books (read and listen)	2	1	6	2	4	6	13	11	26	11	32	23	30	18
Writing	2	2	0	0	2	7	3	12	11	3	5	4	4	1
Spelling	0	0	0	0	0	0	1	1	8	3	9	5	13	8
Arithmetic	0	0	0	0	1	2	3	2	16	14	12	14	14	17
Other (science, social studies)	0	0	0	0	0	0	0	0	0	7	12	11	10	23
Clubs, project, etc.	0	0	0	0	0	0	0	0	0	0	4	2	0	1
Total work	4	4	12	6	25	35	43	43	75	44	77	61	72	69
Creative														
Color	14	5	16	4	11	9	9	3	4	3	1	2	1	0
Paint	7	2	3	1	3	0	1	1	0	0	0	2	0	0
Draw	1	1	0	5	0	3	7	4	3	5	1	2	2	3
Clay	4	2	2	0	1	0	2	1	0	0	2	1	0	0
Other	7	4	6	0	2	4	2	1	1	1	0	0	0	2
Art	0	0	0	0	0	1	2	1	3	5	6	9	6	10
Total creative	33	14	27	10	17	17	23	11	11	14	10	16	9	15
Music	3	0	0	0	0	0	0	1	2	1	5	3	4	1
"Gym"	0	0	2	0	1	1	1	6	1	5	4	5	5	20
Movies and TV	0	1	0	0	1	0	5	3	0	8	2	1	1	2
Pets	0	0	3	0	0	0	0	0	0	0	0	0	0	0
Social	0	2	2	0	0	0	1	0	1	0	1	0	2	0
Help teacher (be useful, etc.)	1	1	1	0	1	0	2	0	2	1	1	0	1	0
Eat	1	1	0	0	0	0	2	1	0	2	3	3	0	2
Recess, go outside	1	2	0	2	2	0	0	0	0	2	3	3	1	2
Nothing, or rest	0	0	1	1	0	1	0	0	0	0	1	1	1	1

[a]Mostly "trucks" in boys at 5 and 5½.

Since responses are so highly varied, tabular results are given in terms of classes of activities rather than in terms of specific individual activities. As Table 84 shows, for girls, coloring and related activities lead at 5 years. Gross motor activity is a close second and steadily increases during the years, with ball play emphasis in boys, and seasonal sports in girls especially conspicuous from 8 years on.

INDOOR SCHOOL PREFERENCES

Trends are clearest here (see Table 85). Play activities lead at 5 and 5½ years whereas work activities show a steady gain from 6 to 10 years. The continued preference for play activities after 6 years of age should be investigated, to judge the extent of a child's immaturity. Similarly a persistent interest in trucks by boys above 6 years of age may indicate immaturity.

Creative activities steadily decrease in girls, although they start from a high level, whereas they hold a fairly constant level in boys. It would be interesting to determine whether the boys who are interested in the creative media, especially in drawing and art, might also be the ones who are having difficulty in reading. Boys' interest in gym shows up strongly at 10 years of age.

In noting some of the separate items, an interest in books shows a steady rise from 7 to 10 years, with more girls than boys mentioning this interest. Arithmetic shows a lesser interest, but is strong from 8 to 10 years. Interest in science and social studies becomes stronger at 9 and 10 years, with twice as many 10-year-old boys as girls mentioning this interest.

Mention of eating, recess, or doing nothing as preferred interests gives one pause and makes one wonder how well things are going for a child who reports about his school life in this manner. The chances are that he is not doing well. Even the child who reports after 5 years of age that he likes best to help his teacher shows immaturity.

OUTDOOR SCHOOL PREFERENCES

Gross motor activities, individual in character, are strongest at 5 and 6 years and decrease sharply in boys, less sharply in girls, from then on. Interest in more organized games, especially ball play, increases steadily in boys from 6 years on.

As to the separate items, swings, the favorite of the 4-year-old, remain a high interest at 5 and 5½ years, especially in girls. The interest in the slide is not as strong but persists through 6 years of age, here again more predominantly in girls. Jungle gym and monkey bars are just as strong in girls as the interest in the slide, and these interests persist in girls into 7 and 8 years of age. In the meantime, boys have shifted to ball play.

TABLE 86 *School Preferences: Outdoors*

	5 years		5½ years		6 years		7 years		8 years		9 years		10 years	
	G	B	G	B	G	B	G	B	G	B	G	B	G	B
Gross Motor														
Seesaw	1	0	0	0	1	0	0	0	0	0	0	0	0	0
Slide	17	11	13	11	20	12	3	3	10	2	3	1	0	0
Swings[a]	31	17	33	30	9	6	9	4	9	5	14	4	7	2
Jungle gym and monkey bars	15	9	12	13	26	14	31	1	17	4	4	2	1	0
Chinning bars	0	0	0	0	7	2	3	0	4	2	3	2	1	1
Bikes	4	4	0	1	0	0	0	0	0	0	0	0	0	3
Total gross motor	68	41	58	55	63	34	46	8	40	13	24	9	9	88
Play														
Play games	2	2	2	1	7	9	10	4	12	7	6	1	13	9
Jump rope	0	0	4	0	1	0	1	0	13	0	13	0	15	0
Hopscotch	0	0	0	0	6	0	10	0	7	0	10	0	7	0
Tag	0	0	0	1	0	1	0	2	0	5	0	4	0	5
Ball	2	5	3	5	2	8	6	28	6	30	18	45	28	74
Total play games	4	7	9	7	16	18	27	34	38	42	47	50	63	88
Imaginative Play														
Pretending, collecting, art, building, sandbox	1	5	4	7	4	3	3	2	0	3	4	2	4	2
"Play"	2	2	1	4	0	5	7	7	3	8	2	2	1	1
Be outside, walk around, etc.	3	1	1	2	7	8	5	8	7	4	8	4	9	11
Do something with teacher or be useful	1	0	0	0	0	2	1	0	2	0	3	0	0	0
Do something with same sex or "friends"	2	3	0	0	3	11	2	9	4	8	6	6	8	3
Do something with opposite sex	0	0	0	0	3	4	1	2	3	0	1	0	1	0

[a]Several complained at 6 that swings weren't up. Or, a typical 6-year-old response is that they like best to play on the swings, but they never get a chance. Somebody always beats them to it.

As might be expected, girls lead in mention of playing games, jump rope, and hopscotch, whereas boys more often mention playing tag, though figures are not sizable. It is ball play that takes over in boys from 7 years on, nearly tripling in interest from 7 to 10 years. No wonder Little League has struck such a responsive chord. The boys' interest in ball play is close to three times that of girls (see Table 86).

INDOOR HOME PREFERENCES

No special single behavior or related group of behaviors stands out among home preferences indoors (Table 87). The highest interest shows up in play with some kind of toy, there being a sharp contrast between the boys' interest in trucks, cars, and trains and the girls' interest in dolls.

Playing games is an interest of both sexes and this increases from 7 to 10 years, showing up most strongly in the 10-year-old boy. Creative activities are mentioned by both sexes with low points at 8 and 10 years.

Reading shows a slight increase at 9 and 10 years but not to the extent one might expect. The choice of television has a stronger and earlier start. By 7 years this interest is gathering strength. It shows a further rise in frequency of mention by both sexes at 9 and 10 years. This bears out earlier research findings of our own and others as to the frequency of TV watching at these ages. (We have often wished that the schools might more effectively utilize this interest in TV in the 4th and 5th grades.)

Doing something with some person or animal shows a steady rise, especially in girls. By 9 and 10 this social interest is twice or more as common in girls as in boys. This is repeatedly evident whenever boys and girls are compared. Girls seem to relate to people; boys to things.

OUTDOOR HOME PREFERENCES

The leading outdoor home preferences are either some kind of gross motor activity or playing games. Gross motor interests remain strong through 7 years and reduce only slightly thereafter. Bike riding remains relatively high throughout. Swings are a strong interest in girls through 7 years of age. Playing games shows a marked increase at 8 and 10 years with special emphasis on ball play in boys (see Table 88).

On the social side (doing something with somebody), the girls show a markedly greater interest than do boys, outdoors as well as in. This interest is substantial throughout these ages of 5 to 10 years.

Another interest is in seasonal sports, especially from 8 to 10 years.

It is difficult to judge the validity of these choices of activity responses. Parents are particularly aware of the possibility of inaccurate reporting, especially of omissions. The very thing a child may be most interested in, he may neglect to mention.

TABLE 87 *Home Preferences: Indoors*

	5 years		5½ years		6 years		7 years		8 years		9 years		10 years	
	G	B	G	B	G	B	G	B	G	B	G	B	G	B
Toys														
Play with toys	3	5	6	8	3	8	0	5	0	2	0	1	0	3
Trucks, cars, trains	0	16	0	9	1	17	0	9	0	10	0	4	0	8
Puzzles	2	2	1	0	0	0	1	2	0	0	0	1	0	1
Blocks, etc.	3	3	1	4	2	3	0	3	0	0	0	1	0	0
Dolls	11	0	11	0	10	0	7	0	11	0	7	0	9	0
Total toys	19	26	19	21	16	28	8	19	11	12	7	7	9	12
Play games	4	8	3	5	7	5	14	7	15	17	18	18	14	28
Creative														
Color, paint, draw	12	3	12	10	11	8	8	3	3	2	6	4	5	2
Make things	2	3	0	3	0	1	2	7	0	5	4	9	3	5
Total creative	14	6	12	13	11	9	10	10	3	7	10	13	8	7
Imaginative[a]	8	3	13	2	8	9	13	10	9	7	5	13	6	7
Gross Motor														
Bikes, ball, rocking horse	2	2	4	2	2	2	2	0	6	1	2	1	5	2
Read, write, work	2	0	1	3	4	2	6	8	7	4	6	12	10	12
TV	2	3	4	9	6	10	14	15	8	18	18	17	18	19
Do something with parents, be useful	2	1	4	3	5	4	4	4	6	3	6	5	8	2
Do something with siblings	2	3	7	5	6	1	6	9	9	6	9	5	9	5
Do something with same sex, friends	3	1	3	3	5	2	1	2	2	3	4	0	3	1
Do something with opposite sex	0	0	0	0	0	0	1	0	0	0	0	0	0	0
Do something with animals	2	1	1	0	2	2	2	0	3	2	4	2	3	1
Music (listen and perform)	2	1	0	0	0	0	2	0	3	2	4	2	3	1
Go outside	1	3	1	2	0	0	0	1	0	1	0	0	0	0
Eat or sleep	4	1	4	0	4	1	1	1	1	1	0	4	0	2

[a] Play house, store, in girls; cowboys in boys.

TABLE 88 *Home Preferences: Outdoors*

	5 years		5½ years		6 years		7 years		8 years		9 years		10 years	
	G	B	G	B	G	B	G	B	G	B	G	B	G	B
Gross motor														
Seesaw	3	0	0	0	4	0	0	0	1	0	0	0	0	0
Slide	3	1	5	2	3	0	1	0	0	0	0	0	0	0
Swings	17	9	11	9	21	4	15	2	9	0	6	0	3	0
Jungle gym, etc.	0	1	0	1	4	0	2	0	0	0	0	0	0	0
Bikes, cars, wagons	8	16	10	12	6	11	14	16	6	7	9	11	17	11
Other	2	0	1	1	2	0	0	3	1	0	3	1	1	2
Total gross motor	33	27	27	25	40	15	32	21	17	7	19	12	21	13
Play														
Play games	3	1	1	0	1	2	2	4	6	5	6	6	8	8
Tag	0	0	0	0	1	2	1	0	3	1	1	0	3	7
Hide-and-go-seek	1	0	1	0	0	0	0	0	0	0	3	1	2	0
Hopscotch	0	0	0	0	2	0	0	0	2	0	1	0	5	0
Jump rope	0	0	2	0	0	0	1	0	1	0	7	0	9	0
Ball	1	4	0	5	1	11	3	22	6	27	4	30	13	50
Total play games	5	5	4	5	5	15	7	26	18	33	22	36	40	65
Imaginative and constructive play	4	0	1	5	9	7	8	6	3	11	3	4	12	8
Sand and dirt	6	5	4	7	5	3	4	2	2	2	1	1	0	0
Toys (mostly trucks)	0	5	0	2	0	4	0	5	0	5	0	1	0	1
Play	1	5	4	4	1	3	1	6	1	1	3	0	4	0
Be outside, walk, run around	2	2	5	2	6	5	4	4	8	5	2	10	7	13
Climb trees	1	1	0	0	1	1	1	1	3	2	1	2	4	5
Do something with parent or be useful	1	3	0	0	0	1	0	4	0	2	2	4	1	2
Do something with siblings	3	2	2	1	1	1	5	3	4	3	4	1	7	1
Do something with same sex, relatives, friends	7	5	12	7	15	8	18	11	11	10	15	9	17	11
Do something with opposite sex	0	0	0	1	0	1	2	0	0	0	0	1	0	0
Do something with animals	0	0	4	4	4	1	3	3	4	1	6	2	6	4
Swim, etc. (summer)	0	1	0	1	0	0	1	1	7	8	9	6	4	7
Sled, skate, etc. (winter)	0	1	1	0	1	3	4	4	15	10	18	18	17	12
Other	3	2	4	2	3	6	3	4	3	10	6	8	8	9

Sometimes the answers to these questions, however, can give an amazingly full picture of the child's interests and activities. One can almost see him moving through his day. With other children the reporting is sparse, not really telling much about the child's life. The more immature child digresses to tell stories that relate to some specific experience, reminiscent of a 4-year-old's reporting.

A warning to the examiner when he is examining a 6-year-old is to anticipate the child's irritability when he thinks he has already answered the questions about home interests in his initial reporting about what he likes to do best. Six will say in his impatient, spitfire way, "I told you already!"

It is then time for the examiner to backtrack, take the blame, make a different attack, add a little humor. This kind of knowledge about what to expect at different ages should also be in the hands of the teacher. She, too, needs face-saving devices, a keener perception of the child, so that she can exercise a surer hand and experience less wear and tear from her job of teaching.

CHAPTER *14*

USEFUL ADJUNCTS TO EVALUATION

||||||||||||||||||||||||||||||||||||||||||||||||||||||||||||||||||||||||||||||||||||

Though not essential parts of the developmental examination as such, there are several additional tests or kinds of observation which are useful to the examiner in reaching a fuller evaluation of the behavior level and individuality of any given child.

Each examiner will in all likelihood work up his own group of supplementary tests or things he likes to observe about each child whom he is examining. Four areas of investigation which have proved useful to us include observation of the child's teething, a check on his vision (when this is practical), an evaluation of his reading ability through use of the Gray Oral Reading Test and the Iota Word List, and a simple measure of individuality and level of emotional development—the Lowenfeld Mosaic Test. Each of these supplementary measures will be discussed briefly in the present chapter.

TEETH

Since we closely relate function to structure, we have always been aware of the remarkable evidence, so obviously present and clear for all to see, of the differences which exist from child to child in the matter of movement of the loss of baby teeth and their replacement with the permanent teeth. Most parents and others interested in the behavior and growth of infants have already, in the child's first two years of life, been interested in relating his teething to the rest of his growth.

They also note, though often more casually, the falling out of baby teeth, and the eruption of the second teeth. But for the most part, people have been very superficial in these appraisals and thus have probably missed many important potential clues that could give much information about any individual child. They might note unusual patterns with interest, but somehow fail to relate these patterns to the rest of the child's behavior and growth.

For example, late teething in the infant, with the upper central incisors first erupting as late as 1 year of age, may seem odd even to the most unschooled. What does it mean? Certainly nearly anyone will suspect that things are topsy-turvy, since the lower teeth are expected to erupt first. Consider the eruption of the lateral upper incisors before the eruption of the central incisors. This again strikes even the untutored eye. Might this imply some difficulty or delay in focal central behavior? If we ourselves saw this evidence in a boy baby we would be concerned about his placement in school when the time came and would want to be sure that he would be allowed to progress slowly enough to have time to catch up with himself.

A second set of teeth gives those interested in observing and helping children a second chance to peer into nature's inner workings. We ourselves have become rather self-conscious at the mere mention of teeth, because so many people believe strongly that there is no relationship between structure and behavior, between, for instance, a child's behavior in school and his teething. But our clinical evidence has been piling up over the years to the point that we are convinced that a definitive study should be made of this relationship.

If, for example, an 8-year-old boy is brought to us because of educational difficulties in the third grade and reveals with his smile of greeting that he still has four upper central baby teeth, we are alerted at once that his teething is below a 6½-year-old level. It is natural to question whether this boy is capable even of second grade work, if the warning of his teeth is taken into consideration. He may more correctly belong at a first grade level. Fortunately, today's concept of ungraded classes is giving such a child more opportunity to be his biological age, rather than pushing him into the expectations of his chronological age.

Another example might relate to a partial delay in teething. Again let us consider an 8-year-old boy in third grade. This time he reveals by his smile that he has his right second central and lateral upper incisors fully erupted, but that his left central and lateral incisors are still his baby teeth. Might this not alert the educator to a potential marked discrepancy in behavior? We have found this kind of eruption to be related to extremes of behavior. On the one hand, the child is right up to his age or better, but he also shows some behaviors markedly below his age. This kind of boy will need the stimulation which his advancement requires, but he will at the same time need to be allowed protection to organize through his basic level which will be much lower.

Anyone interested in the loss and eruption of teeth can witness this drama almost daily in the spring of the kindergarten year. Teachers might well learn from these happenings and allow the children to keep track of their own teething on individual charts. This might of course be hard on the child who is slow in teething. If, however, he were in the grade where he really belonged this same child might find himself in the vanguard as far as teething was concerned.

In our Weston study there was clear evidence that the teething schedule of boys was behind that of girls of the same age. Of the 41% of Weston subjects who were behind the average teething schedule, 73% of these were boys (see Table 89). We also noted especially that boys more often than girls were likely to erupt their second teeth behind their first teeth without losing their first teeth through the absorption of their roots to facilitate their loss. It is with boys that the dentist more often had to pull the first teeth to give the second teeth space to come into good alignment. Does this mean that boys have greater difficulty in transitions, that they are more apt to hold on to their past?

We include two tables from our Weston study with apologies, since only 80 subjects are covered, without any standardizing controls. The first table gives some idea of normative expectancy. Thus we would anticipate some movement of teeth in the 5½- to 6-year-old, either of the lower central incisors or 6-year molars (Table 89). By 6 years of age

TABLE 89   *Average Age of Tooth Eruption*

Age	No Eruption (%)	Beginning Movement (%)	Eruption (%)	Molar (%)	Lower Central Incisor (%)
$5-5^4$	90	25	7	7	7
5^5-5^{10}	50	25	50	25	36
$5^{11}-6^4$	16	14	80	58	78
6^5-6^{10}	5	13	84	81	81
$6^{11}-7^4$	2	0	98	94	98
7^5-7^{10}	0	0	100	98	100
$7^{11}-8^4$	0	0	100	100	100

Age	Upper Central Incisor (%)	Lower Lateral Incisor (%)	Upper Lateral Incisor (%)	Number of Cases
$5-5^4$	0	3	0	28
5^5-5^{10}	7	4	0	68
$5^{11}-6^4$	30	15	5	55
6^5-6^{10}	52	52	18	38
$6^{11}-7^4$	84	72	51	51
7^5-7^{10}	89	80	53	36
$7^{11}-8^4$	96	93	80	29

both lower central incisors and 6-year molars are at a normative level of eruption. Next follow the upper central incisors and lower lateral incisors, by 6½ years of age. By 7 to 7½ years the upper lateral incisors are erupting. By 8 years of age one can anticipate four 6-year molars and four upper and lower incisors. This might well be the badge of readiness for entrance to third grade. There are, however, exceptions as with the 6% of girls who were behind schedule but who were capable of top or A group placement (see Table 90).

In fact we should emphasize that in the case of teething as with other aspects of physical growth, though behavioral maturity more often than not does go along with physical maturity just as behavior goes along with chronological age, there can be many exceptions.

We include a table on correlation between rate of teething and quality of school performance in our Weston subjects. We have found a definite correlation between being ahead of or behind schedule in teething and school performance. In general it will be clear from Table 90 that according to our judgments the majority of those children whose teething was ahead of schedule were doing well in their school work in the grade in which age placed them. Conversely the majority of those children whose teething was behind schedule were doing less well in school.

TABLE 90   *Correlation Between Teething and School Performance*

Teething	Number	Total Group (%)	Boys (%)	Girls (%)
Ahead of schedule	25	31	20	**80**
Behind schedule	33	41	**73**	27
Both ahead of and behind	22	28	45	**55**

School Placement

Those whose teething is ahead of schedule	
Definitely in top group	**60**
Doing well or fairly well	36
Atypical, repeated	4
Those whose teething is behind schedule	
Should have repeated	**54**
(Did repeat)	(22)
Would have profited by repetition	40
Top group—no question of repeating	6 (all girls)
Those whose teething was both ahead of and behind schedule	
Repeated by the school	14
Would have benefited by repeating	**50**
Doing nicely, well placed (described as hard workers)	36

An interesting variable is an irregular eruption pattern which is first ahead, then behind, later ahead again. Twenty-eight percent of our group were in this irregular category. Of these, 64% were either repeated by the school or would have profited by being repeated. However, 36% were doing nicely and were described as hard workers. All of which goes to show that placement cannot be surely judged by one aspect of behavior such as tooth eruption alone, but it does suggest that tooth eruption findings can support and sometimes clarify other evidences of physical and behavior growth.

VISION

Although most schools are probably not overly interested in either the behavioral or physical aspects of children's teething, and although many dentists are probably not very interested in the behavior implications of teething, at least most children in our schools have the health aspect of their teeth very adequately cared for.

Unfortunately the same cannot be said for vision. Every school needs to know much more about the visual functioning of its pupils than most do now. Not only would proper examination and evaluation further the understanding of each child and his visual functioning, but it could also reveal areas in which many children even at these early ages would benefit from immediate visual help.

Teeth reveal an outward manifestation of growth, but vision reveals a more inward manifestation. No other function can tell so much about the child's inner workings as his visual understanding, use of his eyes, and eye measurements. Developmental changes of visual behavior can be documented from birth by observation of visual performance. One especially informative kind of observation is made with the use of a retinoscope during various visual tasks at various distances.

Every child who goes through our clinical service is given a full developmental visual examination. The visual behavior picture usually supports and supplements the findings on the developmental examination, revealing clearly a behavioral age level as well as an individual process of patterning. Such an examination, however, may also reveal specific compensation mechanisms such as myopia, adverse hyperopia, and astigmatism. Lenses and visual training can often be an important therapeutic consideration in guiding visual behavior, both when actual compensations exist and when only behavior patterns are distorted.

We have come to know that these compensations come about in some children because of the function of the child's visual mechanism and restricted visual understanding. It is the basis of restricted or inadequate functioning that we wish to understand and help. These restrictions in function may relate to fixation, to focusing, or to interpreting what is seen and where things are seen. Each of these areas has an age expectancy. The 5-year-old, for instance, *should* be able to track a moving target. If his eyes cannot posture easily and accurately to fixate the target and hold on to it as it is moved, but rather dart ahead or lag behind, or lose contact, then he is in visual trouble.

If the child cannot shift his focusing posture from a far point such as the chalkboard to the near point of his desk by 8 years of age, he is also in visual difficulty. Misinterpreting what is seen and where things are seen can show up in different ways at any age and needs to be related to the performance patterns of the various age expectancies.

We cannot include visual findings or methods of examination in this volume, but we would like to alert the educator to the importance of obtaining such findings. We have given some idea of the correlation of visual developmental findings with other findings from other tests in our Weston study in Chapter 3. The correlation was very high. That is, children who showed themselves visually ready for the grade in question were also, as a rule, ready on the basis of other kinds of tests.

We know that eventually fuller visual coverage will be needed for all children than is now available. Information obtained from Snellen Acuity charts barely scratches the surface and reveals only some of the gross difficulties. We do not consider it an adequate measure of a child's visual functioning. Schools need to know much more about vision than this test reveals.

We also know that visual experts need to be trained more fully in the principles of visual behavior and developmental vision. Though it may be some time before school systems will include a visual specialist as part of their regular staff, the service of such a specialist should be available to all school systems. All need to know more than most now do about the visual functioning of their pupils.

READING TESTS

After the child has begun to read, it is useful for the examiner to obtain some knowledge of his reading progress. Reading ability can be tested at the end of the developmental examination. This is done not only to secure a reading score, but also to note the quality of the child's method of reading.

We use the Gray Oral Reading Test in its original form. It is both easy to administer and easy to score.[1] The test allows the child to show

[1] This test and directions for scoring can be ordered from The Bobbs-Merrill Co., Inc., 4300 West 62nd Street, Indianapolis 6, Indiana.

his level of reading clearly; at the same time each age group reveals difficulties as well as special methods of attack.

Thus, the 6-year-old may need to keep his place with his finger. He may lose a line as his eyes drop down too far. (A marker could prevent this.) He is apt to repeat words he has read in a story, such as "little" or "long" when they do not recur. He needs considerable help and clearly shows his satiety point.

The 7-year-old has an easier time keeping his place, but as the reading gets harder he tends to hold the page closer to his eyes, thus revealing focusing difficulty. He often reads in a mechanical way, linking sentence to sentence and paragraph to paragraph. If he does shift his voice at the end of a sentence his inflection is usually upward. He is especially interested in the meaning of what he is reading and does not wish to linger over difficult words to figure them out. He wants somebody to supply the words he cannot read. Since the meaning of what he reads is more important to him than the exact words, he may translate a word which is hard for him into something he knows, thus reading "birthday" as "surprise." Rather than inserting extra words as he did at 6, he is more likely to omit words.

By 8 years of age the child is able to read with greater fluidity and inflection. Sentences are now separated naturally, ending with a downward inflection of the voice. EIGHT has a capacity to attack new words and can work over them phonetically. He doesn't lose his contact with the meaning of the story as he stops to work out a word. If he can read the words "Pray, Puss" (paragraph 3 of the Gray Oral Test), we judge him to be at a third grade level. This may seem like an unwarrantedly simple conclusion, but our experience has shown that the ability to read this phrase does reveal that the 8-year-old can accept the unusual and can work it out phonetically as well as in context.

These three capsule age summaries suggest that the child reveals himself in whatever he does. When an 8-year-old is reading like a 7-year-old, he may merely need to progress at a slower rate. He does not necessarily need extra remedial help. Perhaps we are producing many of our reading problems because we do not allow the child to respond from his own base and at his own rate. We may be merely confusing him when we face him with material which is beyond his capacity.

Along with the Gray Oral paragraph reading we also use the Iota Word List or any selected list of single words. It is interesting to contrast the child who has an easier time reading within the context of a paragraph and the one who reads single words better. This kind of information about a child can give the teacher a clue to facilitate his reading.

With single words, as with reading in context, the child clearly reveals his age. The 6-year-old either knows a word or doesn't know it.

He builds up his knowledge of words by the way they look. Often he gets his clues from the letter they begin with. The 7-year-old has considerable trouble with vowels. Tap becomes tip, ball becomes bell. He may read words backwards. By 8 years of age most are willing to tackle any word; they now have usable phonetic tools. Many get into trouble with silent letters, however.

LOWENFELD MOSAIC TEST

One of the most popular of all the many so-called projective tests now in vogue in this country is the Lowenfeld Mosaic Test. It is easy to give, easy to record, and very well received by subjects of all ages from the preschool years right through old age.

The one chief difficulty with this test is that to date no generally accepted formal scoring system has been worked out for it. Thus, as is actually the case with most of the tests proposed in the present volume, the examiner is required to *evaluate* the child's response rather than simply score it.

In spite of this difficulty, we consider the Mosaic useful enough, both clinically and for research purposes, to include it routinely when we examine.

It is hoped that the widespread administration of this test by examiners who will be using the present volume will result in a body of data which will add to our knowledge of its possibilities and significance. Until then, this potentially valuable test remains in its infancy.

Materials[2]

The standard Mosaic set consists of a box of 456 plastic pieces, $\frac{1}{16}$ inch thick. These pieces come in 5 different shapes—square, diamond, and equilateral, right-angled isosceles, and scalene triangles; and in 6 different colors—black, green, yellow, red, white, and blue.

The dimensions of the pieces were determined in relation to the square: the diamond's sides are equal in length to those of the square; each right- isosceles triangle is equal to half a square. The sides of the equilateral triangle equal the diagonal of the square or the hypotenuse of the right triangle. The scalene triangles are bisected equilateral triangles.

The number of each type available are: 8 squares of each color, or 48 squares in all; 12 equilateral triangles of each color, 72 in all; 16

[2] The Mosaic materials can be ordered from Badger Tests Co. Ltd., Liverpool House, 15–18 Eldon Street, London, E.C. 2, England. The standard size box is priced at $55.00; the small or half-box is $35.00.

diamonds of each color, making 96; 16 right-isosceles triangles of each color, making 96; and 24 scalenes of each color, or 144.

The working surface on which the patterns are to be made is a sheet of white paper which covers the surface of a rectangular wooden tray having a raised rim on three sides, with the side placed nearest the subject being rimless. The standard size of this working surface is 10¼ by 12⅜ inches.

Administration

The subject should be seated before a table on which is placed, directly in front of him, the tray covered with a piece of white paper. The open Mosaic box containing the Mosaic pieces is at his left.

The examiner says, "Here is a box of pieces, all different colors and all different shapes. I want you to make something with some of these pieces on this paper, anything you like. But first I'm going to show you all the different kinds." (If the subject starts right away to reach for one of the pieces, the examiner holds his hand over the box, protecting the pieces as he demonstrates.)

Examiner demonstrates one piece of each kind—equilateral triangle, square, isosceles triangle, diamond, and scalene triangle, in that order. As the examiner holds up the large triangle, he comments, "This comes in all these different colors" (showing). As he holds up the square, he says, "And this, too, comes in all the different colors," and so on for each piece.

After demonstrating and commenting on each shape, the examiner refers to the second half of the box, away from the child: "And here are extra ones in case you need more." (That is, the box is divided into two halves, each containing 228 pieces.) "Now I want you to take some of these pieces out of the box and put them onto the paper and make something—anything you like. You may take as long or as short a time as you like. You may make a big thing or a little thing, and you may use a lot of pieces or just a few. You may start now."

If the subject hesitates, the examiner may encourage him with, "Which one are you going to start with?" Further encouragement is seldom necessary.

The general wording of these instructions will need modification in nonessentials to suit the age of the child, but the essentials which must be retained are that the contents of the box should be explained to the subject, and that the pieces used for demonstration should be put back into the box—not left on the board to serve as a suggestive starting point.

Examiner records as much detail as possible, both as to what the subject does and what he says as he works. If the subject inquires about what the examiner is writing, examiner answers, "I'm just writing down what pieces you use."

Examiner should avoid leading comments such as guessing what the child is making, though he should respond in a friendly way to any comments addressed to him. When the subject asks for pieces not available, such as round pieces, or brown pieces, examiner merely indicates that we do not have those.

When the subject is finished, examiner says, "Now tell me about what you have made." This should be asked in a friendly and interested way, but not in a perplexed manner.

Unless the subject works for more than 20 minutes, he is permitted to take as long as he likes.

After the entire test battery is finished, the examiner traces around each Mosaic chip which the child has placed on the board, indicating its color. The recorded design is then colored in with crayons or pasted over with colored pieces of gummed paper[3] representing the different shapes and the different colors. One of the many advantages of the Mosaic test is that an almost exact replica of the child's own product remains available for later analysis.

Findings

Interpretation of Mosaic results does not require the high degree of specialized skill needed for the interpretation of the Rorschach. Nevertheless, it is not a task for the beginner. Thus we recommend that any examiner who intends to include the Mosaic in his readiness battery, consult our technical book on this test.[4]

Findings are presented briefly here in Table 91 which follows. As will be seen, responses are divided into three main classes (each with its own subclasses); nonrepresentational designs without pattern, nonrepresentational designs with pattern, and representational designs. As this table shows, representational designs lead at every age, and increasingly. Conversely, nonrepresentational designs without pattern decrease with increasing age.

To give the reader or examiner who is not already familiar with the Mosaic test a more concrete view of the kinds of responses which we expect from children of different ages, we have summarized briefly the outstanding kind of responses which we consider characteristic of the individual ages from 4 to 10 years.

[3] The colored pieces of gummed paper representing all the different shapes and colors are not sold commercially, but can usually be obtained from a local printing establishment.

[4] Louise B. Ames and Frances L. Ilg, *Mosaic Patterns of American Children.* New York: Hoeber-Harper, 1962. For further studies on the Mosaic, see page 354.

TABLE 91 *North Haven Mosaics: Type of Structure at Different Ages*
(Number Each Type of Response)

	5 years			5½ years			6 years			7 years			8 years			9 years			10 years		
	G	B	All	G	B	All	G	B	All	G	B	All	G	B	All	G	B	All	G	B	All
A. Nonrepresentational without pattern																					
Just drop or pile																					
Scatter singly	2	7	9	3	1	4	1	1	2	1	0	1									
Prefundamental	3	2	5	2	3	5	4	1	5												
Slab, small, large	7	4	11	8	8	16	8	8	16	13	8	21	7	5	12	3	5	8	3	3	6
Overall	2	1	3	1	1	2	1	0	1	3	0	3	1	0	1						
All A	14	14	28	14	13	27	14	10	24	17	8	25	8	5	13	3	5	8	3	3	6
All A except slab	7	10	17	6	5	11	6	2	8	4	0	4	1	0	1	0	0	0	0	0	0
B. Nonrepresentational with pattern																					
Fundamental	2	1	3	1	3	4	0	2	2	2	2	4	2	2	4	3	0	3	0	0	0
Central design	7	2	9	8	1	9	6	3	9	6	8	14	6	5	11	8	11	19	9	6	15
Design along rim	0	0	0	1	0	1	0	0	0	0	0	0	0	1	1	0	0	0	0	0	0
Fills tray																					
Frame	1	0	1	0	1	1	1	0	1	0	0	0	0	1	1	0	0	0	0	0	0
Whole pattern	0	1	1	2	1	3	0	0	0	1	0	1	0	1	1	2	0	2	0	1	1
Separate design	0	0	0	1	0	1	3	0	3	0	0	0	2	0	2	2	2	4	0	2	2
All B	10	4	14	13	6	19	10	5	15	9	10	19	10	10	20	15	13	28	10	8	18
C. Representational																					
Object	24	**29**	**53**	15	**22**	**37**	20	**27**	**47**	13	**21**	**34**	**26**	**27**	**53**	**27**	21	**48**	21	**28**	**49**
Scene	2	2	4	8	9	17	4	5	9	9	9	18	4	7	11	4	10	14	15	11	26
All C	**26**	**31**	**57**	**23**	**31**	**54**	**24**	**32**	**56**	**22**	**30**	**52**	**30**	**34**	**64**	**31**	**31**	**62**	**36**	**39**	**75**
D. Mixed	0	1	1	0	0	0	2	2	4	2	2	4	2	1	3	1	1	2	1	0	1

NOTE: Boldface figures are the leading items at each age, rather than normative items.

FOUR-YEAR-OLD

He typically combines some pieces, and names what he has made, even though his products seldom resemble real objects to the adult eye. Most typical of FOUR is a circular shape made of six large triangles, often all of the same color. Otherwise attention to color is only spasmodic, even though more blue is used than any other color. Some at this age line up pieces, all of the same kind, in a vertical row.

Simple as 4-year-old Mosaic products may be, there is at 4 a tremendous advance over 3-year-old responses. Four is the first age at which nonrepresentational products without design are no longer normative. In fact, any 4-year-old who still merely drops or piles the pieces, or combines merely two or three pieces without naming, is showing patterns below his age.

The 4-year-old uses the large triangle more than any other shape.

Four-year-olds are likely to joke and to behave in a somewhat silly manner as they work with the Mosaic pieces. Conversation either about what they are doing or even about entirely extraneous matters is almost constant. FOURS are very likely to address the Mosaic chips in a silly manner: "Hey there! Where are you going?" Most FOURS seem to enjoy this test very much.

FIVE-YEAR-OLD

He shows a marked advance in that now 53% of all subjects make some kind of object. These objects are almost equally divided among those in which the pieces are used as paint, or two to five pieces combined (often cleverly and effectively) in small patterns, and good, large, or complex objects which include large, open square structures, especially houses.

Others merely line up pieces, or produce some kind of elaboration of the 4-year-old circle of six large triangles. Blue remains the leading color. The square is now the outstanding shape.

Most importantly, perhaps, only 28% of subjects now make nonrepresentational designs with no pattern.

FIVES are much less silly, less talkative, and altogether quieter than are most FOURS. Conversation is for the most part quite to the point and chiefly concerns the thing they are building.

FIVE-AND-A-HALF- TO SIX-YEAR-OLD

One of the Mosaic products which we think of as most highly characteristic of this age period is the simple scene which resembles the kind of drawing a child customarily makes at this age. That is, there are horizontal layers of sky (including sun), trees, houses, and grass or ground. Color is used effectively in these scenes with blue sky, yellow sun, green grass.

Nearly half the children, however, make simple single objects, chiefly houses, but also, conspicuously, arrow, rocket, kite. Houses are either simple two-piece affairs or large, open structures made chiefly of squares. There is much experimenting at this age with different kinds of combinations of pieces. This may be of different forms, different colors, or different positions of pieces.

Nearly one-fourth of subjects still make some sort of nonrepresentational design without pattern. Most of these are so-called "slabs" and except for slab patterns we consider these an immature product at this age. Good central designs are made by only 9% of both 5½- and 6-year-olds.

As to use of color, superior subjects place considerable emphasis on color in designs as well as in scenes, and some take pains to use all six available colors. In fact, there seems to be not only planned use of color but as noted above, some experimenting with different color combinations. But this is seen chiefly in children of superior endowment.

Squares are the leading shape used; blue, the leading color.

The 6-year-old is characteristically more talkative as he works than was the 5-year-old, and many SIXES chatter away in such an expansive manner that their talk interferes with their work.

SEVEN-YEAR-OLD

The response which we consider most highly characteristic of the 7-year-old is a serial, horizontal lining up of pieces or groups of pieces, often all of the same shape but of different colors. Forty-six percent of subjects show at least some degree of this serial placement.

Scenes are still conspicuous (18%), but different from the 6-year-old scene in that they tend to be more sketchy in appearance. There is usually less massing of pieces, and the sky area is becoming restricted to the very top of the paper.

One-third of subjects make an object of some sort, especially houses or other buildings, vehicles, things seen in nature. Only a few objects are still made at the simple 2–4 piece level; most are made with more pieces and in a more complex manner.

Central designs, sometimes quite accurately made, have increased to 14%. Though nearly one-fourth of subjects still make some sort of nonrepresentational pattern without design, these are mostly slab patterns and we consider any nonrepresentational pattern without design, except for slab, to be definitely immature at this age.

The square is the leading shape; blue, the leading color. Color is used effectively and naturalistically in scenes, and as at 6 years, considerable attention is paid to the systematic variation of color used in linear products.

SEVENS are characteristically much quieter than SIXES as they work, and many merely whisper to themselves and do not talk to the examiner.

EIGHT-YEAR-OLD

Though objects are the outstanding product made by 8-year-olds (53% of all responses), scenes continue strong. A typical 8-year-old orientation is that the child now seems to be trying, even though rather unsuccessfully, for perspective, and thus houses, for instance, may be placed anywhere on the page instead of being lined up in rows as earlier.

Houses continue to be the chief object made. They are no longer large, open squares as earlier, but now consist mostly of two pieces only, or at the other extreme they are becoming larger and more blocky. Other leading objects are arrow, rocket, and car for boys, and trees, grass, and flowers for girls.

Products at this age are mostly larger, cover more of the page and are much more variable than at 7 years, making it more difficult to define central trends. In fact, variety and multiplicity may be considered two of the outstanding characteristics of the products of the 8-year-old.

We do not expect to find nonrepresentational products without pattern except for slabs, at this age. Patterned designs are still at only a 20% level of occurrence. Squares still predominate as to shape; blue as to color.

EIGHT is again very talkative during the testing session. He explains, boasts, jokes, and even addresses the pieces directly, "Hey, you dumbbells, stay together!" Verbalization, as with the preschooler, is often more imaginative than the actual products themselves.

NINE-YEAR-OLD

Nine is a somewhat contradictory age so far as the Mosaic product is concerned. Some NINES seem to continue the trend started at 8 and make very large intricate designs, filling almost the whole board and often of surprising accuracy both as to colors and shapes used.

At the opposite extreme are those subjects who make very small designs or objects, sometimes consisting of only two or three pieces and often of a dark color (black or blue).

This wide variation in size of product, as well as the fact that patterned nonrepresentational designs have now markedly increased (28%)

and thus appear about half as often as do representational designs, make us suspect that variety and unpredictability are the keys to the 9-year-old performance, even more so than was the case at 8 years.

We may expect almost anything of the 9-year-old, but the one thing we do not expect is the nonrepresentational nonpatterned product which, except for slabs (which come in this category), should have dropped out long since.

The square is still the leading shape used by girls, but in boys the diamond now leads. Black and blue are the leading colors—black leading in girls, blue in boys.

The 9-year-old is again quieter, much less talkative than he was a year earlier.

TEN-YEAR-OLD

Although the Mosaic product of 10-year-old girls continues to be highly varied, the boys quite characteristically make a large, solid, and bulky, rather square-shaped product (object or design), constructed chiefly of squares. Actually more pieces are used on the average by both girls and boys than at any other age to date.

Ten seems to be a highly representational age with many objects and more scenes than at any earlier age. Scenes are becoming much more imaginative and variable than earlier—the ubiquitous house is dropping out and in boys especially, people, animals, vehicles are coming in, with action strongly mentioned.

Phallic-looking men and missiles are quite strong in boys, and will be even more prominent at 11. Central designs when present tend to be of good design.

As to predominant shape, girls use scalenes most, boys use squares. In girls' scenes naturalistic use of color is excellent. Boys show good color pattern in their patterned designs. As at most ages, blue is the leading color.

Most conspicuous in TEN is the easygoing, undemanding attitude the child shows toward his product. He is even easy on himself when he makes errors: "Oh, well. A little must overlap," "Oh well. Guess I'll manage somehow." However, as so often with TEN, along with his casualness, we frequently note a lack of any clearly formed plan of procedure.

These brief age sketches will give the beginning examiner an idea of what to look for. Also useful in getting an orientation toward this test will be the normative detail for each age given in the separate age chapters. These tabular summaries list in specific detail the kinds of patterns which we consider below age, at age, and above age for each successive age level.

General Comments

We consider any projective test as *supplementary* to the basic battery of developmental tests. The Mosaic differs from the developmental tests in that even though it gives in most cases a good clue as to developmental level, it is primarily a test of individuality.

There are some children so poorly endowed that at all levels of development they give an extremely sparse response. This sparsity of response, unless very carefully evaluated, might in some instances be confused with a low developmental level. Thus, if a 6-year-old boy makes a typical 4-year-old circle of six large triangles, we cannot always be certain whether he is performing at a 4-year-old level now but may catch up later, or whether he is merely showing a limited personality make-up and possibly low intelligence.

Or consider a two-piece "house" made of a square capped by a small triangle, such as is frequently made by 5-year-olds. Many normally developing and well-endowed children go on past this simple house response by 6 years, certainly by 7. However, it might be possible for a child of low intelligence to continue with this two-piece house well into 9 years of age. The paucity of response might, in this instance, be indicative of sparse individuality factors, rather than immaturity of development.

Therefore we prefer to use the Mosaic as an additional rather than a primary clue to developmental level. A poor Mosaic in a child whose developmental level as indicated on other tests seems high, can be a warning as to possibly limited potential in spite of normal maturity. A good Mosaic in a child whose developmental level is low, might be a clue that the child falls in what we term the "superior-immature" category—that is, he is a child of potential or present superiority who is nevertheless developing at a slower than average pace.

In spite of the fact that it is not always possible (at this stage of our knowledge) to distinguish immaturity from basically meager endowment, our experience has shown that the Mosaic test seems to agree well with other tests in indicating school readiness or unreadiness, especially in the 5- to 6-year-old, even though by 7 years and thereafter it is somewhat less useful.

In the first 6 years of life the Mosaic, whatever it may tell about individuality, seems clearly to show developmental status. It is reasonably easy for the experienced examiner to distinguish between 2-, 3-, 4-, 5-, and 6-, and in many instances, 7-year-old products.

Thus, as far as 5- and 6-year-old children (kindergarten and first grade beginners) are concerned, the Mosaic can clearly indicate those children who are not up to a 5- or 6-year-old performance. Though somewhat less clear-cut in distinguishing developmental level for 7 or 8 year olds, the test is extremely useful in giving clues to highly atypical development as well as atypical personality patterning.

Some examiners may wish to give the Mosaic directly at the end of the individual developmental examination. However, others may find that it can be used most effectively to get the feel of a total group. Thus, rather than including this test as part of the regular battery, an examiner using two half-days should be able to cover an entire kindergarten class of 25 or 30 children, since any one child may take no more than 2 to 5 minutes in his response.

A special advantage of the Mosaic test, as we have noted, is the almost exact replica of the child's own product which remains available for later analysis. When all the products have been completed for the entire class the teacher can then lay them out before her. She can sort out the less and the more mature products, and can thus easily get a notion of where any one child's performance falls with relation to that of the other children in the class.

By such a method she might be able to feel the texture of her group, and the potential capabilities of its members. After she knows her class better she might again review these products to get additional clues as to individual personality, as well as relative standing within the group.

PART III
THE AGES

IN THE PRECEDING SECTION WE HAVE ATTEMPTED TO GIVE THE longitudinal flow of each of the tests in the developmental examination for the years from 5 to 10. Such an approach gives the movement of growth but it often blurs the outline of a specific age. Therefore in this section we shall endeavor to provide stopping points, and shall shift our view from the age changes of a specific developmental item to the way in which each age cuts through or defines each item. At times we may appear more didactic than we would wish to be, for the sake of clarity.

In dealing with each age we shall first introduce the age with a general picture of behavior, highlighting any educational implications when possible. We should like the reader to begin to feel that each age has its own essence, that there is such an entity as 5-year-oldness, 7-year-oldness, 10-year-oldness. It is through this greater awareness that we shall be better able to place children where they belong in school.

CHAPTER 15

FIVE YEARS

‖‖

Behavior Characteristics

"Good" is the word that describes FIVE best—and what's more his greatest desire in life is to be good. Age changes taking place at 5 make it easier for the child to achieve this aim. He has given up his exuberant 4-year-old ways, ways which needed both to be controlled and to be given leeway. Maybe he was more exciting at 4, but his 5-year-old calmness is extremely relaxing. He not only feels good, but his health is good. There may be quite an improvement from his feelings of sickness and his frequent stomach aches at 4, along with his tendency to have one cold right after another.

FIVE is like a nice rounded whole. He seems all put together. This is evident in the surety of his movements, and he can be recognized from the rear as he walks with a sure, firm step. Gone are his far-flung, out-of-bounds, 4-year-old ways when he might fall and knock out his front teeth or even wander off and become lost.

FIVE wants most to be at home, close to his mother. He likes best to be with her in the kitchen, talking with her, helping her, working at his own table and chair in sight of her. This is a happy time for both mother and child. The mother recognizes the child's desire to please and she is relieved by his urge to ask permission even when it isn't necessary.

Sometimes he even confines and restricts his activities too much. He can sometimes become stuck in a pattern of action or thinking. Jarring him loose may be accomplished in many different ways. One mother slapped her stuck 5-year-old one day in exasperation. Whereupon this 5-year-old turned to his mother and said, "Thank you." It was the mother who dissolved in tears.

Perhaps no place can better provide FIVE's needed expansion than kindergarten. He wants to be told what to do. He wants to obey. And above all, he wants to help. Though he loves home and wants to be with his mother, he anticipates the time when he will be ready for kindergarten. His main demand related to home, once he has started school, is that his mother will be there waiting for him on his return.

More thought should be given to this separation from home, and to the way in which a child gets to and from school. In days when the neighborhood school was closer to home, FIVE walked happily to and from school, possibly being met on the way home by his mother. But nowadays with bus travel, FIVE can feel engulfed by bigness, noisiness, and just too many people. Many FIVES would be happier if they could be transported separately from the older children, and in smaller groups. For each child to be transported by his own mother could be best of all.

FIVE thrives best in a morning session of school. The hardship of having to wait until an afternoon session, when he should be resting or taking a nap, can disrupt his entire adjustment.

In spite of extra adjustments which FIVE must make, he is ready for the group activities and the new intellectual challenges that school can provide. He knows his letters, in part at least. He can count to 20. He is alert to new words, and repeatedly asks their meaning. He listens well and wants to carry out instructions. In truth, FIVE is a real kindergartener.

EXAMINATION

FIVE may appear shy when he is approached by the examiner in his classroom and is asked to come and play games with her. At the same time he is ready for new adventures and has that look of adventure and conquest in his eyes. The examiner instinctively reaches a hand out to him. He usually responds in kind and this makes him feel more secure as he walks down the corridor with the examiner to the examining room.

He may respond to some of her queries, but on the whole he has lost his bubbling 4-year-old enthusiasm and isn't ready yet to make some of his 5½-year-old jagged thrusts. He is most comfortable as an obedient person. In fact, his too great obedience can at times be a handicap, for FIVE sometimes becomes stuck in situations, waiting for a new directive from the adult to release him.

After seating himself in the examining chair at the table (both chair and table suited to his size), it may be difficult for him to find his tongue. It is with the 5-year-old that the expertness of the examiner is put to the greatest test. She needs to know how and when to shift her approach and when to give up. She needs to realize that at this age a final score on any specific test is far less important than maintaining rapport and securing some response to the entire examination, minimal as this might be.

Because of FIVE's being so easily distracted, it is important to have an examining room in which outside noises are kept at a minimum. There is no reason, however, why FIVE and the examiner cannot momentarily stop to contemplate sounds, such as the far-off sounds of a train or the voice of a teacher, recognized as she is passing by.

Interview

AGE AND BIRTH DATE

Most 5-year-olds give their age with ease, often telling it without being asked. A few gesture the number five with their fingers, a typically younger response. Some may need to count their fingers to arrive at their age.

A surprising number (40% G, 30% B) know the month of their birthday. A more typical response, however, is "I already had it," or "I just had mine." The past is past—"It was on already. It's all over now." FIVE has a way of isolating. His birthday is past and he is interested in "now."

A few cling to the time when they were 4. "I was 4. Now I'm 5. I ain't 4 no more." Their very method of expressing themselves shows that they are trying to release their past.

A few say they have forgotten their birth date and still another few put the blame on their mother. "Mother didn't tell me." But the majority make the simple statement, "I don't know."

BIRTHDAY PARTY

Reporting on a party is used as a topic which will interest most FIVES. Favorite activities and presents reported are highly varied. Playing with the toys received is a fairly typical general statement of the things FIVE liked best to do. Favorite presents are clothes, doctor kits, balls, trucks, all so dear to the heart of a 5-year-old. The party itself with the cake and candles is still without inward meaning to most FIVES. Another year needs to pass before this true symbol of his age will become meaningful and of primary importance to him.

BROTHERS AND SISTERS

FIVE often gives a single total answer such as "four." He will respond to the further questions about their names and ages, but only one at a time, first naming their ages. If he doesn't know the ages of his siblings, he will often refer to their size, as to whether they are bigger or littler than he is. FIVE thinks often of his family group and of course includes himself.

FIVE may still refer to siblings as boys and girls, or he may refer to them as brothers and sisters. A mature FIVE will group his siblings: "I have three brothers and two sisters." A hallmark of FIVE is the use of the words "just" or "only." He reports, "I have only five brothers" or "I just have one sister." Often he refers initially to what he doesn't have: "I don't have any brothers." Sixty percent give ages of siblings correctly and nearly all give their names correctly.

FATHER'S OCCUPATION

FIVE's most common answer about his father's occupation ("What does your Daddy do?") is the single word, "Works." When asked further about what his father does, the less mature FIVE may refer to his activities around the house—"He works down cellar," or "He works outside." In general, however, FIVE has the concept of his father going to work. He often refers to the place of his work, such as a farm or bank. He may also refer to what his father does specifically such as "Pumps gas" or "Makes cakes." A few FIVES can name their father's profession, such as electrician or doctor. Most FIVES know that their father works to get money.

Paper and Pencil

FIVE is able to inhibit his approach to the paper and pencil which awaits him on the table. He is able to answer the interview questions without being distracted by the paper and pencil. If he should be distracted, wanting to jump right in, this behavior is closer to that characteristic of the 4-year-old.

GRASP OF PENCIL

FIVE picks up his pencil directly with his dominant hand, not picking it up first with the nondominant hand and then transferring it to the dominant hand as he did at a younger age. His grasp of pencil is usually an easy three-finger grasp near the tip of the pencil. The shaft of the pencil is directed obliquely upward.

If the child still holds the pencil high on the shaft, or the shaft is held perpendicularly upward, he is still acting like a 4-year-old. Another evidence of remnants of 4-year-old behavior is when the pencil is held in a pronate way with all fingers encircling it and the shaft extending horizontally outward.

NONDOMINANT HAND

The characteristic posture of FIVE's nondominant hand is easily recognized. It is placed flat on the table, fingers close together, very close to the dominant hand. The nondominant hand moves as the dominant hand moves.

Printing Letters and Numbers

FIVE often confuses letters and numbers and he understands "print" better than "write." He may say he can't print any letters, but when asked to print his name he readily complies. The typical 5-year-old can print his first name (especially his nickname), but only 16% of girls, 8% of boys can print their whole last name.

FIVE may or may not know the names of the letters he prints. He prefers to print capital letters. If he is taught small letters, he uses them as capitals. FIVE tends to reverse some of his letters. The more common loose, big capitals of the boys, in contrast to the small sharply formed capitals of the girls, already give clues as to a basic difference between the sexes in the rate of growth.

Placement on the page is highly varied, though letters may be placed either in the lower half of the page or in the middle of the page. The size of FIVE's letters is not consistent, and the base line of his name is wavy.

FIVE has some idea of writing numbers up to 5, though he may not write them in correct sequence. He is likely to omit some numbers, especially the ones he cannot write. In general, he places his numbers in the lower half of the page, more often at random. The size of his numbers is not only large (½ to 1 inch), but often very large (1 to 2 inches). FIVE devises his own special ways of executing his numbers, more often in pieces, as two circles for an 8. His numbers may reverse, or the ones with which he is having difficulty may become much larger.

Copy Forms

FIVE often names a form before he draws it, i.e., "round circle," "square." He tells you how he feels about a form—"easy," "simple," or "kinda hard." When it seems very hard, as with the divided rectangle, he may explode with "Wow!" or "Whew!" He may initially refuse by saying, "I can't do that one," but a little encouragement usually gets him started. ("You could try." "How would you like to start?")

Some produce a running critical commentary about their own abilities: "Sometimes I make mistakes," or "I can't draw very straight." They no longer need to throw bouquets at themselves as they did at 4 when at the very moment of their failure they will say, "I'm smart," or "I can do anything." FIVE says very clearly, "That's all I can do" or "That's the best I can do." He shows his straining by lip pursing, blowing, groaning, and sighing—such big sighs! At times he lifts his buttocks from the chair, but as a rule he stays at the table doing what he can.

The conquest of the circle, cross, and square have been relatively mastered within the past two years even though the quality of response has changed with age.

CIRCLE

The circle is now executed top down in a CCW direction by the majority of girls, but more often from the bottom up in a CW direction by boys.

CROSS

The cross is most often made with two lines, the vertical first from the top down and the horizontal second, from L to R. Boys are more likely than girls to make the vertical stroke from the bottom up. The finished product tends to be vertical or lopsided.

SQUARE

The more typical 4-year-old square of vertical shape with two long vertical lines crossed by two horizontal lines with poor closure points has given way to a fairly tidy, well-proportioned square made often in one continuous stroke starting from the left side down in a CCW direction. Girls more than boys may break up the continuous line. Boys may draw in a CW direction with a continuous stroke, earlier than and more frequently than girls.

TRIANGLE

It is the triangle that taxes the powers of the 5-year-old and it is here that his growing edge is most evident. How to make the point of a triangle, how to produce the oblique sides become knotty problems for most FIVES. As a 4-year-old, the child more often started at the bottom, drawing the sides vertically upward and ending with an open square at the top. By 5, most are able to angulate the side lines toward a point if they start from the bottom.

If they start from the top, the initial line (the left side) is often vertical. The child then draws an oblique or curved line on the right side, followed by a base line drawn obliquely upward. The finished product gives the impression of resting on a point. Many different methods can be used, but the semblance of a triangular form becomes definitely evident. Girls use mostly two lines; boys, three.

DIVIDED RECTANGLE

If the triangle was hard to solve, the divided rectangle may be judged as doubly difficult. But this is not necessarily true. Its four-sided structure puts it within the realm of many 4-year-olds. FOUR is most likely to draw a vertical square bisected by a vertical central line with many horizontal lines radiating out from either side of this central vertical line in what we classify as a "ladder" formation.

Boys' patterns vary greatly, but girls and some boys make a square or rectangular outside form. Girls make this in a continuous line (46%), mostly in a CCW direction (30%). The inner patterns are usually unsuccessful, but a fair proportion produce a vertical cleavage pattern similar to the 4-year-old response (34% G, 32% B). FIVE differs from FOUR in that he makes only three lateral lines, most often horizontal, on each side of the vertical central line. Top and bottom lines may be made slightly oblique, pointing toward a central area. A few FIVES (12% G, 6% B) make a central star pattern with lines radiating out from or into a central point.

DIAMOND

Horizontal. The majority of both sexes make some type of younger (i.e., unsuccessful) pattern.

Vertical. The majority of both sexes make some sort of younger (i.e., unsuccessful) pattern.

CYLINDER AND CUBE

The majority copy the cylinder as a circle and are not ready for the cube.

ORGANIZATION OF FORMS ON PAGE

Girls. Size of forms is highly variable (42%). Seventy-eight percent use half page or more, including 44% who use more or less the whole page. The largest number (42%) make forms in a crude circular order though mostly out of order. Of the few (28%) who make the forms in horizontal order, the largest number use three rows.

Boys. Size is variable in over half the subjects (54%). More than half (54%) use more or less the whole page with 78% using half page or more. In fact, 10% use more than one page. The largest number (42%) make forms in a crude circular order though they may be out of order, and in 32% of subjects order appears to be completely random.

Incomplete Man

GIRLS

Number of parts. 9.96.
Arm. Upper third of body line, straight out, too long.
Fingers. Varied.
Leg. Too far out on body line, too straight down, too short.

Foot.   Pointed correctly, but too long.

Eyes.   Too low, but matching and placed evenly. Mostly large open circles or small filled circles.

Ear.   Too low, too small, poor shape.

Hair.   Too few, too far around, too long.

Neck treatment.   Mostly body line only.

Extras.   Thirty-four percent add some extras, especially buttons or marking on nose or mouth.

Naming.   Nearly all name; "man" is name most often given.

Facial expression.   Subjects fail facial expression or "How looks," but 52% can tell how he feels. Most say that he is "smiling, happy, fine, good, or nice."

BOYS

Number of parts.   8.12.

Arm.   Upper third of body line, pointed upward, too long.

Fingers.   Thirty-two percent have two fingers, mostly too long.

Leg.   Too far out on body line, too straight down, too short.

Foot.   Pointed correctly, but too long.

Eyes.   Too low but matching, and placed evenly. Mostly large open circles.

Ear.   Too low, too large, poor shape.

Hair.   Too few, cover too little space, too long.

Neck treatment.   Mostly body line only.

Extras.   Thirty-two percent make some extras, chiefly buttons.

Naming.   Nearly all name; "man" is name most often given.

Facial expression.   Subjects fail facial expression and "How looks," but 46% tell how he feels. Most say that he is "smiling, happy, fine, good, or nice."

Visual One

GIRLS

Fifty-eight percent respond correctly to ten or more of the forms, but only 14% get all correct. Closure is fair in 50%, but good in only 16%. The largest number, 46% start at the bottom for more than half the forms. The majority of forms are made CW. Fifty-six percent of girls make more than half their figures CW.

BOYS

Fifty-two percent make ten or more correct, though only 8% get all correct. Forty-six percent make fair closure. More than half the figures are started from the bottom in 60% of subjects. Forty-two percent make all circles CW and in 78% of subjects more than half the figures are made CW.

ERRORS

Five-year-olds have various difficulties in response.

Thirty-four percent of the 5-year-old girls and 40% of the boys have trouble starting. Eight percent of the girls and 18% of the boys encircle both forms, rather than selecting one.

Some choose all top forms. Thus, 8% of the 5-year-old girls choose all top figures; 10% choose all top figures in the last row. Twenty-four percent of the boys choose all top figures in the last row. Thirty-two percent of the girls and 52% of boys lose their place and need help in getting reoriented.

Visual Three

Average number correct: girls, 3.6; boys, 3.3.

Average number of lines used: one.

Fifty percent or more respond correctly to: none.

Fifty percent or more attempt: Form One on Cards I and III. Also, girls attempt Form Two, Card I.

Right and Left

NAMING PARTS

Fifty percent or more of FIVES can name eye, eyebrow, palm (calling it hand), elbow, thumb. Over 50% give little finger some correct name (little, baby, pinkie).

NAMING RIGHT AND LEFT

Thirty-six percent of girls, 34% of boys show or name all correctly; 14% of girls, 24% of boys, all opposite.

For right hand only, 18% of girls, 20% of boys name correctly. Added to these are 42% of girls and 28% of boys who show right hand correctly.

The main reason given for knowing one side from the other is that their mother told them.

SINGLE COMMANDS

All can obey the six selected commands. Average time of response per command is 3.0 seconds.

DOUBLE COMMANDS

Only commands 1 and 7 are given at this age. Mean time of response per command is 13.3 seconds.

Naming Animals

GIRLS

Only 29% can name for a minute. Mean number of animals named is 6.8. Domestic animals (dog) lead. Forty percent precede name of animal with "a."

BOYS

Only 28% can name for a minute. Mean number of animals named is 6.10. Zoo animals (lion) lead. Thirty percent precede name of animal with "a."

Home and School Preferences

Indoors at school, 5-year-olds prefer some kind of "play" (dolls, toys, blocks, puzzle), mentioned 42 times[1] by girls, 55 times by boys; followed by some sort of creative activity (33 mentions in girls, 14 in boys). Outdoors at school, gross motor activity leads (mentioned 68 and 41 times by girls and boys respectively).

Indoors at home, FIVES prefer play with toys (19 mentions by girls, 26 by boys). Outdoors they prefer some kind of gross motor activity, mentioned 33 times by girls, 27 times by boys.

As to what they like to do best of all, for girls coloring leads, for boys some sort of gross motor activity.

Mosaic

BELOW AGE

Just drops or piles.
Scatters singly.
Lines up pieces.
Prefundamentals.[2]
Four-year-old circle without elaboration.[3]

AT AGE

Fundamentals:[4] elaboration of 4-year-old circle; four squares combined into a basic square.

[1] Figures in home and school preferences refer to the number of times a specific activity or group of activities is mentioned. When a number of activities are grouped together (as gross motor activities, or playing games), this number may be greater than the number of different children involved, since one child might mention several different kinds of gross motor activity, or several different kinds of games.

[2] Prefundamental: any simple combination of two or three pieces, usually of the same type, in combinations approaching, but not reaching, a fundamental.

[3] Four-year-old circle: circle made of six large triangles.

[4] Fundamental: the simplest patterns that can be made with each piece, as a square of four squares, square of two small triangles, triangle of four large triangles, arrow or diamond of four diamonds, star of eight diamonds, etc.

Horizontal lines of some one shape, some attention to color.

Slabs:[5] mean of three different colors, three to four different shapes, poor fit, not pleasing.

Central designs: simple effort, may not be successful.

Object resembling thing named:

> Mostly houses: two-piece or crude open square.
>
> People, mostly of six pieces with triangle or square body, scalene appendages (G); may not actually resemble people (B).
>
> Pieces lined up to form "stair" or combined to make "box."

Object not resembling thing named:

> Slab structure, but named as object.
>
> Large or small masses of pieces called "building" or "house."

Large triangle is the leading shape; square comes second.

Color: blue used most, black second. No good total plan in use of color but there may be pairs, clusters of lines of matched or alternating colors, probably chosen intentionally.

ABOVE AGE

Any scene resembling scene.

Effective complex central design.

---

[5] Slab: pieces of different shapes placed one against the other to form a more or less compact figure in which no over-all meaningful pattern of design can be recognized.

CHAPTER 16

FIVE-AND-A-HALF YEARS

||||||||||||||||||||||||||||||||||||||||||||||||||||||||||||||||||||||||||||||||||||||||

Behavior Characteristics

Half-year intervals still show striking changes, and the 5-year-old has changed a great deal by 5½. Parents are the first ones to recognize the changes, and the significant question they ask is, "What has gotten into him?"

What has happened is that their darling little cooperative 5-year-old is beginning to explode, to oppose, to demand. This stage, just beginning at 5½ and rising to a crescendo by 6, often takes parents unawares. They tend to combat force with force and by doing so only add fuel to the fire.

It is important to recognize that new, uncontrolled, unmodulated emotional forces are welling up in the 5½-year-old. This is a time for strategy, not for open warfare. A mother needs to develop a certain amount of detachment, so that she may be ready for her child when he strikes out. His sudden shift from "I love you" to "I hate you" will inevitably produce its sting, but there is often a humorous aspect to the child's very intensity.

That he needs to make so much of so little (perhaps the mere misplacement of one of his belongings) should make a parent pause and wonder. It soon becomes evident to the discerning parent that the child of this age is worst to and with his mother. He behaves much better with his father or, in fact, with anyone else. Therefore letting someone else take over can relieve the strain.

Girls are likely to hit this stage earlier than boys, in fact some boys may never express this stage to any great extent. These are the boys in whom intellectual rather than emotional forces predominate.

The injection of emotions as it were into the good, cautious, and obedient 5-year-old releases him from any stuck positions he may have taken earlier. Initially 5½ may be as strongly stuck in opposition as he was earlier in an inability to move. However, this will eventually lead to a more fluid position, an ability to see things from different sides and to be receptive to different points of view.

FIVE-AND-A-HALF is gathering a new kind of stamina, a new ability to stand up for himself. The older kindergarten children, those in the 5½-year-old realm, show their tougher readiness for school as compared with their 5-year-old classmates. They know how to speak up, to ask questions and to carry out commands after only an initial instruction. They become fun to teach because they are developing an easy give and take.

Children of this age are less likely to show the extremes of their personality at school. Teachers are, in fact, often a bit shocked when they hear about a child's bad behavior at home—the very child whom they may consider a delight. But when teachers themselves hear that FIVE-AND-A-HALF reports only on the *bad* things other children do at school, it may help them to recognize his propensity for producing trouble.

EXAMINATION

The 6 months that have intervened between 5 and 5½ years have left their mark. Now the child is more ready to give and take in a way for which he was not ready at 5. At 5 he was more on the receiving end, wanting to do what was asked of him and to do things right.

But now at 5½ he is beginning to express himself more freely. His shyness has left him as the examiner approaches him to come and play games with her. He is quite ready to drop what he is doing. Though he may accept the examiner's hand initially, very soon he releases it, wishing to be on his own. The examiner is less conscious of needing to protect him. His body now moves with a looseness, having lost the stiffer erectness characteristic of 5. He slips into the chair at the examining table quite naturally, and is ready and eager to do whatever is asked of him.

Interview

AGE AND BIRTH DATE

The child now definitely knows that he is 5 when he is asked, and he no longer refers to the time when he was 4. A few give their age as 5½, showing a good number concept. FIVE-AND-A-HALF is beginning to grasp the idea of a birth date, especially the month in which his birthday occurs (46% G, 32% B). A fair number can also give the day of the month (26% G, 16% B). It is interesting to note which children refer to the past, "I already had it," and which refer to the future, "Next year." The former response is perhaps more related to 5 and the latter to 6.

The 5½-year-old reports more spontaneously about his brothers and sisters. You don't have to tease information out of him as at 5. He is quite accurate in reporting ages of siblings (82% G, 70% B), and all give the names of siblings correctly.

FATHER'S OCCUPATION

His father's occupation is now a matter of real interest. He can specify that his father prints, builds, fixes things, makes plans for boats, rolls down roads, etc. He can surprise you with detail such as locating his father's place of business: "Trust Company, Main Office." The concept of a profession is still tenuous and is reported only by a few.

Paper and Pencil

POSTURE

FIVE-AND-A-HALF'S posture and placement of the paper is similar to that seen at 5, but there are definite evidences of a breakup. The head often shifts from side to side, giving a marked clue as to why letters and numbers are likely to shift. The free hand is not held as tight and flat as formerly. The little finger may separate off, moving outward.

OVERFLOW

The tongue extends and sweeps over the lips, participating fully in the act of writing, clearly showing points of increased strain. It is this tongue posture and activity that are so typical of this age. There is more wiggling in the chair than earlier. Eyes are no longer staring but show a freer movement.

WRITING NAME

Ninety-six percent of girls, all boys, print their first name; and over half can now make either their last name or at least the first initial of their last name. Base line is still uneven and size only "fairly" consistent.

However, now 76% of girls, 74% of boys use capitals and small letters correctly. There is still no cursive writing. Some children (10% G, 36% B) still reverse and 20% of girls, 22% of boys use substitutions. Placement is still highly varied.

Copy Forms

CIRCLE

The majority of both sexes, here and through 10 years, draw in a CCW direction, with one line, starting at the top.

CROSS

The majority of both sexes, here and following, use two lines, drawing first a vertical line from top to bottom and then a horizontal line from L to R.

SQUARE

The majority of both sexes use one line only and start down the left side. Seventy-eight percent of girls and 82% of boys draw in a continuous direction—54% of girls, 48% of boys draw in a continuous CCW direction.

TRIANGLE

There is still marked variation in the way the triangle is drawn. Number of lines used varies greatly. Sixty percent of girls and 46% of boys start with a line down the left side. Younger (unsuccessful) patterns are dropping out. Most draw noncontinuously.

DIVIDED RECTANGLE

Outside pattern. Most draw a single continuous line and 44% of each sex draw continuously in a CCW direction.

Inside pattern. Younger (unsuccessful) patterns still predominate in girls but not in boys, where performance is better than that of girls but highly variable. Boys make mostly some variation of two sets of lines, crossing.

DIAMOND

Horizontal. The largest number make some nearly correct reproduction of the form, but the method of drawing varies widely from child to child.

Vertical. The largest number make some almost successful effort to copy the diamond correctly, but method varies widely from one child to another.

CYLINDER AND CUBE

The largest number (44% G, 48% B) copy the cylinder as a circle. The majority copy the face-on cube as a square and do not attempt the point-on cube.

ORGANIZATION OF FORMS ON PAGE

Girls. Size is variable in 40%. The largest number (42%) now place forms in a horizontal sector of the page—and order is largely horizontal though not in correct sequence (32%). The largest number still use three horizontal rows. Fifty-eight percent use half page or more and of these 8% use more than one page.

Boys. Size is still highly variable (46%). The largest number use a horizontal sector of the paper though 60% still use half page or more. Placement is chiefly horizontal in correct order (38%), boys like girls using mostly three rows.

Numbers

GIRLS

One to ten only, or fewer. Over ½ inch in size. The majority (86%) use front of paper. Sixty-two percent reverse some figure or figures: 34% once, 28% more than once; 3 is reversed the most. Only 2% reverse order. The largest number (8%) have trouble other than reversal with 5. The largest numbers (30% each) make either half line or one line. First line breaks most often (18%) at 10. Base line, spacing, and relative size of figures are all uneven.

BOYS

One to nine only, and some make fewer. Over ½ inch in size. The largest number use front of paper. Sixty percent reverse some figures, 28% once, 32% more than once—7 and 9 most. The largest numbers have trouble other than reversal with 2 (10%) and 5 (10%). Only 4% of boys reverse order. Largest number (48%) make only half line or less. First line breaks at 7 (14%) or 5 (12%).

Incomplete Man

GIRLS

Number of parts.   9.08.
Arm.   Upper third of body line; pointed upward, too short.
Fingers.   More or less correct shape, but too long.
Leg.   Too far out, too straight, variable length.
Foot.   Pointed correctly and may be of good length.
Eyes.   Placed variably but matching, and placed evenly. Mostly small filled circles.
Ear.   Too low, of variable size, poor shape.
Hair.   Too few, placed too far around, too long.
Neck treatment.   Ninety-eight percent either neckline, neck, or bow. Twenty-two percent make body line and neck.
Extras.   Only 18% add any extras, mostly buttons.
Naming.   The majority call the figure "man," but 38% (the high point) call it "boy."

Facial expression. Subjects fail facial expression, how looks and how feels, but 78% can tell whether he is happy or sad. The largest number give both emotions in some way, i.e., looks good but feels sad. Forty-six percent can tell how they know this—in 30% it is by the mouth.

BOYS

Number of parts.   8.92.

Arm.   Upper third of body line, pointed up, too long.

Fingers.   More or less correct shape, but too long.

Leg.   Too far out, too widespread, too long.

Foot.   Pointed correctly, and may be of good length.

Eyes.   Forty percent placed correctly, even, and matching. Mostly small filled circles.

Ear.   Placed too low, too small, poor shape.

Hair.   Too few, too far around, too long.

Neck treatment.   Most make body line only.

Extras.   Only 26% make extras, mostly belly button, buttons, or marks on mouth.

Naming.   The majority name figure some kind of man, though 30% (a high point) call him "boy."

Facial expression.   Subjects fail facial expression and how looks. 36% can tell how he feels and 36% tell whether he is happy or sad. Some positive emotion leads (28%) or both positive and negative (24%). The majority can tell how they know—it is chiefly because of the mouth (42%).

Visual One

GIRLS

The majority now respond correctly to all 12 forms. Closure is fair in 52%. Forty-two percent start at the top for more than half their figures. And now 66% make more than half their figures CCW.

BOYS

Sixty-six percent respond correctly to all 12 forms. Closure is fair in 46%. Forty-eight percent still start more than half their circles at the bottom, but 50% now make more than half CCW.

Visual Three

Average number correct: girls, 4.9; boys, 4.2.

Average number of lines used: the largest number of girls (32%) use four lines; largest number of boys (38%) still use one line only.

Fifty percent or more respond correctly to: none.

Fifty percent or more attempt: Form One, Card I; Form One and Form Two, Card II; Form One, Cards III, IV. Also girls attempt Form Two, Card I.

Right and Left

NAMING PARTS

Fifty percent or more of 5½-year-olds can name eye, eyebrow, palm (calling it hand), elbow, thumb, pointer finger (after demonstration). Over 50% give little finger some correct name.

NAMING RIGHT AND LEFT

Seventy-four percent of girls, 82% of boys show or name all correctly; 18% of girls and 6% of boys get all opposite.

For right hand only, 12% of girls, 22% of boys name correctly. Added to these are 66% of girls and 60% of boys who show right hand correctly.

Main reason given for knowing one side from the other for girls is that their mother told them; for boys that they "just know."

SINGLE COMMANDS

All can obey the eight commands. Average time of response is 2.8 seconds.

DOUBLE COMMANDS

Mean time per command is 8.4 seconds.

Naming Animals

GIRLS

Forty-three percent can name for a minute. Mean number of animals named is 7.7. Zoo animals (lion) lead. Name of animal may still be preceded with "a."

BOYS

Only 36% can name for a minute. Mean number of animals named is 7.5. Zoo animals (lion) lead. Name of animal may still be preceded with "a."

Home and School Preferences

Indoors, at school, both sexes still prefer some sort of play with object (33 mentions by girls, 47 by boys). Outdoors, both prefer gross motor activities (58 mentions by girls, 55 by boys). Indoors, at home, both prefer play with toys (19 girls, 21 boys). Outdoors, gross motor activity still leads (27 mentions by girls, 25 by boys).

As to what they like to do best of all, both choose some kind of gross motor activity.

Mosaic

BELOW AGE

Scatters singly.
Prefundamentals.
Pieces lined up along edge.
Slabs: entirely ill fitting.
Collection of pieces named object, but in no way resembling object.
Fundamentals: basic 4-year-old circle or square of four squares.

AT AGE

Horizontal line of single pieces, some attention to color.
Slabs: at least some pieces fitting on some sides; mean of 4 to 5 different colors; somewhat pleasing. Larger than at surrounding ages.
Objects more likely to resemble thing named than at 5 years.
Objects, pieces used as paint.
Or objects: especially houses, mostly two-part or open squares. Simple correct use of pieces in people, rockets, etc. Or "square," "decoration," "puzzle," etc.
Over-all design: nonpatterned but neat.
Central design: any effort, may be failure.
Scene: very simply constructed, covers much of page, may include sun and/or sky.
Square is the leading shape used.
Color used: blue most, black second. The largest number of subjects combine or alternate colors successfully.

ABOVE AGE

Fundamentals beyond basic 4-year-old circle or square of four squares.
Any successful or nearly successful central design.
Successful separate designs (several) with pattern.
Whole pattern filling tray.
Objects: houses beyond two pieces or open square houses. May be made solidly or with effort at fitted roof.
Objects: any clever fit or imaginative or complex use of pieces.
Scenes with good sky, grass, sun.

CHAPTER *17*

SIX YEARS

||||||||||||||||||||||||||||||||||||||||||||||||||||||||||||||||||||||||||

Behavior Characteristics

SIX is the full-blown picture of behavior seen in its beginning in the 5½-year-old. A mother may have needed to detach herself from her child in the previous 6 months, for her own sanity. But he has also been steadily detaching himself from his mother in these same past 6 months. Mother may have been the center of his world when he was 5 years of age, but now he himself is the center of his world.

SIX calculates as it were from his own center as he tries to tell you how big a fish was, stretching his arms out laterally and using his arms and trunk as a measuring device—which, of course, turns out to be not big enough. So often he is spoken of as selfish—wanting the biggest piece, wanting to be first, always wanting to win.

Everything he does he feels deserves praise. Perhaps there is no age when praise is more welcome and more helpful. He can never get enough of it. Praise to the 6-year-old is like water and sunshine to a plant. Parents and teachers need not fear that too much praise will spoil him. Nor will winning spoil him, especially at home. He will slowly learn the steps of playing the game in the next 2 or 3 years. This is no time to upset his equilibrium further by demanding that he be fair and reasonable, when he is barely held in balance as it is.

He himself is very much concerned with balance, possibly because of his own imbalance. The nice straight sure walk so characteristic of FIVE has broken up into an outflinging of arms and legs. SIX is said to trip over a piece of string. No wonder he craves balancing acts such as walking on fences. When he falls he is apt to break his fall with his arm, and may break his arm in the bargain.

Whatever he does, he does with impulsive enthusiasm. His exuberance is contagious. When he is ready to use his forces positively he draws

274

delightful scenes with paint or crayon, or he listens to stories with avidity, and spontaneously wishes to dramatize them, or he gives himself to any intellectual pursuit offered him. He is characteristically eager to learn.

If, however, he is not ready to use these forces positively, he may become a disruptive element in the classroom. He will distract others. He will clown. It soon becomes evident when he is beyond his depth and could use his abilities more positively in kindergarten.

Another interesting misuse of the 6-year-old's talents may be exercised in his tall tales. His imagination can reach shaky heights. Parents need to be warned that when a 6-year-old comes home telling about the awful things his teacher has done to him, such as spanking him or making him eat large quantities of food in the lunch room, they had better not act until the real truth has been fathomed. Some story the child has heard at school may have triggered his imagination, and since he is the center of his own attention, these things can so easily be shifted as happening to him.

Six's enthusiasm needs necessarily to be counterbalanced by its opposite, a real lack of energy. Though he no longer needs to nap, he definitely needs to rest during naptime. It is unfortunate when the educator does not recognize this low afternoon period when six appears to wilt. The demands on his body may be such that he even has a slight temperature. He could recover his energy far better if his schedule permitted a play nap at home in the early afternoon.

The 6-year-old's day may not seem too long and demanding to the school authorities, but the release of tension which takes place on his arrival at home suggests overstrain. This tensional release is expressed in various ways by different children. Some run around the house wildly. Others explode in temper tantrums. Still others cry or pick fights. Eventually illness may intervene. When six is ill he does not easily contain his illness. A cold may rapidly spread to his ears or his lungs.

A perfect school day for a 6-year-old (actually in effect in some European countries) would be from 10 to 2 o'clock with a happy time out for lunch at school. This would give him good time to dawdle at home before going to school in the morning, and would also give him time for a play nap in the afternoon on his return home after school.

EXAMINATION

Six is eager to have his turn. If the examiner enters his classroom to fetch another child, the 6-year-old tends to clamor for his own turn. Children of this age are sparkling in their enthusiasm and tend to run along ahead of the examiner. It is the examiner who needs to keep up with six, both on the way to the examining room and in the examination.

Interview

Six gives his age with ease and also gives the correct month of his birthday. Girls know the day, but boys will need to wait another year before they know the more precise date of their birthday. Six reports with the feeling of remembered experience about his birthday party. No one likes a party better than a 6-year-old. Blowing out the candles and playing the games intrigue him most.

When asked about siblings, six is still likely to report on the siblings he doesn't have, as "I don't have any brothers, just three sisters." Girls are a little more accurate in giving the correct ages of siblings (96% G, 78% B).

Paper and Pencil

POSTURE WHEN WRITING

Six may not shift his paper toward the nondominant side, but he does tilt his head to the nondominant side. His free hand is placed flat on the table or on his paper, with fingers spread. If he makes an error or a poor start he is apt to scribble over it rather than erasing it as he will do at 7.

OVERFLOW

Six does not sit quietly. He is likely to balance on the back two legs of his chair, and if he tries to balance on one, as he may do, he is likely to fall off. His tongue is more controlled than at 5½. Now he tries to inhibit it by pushing it against his lower lip or cheek. Fingers frequently are brought to the mouth, especially the two little ones. The 6-year-old not only clamps down on his fingers, but he chews his pencil and any loose tabs of clothing available, especially a collar or a sash. He presses so hard as he writes that he is apt to break his pencil.

Throat clearing can become so marked in the child of this age that it may be like a tic. This, however, occurs in the less typical or less mature child, the one who needs protection.

Six often accompanies his responses with hand gestures, rotating his hands outward. His eyes sweep laterally.

A delightfully typical 6-year-old response is the use of the expletive "Oh!" This indicates a sudden insight, a sudden breakthrough. Five was often stuck and needed to be shown laboriously piece-by-piece or bit-by-bit how to extricate himself. Six releases on his own.

WRITING NAME

Here and from now on, all children can print their first name, and over half (58% of boys, 66% of girls) print whole last name as well. Base line is predominantly wavy, size still only "fairly" consistent.

Nearly all (94% G, 92% B) use capitals and small letters correctly. Only 6% of girls, 2% of boys still reverse, but 22% of each sex still make substitute letters.

Placement is moving toward the left upper corner of the page. More than half place last name correctly in relation to first name and 30% of girls, 42% of boys leave a correct space between names.

Copy Forms

CIRCLE

Ninety percent of girls, 66% of boys start circle at the top. Nearly all use one line only and the majority of girls, 60% of boys, draw in a CCW direction.

CROSS

Virtually all use two lines. Vertical line first downward, horizontal line next L to R.

SQUARE

Most girls, 68% of boys use one line only. Starting side is left downward. The majority use a continuous CCW line.

TRIANGLE

Number of lines used varies from child to child. Most start with a downward stroke at the left side. The majority draw in a noncontinuous direction.

DIVIDED RECTANGLE

Outside pattern. By far the majority draw one continuous line. Fifty-six percent of girls and 44% of boys draw this line CCW. The majority draw their first line down the left side.

Inside pattern. Responses are highly varied but for the first time the majority of both sexes (66% of girls, 58% of boys) use some four-line variation.

DIAMOND

Horizontal. A highly variable response though the largest number of both sexes draws some type of continuous line.

Vertical. Same.

CYLINDER AND CUBE

The largest number still copy the cylinder as a circle, the face-on cube as a square, and do not attempt the point-on cube.

ORGANIZATION OF FORMS ON PAGE

Girls. Size is, for the last age, variable (38%). Forty-six percent of subjects use a horizontal sector of the page, though 64% use half page or more. Thirty-six percent place forms in horizontal order, mostly in correct order. The largest number use more than three horizontal rows.

Boys. Size is variable in 30%, but another 30% make figures which increase gradually in size. The largest number (36%) use a horizontal sector of the paper, though 52% still use half page or more. Forty-four percent now make forms in horizontal order, mostly in correct order and in three+ rows.

Numbers

GIRLS

Forty-two percent of girls write numbers from 1 to 20. Still ½ inch or more in size. The majority (64%) use front of paper. Forty-four percent reverse some figures: 18% once, 26% more than once. Figures reversed most frequently are 7, 3, and 9. Ten percent write 20 as 02. Only 4% reverse order. Largest single number make one line only (26%). First line breaks at 10 (14%), 12 (12%), or 13 (12%). Base line, spacing, and relative size of figures are all uneven. It is the superior child at this age who has no reversals.

BOYS

One to twenty, now and at all following ages. Still over ½ inch or more in size. The largest number (64%) use front of the paper. Only 34% reverse any figures: 22% once, 12% more than once. Figures 9 and 7 are reversed most often. Sixteen percent write 20 as 02. Only 2% reverse order. The largest number (34%) make one line. First line breaks at 20 (20%) or 10 (14%). Base line, spacing, and relative size of figures are all uneven. Six percent orient figures vertically; and 12% turn page sideways to make figures.

Incomplete Man

GIRLS

Number of parts. 9.96.

Arm. Upper third, pointed up but still too long.

Fingers. More or less correct shape but too long.

Leg. Forty-two percent each place leg correctly or too far out. It is too straight and too short.

Foot. Pointed correctly, good length.

Eyes. Placed correctly, even, matching. Mostly small filled circles.

Ear. Too low, good size, or too small, poor shape.

Hair. Too few, too far around, more or less good length.

Neck treatment.   Forty-six percent now make neckline, neck,and bow.

Extras.   Only 24% add any extras, mostly buttons or marks on nose or mouth.

Naming.   Most name figure "man."

Facial expression.   Most fail facial expression and how the man looks, but 68% can tell how he feels. Some negative emotion leads. Fifty-two percent can say how they know—42% saying because of the mouth.

BOYS

Number of parts.   9.56.

Arm.   Upper third of body line, pointed up, too long.

Fingers.   More or less correct shape, but too long.

Leg.   Too far out, too widespread, too short.

Foot.   Pointed right, but too long.

Eyes.   Placed correctly, even, and matching. Most are small filled circles, large open circles or small open circles.

Ear.   Placed correctly (48%), too big, 44% with some kind of indent.

Hair.   Too few, placed either more or less right or too far around; either too long or more or less correct length.

Neck treatment.   The majority make neckline, neck, or bow, with 32% making all three. Twenty-eight percent making neckline and neck only.

Extras.   Only 20% make any extras.

Naming.   Most name figure "man," though 24% (a high point) call him "boy."

Facial expression.   Most fail facial expression and how the man looks, but 48% can tell how he feels. Thirty-four percent give some positive emotion; 36% some negative emotion.

Visual One

GIRLS

Eighty-six percent now respond correctly to all 12 forms. Sixty-eight percent make fair closure. Sixty percent start more than half their circles at the top and 66% make more than half CCW.

BOYS

Ninety percent respond correctly to all 12 forms. Fifty-six percent make fair closure. Sixty-four percent start more than half their circles at the top and 62% make more than half CCW.

Visual Three

Average number correct: 5.7, both sexes.

Average number of lines used: the largest number (42% G, 44% B) use all four lines.

Fifty percent or more of 6-year-olds can name eye, eyebrow, elbow, One, Card III.

Fifty percent or more attempt: Forms One and Two, Card I; Forms One and Two, Card II; Form One, Cards III and IV.

Right and Left

NAMING PARTS

Fifty percent or more of 6-year-olds can name eye, eyebrow, elbow, thumb, and pointer finger (with demonstration). Over 50% give middle finger some correct name (middle, tall); and over 50% give little finger some correct name.

NAMING RIGHT AND LEFT

Fifty percent of girls, 62% of boys, show or name all correctly; 18% of girls, 20% of boys give all opposite.

For right hand only, 34% of each sex name correctly; added to this are 36% of girls and 34% of boys who show right hand correctly.

Reasons for knowing one side from the other: girls say either their mother told them or they write (or eat) with it. For boys the main reason is that their mother told them or because they pledge allegiance with right hand.

NAMING EXAMINER'S RIGHT HAND

Sixty-four percent named correctly.

SINGLE COMMANDS

All can obey all of the commands. Average time of response per command is 2.3 seconds.

DOUBLE COMMANDS

Only commands 4, 6, 7, and 8 are executed correctly by the majority at this age. Average time per command is 7.1 seconds.

Naming Animals

GIRLS

Now 64% can name for a minute. Mean number of animals is 8.2. Zoo animals (lion) lead as a class though "dog" is the largest single item. Forty percent still precede name of animal with "a."

BOYS

Seventy-four percent can now name for a minute. Mean number of animals named is 9.2. Zoo animals (lion) lead. Twenty-six percent still precede name of animals with "a."

Home and School Preferences

Indoors, at school, both sexes prefer some work activity (25 mentions by girls, 35 by boys). Outdoor, both still prefer gross motor activities (63 mentions by girls, 34 by boys). Indoors, at home, play with toys leads (16 mentions by girls, 28 by boys). Outdoors, gross motor activities lead in girls (40 mentions by girls). Gross motor and playing games tie in boys (15 mentions each.)

As to what they like to do best of all, girls favor a variety of activities: gross motor, some sort of creative activity, or playing games, in that order. Boys clearly favor some sort of gross motor activity.

Mosaic

BELOW AGE

Scatters singly.
Prefundamentals.
Horizontal line of single pieces, spaced or touching.
Slabs: little or no fit.
Fundamentals: 4-year-old circle or square of four squares.
A single two-piece house.

AT AGE

Slabs fitting on two sides or better; mean of three (B) or five (G) different colors.
Simple central design, successful or slightly unsuccessful.
Separate designs.
Object resembling thing named, especially:
Houses: square open house with windows and/or door and slanted roof; or several two-piece houses.
People: mostly seven-piece people.
Any simple object reasonably resembling thing named, as airplane, arrow, rocket, flag, flower.
Scene: rows of earth, houses, sky (and sun); made in horizontal rows of pieces.
Diamond, leading shape (G); square, leading shape (B).
Color use as at 5 years, less advanced than at 5½.

ABOVE AGE

Complex central design, successful in both form and color.
Fundamental: any beyond basic circle or square of four squares.
Object: cleverly fitted.
Scene: any elaborate scene beyond the 6-year-old rows of pieces.

CHAPTER 18

SEVEN YEARS

|||||||||||||||||||||||||||||||||||||||||||||||||||||||||||||||||||||||||||||||

Behavior Characteristics

The coming into good working form and enjoyment seen at 6½ years is soon to be superceded by further pulling in, even to the point of withdrawal, at 7. This withdrawal serves well to protect the 7-year-old from striking out as he did at 6 and fighting, supposedly, for his "rights." SEVEN may complain that things are unfair, but he takes his discontent out on himself rather than on others.

SEVEN can be happiest when he is off by himself. He longs for a room of his own and wants his possessions to be protected from younger siblings. A high hook on his door may be needed to keep others out.

SEVEN especially loves to draw. His drawings are full of action. He particularly likes to draw with a pencil. He likes the precision of line the sharper point of a pencil can produce. If he reads, he may become a chain reader, moving from one book to the next, each in a different stage of completion. Television can also absorb his interest.

His fears are predictable and often hard to shake. He may spend the whole summer before he goes to second grade fearing that it will be too hard for him. Knowing his teacher ahead of time and knowing where his room will be can often alleviate this fear. Once he starts to school he may worry that he will be late, since he is becoming more aware than before of clock time. The thing that finally dispels this fear of being late is actually crossing over the threshold of his classroom. His teacher would never guess his fear—he sheds it so fast when he has reached his goal.

Although SEVEN may have trouble in finishing things, completion is his greatest interest. He is so geared to finish that he is apt to continue any activity until he is exhausted. For his own protection he needs to be given limits, stopping points within his powers of sustaining. At times when he hasn't been able to finish a task at school he should be allowed to take it home to finish.

Parents complain that their 7-year-old would sit up all night to hear the end of a book they are reading him. Fortunately most books for SEVENS are broken up into chapters which allow for numerous completion points. Even SEVEN's interest in being last, as last in line, rather than first as at 6, is probably because last relates to end or completion.

SEVEN loves to write. His letters are smaller than earlier and well-formed. He is a perfectionist and craves to get 100. Any paper below 100 is not worthy to be taken home. These unworthy papers so often manage to get torn up or lost on their way home, but perfect papers are proudly saved. The morale of a 7-year-old is greatly heightened by this kind of success. Sad is the life of a SEVEN who never manages to get 100.

The greater surety of SEVEN's writing stroke, along with his smaller printing, suggest a new intellectual awareness. "Think" is one of his favorite words and his favorite activities. He may even call his brain his "thinker." Sometimes he thinks so hard that his "thinker" hurts and he develops a headache. His increase in vocabulary and understanding of words is shown by his comprehension of such words in the examination as "palm," "address," "least," and "facial expression."

He works laboriously, tries so hard, and often takes a longer time than is anticipated. Any school task is made harder if he has to transfer work from the board to his desk. His visual shift of accomodation is often slow and laborious and this makes the task of transfer very demanding. He would prefer *either* to work at his desk or at the board. How he loves to work standing at the board! He would like all the walls of his second grade classroom to be covered with blackboards so he would be certain always to get his turn working at the board.

SEVEN shows real control in all sorts of ways—control of his temper, control of striking out, control of his stroke, and control of his voice. He can now control his voice to a whisper. This was impossible at 6 years when he simply had to talk out loud. SEVEN is very aware of being yelled at, even though he can produce a penetrating scream himself.

SEVEN can develop strong deep emotions either for a classmate of the opposite sex or for his teacher. He tugs at loose pieces of his teacher's clothing to secure her attention so that he may whisper his request. Happy is SEVEN when his teacher responds to his demands and smiles upon him. He is more dependent on the teacher than his quiet ways would lead us to expect. That is one of the reasons why he can be so lost and tends to daydream when he is overplaced in third grade.

SEVEN's exhaustion is not as apparent at school as it was at 6. But he often collapses as soon as he reaches home. When he becomes ill he often has a prolonged illness. Like the 6-year-old, he too would profit by a half day at school up until Christmas. From January on, afternoon attendance can be slowly increased from two afternoons a week to a full-day attendance by spring, when he is showing a hardier stamina as he approaches 8 years of age.

EXAMINATION

SEVEN readily finds his way to the examining room alone if he has been taken there before. Since he may linger along the way, the examiner may need to check on him. He is likely to saunter. The entire tempo of the examination, in fact, tends to be slow and laborious. It may take longer than the anticipated half-hour. SEVEN doesn't like to be rushed. He wants to take his time. If he is a perfectionist then he takes extra time.

Interview

The interview is accomplished with relative speed because SEVEN knows the salient answers. He knows not only his age, but also the month and day of his birth (78% G, 76% B). Likewise he gives the current day and month correctly (78% G, 74% B). He groups and names his siblings and their ages with order and planning. SEVEN likes to classify.

Paper and Pencil

POSTURE WHEN WRITING

SEVEN shifts both his paper and his body to the nondominant side. His free hand is relaxed and he often pins down the upper corner of the paper on the nondominant side with index or middle fingers. His head may be bent way over, even down to the table top. His pencil is held tightly, close to the tip.

OVERFLOW

Overflow is especially evident during the pencil and paper tests. Under increased demands, the free hand, which was initially poised and relatively relaxed, takes on the flat spread-finger posture of the 6-year-old. On further demand, it fists. This is evidence that the child is struggling. (In a classroom situation the teacher needs to decide whether a shift in activity is indicated or whether the child should be helped to push through to completion.)

The tongue is now still, but the lower lip is drawn in. In fact it may be drawn in so much that it becomes chapped. SEVEN makes many mouth noises, often to the annoyance of others. (Time out for whistling in the classroom might satisfy this urge.)

Eyes sweep to the side and up, or move directly in an oblique upward direction. This is especially observed as a child is concentrating, as in oral arithmetic.

SEVEN shows his extreme inner fatigue by yawning. This has nothing to do with lack of sleep as a rule, especially when it is triggered specifically by an unusually difficult task.

WRITING NAME

SEVEN usually places both first and last names at the upper left hand corner of his paper. He may crowd them way to the top. Capitals and small letters are used correctly from now on. Letters are medium sized ($\frac{1}{4}$ inch) (82% G, 56% B) and consistently even (77% G, 54% B). The base line is becoming straight (50% G, 38% B) and there is good spacing between the first and second names (76% G, 74% B).

WRITING DATE

Thirty-two percent of girls, 34% of boys write the date, nearly all of these giving month and year, most giving the day. Nearly all give the correct date. Placement is highly varied; in the largest number it is written right under the name.

Copy Forms

CIRCLE

All girls and 94% of boys draw a circle top down. Most girls and 82% of boys draw in a CCW direction. Nearly all use one line only. The advanced performance of the girls is also shown in the quality of a well-shaped circle.

CROSS

Nearly all use two lines—a vertical line first drawn from top down; a horizontal line next from L to R.

SQUARE

This is the last age when the majority of both sexes use one line only. The starting side is left downward, and the direction CCW.

TRIANGLE

The number of lines varies though most use two lines. The starting side is predominantly left down. The majority draw in a noncontinuous direction. A good triangle is achieved by most (56% G, 68% B) with a good, straight base line.

DIVIDED RECTANGLE

Outside pattern. This is the last age when the majority of both sexes use a continuous line. The starting point for these continuous shapes is predominantly left side down, CCW (36% G, 56% B).

Inside pattern. Some variation of two sets of lines, crossing (70% G, 58% B).

DIAMOND

Horizontal. This is the last age when younger patterns occur. Both horizontal and vertical positions are drawn correctly (76% G, 60% B). There is great variation in manner of drawing, but most (54% G, 56% B) do draw in a continuous direction.

Vertical. Great variation though the largest number of girls (44%) have a horizontal or vertical split. Most boys (54%) draw in a continuous direction.

CYLINDER AND CUBE

The largest number copy the cylinder either as two circles in vertical orientation but separated and connected by two vertical lines down the sides, or in a fairly good form but with a flat bottom. Face-on cube is still copied as a square. Point-on cube is copied as a diamond.

ORGANIZATION OF FORMS ON PAGE

Girls. For the first time forms are of even size in nearly half the subjects (48%). Sixty-two percent still use half page or more. Figures are made horizontally and in correct order in 52%. The largest number use more than three rows.

Boys. Size of forms continues variable (34%). Placement is generally horizontal (42%). Fifty-six percent of boys use less than half the page. This compression is not maintained in following years. Forty-eight percent make forms in horizontal order.

Numbers

GIRLS

One to twenty, now and at all following ages. *Under ½ inch in size and at all following ages.* Nearly all (88%) use front of page. Only 12% reverse any figures, mostly writing 20 as 02. *No reversals of order, here and from now on.* Largest single number make 1+ lines (38%). *Base line and relative size are even here and at all following ages.* Spacing is still uneven (in 60%).

BOYS

The majority, now and hereafter, make figures under ½ inch in size. The largest number (94%) use front of paper. Only 12% reverse any figures—mostly reversals of some teen figures as 61, 71, etc. No reversal of order. The largest number (32%) make one line +. Base line and relative size now even. Spacing uneven (68%). Six percent orient figures vertically; 6% turn paper sideways to make figures.

Incomplete Man

GIRLS

Number of parts.   9.86.

Arm.   Upper third, pointed up, but too short.

Fingers.   More or less the right shape, but too long.

Leg.   Placed correctly, but too straight and too short.

Foot.   Pointed correctly, but too short.

Eyes.   Placed correctly, even, and matched. Small filled circles or pupils in an open round circle.

Ears.   Too low and a good size. Twenty-eight percent have some indentation.

Hair.   Too far around and more or less a good length, though too few.

Neck treatment.   For the first time the majority give all three parts—neckline, neck, and bow, though poorly formed.

Extras.   Only 12% add any extras.

Naming.   Sixty-four percent name figure some kind of man.

Facial expression.   Most fail facial expression, how looks and even how feels. Forty-four percent can tell that he is happy or sad. (This is less advanced than at 6 years). Some negative emotion prevails. Sixty-two percent can tell by his mouth.

BOYS

Number of parts.   9.70.

Arm.   Upper third of body line, pointed up, too long.

Fingers.   Either correct, or correct shape but too long.

Leg.   Placed too far out, too straight, and the largest number, 42%, are still too short.

Foot.   Pointed correctly with the largest number (44%) good length.

Eyes.   Placed correctly, even, and matching. Thirty-four percent now have pupils, pupil in open round circle being the leading type (22%).

Ear.   Most (46%) placed correctly. Size is correct in 44%, but shape is poor.

Hair.   Too few, more or less in the right place. Sixty percent have length more or less correct.

Neck treatment.   For the first time 50% make all three parts.

Extras.   Twenty-four percent still make extras, mostly marks on mouth.

Naming.   Some kind of man named by 58%.

Facial expression.   Most fail facial expression, how looks, and how feels. Sixty-two percent can tell whether man is happy or sad. Some negative emotions prevail. Subjects tell about emotion by the mouth (62%).

Visual One

GIRLS

Eighty-four percent respond correctly to all 12 forms. The majority (56%) make fair closure, but 40% now make good closure. Sixty-eight percent start more than half their circles at the top and 48% start all circles at the top. Sixty-four percent make more than half CCW.

BOYS

Ninety-six percent respond correctly to all 12 forms. Closure is fair in 60 percent, good in 40 percent. Fifty-four percent start more than half their circles at the top; 72% make more than half CW.

Visual Three

Average number correct: girls, 7.5; boys, 7.8.

Average number of lines used: all four lines.

Fifty percent or more respond correctly to Forms One and Two, Card I; Forms One and Two, Card II; Form One, Card III.

Fifty percent or more attempt all four figures, Card I; Forms One, Two, and Three, Card II; Form One, Card III; Forms One and Four, Card IV.

Right and Left

NAMING PARTS

Fifty percent or more of subjects can name eye, eyebrow, palm (calling it hand), elbow, and thumb; 39% can give index finger some correct name (index or pointer finger) without demonstration. Thirty percent name middle finger correctly without help; 63% can name ring finger correctly. Twenty-eight percent can name little finger as such, though over 50% call it little, baby, or pinkie.

NAMING RIGHT HAND

Eighty-two percent of girls, 68% of boys name right hand correctly; plus 10% of each sex who can show it correctly. Main reasons for knowing: for girls, that they write (or eat) with right hand; for boys, that they pledge allegiance, write, or eat with it.

NAMING EXAMINER'S RIGHT HAND

Seventy-four percent succeed in naming correctly.

SINGLE COMMANDS

Average time per command for the ten single commands is 2.1 seconds.

DOUBLE COMMANDS

Average time per command for the ten double commands is 6.4 seconds.

Naming Animals

GIRLS

Now 80% can name for a minute. Mean number of animals named is 10.9. Domestic animals (dog) now lead. Last age when name of animal may be preceded with "a."

BOYS

Eighty-eight percent can now name for a minute. Mean number of animals named is 12.5. Zoo animals (lion) still lead. Twenty-six percent still precede name of animal with "a."

Home and School Preferences

Indoors, at school, both sexes prefer some kind of work activity (43 mentions by each). Outdoors, girls still prefer gross motor (46 mentions), but boys now like to play games (34 mentions, 28 of these being some kind of ball play).

Indoors, at home, girls like most to play games or watch TV (14 mentions of each). Boys prefer play with toys (19 mentions). Outdoors, gross motor still leads in girls (32 mentions); playing games is preferred by boys (26 mentions).

As to what they like to do best of all, girls like best some gross motor activity; next best, some activity with parent, sibling, or friend. Boys clearly favor gross motor activity.

Mosaic

BELOW AGE

As at 6 years.
Failed simple central design.
Six-year-old scene with rows of grass, sky, houses, etc.
Single two-piece house.

Any simple serial placement.

Slabs: many pieces fitting on two to four sides; mean of four different colors, four to five different shapes. Variably pleasing, fit still questionably good.

Fundamental: arrow of four diamonds.

Central design: successful simple or failed complex.

Object (may be several, unrelated, on a page):

Houses: beyond open square house. Mostly solid combinations of squares or rows of two-piece houses.

People: well-constructed, scalene limbs usually one-piece limb.

Arrows and rockets of rows of paired diamonds.

Scene, especially things lined up in serial placement. Sky area diminishing.

Squares and diamonds are the leading shapes.

Full color pattern repeating form is the leading type of color use.

ABOVE AGE

Fundamentals: diamond of four diamonds or star of eight diamonds.

Successful complex central design.

Object: complex, nicely fitted pieces, good proportion.

Objects: any with clever fit.

Scene: complex effective total design.

CHAPTER 19

EIGHT YEARS

IIIIIIIIIIIIIIIIIIIIIIIIIIIIIIIIIIIIIIIIIIIIIIIIIIIIIIIIIIIIIIIIIIIIIIIIIIII

Behavior Characteristics

EIGHT does indeed have a hardier stamina than did SEVEN. He is no longer the gentle reed who needed protection and special planning. Most marked is the improvement in his health. Now if he catches a cold he seems able to throw it off in no time. He can bounce back.

There is a new kind of flow in him, a flow of ease in expression, and ease in communication. He reports fully on the happenings at school when he reaches home. This delights his mother who may earlier have felt decidedly out of touch.

EIGHT feels a part of his school group whether he is in a reading group or a sports group. He can now bide his time and take his turn. Participation in a group means more to him than just getting his own turn, though he still wants to have his chance. He is beginning to project beyond his own immediate needs, recognizing that other people have lives apart from him—that things don't happen just for him.

He is equipped to take on this new role with his new capacity of speed and his new swift encompassing of wholes and seeing things in a flash. His ease of shifting his focus from far to near, from blackboard to desk and back again to board gives further evidence of a new capacity.

Whereas earlier the job had to be carefully geared to the child's capacity and tailored to his method of operation, more leeway is available at 8 years. As he reads, for example, he can attack a word effectively, working it out phonetically without losing the meaning of what he was reading as he was apt to do at 7. He can also stop in the middle of a passage, talk about its meaning and bring in new material, and then return to his reading without losing the sense of the whole.

A third grade especially needs to operate as a group. It is unfortunate when any one child still operating in a laborious 7-year-old fashion is allowed to drag on the group. EIGHT is quick to criticize and is not averse to naming a slow child "stupid." It is hard to curb EIGHT's pronouncements, nor should we, if he speaks the truth. Rather the out-of-place child should be removed to where he belongs. He shouldn't be subjected to taunts which only tend to make him withdraw more than he would naturally, and make him feel miserable and out-of-place.

There is also the 8-year-old misfit who, feeling his own inadequacy, tends to bully younger children. These are the hat snatchers; they especially snatch the hats of vulnerable first grade children. These bullies seem to sense the very ones they can annoy the most and they make the lives of these younger children miserable.

These boys should be spotted early and not allowed to reach the stage of bullying. They are often remedial educational problems, needing special attention. A developmental appraisal will tell us more about such boys and about the real difficulties they are in. When we see them more clearly, our compassion rather than our ire will be stimulated.

EXAMINATION

EIGHT likes to be examined. He likes tests. He has acquired a social ease and a more direct approach that make him a delight to examine. He expresses himself easily and emphatically with his "Yow!" and his "Yikes!" The examiner can be quite natural with him, needing neither to protect him nor to goad him on. EIGHT may be sloppy in his performance, but he is no longer laborious as he was at 7. He is more ready to accept life as it is without straining for perfection as he so often did at 7. He can even laugh at himself.

Interview

The interview is dashed off with ease. EIGHT has his answers readily available. He doesn't have to stop and think about the interview questions because they relate to intimate, everyday parts of his life.

EIGHTS can give their age and the day of their birthday (already established at 7). They are well-oriented to time and give day, month, and year of the date.

From EIGHT's report on his birthday party, it becomes evident that home and birthday cake no longer occupy prime importance. It is the activity of the party, perhaps something such as going bowling, that is remembered best.

EIGHT groups his brothers and sisters nicely and reports directly: "I have three sisters and one brother," and then proceeds to name his siblings in an orderly fashion from the oldest to the youngest, giving not only their ages, but perhaps what they are going to be next. There is nothing static about EIGHT. He is in movement in his thinking, as well as in his actions. He reports readily on his father's occupation, even giving some idea of any special aspects of his father's work.

Paper and Pencil

POSTURE WHEN WRITING

EIGHT has lost the tenseness of his 7-year-old self when he may even have tended to tremble. His muscles, the relationship between his extensors and his flexors, are in better balance. He is more symmetrical as he works with paper and pencil than he was at 7. He shifts his paper and also his head slightly to the nondominant side, but he tends to place his paper and to work opposite his dominant shoulder. His pencil is now held more like a tool, in an adult fashion rather than with a tight grip at the tip as if it were an extension of his fingers, as it was at 7.

OVERFLOW

EIGHT shows much less straining than he did earlier. His mouth overflow has ceased. In fact his mouth may be in such repose that it may even be a little gaping. It is the often dramatic rolling of the eyes which gives EIGHT a new area for release of tension and which also gives some clue as to the mental processes that may be stimulating such movement. These processes are fluid, sparkling, and often original.

WRITING NAME AND ADDRESS

EIGHT tends to place his whole name in the upper left hand corner of the page. He is now writing cursively (54% G, 60% B).

Size is consistent and capitals and smaller letters are used correctly, at least for the name. There are no reversals or substitutions. Last name is placed properly in relation to first with good spacing between.

Though EIGHT knows his address, the correct writing of his full address is barely normative (54% G, 46% B). He has some trouble with spelling and capitals, but most trouble with punctuation. He tends to string his address out after his name on one or two lines (60%). Though he can write his name cursively, he tends to shift into printing as he makes his address.

WRITING DATE

Nearly all can write day, month, and year, with only 10% of girls making an error as to the day. Place is chiefly top left or top right of paper. The largest number, about one-third of both sexes, write the date under their address. There are occasional errors in punctuation.

Copy Forms

CIRCLE

Nearly all start the circle at the top and draw with a single line in a CCW direction. The exception is that only 74% of boys draw CCW with a single line, others drawing CW or with two lines.

CROSS

Virtually all draw with two lines, vertical line first, downward; horizontal line next, L to R.

SQUARE

Half the girls draw in a single continuous line. Boys are evenly divided between one line and two. Nearly all start with the left side in a downward direction. More than half the girls, 40% of the boys, draw in a continuous direction.

TRIANGLE

Number of lines used varies, but 50% of girls, 42% of boys use three lines. Most start with left side downward. The majority draw with several lines, left side or right side downward first, in a noncontinuous direction.

DIVIDED RECTANGLE

Outside pattern. Response is now highly varied. For the first age since 5 years, drawing in a continuous direction fails to predominate. Most start downward at the left side, but response is highly varied.

Inside pattern. Response is highly varied but 80% of girls, 72% of boys, draw some four-line variation.

DIAMOND

Horizontal. The majority of both sexes draw a successful horizontal diamond, but response is still highly varied and individual.

Vertical. A successful vertical diamond is now normative. Over half (54% G, 52% B) draw with either a horizontal or vertical split.

CYLINDER AND CUBE

Response to the cylinder is extremely varied, though a substantial number copy it correctly except that the bottom may still be made as a straight line. Face-on cube is still copied as a square. Point-on cube is still chiefly copied as a diamond.

ORGANIZATION OF FORMS ON PAGE

Girls. Forty-eight percent of girls make even figures as at 7 years. Placement is horizontal (54%). The majority (52%) still use a half page or more. Fifty percent arrange forms in a horizontal alignment, in correct order. The largest number make three rows.

Boys. Boys' forms are less even in size than are girls'. The largest number (32%) are variable. Placement is now horizontal in 44% of cases. Sixty-six percent use half the page or more. The largest number, but still less than half (42%), arrange forms horizontally and in correct order. The largest number still make three+ rows.

Numbers

GIRLS

From now on all make figures from 1 to 20. Nearly all figures ¼ inch or less. Nearly all (92%) on front of page. No reversal of figures, here and from here on. No reversal of order. The largest number (10%) have trouble other than reversal with number 20. The largest number make one line (38%) or one line+ (36%). The first line breaks at 19 (36%). Base line and relative size all even here and from here on spacing is good in 48%. Four percent orient vertically; 6% turn page and write figures.

BOYS

All figures from 1 to 20 here and following ¼ inch or less. The largest number (84%) use the front of the paper. *No reversal of figures or of order here or following.* The largest number (36%) make one line only. First line breaks chiefly at 19 (28%). *Base line, spacing, and relative size all even here and following.* Sixteen percent orient figures vertically.

Incomplete Man

GIRLS

Number of parts. 10.52.
Arm. Upper third of body line, pointed upward, too short.
Fingers. Good shape and length.
Leg. Placed well, too straight, either good length or too short.
Foot. Pointed right direction, but up too much, too short.
Eyes. Placed well, even, and matching. Forty percent now have pupils and 34% eyebrows.
Ear. Placed either correctly or too low; good size (44%). Shape very varied. Twenty-eight percent have good shape, but no indentation.
Hair. Too few hairs, placed either correctly (44%) or too far around (46%), reasonably good length.
Neck treatment. All three neck parts.
Extras. Sixteen percent make extras, mostly buttons or marks on nose or mouth.

Naming.   Fifty percent name some kind of man.

Facial expression.   For the first time, over half the subjects can give facial expression. Some negative emotion predominates.

BOYS

Number of parts.   10.17.

Arm.   Upper third of body line, pointed up, good length.

Fingers.   Correct.

Leg.   Placed well, too straight, good length (48%).

Foot.   Pointed correctly, and good length in 44%.

Eyes.   Placed well, even and matched. Forty-two percent have pupils.

Ears.   Placed well, variable size, some indentation in 36%, though not accurate.

Hair.   Too few hairs, placed well, more or less good length in 42%.

Neck treatment.   Fifty-two percent add all three parts.

Extras.   Twenty-two percent add extras, mostly marks on mouth.

Naming.   Fifty-four percent name some kind of man.

Facial expression.   Thirty-six percent now can give facial expression and 38% more tell how man feels. Some negative emotion predominates. Forty-six percent can tell because of mouth.

Visual Three

Average number correct: girls, 8.8; boys, 8.9.

Average number of lines used: all four lines.

Fifty percent or more respond correctly to: Forms One and Two, Card I; Forms One and Two, Card II; Form One on Cards III and IV.

Fifty percent or more attempt: Forms One to Four, Cards I and II; Forms One and Four, Card III; Forms One and Four, Card IV (also boys attempt Form Three, girls attempt Form Two).

Right and Left

NAMING PARTS

Fifty percent or more of subjects can name eye, eyebrows, palm, elbow, thumb, index finger (calling it index or pointer finger), and ring finger. Only 37% can name middle finger. Only 41% call little finger "little finger" on first trial, but over 50% call it little, baby, or pinkie.

NAMING EXAMINER'S RIGHT HAND

Ninety-five percent give correct answer. Main reason for knowing is "Facing a different way," or "My right is opposite yours."

Average time per command for the ten single commands is 1.8 seconds.

Average time per command for the ten double commands is 4.5 seconds.

Mean time per picture is 24.9 seconds.

Mean time per picture is 20.0 seconds.

Naming Animals

GIRLS

Now 92% can name for a minute. Mean number of animals named is 11.8. Domestic animals (dog) now lead.

BOYS

Ninety-six percent can name for a minute. Mean number of animals named is 14.5. Zoo animals (lion) lead as a class, though "dog" is the largest single item.

Home and School Preferences

Indoors at school, some sort of work activity clearly leads (mentioned 75 times by girls, 44 times by boys). Outdoors at school, gross motor activities still lead in girls (40 mentions), but playing games leads in boys (42 mentions with 30 of them playing ball).

Indoors at home, behavior is almost completely varied from child to child, though playing games leads in girls, TV in boys. Outdoors at home some sort of playing game (tag, hide-and-seek, jump rope, ball) leads, with ball play alone the leading single activity, occurring in 27 of the 50 boys.

As to what they like to do best of all, for the first time, winter or summer sports lead in girls, with some activity with parent, sibling, or friend second. Boys still prefer gross motor activity, especially some kind of ball play.

Mosaic

BELOW AGE

Any unpatterned products except slabs.
Ill-fitted slabs.

Fundamentals: basic 4-year-old circle, square of four squares, or arrow of diamonds.

Failed central design.

Failed object or very simple object as "box," two-piece house. Or open square house of squares.

Strong serial placement.

AT AGE

Slabs: colors attractive, many pieces fitting on three or more sides. Mean of four to five different colors. Mostly pleasing.

Fundamentals: diamond of four diamonds, star of eight diamonds.

Successful central design: color and pattern accurate.

Whole pattern, accurate or nearly so.

Objects: symmetric and well-formed, becoming larger. People are rather angular, or solid and symmetric, made of more pieces than at 7. Body often consists of a diamond. Limbs may have several segments, or faces or houses of two to three pieces, or large, solid, and square.

Objects: boys make mostly masculine objects as rocket, steam shovel, truck, car.

Scenes: light and airy, mostly houses and trees. Eight-year-old orientation, all over page, giving impression of perspective.

Squares the leading shape; diamonds next.

Color: blue leads in both. White second in girls; black in boys. Leading color use in girls is naturalistic; in boys, full color repeating form.

ABOVE AGE

Fundamentals: diamond of nine diamonds or circle of twelve scalenes.

Object: cleverly designed or with ingenious touches, or people in action.

Highly complex, balanced central design, correct as to color and form.

Single pieces stand for objects.

Scenes, attractive, effective, and beyond 8-year-old orientation.

CHAPTER 20

NINE YEARS

〰〰〰〰〰〰〰〰〰〰〰〰〰〰〰〰〰〰〰

Behavior Characteristics

It is NINE's independence that characterizes him best. He is less dependent on the adult than he was at 8, both at home and at school, and needs far less control and supervision.

Now the child is busy with his friends, with his activities, and with his hobbies. He is less interested in being with his parents, and more interested in being with his friends. He especially enjoys competing with his friends to try out his skills. He can spend hours perfecting a skill.

His reading comes within this area of perfecting. Though there are many early readers, this is the first age when the majority of children begin to read silently on their own.

NINE's interests are so varied and so numerous that his days are almost too full. Each afternoon is filled with some activity—music lessons, dancing, Cub Scouts or Brownies, choir practice—always something. He is driven by time, but he hates to give anything up.

NINE's main problem is that he worries and tends to complain. Any task that he doesn't wish to do, any task which seems hard to him, will not merely be refused as earlier. Now he gives some plausible reason why he can't do it. His complaints are usually related to some required task. If he is to practice the piano, his hands hurt. If he is to eat some food he dislikes, his jaw hurts him. If he is to study his homework, his eyes hurt. One usually can ride over these complaints, but not always.

There are some abdominal complaints of pain which, if they *persist*, should be looked into. A differential diagnosis between an acute appendicitis and enlarged mesenteric nodes may be needed to determine whether an operation should be performed.

Fourth grade should ideally be a grade of high achievement. NINE's interest and ability to work out the process of his thinking, along with his interest in perfecting his skills, allows for independent work. Reading is now on sure ground and is moving independently. NINE not only can figure out words on his own, but can look up their meaning in the dictionary.

To observe a 9-year-old group at work is indeed a pleasure. Two or three children might be working on a map project, another two or three might be looking up information in an encyclopedia. Others are busy at their desk work, so concentrated that they may not even notice a visitor.

These are the NINES who are ready for the demands of the grade. These are the NINES who are capable of independent work, both at school and at home. They are like cream that rises to the top. Alas, those who are not ready are truly the dregs which fall to the bottom. Such children should be rescued from a situation where they do not fit, and replaced in a situation where they too can strive.

This discrepancy of ready and not ready is clearly seen in fourth grade. The unready are not capable of independent work. One can pick them out quickly in a fourth grade classroom, watching them trail their teacher, asking many questions about what they are to do and how they are to do it. Such children are a drag on the class and on themselves. NINES are not as cruel as EIGHTS in criticizing other children or in calling them stupid. NINE's thoughts are actually concerned more with ability than with lack of ability. He knows who is best in math, best in drawing, best in sports. He makes these pronouncements as facts.

Fourth grade is no situation for an immature 9-year-old who should be in third where he can more readily mesh with the group and where his inabilities will not stand out so strongly. In fact, these inabilities may only be related to an excessive demand. Properly placed in third grade such a child may achieve well.

EXAMINATION

NINE shows the same enjoyment in being examined that EIGHT does. He is ready and eager to test his skills. He likes the challenge of being timed.

Interview

NINE is capable as was EIGHT of responding correctly and quickly to questions about his age, birthday, and names and ages of siblings. He gives away his age when he reports on his birthday party. Boys will have nothing to do with girls at their parties. They would prefer to do something special with one or two friends. Girls exclude boys, but with less passion. They, too, may prefer doing something special with one or two friends rather than inviting a large group of friends. However, if they do have a large group the fun of a party with lots of relay races is very challenging to them.

Paper and Pencil

POSTURE WHEN WRITING

NINE may not have shifted much from his 8-year-old posture. However he tends to shift his paper markedly, almost through 90 degrees, thus making the vertical side of his paper parallel with the table edge. At the same time he shifts his trunk so that his legs and feet point to the side. His free hand usually steadies his paper half way down the edge.

His head initially is bent to the nondominant side, but as he writes across the page his head moves through an arc ending up on the dominant side as he reaches the edge of his paper. This shift in posture repeats itself as he traverses succeeding trips across the page. His pencil grasp is sure and may differentiate in special posturing. This gives him excellent control of his stroke, which may acquire the perfection of copy book.

OVERFLOW

NINE does not show much overflow. He may pick at his teeth in his precise way. Or he may piano his fingers, but he no longer rolls his eyes as he did at 8. Rather, eyes fixate sharply.

WRITING NAME AND ADDRESS

NINE is schooled in the practice of writing name and address, with town and state included. Placement is for the most part in the upper left hand corner of the page (78% G, 76% B) on three lines. NINE writes not only his name cursively, but his entire address (70% G, 68% B), often forming his letters in a tight but rounded fashion so characteristic of the acquired skill of his age. There is a consistency of size, straight base line, and good use of capitals. Correct punctuation still needs to be mastered.

WRITING DATE

Nearly all write day, month, year with only an occasional error as to the day. Place of writing is chiefly top left or top right of the page. Most write either directly under the name or directly under their address. There are still a few errors in punctuation.

Copy Forms

CIRCLE

Nearly all draw the circle with a single line CCW, starting at the top.

CROSS

Virtually all use two lines, vertical first downward, horizontal next L to R.

SQUARE

Number of lines varies. Most draw left side downward first. Pattern is highly varied.

TRIANGLE

For the first time use of three lines is normative. Most draw left side down first, and draw in a discontinuous manner.

DIVIDED RECTANGLE

Outside Pattern. Response is becoming increasingly varied. Most use two or more lines. Only 18% of girls and 26% of boys draw in a continuous direction.

Inside Pattern. Nearly all use some variation of

DIAMOND

Horizontal. Half the girls, 40% of boys, draw with either a horizontal or vertical split. This type of response is increasing.

Vertical. Most (66% of girls, 64% of boys) make either a horizontal or a vertical split. This type of response is increasing.

CYLINDER AND CUBE

The cylinder is now copied correctly by the majority except that the bottom line still tends to be a straight rather than a curved line. Face-on cube is chiefly copied as two or three squares in vertical alignment. Point-on cube is now copied correctly by a third of subjects except that bottom line is straight across. However 30% of boys make it correctly.

ORGANIZATION OF FORMS ON PAGE

Girls. Fifty percent of girls now make even figures. Nearly half (48%) place forms horizontally. Figures are large—86% use one half page or more. The majority (52%) arrange forms in horizontal order, 44% in correct order. The largest number again use three+ lines.

Boys. Less than half but the largest number (36%) make forms of even size. Forty-six percent place forms horizontally. Sixty-four percent fill one half page or more. The largest number (40%) arrange forms horizontally and in order. Most use three lines only.

Numbers

GIRLS

All complete figures one to twenty. All figures are ¼ inch or less. Eighty-six percent use front of page. No reversal of figures or of order. First line breaks at 19 (26%). Base line, spacing, relative size all even. Largest number (40%) make one line. Highest vertical orientation on page of any age. Ten percent orient vertically; 2% turn page to write figures.

BOYS

One to twenty: all figures ½ inch or less, largest group 3⁄16 (28%). Largest number (86%) on front of page. No reversal of figures or order. Twenty-six percent use one line only. First line breaks at 19 (30%). Six percent orient figures vertically; 6% turn paper sideways.

Incomplete Man

GIRLS

Number of parts. 10.56.
Arm. Upper third of body line, pointed up, good length in 46%.
Finger. Good fingers.
Leg. Good placement, too straight down, good length.
Foot. Pointed correctly but up too much; good length in 46%.
Eyes. Placed well, even, and matching. Forty-eight percent now have pupils, and 36% eyebrows.
Ears. Placed well, good size, and 36% have good shape.
Hair. Too few, good placement, good length.
Neck treatment. Fifty-eight percent give all three parts.
Extras. Thirty percent add extras, mostly buttons or marks on nose or mouth.
Naming. Sixty-two percent name some kind of man. Twenty-six percent (a high point) name "person."
Facial expression. Eighty percent now can answer facial expression, but response is varied. Thirty-eight percent still give some negative emotion only. Fifty-four percent tell by the mouth.

BOYS

Number of parts.　10.50.

Arm.　Well placed, pointed up, but length variable.

Fingers.　Good fingers.

Leg.　Forty-two percent place leg well (slightly fewer than at 8 years). Leg is too straight, variable length.

Foot.　Pointed correctly, good length in 48%, pointed up too much in 46%.

Eyes.　Placed well, even, and matched. Fifty percent have pupils.

Ears.　Placed well, good size, 38% have some indentation.

Hair.　Too few, good place, good length.

Neck Treatment.　Sixty percent give all three parts.

Extras.　Thirty percent make extras, mostly marks on mouth.

Naming.　Fifty-six percent name some kind of man.

Facial Expression.　Eighty-six percent now can give facial expression, the first age this number exceeds 50%. Some negative emotion predominates. Subject tells because of the mouth.

Visual Three

Average number correct: girls, 10.5; boys, 10.3.

Average number of lines used: all four lines.

Fifty percent or more respond correctly to: All four forms, Card I; Forms One, Two, and Four on Card II; Form One on Cards III and IV.

Fifty percent or more attempt: Forms One through Four, Cards I and II; Forms One and Four on Card III (also boys attempt Form Two, girls attempt Form Three); Forms One, Two, and Four on Card IV.

Right and Left

NAMING PARTS

Fifty percent or more of subjects can name eye, eyebrow, palm, elbow, thumb, index finger (calling it index or pointer finger) and ring finger. Only 37% can name middle finger. Only 41% call little finger "little finger," but over 50% call it little, baby, or pinkie.

EXAMINER'S RIGHT

Ninety-six percent now give correct answer. The main reason for knowing is "Facing a different way" or "My right is opposite yours."

SINGLE COMMANDS

Average time per command for the ten single commands is 1.2 seconds.

DOUBLE COMMANDS

Average time per command for the ten double commands is 2.6 seconds.

RIGHT AND LEFT PICTURES, VERBAL RESPONSE

Mean time per picture for the three pictures is 14.9.

RIGHT AND LEFT PICTURES, MOTOR RESPONSE

Mean time per picture for the three pictures is 18.9.

Naming Animals

GIRLS

Now 90% can name for a minute. Mean number of animals named is 14.7. Domestic animals (dog) lead.

BOYS

Ninety-two percent can name for a minute. Mean number of animals named is 13.7. Zoo animals (lion) lead as a class, though "dog" is the largest single item.

Home and School Preferences

Indoors at school, some sort of work activity clearly leads, with 77 mentions by girls, 61 by boys. Outdoors at school, playing games leads (47 mentions by girls, 50 by boys). There are 45 mentions of some kind of ball play by boys.

Indoors at home there continues to be great variety as earlier, though playing games and TV lead. Outdoors at home, playing games leads, with 30 mentions of ball play in boys.

As to what they like to do best of all, girls still favor winter or summer sports. In boys, gross motor activity, especially some sort of ball play, is by far the favorite.

Mosaic

BELOW AGE

Any unpatterned designs except slabs.
Fundamentals below level listed here as at age.
Failed object or central design.
Open square house.
Any 7-year-old (serial) or 8-year-old (odd orientation) scenes.

Slabs, multicolored, pleasing, good fit; larger and beginning to open out slightly. Most use all shapes.

Fundamentals: eight-piece star or nine-piece diamond of diamonds, or circle of twelve scalenes.

Central designs: successful or nearly so as to both form and color. Becoming larger, more solid and much more complex.

Several separate central designs.

Occasional pieces placed over others for emphasis.

Patterned design filling whole tray.

Objects, varied, successful. Some solid; some angular use of scalenes and diamonds.

Objects:

> People made of more pieces than earlier, 7–19 pieces. Bodies may be made of squares.
>
> Rockets may resemble people.
>
> Houses: Two-piece, alone or in rows; or solid squares.

Scenes: beyond 8-year-old orientation. Very varied. Some all blue or black. Action in some.

Diamonds are the leading shape, squares are second in girls; boys, the opposite.

Color: blue leads, black second. Level of color use predominating is naturalistic in girls, full color pattern repeating form in boys.

Solid 10-year-old object or design, mostly of squares.

Well-planned, attractive scenes.

CHAPTER *21*

TEN YEARS

‖‖

Behavior Characteristics

The tense achievement of 9 is relaxed at 10. "Casual" is the word that best describes the 10-year-old. Like his 5-year-old self, he once again likes to be close to home and mother. He may spontaneously wish to give up many of his afternoon activities. He needs to be helped to pick and choose what would be best to give up and what would be best to continue.

TEN likes to anchor near home, possibly within a radius of a few blocks. He moves around this area freely on his bike. It is the casual activity and meeting which he enjoys most, more than things that are highly planned and structured. He likes to linger in his contacts without needing to meet a time schedule. He likes to rule time, rather than being ruled by it.

Issues that needed to be tackled at younger ages can now be passed over, because he is so good-natured and nice to have around the house. There is, though, one issue which eventually needs to be faced head on by most parents. TEN's casualness usually extends too far within the realm of not wishing to bathe.

The old-fashioned Saturday night bath would be most congenial to him, but two or three baths a week will keep him cleaner. Planning and forewarning produce the best results. The wise parent will warn TEN before dinner that tonight is bath night. This warning, along with less frequent demands for bathing and perhaps adequate shower equipment for boys, takes away TEN's tendency to argue back about this important function.

TEN has surprising scope in his interests. He seems capable of absorbing many different areas. He is an avid television watcher and retains so well that he may be able to retell every detail of what he has seen. However, he is apt to retell so literally without any highlights that his rehearsal can go on too long. His memorizing powers can be utilized in more effective ways. This is a time for more oral than written work. Give TEN the chance and he'd return to school on Saturday morning if he could just have the chance to talk.

Reading may be as important to him as talking. This is the age when flashlights are used for reading under the covers in bed after the official lights are out. (This will be worse at 11.) Books about great men intrigue the child of this age. He especially likes to read about their childhoods. He identifies with them and experiences his first real taste of hero-worship.

Though the act of writing itself is not too difficult for TEN, organizing his thoughts for writing is not easy. He is also more easily distracted than he was at 9, and less critical of himself and of his accomplishments. A book report of two or three lines may seem adequate to him. Talking into a tape recorder might suit him better. Then he could more easily expand and embellish.

TEN's fondness for his teacher is like that for his parents. In fact, he may inadvertently call his teacher "Mommy." He likes it when his teacher provides a casual atmosphere resembling that of home. This casual atmosphere can permit the spread of interest that TEN needs, and much can be accomplished at school especially if not too much polish and perfection are demanded.

EXAMINATION

TEN's casual nature is evident in the examination situation and this causes the examiner to treat him in a more adult fashion.

Interview

The interview is tossed off with ease and accuracy. TEN gives the same casual attention to reporting on any birthday activities that he does to life events in general.

Paper and Pencil

POSTURE WHEN WRITING

TEN returns to an earlier more symmetrical posture, giving up the strong tendency to shift both his paper and his trunk to one side so characteristic of 9. His arms may be held akimbo.

WRITING NAME AND ADDRESS

TEN shows both ease and individuality in writing his name and address, placing them usually in the left upper corner of the paper on three lines as when addressing an envelope. Cursive writing is now well established (75% G, 86% B) and the structure of writing is loosened, having lost the tight form of a year ago. TEN maintains a straight base line, good size consistency, good spacing between words, good use of capitals, but punctuation still tends to be faulty.

WRITING DATE

All children write day, month, and year correctly. The largest number write at the top left of the paper and most write directly under the address. A few still make errors in punctuation.

Copy Forms

CIRCLE

Nearly all start at the top, use a single line, and draw in a CCW direction.

CROSS

Ninety-four percent of girls, 96% of boys use two lines, draw vertical line first downward. Eighty-six percent of both sexes draw horizontal line L to R.

SQUARE

Response is highly varied. Forty-four percent of girls, 30% of boys use one line only. However, many, boys especially, use either two or four lines. Most start with left side down, but fewer (44% G, 36% B) draw in a single continuous direction.

TRIANGLE

Use of three lines is normative for both sexes as at 9 years. Nearly all make the first line down the left side. By far the majority draw in a noncontinuous pattern.

DIVIDED RECTANGLE

Outside pattern. Responses are highly varied. Only about one-third draw in a continuous manner. About a third more use some one of the more common multiline variations (see Table 23, p. 88).

Inside pattern. For the first time some type of

pattern is normative in both sexes. With few small exceptions this method of drawing has been increasing steadily.

DIAMOND

Horizontal. A horizontal or vertical split is normative in girls. Responses of boys are still highly varied.

Vertical. A horizontal or vertical split is normative in both sexes.

CYLINDER AND CUBE

A substantial number of girls and over half the boys copy the cylinder correctly except that some use more or less than the conventional four lines. Face-on cube is still made in a highly varied manner, only 2% of girls and 20% of boys copying it correctly. Point-on cube is made correctly by over half except that the bottom line may still be straight across. However 34% of girls and 46% of boys copy it correctly.

ORGANIZATION OF FORMS OF PAGE

Girls. Seventy percent now make forms of even size. Sixty-six percent place them horizontally. For the first time over half (60%) use less than one-half page. Orientation is horizontal and in correct order in 54%. Most use three rows.

Boys. Nearly half (46%) now make forms of even size. Placement is horizontal (54%), but boys (66%) still use one-half page or more. Orientation is horizontal and in correct order in 52%. Most use three lines.

Numbers

GIRLS

All complete figures 1 through 20. All figures ¼ inch or less. Ninety percent use front of page only. No reversals of figure or order. First line breaks at 19 (16%).

Base line, spacing, and relative size all even. Twelve percent use commas between figures—the only age for conspicuous use of commas.

BOYS

All complete figures 1 through 20. Ninety-eight percent of figures ¼ inch or less. Largest number (72%) on front of page. No reversal of figures or order. First line breaks at 19 (26%). Base line, spacing, and relative size all even. Twelve percent use commas between figures, the only age for conspicuous use of commas.

Incomplete Man

GIRLS

Number of parts. 10.24.

Arm. Upper third of body line, pointed up, good length.

Fingers.   Good fingers.

Leg.   Forty-six percent place leg correctly. Forty-six percent each have it slanted correctly and 46% too straight. Length is good.

Foot.   Pointed correctly; good length.

Eyes.   Placed correctly, even, and matched. Fifty-four have pupils, 42% eyebrows.

Ear.   Placed correctly, good size, 40% are of good shape.

Hair.   Too few, but placed correctly and of good length.

Neck treatment.   Neck and bow only now predominate (58%).

Extras.   Twenty percent add extras, mostly marks on mouth.

Naming.   The majority (60%) name figure some kind of man.

Facial expression.   Ninety-four percent can now give facial expression. Negative emotions predominate (34%).

BOYS

Number of parts.   10.44.

Arm.   Upper third, pointed up, good length.

Fingers.   Good fingers.

Leg.   Placed well, slanted correctly; good length.

Foot.   Pointed correctly, good length, but 42% point up too far.

Eyes.   Placed correctly, even, and matching. Forty-two percent have pupils.

Ear.   Placed correctly, good size, 30% are of good shape and 42% do have some sort of indentation.

Hair.   Too few, good place, good length.

Neck treatment.   Sixty-six percent make all three parts.

Extras.   Thirty-two percent add extras, mostly marks on nose or mouth, or buttons.

Naming.   Sixty-six percent name some kind of man.

Facial expression.   Ninety percent now can give facial expression. Some positive emotion now predominates (44%). Expression is told by the mouth.

Visual Three

Average number correct: 11.2.

Average number of lines used: all four.

Fifty percent or more respond correctly to: all forms on Cards I and II; all but Form Two on Card III; Form One on Card IV.

Fifty percent or more attempt: all.

Right and Left

NAMING PARTS

Fifty percent or more of subjects can name eye, eyebrow, palm, elbow, thumb, middle finger, ring finger, index finger (calling it index or pointer finger). Thirty-six percent name little finger "little finger;" but over 50% call it little finger, baby finger, pinkie, or small finger.

EXAMINER'S RIGHT

All now can give a correct response. The main reason continues to be "Facing a different way" or "My right is opposite yours."

SINGLE COMMANDS

Average time per command for the ten single commands is 1.1 seconds.

DOUBLE COMMANDS

Average time per command for the ten double commands is 2.3 seconds.

VERBAL PICTURES

Mean time per picture is 12.2 seconds.

MOTOR PICTURES

Mean time per picture is 12.4 seconds.

Naming Animals

GIRLS

Now 96% can name for a minute. Mean number of animals named is 15. Domestic animals (cat, dog) lead.

BOYS

Ninety-eight percent can name for a minute. Mean number of animals named is 16. Zoo animals (lion) lead as a class, though "cat" is the largest single item.

Home and School Preferences

Some sort of work activity still leads as the favorite indoor school activity (72 mentions by girls, 69 by boys). Outdoors, at school, playing games leads (63 mentions by girls, 88 by boys), with ball play by far the leading single item as usual, mentioned 74 times by boys.[1]

Indoors at home, play varies widely. Outdoors at home, playing games (40 mentions by girls, 65 by boys) leads with 50 of these mentions by boys being some sort of ball play.

[1] This number exceeds the total number of boys since different kinds of ball play might be mentioned by the same boy.

As to what they like to do best of all, some sort of gross motor activity leads in both sexes, with horseback riding beginning to be popular for girls.

Mosaic

BELOW AGE

Any unpatterned designs except slabs.
Any fundamentals.
Failed designs or objects.
Open square house or two-piece house.

AT AGE

Slabs: most opening out, most pieces fitting on most sides. Pleasing. Mean of six different colors.
Central designs: complex, well-patterned, accurate color use.
Successful design filling whole tray.
Objects successful. Mostly rockets and people. Men and rockets may resemble each other. Houses fairly solid combinations of squares. People's bodies mostly squares. Some "clever" designs as "fireplace with fire," "octopus," "bird."
Many scenes, more complex but still not well-proportioned or attractive as in the teens. Houses frequent. In boys, rockets in action the main theme.
Very strong use of squares which lead in boys, with diamonds second.
Color use is naturalistic in girls. In boys, full color pattern repeating form.

ABOVE AGE

Complex central designs, open and spaced. Color may add complexity to form.
Several separate, successful, patterned designs.
Extremely clever use of pieces.
Attractive and well-proportioned scenes.
Symbolic or abstract productions.

PART IV
TO PARENTS AND EDUCATORS

THERE ARE THREE PEOPLE VITALLY IMPORTANT TO THE LIFE AND well-being of the school-age child—the parent, the teacher, and the principal. The relationship of these three can be very smooth and productive when all goes well. When problems arise, however, this relationship can sometimes reach the breaking point.

Often problems arise because these three persons are looking at the child from different points of view. A parent may be demanding a child's legal rights without judging his capacity to fulfill these rights. The educator, represented either by the teacher or principal, may be thinking too much about a child's seeming resistance to learning or his disruption of a group, without sufficiently considering the why of his behavior. As with the parent, the educator may also fail to judge correctly a child's capacity to do what is being asked of him.

Both camps of home and school need to be brought together so that they are looking at the same child *as he is* and not as they want him to be. It is to help both that we have devised the developmental examination, which can usually be viewed and understood by both if each has the willingness to look.

Fortunately, a child reveals himself truly in his response to the developmental examination. He cannot be trained to pass it. He may be taught some single bits of behavior, but he gives himself away in so many other ways that his response inevitably gives a true picture of his capacity. Thus the child shows us his true self, the very self we are after, the very self that determines our choice of what we need to provide for him educationally.

Those parents who sometimes attempt to coach their children to pass examinations do so because they are not sufficiently informed about the laws of growth. It is for the educator to devise a method and a means by which a parent can become a partner, rather than a possible hindrance in the education of his child.

It is for this reason that we propose a fourth person who can be of basic importance to the child in school. Initially we may consider the task of this fourth person to be mainly in the field of developmental examining. We may call him (or her) the developmental examiner. His duty is to give us a summary picture of a child's rate and method of growth, and of his level of behavior growth—as to quantity and quality.

A developmental appraisal can become a talking link between home and school, but it is still only one contributing factor toward arriving at a final decision as to what is best for a child. The child needs also to be judged by his behavior both in his home and in his school group. This is why we might suggest enlarging the scope of the developmental examiner into a larger role of what might be termed a "developmental guidance coordinator." It is the kind of assignment that a person would need to grow into.

The work of such an individual would include not only developmental examination of the individual children, but also observations in the classrooms and conferences with each teacher. In addition, interviews with the parents would enable the coordinator to find out more about each child's home behavior and his past development, and to interpret developmental findings for the parent. The final coordinating task would come in imparting all of this information to the principal, who would then be ready to make any final decision about the child.

Each of these four individuals will be discussed separately in an attempt to present our version of their separate roles and to suggest ways and means by which they can support each other for the ultimate good of the child. They will be discussed in the order of their importance to the child: the parent, the teacher, the developmental examiner, and the principal. However, in the final analysis, the decision of the principal may be the most important for the educational welfare of the child.

CHAPTER 22

PARENTS

‖‖‖

This chapter is addressed primarily to parents of kindergarten, first, and second grade children. This is because the principles of this book—that all children should have the privilege of starting school when and only when they are ready, that they should be correctly grouped and that they should be allowed to proceed at a rate which fits their own individual development—are most effectively put into practice in these earliest school years.

For those parents whose children are already past these earliest grades, the same educational principles hold true. We hope that if any readers whose children may be beyond these early grades suspect from what we have to say that their children may be having school difficulties as a result of being, even in the upper grades, overplaced or wrongly placed, they will at least check carefully on this possibility with the teacher or principal.

Parents on the whole are deeply interested in the education of their children. Up to a child's entrance into kindergarten they have been the chief guardians of his growth and education. Nursery schools have given much to the life of the young child, but they have acted somewhat as an extension of the home. When that moment comes for a child to be ready to enter the big public schools, new expectations often arise in the minds of most parents.

Sometimes these expectations are unrealistic and overdemanding. On the other hand, the close relationship between parent and child alerts the parent to the child's true capacity and needs, and helps him to know what might be reasonable to expect for his child from a school experience. Parents have a great deal to contribute in the area of education, and some of the most effective reforms that have taken place in this area may be traced to the demands of parents. Certainly their capacity and willingness to pay local taxes have enabled public schools to provide facilities that could not have been provided otherwise.

There was a time when the education of young children was almost completely in the hands of their parents. (Some children even now would profit by a slower induction into school and more planned home activities until they were as much as 7 or 8 years of age.) This was followed by a time when the child was given over almost completely to the educator. The parent was called in only when there was trouble.

Things have indeed changed, and now both parents and schools work together in this important matter of the education of the child. The effectiveness of their cooperation, especially in the early school years, may well determine the entire course of the child's education.

What has happened to a child in the years before he enters kindergarten or first grade will, of course, determine to a large extent how he will adjust and what he will bring to school in the way of experience. This does not mean that if he has attended a nursery school or kindergarten, he will be that much ahead and thus ready to enter school before the allotted time. Parents must keep reminding themselves that growth takes its own time. It cannot be hurried. Cultivating speed for its own sake has the inherent danger of producing a crash later on.

Nursery school can provide new meaning to the preschool years. The movement to provide more and better nursery schools has been a real boon to both parents and children. Many nursery schools consider that three years is a good age for starting. It is a time when the child is both able to separate emotionally from his parents and also to begin to adjust to a group. Three mornings a week, in our opinion, are not only adequate but probably better for the child than daily attendance. With a three-morning-a-week schedule, he is not moved too far from home base, but is provided with new interests and experiences.

Nursery school may, in many ways, be one of the most ideal educational opportunities which a child will have. Because of the small classes which most nursery schools maintain, and the minimum demands it is necessary to make of the child at that age, the nursery school can better adapt its requirements to the abilities of the child.

Both individual and age differences in ability can be considered. The child is not allowed to do anything he wants to or to behave in any way he wishes, should it be disrupting to the group. Nevertheless, for the most part, he can be permitted to perform at the level at which he functions most comfortably.

A responsible school will attempt to help the preschooler move toward the next level of ability, but, at the same time, will respect his need to function *where he is.* A child may not be ready to join the group, to share, to take his turn, to cooperate fully in routines, and to come to school at every scheduled session. These immaturities will be fully respected.

Nursery school can also be a learning experience for parents. Even though a child is old enough to attend nursery school, his life as a preschooler is still filled with crucial moments—accidents, illnesses, emotional outbursts, and inability to separate from his parent. These moments demand a constant flow of communication between parent and teacher. One needs to inform the other about the life of the child when the other is not present. So much can be ironed out or dealt with quickly if both parent and teacher are fully informed. It is not only the difficult moments, however, that need to be considered. There are also the positive, happy, growing moments that should be communicated. Nursery school can be a happy and rewarding time for the child. It is a separation from the home which can still be shared with the home.

A public school situation, even a kindergarten or first grade, will need to make somewhat more demands, but the early primary grades have much to learn from the more flexible atmosphere of the nursery school.

The public school might also well take heed of the productive and satisfying communication between parent and nursery school teacher. All too often the parent feels excluded as soon as his child enters the public kindergarten. The snatched moments of communication when a parent picked up her child at the end of the school morning are no longer possible in those schools which furnish bus transportation. Most parents need to be satisfied with a scheduled conference with the teacher, or a PTA meeting. Even when parents know things aren't right with their child, they may be slow to report, fearing criticism or an adverse attitude toward the child.

Something should be done to increase opportunity for communication between parents and teachers. The parent should be given easier access to the school, both to question and to inform. This need is more definite at the kindergarten and first grade level, but also extends up into second grade.

Much unnecessary and unwarranted criticism of the schools could be alleviated if parents were really informed about what is going on in school and even given a chance to speak up. More communication between parent and school could help parents to understand why their children are experiencing difficulties. As we consider the basis of some parental decisions and demands, we realize how much more information parents need about what is really going on.

There will undoubtedly be many adjustments and some disappointments for any parent during the course of his child's school career. That is one of the reasons why it is so important to establish good and continuous communication between home and school in these early school years. Actually, the educator, to carry out his task effectively, needs the parent as much as the parent needs the educator. The teacher needs to be informed about a child's home behavior. Does behavior at home suggest that school is a good experience for the child? Does he show an eagerness to go to school? Or the opposite?

Not only do teachers need to know about the child's immediate response to school, but they would profit from knowing more about his early development in the years before he entered school. This kind of information may best be obtained by the developmental examiner who should be trained in this type of interviewing. Knowledge of a child's early motor development, his language development, his adjustment to the routines of life all add to the total picture. Even such knowledge as whether he reads road signs or listens well when read to, gives a very good clue to a child's potential approach to reading.

Once the child starts school, his teachers should be informed about many aspects of his life at home. It is particularly important for them to know of any fears which he may be experiencing, especially those which may have arisen in relation to some school experience. Maybe a fear was stimulated by the reading of a story. Maybe the child couldn't put on his rubbers. Maybe toilet facilities trouble him, especially when he is 7 and the lack of a full door which he can close fails to insure his needed privacy. All sorts of problems arise that could and should be discussed with the school. Someone needs to be available for these discussions.

An excellent natural time of communication could be fostered between home and school if a 5- or 6-year-old's afternoon play nap could be allowed for by the school schedule. This would mean that there would be no afternoon kindergarten sessions and that first grade would be dismissed early. Some FIVES still need to sleep. Most SIXES need a rest time. Their fatigue is very evident in school during the afternoon session.

It would be far better for children of these ages to be at home, enjoying and benefiting from a play nap. Some of the school equipment might be allowed to be taken home just as library books are taken home. Mother and teacher might use this afternoon time to talk things over with each other in personal conference or by phone. This interest on the part of the teacher would make it easier for the mother to communicate and difficulties could be taken care of as they arise.

Parents are often accused of wanting to get their children off their hands. It is argued that they oppose reduced first grade sessions because they would have to look out for their children that much longer. This may be true in isolated cases, but most parents think first about what is best for their child. If it became a custom for 5- and 6-year-olds to have an hour's play nap in the afternoon, this would not only provide extra time for the parent but would revive the child and make him ready for his afternoon play and other activities. The interest the school would take in the child's home activity would add a new bond between home and school.

Parents also need to know as much about what is going on in school as the teacher needs to know of what is going on at home. The child is not an adequate source of information on either score. Some parents have also complicated the decisions of the school by not facing the reality of their children. Some have been more concerned about what they want their children to be, than what they actually are. Some almost seem to treat their children and their children's educational activities as status symbols.

It is indeed a sad state of affairs when parents so view their children, pushing them into college, professions, or social activities they neither wish for or are suited for, in order that parental pride be satisfied. Much of the misery experienced nowadays at the college level is produced through pressures and false hopes on the part of the parents. These may, of course, be only one factor, but a vital enough factor to make it important for parents to check on themselves and to take stock of their attitudes and their demands.

Fortunately many parents have recognized the adverse influence on children when experiences, either social or educational, come to them before they are ready. Parent groups are now banding together to define rules and regulations in order to set in motion a decelerating process which is needed to counteract the accelerating process which prevails in many communities. These parents realize, for instance, that social dancing doesn't need to begin at 9 years of age. Twelve is quite early enough. Interestingly enough, the children have not rebelled at this idea of going more slowly socially. Rather, most have slipped back quite comfortably into a childhood they were being asked to forfeit.

This same type of pushing has taken place in the matter of getting children into school early. The earlier a child is admitted to kindergarten, ready or not, the happier some parents have been. In some communities there is a constant war on between parents and school in relation to legal entrance date. These dates vary, as we have already noted, from September 1 to the following January 1. Deadlines have their place, of course, but they should be related to growth expectations. A September 1 deadline for entrance into kindergarten at least relates to a growth expectation as we know it.

This tendency to push their children and to treat them as status symbols is by no means characteristic of all parents. Let us, at this point, bow to those parents who have been in the vanguard, who have seen their children as they really are. Such parents have often fought their battles alone, trying desperately to arrange for their children to go a little more slowly than the expected rate, trying to have them replaced in the grades in which caution suggested they belonged.

It was in large measure just such parents who alerted us to the need of correct school placement, and who inspired us to undertake the research which has culminated in the present volume. This research, as earlier chapters of this book have explained, has made it clear that neither age in years nor sheer intelligence as measured by intelligence tests, is an adequate measure for determining a child's readiness either to start school or to be promoted from one grade to another.

How a parent will accept the school's decision as to his child's readiness or nonreadiness for kindergarten will depend on many factors. Pride or disappointment will continue to be stimulated until we all are able to view each child in his own right. It is unfortunate that the response of some parents, understandable as it may be, still makes it necessary for schools to try to disguise the true identity of different groups, trying to conceal the fact that one group at a certain grade level is more advanced than another.

It is the child's adjustment to the group that should be paramount. Correct grouping is fully as important as starting the child at the right time for him. We have seen the change in a child originally misplaced in a top group in our North Haven applied study, after he was finally properly replaced in a lower group whose demands were more suited to his abilities. An unhappy, lost child not wanting to come to school can turn into a happily functioning child who loves school, when he is properly placed.

A parent's willingness to accept the fact that his child may not be ready to start kindergarten, or may be ready to start, but not necessarily in the most advanced group, is essential in permitting a comfortable and pleasant beginning school experience for the child. Even more vital is the parent's acceptance of the fact, when such is the case, that a boy or girl may be going to need to repeat a grade.

If our findings in both Weston and North Haven as to the large percentage of children now overplaced in our public schools should turn out to be true of schools throughout this land, many readers of this book will be the parents of children who are currently overplaced in school. Ideally, as schools become increasingly aware of the need for correct grade placement, they will suggest that many of these children be put back a grade. (Eventually when the schools place all or nearly all children correctly from the time of entrance in kindergarten, there will be much less need for repeating. Some children may need to progress more slowly than the average, but this could be provided for by half-year intervals.)

Other than seeing that a child doesn't start school too early, there is probably no greater single contribution a parent can make toward his child's successful schooling than to help him accept the wisdom of the school's decision to have him repeat a grade—should such a decision be made.

Parents all seem to share the quite reasonable worry that it will make their child unhappy if he finds that he must repeat. We have been amazed how easily this adjustment can be accomplished, dependent in part on how the school has handled it. The parental fear that repeating a grade will cause great and lasting emotional disturbance in the child is, in our experience, quite unfounded.

The ways of adults must often seem arbitrary and strange to the child. But most children basically accept their parents' decisions about important matters such as school. Time and again we have observed that boys and girls put back into the grade where they belong—the grade whose demands actually match their behavior abilities—are so much happier and more successful that both home and school often describe them as "a changed child."

More than that, however, we have found that if the parents themselves *really accept* the importance of having the child in a grade which suits his abilities, that in most cases it is remarkably easy for them to convey this acceptance to the child. If a child is doing something his parents really believe in, and if, with even a minimum of tact, they assure him that they and the school have made a mistake about the grade he should be in, but that they now are going to correct that mistake, most children will accept the explanation and the shift in the grade not only calmly, but with relief.

With a smoother working relationship between home and school, undue criticism of parents by the school may be alleviated. Parents have, for instance, been subjected to unfair criticism from the school about what they teach their children at home, especially if the school feels that the parent is encroaching on its territory. There was a time when the schools frowned upon a parent teaching his child the alphabet. But home is the very place where the young child shows this kind of interest most. By 4 many want to print a few letters. By 5, they like to read letters on cereal box tops or in television commercials. They enjoy looking through magazines, picking out the letters they know in advertisements. There is no reason whatsoever why such activities should not be permitted and encouraged. They make an exciting game which many a child enjoys.

This very phrase, "an exciting game which he enjoys," is the key to any successful early or later home teaching. Let the school, when the time comes, be responsible for the more didactic, formalized teaching, but let the home teach through games and through the experience of sharing. If the child wants to learn to read at home before reading is offered at school, by all means let him. A parent can quickly judge when a child has had enough. A parent also needs to distinguish between a child's interest in recognizing single words or in learning to spell words, and his readiness for formal reading instruction.

Much, in fact rather too much, has been written about the formal teaching of reading in the preschool years. Certainly any mother will quite naturally let her child go as far as his spontaneous interests suggest along these lines. Research has shown, however, that most efforts at setting up formal reading instruction in the preschool years do not succeed in teaching the child to read. Even if they do, such a child's advancement over his contemporaries is usually not maintained. Other bright members of his class group will very quickly catch up or even surpass him once the class has reached the customary time for learning to read. Play is the preschooler's work. Let's not worry that he is wasting his time.

Allowing a child to learn is one thing. Formal teaching in the preschool years is another. It is unfortunate when a parent thinks only of teaching a child. He then loses the quality of living, the experiencing together that is the stuff of their relationship. Not that a child may not choose certain areas to experience with his parent, especially as he moves into first grade. Who is more eager for homework than the first grader? Some feel cheated if not given some homework, at least now and then. This homework he may very much enjoy sharing with his parent.

Homework can, unfortunately, in later years, become a tremendous burden for both parent and child. The very school that may have criticized the home for teaching the child before he came to school, may later on place a heavy burden on the home in the way of homework. The terrible load of homework, which is as often a load on the parents as on the child, needs to be seriously reassessed by our schools. Correct school placement will reduce this problem to some extent. The home should be used to enrich the school program, but it should not be expected to replace it or to substitute for it.

The quality of the child's life at home becomes evident to a teacher. Even as early as kindergarten, it is easy to tell what kind of a home he has come from. Responsible parenthood is not an easy job, but it is an essential one. The best parents tend to be those who have the greatest appreciation for the difficulties the school faces, and for what it is trying to accomplish.

Conversely, it is often the most demanding parents, from the school's point of view, who turn out to be the least responsible. Of course, a poor parent isn't going to turn into a good one overnight. When the school offers a helping hand, however, and proves to a parent that a child placed in a suitable school environment can become a more rewarding child to rear, more can gradually be asked of the parent.

It is essential for the parent to realize that what has happened and will continue to happen to the child at home becomes important in his adjustment and success at school. Of course what happens to the child at home relates as much to his growth rate and his individuality as to what his parents have provided for him, but there is still much that parents can do to help every child function at his very best level.

Perhaps the biggest step, so far as the parent is concerned, is to cooperate with the school in the determination of how ready the child is for what it has to offer, and what grade or group the child should be placed in. A perceptive parent may already know the answer to these questions even before the school discusses its decision as to grade placement. A perceptive mother is usually very quick to know whether her child is up to, or behind, others of his age so far as general behavior maturity is concerned.

Most schools are happy to have the parents' confirmation or comment on their own findings. Together, school and parent can then put their decision to a practical test. Early and initial cooperation can mature through the grades until school and parent can really be classed as true partners in helping each child to make the very most possible of his years in school.

The irony of any chapter such as this is that those parents who are interested enough in their children's education to read a technical book of this sort are, almost without exception, parents who already have a sincere, sensible, and practical approach to educational problems.

The same principle holds true for PTA meetings and lectures on school readiness, grade placement, and similar subjects. So often teachers and school administrators remark after a lecture, "If only the *other* parents had been here! The ones who come to these meetings are usually our best parents. They are the ones already willing and even determined that their children should be correctly placed in school and not pushed beyond their ability. These are the ones who cooperate fully with any suggestions we make. It always seems to be the parents who don't need the information who come to the meetings."

We, too, wish that we could reach these *other* parents—parents who sometimes fear that recognition of individual differences and correct grouping means discrimination. If they would only realize that teaching a child at the level he is ready for is not discrimination, but privilege.

Parents are perhaps the strongest pressure group in the world, because their demands that their children have the best possible education are supported by their strong emotional need to see their children functioning happily and effectively. Those parents who have seen their own child released from the struggling and suffering of a grade whose demands far exceeded his abilities, and become a comfortable and effective student in a grade which fitted him, are in a position to do a great service for other parents. They can do this service by telling others of their own experiences and by strongly supporting their own school in its efforts to see that all its students are correctly placed and correctly grouped.

CHAPTER 23

THE TEACHER

|||||||||||||||||||||||||||||||||||||||||||||||||||||||||||||||||||||||||||||||

A child's life often revolves around his teacher, especially in the early grades. A teacher can make or break his school year. Likewise, the child can sometimes make or break the teacher's year.

There has been much written about the poor caliber of our teachers and about the poor training. No one seems concerned, however, with the overburdening of the teacher, with the fact that many a teacher has to put up with impossible situations day after day. It is no wonder teachers have developed a special syndrome of week-end illnesses. This is the only time they can afford to be ill. Their dedication to their work, which is true of most teachers, insures their recovery by Monday morning. Some, however, cannot take the frustrations of their attempts to teach children at a grade level for which many of these children are not ready. Exhaustion mounts in these teachers; eventually they have to give up their chosen profession. Our teacher shortage is unquestionably increased because of those who have had to leave the profession.

It is often said that good teachers are born. As early as 6 or 7 years of age girls especially are already plying the trade as they play school; and many have their hearts already set on becoming teachers. There is perhaps no profession whose members are as dedicated and optimistic as the teaching profession. Teachers have the right to both of these attitudes when one considers the pliable material with which they work —young children and their growing minds. Unfortunately, they may be forced into the misuse of these high attitudes when they are made to attempt things that can't be done.

We have found that most teachers have a very good capacity to judge the readiness of their children. This is especially true at a kindergarten level when it is easier to spot the unready child. An adjustment

327

difficulty, such as a child crying day after day, clearly suggests an emotional immaturity. A child who can't follow directions or stay with a task is quickly spotted by a kindergarten teacher. She soon comes to know what can be asked of each child and which ones can work best together.

Often a teacher has little preliminary material about the child and thus has to work through trial and error. Much of this work would be unnecessary or could be made more effective if she had the help of a developmental appraisal of each child. If the children are also grouped correctly to begin with, they can achieve together, and an effective class program can begin to move earlier in the school year.

In our studies we have often been amazed to note how closely our developmental findings coincided with the teacher's judgment, especially at the kindergarten level. The teacher is, after all, dealing with the maturity of the child. She comes to realize that, more than any other factor, maturity or readiness can determine the child's adjustment to the grade he is in.

Beyond the kindergarten level, teachers' judgments as to readiness may lose their clear-cut accuracy, in part because as the children grow older, the teacher becomes more involved in educating them. We discovered this in our Weston study. Part of the teacher's job is to support, to cajole, to encourage, to hope. We have been able to recognize this supportive attitude as we trained teachers to become developmental examiners. Slowly we have had to help them give up this teacher attitude, which can interfere with their objective examining procedures. To determine the level at which a child is operating is different from finding out how much he can respond to and learn.

We have often seen a teacher shift to what seemed to us a more realistic appraisal of a given child's readiness as soon as she has been more fully informed about his developmental level. It has seemed that she needed this kind of factual support to confirm and to refine her own judgments, which without such help sometimes tend to be over-optimistic. We have been amazed by the rapid sharpening of teachers' evaluations as soon as they were given this developmental material about their children. This is indeed an area where teacher-training could be advanced. This training should help a teacher to spot a misplaced child more quickly. As teachers come to know more about the laws of growth they will realize that decisions about a child's placement should not be put off in the hopes that he will eventually improve. The facts must be faced and immediate decisions made as to what is best for him.

Teachers have not only had to put up with the misplaced child and with the child who is hard to teach, but also with the disruptive child. To support the burden of a disruptive child is asking too much both of the teacher and of the group. We have clocked the time a teacher has spent during a morning with a disruptive child. It can amount to a good 25% of her time. This is not teaching; it is custodial care. The rest of the class is not only being disrupted, but is being deprived of the teacher's attention, which they are entitled to receive. A solution of proper placement of disruptive children needs to be found, not only for the sake of the teacher and the class, but also for their own sakes.

If a group is really ready for the work of a grade, then the teacher can use her energy constructively. All of her otherwise wasted energy, often needed to combat and to discipline unnecessarily, is now available in a new kind of way. We have barely tapped the creative potential of many teachers, either because their energy is used up in dealing with disruptive or unready children or because they have to use a rigid programming to hold a group together. It is not only the teacher's creative forces that become available when a class is grouped correctly, but also the creative forces of the group itself. When a group is working well together it generates its own energy and ideas. Under such circumstances teaching can become a challenge and the interplay between teacher and group can produce an atmosphere that is conducive to learning at its best.

It is just this atmosphere which seems to us in danger of being lost in the team teaching experiments now under way in some of our primary schools. By team teaching we mean the use of a different teacher for every subject; the children go to a different room for each subject which is taught by a teacher who is supposedly a specialist in that subject. Very large groups of students, as many as 80 or 100, assemble from time to time in a home or base room, under the supervision of a single teacher.

This plan seems to us to have several serious disadvantages. To begin with, children, especially in the earlier grades, need to feel a continuing relationship with their teacher and with their special group of classmates. This is lost as they go from room to room. Also, bigness upsets them, and their basic homeroom group is large indeed. Furthermore, too much change disorients them. As one bright little girl recently commented of team teaching, "It's kind of confusin'."

The atmosphere generated when there is a good relationship between teacher and child becomes the basis for a good school spirit, a spirit which is sadly lacking in so many schools today. Parents come to know when the school spirit is good. They can feel it in their children. They, in turn, enter into the spirit and are ready to foster it in any way they can.

We have already mentioned the need for closer communication between home and school, especially in the early grades. There should be time allowed for parents to communicate with teachers, and teachers to communicate with parents. This time needs to be provided. That is why it is asking too much of a kindergarten teacher to be responsible for two groups, one in the morning and the other in the afternoon. She cannot possibly give the attention and time needed to plan for 50 children when she should be responsible for not more than 25. With correct school placement, however, she might be able to handle a larger single group if adequate space and a helper were available.

All kindergarten activities need more planning time, not only those that will be conducted in the schoolroom, but also those which can relate the 5-year-old to his community. Such excursions need special planning. The kindergarten teacher becomes increasingly aware of the facilities of the local community as she has more time to consider such facilities. She becomes aware of the new construction sites, of the stores that would welcome a small group of children, of the factories, and hopefully, the farms. As she sees the meaningful expressions of these experiences in the children's play at school, she will know that the effort of planning and execution were more than worthwhile.

Similar planning is needed for first and second grades. Learning is so much more related to context in these early grades. Here again a teacher needs time for planning. When she has a group truly ready for the grade and ready to absorb her planning, the rewards of education are felt both by the teacher and her children.

A teacher should not be working alone in her planning. She needs the opportunity to discuss each of her children with the developmental examiner and thus to conjecture what kind of activities would be most meaningful to her special group. She needs the support of her principal, both in giving ideas and in providing needed equipment and extra personnel as needed.

A young kindergarten group which is operating at a preschool or 4-year-old level needs an extra pair of hands. Providing this needed help can become a real problem. The true recognition of its need might allow for the provision of an extra half-day staff member. Student teachers can provide the necessary help and receive good training from such a group. Also in the school itself, if the 11-, 12-, and 13-year-olds were still connected with the elementary unit, there would be many girls, especially 12-year-olds, eager to help in a kindergarten setting.

Eventually we would like to have those teachers who would be interested to do so, try their hand at developmental testing under supervision. They could, for instance, re-examine those children whose level and rate of growth has already been determined at the time of school entrance and whose course is pretty well-established. Such children do not necessarily need to be fully re-examined, but a check on their developmental progress would be valuable to have. This would also reduce the heavy load of examining for the official developmental examiner who could, for these older children, restrict himself to helping with the interpretation of the records. If the first and second grade sessions were shorter, some of the afternoon time could be used by a teacher for this kind of examining.

As a starter, so that a teacher could feel the developmental level of her group, she might restrict herself to a very short individual examination, with each child being asked to write his name and the numbers from one to twenty. As they write, the teacher should take time to observe each child individually so that she can become aware of the child's posturing, overflow behavior, grasp of the pencil, response to difficulties, and other factors.

After each child in the entire class has written his name and the numbers, the teacher can analyze each record and seriate them, comparing children. One small experience like this can help her to respect development and to have a new feeling for the individual child, seeing him not only in his own right, but also as his abilities relate to those of the rest of the class.

By no means do we propose to add another function to the work of already overburdened teachers. The formal task of giving a developmental examination and evaluating it in order to determine each child's readiness or unreadiness for the class proposed is clearly the work of a special individual, specially chosen and specially trained and with time made available for this important task. Though it can be extremely useful to the classroom teacher to obtain a better perspective on the relative standing of each pupil, she should not be responsible for the bulk of developmental examining.

CHAPTER 24

THE DEVELOPMENTAL EXAMINER
AS A KEY FIGURE IN A
DEVELOPMENTAL PLACEMENT PROGRAM

The Gesell developmental examination, as we have described it in this volume, has many possible uses. It has proved extremely valuable in a clinical service, to help us know more about the child we are examining. It can be of great help when a child is having trouble in school, by giving information about his actual developmental level and identifying instances of gross misplacement.

However, to be capable of conducting and evaluating a developmental test is one thing; to put it to practical use is quite another. As we have used these developmental tests in our own clinical service we have often had difficulty in putting into practice the course of action which developmental findings might suggest. If the problems which a child revealed on such an examination were outstanding, then something should, of course, be done for him as, for instance, replacement into a lower grade.

Often, however, replacement was extremely difficult to effect in the existing school setup. Often the only way it could be effected was to shift the child to another school. We frequently found ourselves saying, "He should be replaced in his present school setting and could be if there were a total school shake-up." By this we were inferring that there were many other children in the school who also needed replacement and that if this could be arranged for all the children who needed it, then the child in question could be replaced without separating him out as the unusual one.

It is this total school shake-up we are now recommending. We would like to see the schools begin to make a more effective approach than many do to the problem of adequate class grouping and correct grade placement of all the children, based on their actual behavior level as revealed by a careful developmental examination.

Thus, at the present stage of our thinking we see the developmental examination being used most effectively as part of a total school-placement program.

The developmental examiner is a key figure in any such developmental placement program. A fully trained, full-time examiner for each school unit of 600 pupils might be the ideal in putting such a program into operation. But smaller beginnings are possible. Often the growth of a program such as we are advocating is surer if it begins as a response to a school's recognition of a need of better grouping and better placement for each individual child.

The essential ingredient of a developmental placement program, after all, is the point of view, and the essence of that point of view as we see it is *a respect for the child's behavioral age.* This age can, it is true, be evaluated by other means than a developmental examination. A teacher's judgment, as discussed in the previous chapter, can often quite accurately define a child's behavioral level, especially in kindergarten. Too often, however, a teacher's judgment is not sufficiently convincing and is shelved, awaiting further proof. Findings from a developmental examination are extremely useful in supporting the teacher's judgment.

It is a repeated delight for us to observe a teacher's response when a developmental examination of one of her children is discussed with her. A teacher once remarked to us, "It has taken me 8 months to understand what you have revealed through a half-hour examination." It would be fortunate if all examinations could be thus revealing and conclusive.

Who Should Examine

The choice of the examiner and the training of such a person immediately poses a problem. Our present thinking leads us to believe that he or she might best be someone chosen out of the educational ranks, someone with a background of close contact with groups of children. In the end it is not just a child's behavioral age both in rate and quality level that we wish to determine, but also what type of grouping would best fit his needs.

Grouping will, of course, eventually depend upon the children involved. Therefore each school will need to work out its own system of grouping which will depend on the behavioral levels of each individual child and the number of children involved. It might actually be easier to group 100 children at a grade level than 50. The larger numbers allow for more quality gradations, but any group, however small, can take into account a child's rate of growth, even though he might be the only one at that level.

The examiner needs to balance two factors at all times, first the individual child in his own developmental right and this same child in his adjustment to the group. We would wish the examiner not only to know the child individually through the developmental examination, but also to observe him in a group situation. That is why we might prefer the background of the examiner to be in education, so that he could at times substitute for the teacher and experience each child's adjustment to the group firsthand.

His past experience has also given him close contact with the administrative staff as well as with parents. These are all to his advantage. Thus, if a developmental examiner is chosen from among the teaching staff, his new role as developmental examiner is enriched by his background.

There is one shift, however, which such an examiner must be willing to make. He needs to shed his more involved role as a teacher and take on the more detached role of an examiner. He needs to realize that the examining situation includes teaching only incidentally. He needs to keep in mind that the main purpose of the examination is to make an evaluation of how a child is functioning, where he is behaving. A certain amount of praise may be given in a perfectly natural way, but in general the new teacher-examiner needs to curb the elaborate praise and encouragement which is so much a part of a classroom learning situation, so little a proper part of an examining situation.

There was a time in our early planning for developmental examining when we thought each teacher might be able to examine the children in his own class. Since the examination is a fairly simple one and each teacher would be using the examination within the confines of his own grade demands, we thought that this might present a fairly easy solution. However, we immediately ran into the need for a release of time to conduct the examinations. We also soon realized that the adequate interpretation and evaluation of the examination needed a very special background of training.[1]

[1] The one area which might give trouble to the former teacher trained as an examiner but without any special psychological background, could be an instance where a child being examined has some special psychological or emotional handicap with which such an examiner, at the beginning of his career, might not be familiar. Thus a child suffering from a minimal brain injury or a slight degree of autism might give an unusual, inadequate, or otherwise atypical response. Any examiner without special psychological training should make it a rule always, in the case of a markedly atypical response, to refer the child to a qualified psychologist.

Still more important, someone has to be equipped to see the total over-all view, not of just one class, but of all the classes of one grade level; and these in turn as related to the grade level above and the grade level below. For effective developmental placement there must be fluid interplay between groups. There is not just one obvious answer as to what group will best suit a given child. Much will depend upon how the groups form.

We also have considered the extreme opposite solution to the problem of who can most effectively give the developmental examination. This would be to put the examination into the hands of an already trained person such as the school psychologist, who could readily absorb the needed training to become an effective developmental examiner. However, this solution could have the disadvantage of placing an extra burden on the psychologist in addition to his already heavy duties.

Time will be the judge as to who can best fit this new educational role of developmental examiner and the answer may well be different in different school systems.

Training of the Examiner

We have been most fortunate ourselves in having the experience of training two developmental examiners[2] who are now in their third year of our applied project in placement at the North Haven schools. These two examiners, both women, were chosen from the ranks of their separate school staffs, one a second grade, the other a fourth grade teacher. Each had been very successful as a teacher. Neither had had any special psychological background or training.

They were initially trained in the fall of 1962 at a two-week workshop held at the Gesell Institute, during which time they became familiar with the tests, both in relation to procedures and interpretations. They also observed considerable testing of children from 5 to 10 years of age. Following the workshop they received close supervision as they themselves examined, and further training in the interpretation of their findings.

Summarizing their findings in writing was not easy at first, but they soon discovered that they would lose their total impression of a child if they did not analyze and summarize his record, preferably on the same day that he was examined.

A word here as to just how one goes about evaluating the child's response to the developmental examination. As we have just commented,

[2] Two examiners have been thoroughly trained by us for work in our demonstration project in North Haven. Several dozen other examiners have been trained, though less intensively, in a series of two-week workshops which are being held twice a year for qualified school personnel, at the Gesell Institute.

this kind of examination does not yield a single numerical score. Rather, the child's response to each part of the examination is matched against age norms for that test. At first the examiner will need to consult the tables and test description of each test as given in detail in Part II of this book, or the more succinct capsule age summaries in Part III.

Eventually as he gathers experience, he will need less and less often to consult the text. He will "know" what to expect of the 5- or the 6- or the 7-year-old. As he gains familiarity with each of the tests and the responses expected at the different ages, he will also become increasingly interested in the longitudinal flow of behavior in response to any given test. He will actually see in his mind's eye the arm of the Incomplete Man, for instance, as it moves upward on the body line, turns increasingly upward and shortens in length. Knowledge about the longitudinal or age flow and the direction in which behavior changes will help the examiner substantially in determining the age placement of each individual response.

Since responses to most of the developmental tests can be measured with respect to several variables, even the child's response to a single test may fall variably at several different age levels. Added to that, a child may respond much more maturely to some one test in the battery than to others.

However, scoring, though important, is only one part of the total evaluation of the examination. It is the synthetic capacity to put the child together in a total that is essential. This unity is best expressed by giving the child a behavioral or developmental age, around which all of his responses may be seen to cluster. When the range of a child's behavior is wide, not only in different tests, but also within a single test, it may not be easy to define the basic age where behavior clusters. This ability comes only with practice.

There are some examiners who even with experience find it difficult to make this kind of final total appraisal. They prefer to hold to specific scoring and in fact prefer the kinds of tests which yield a specific numerical score. The developmental examination, which requires a total appraisal rather than yielding a clear-cut score, is not a good tool for such examiners.

One of our examiners reported after a month of examining 5-year-olds that what she was really after suddenly hit her like a bolt of lightning. She began to feel the essence of 5-year-old behavior, of 5½-year-old behavior, and of the leftover remnants of 4-year-old behavior. From then on she examined with greater surety, and was able to make rapid and effective appraisals. Within a year's time both examiners became extremely proficient in examining and in appraising.

It is interesting to observe the ways in which different examiners build up their individual methods of appraisal. Different parts of the examination say different things to different people. Some get most out of the Incomplete Man test, others out of Right and Left, and still others out of memory-for-designs (Monroe Visual Three). Each separate part tells its own story so that the examiner is never at a loss for pertinent material. It is as the examiner comes to realize the way in which one part of the examination supports and confirms another part that a final effective appraisal can be made.

There is nothing automatic about a developmental examination. That is why it is so unsatisfactory to those examiners who wish to come out with a single numerical score. Behavior elicited by the developmental examination forms a living whole. The structure of behavior is intricate and yet it functions relatively smoothly as a whole. As Dr. Gesell has often pointed out: behavior has shape, behavior grows. The Copy Forms test may some day reveal the brain as a computer system far more intricate than any man-made machine.

The examiner can be fatigued but exhilarated when he finally summarizes the behavioral essence of a child from a developmental examination, and the examination is of use mainly when this kind of meaning can be secured. This can then be communicated to the parent, to the teacher, to the principal. Scores alone do not tell the story. It is the living, working texture of the child and his behavior that must be understood and explained.

Use of the Developmental Examination in a School Placement Program

A school will provide for a developmental examiner in its budget only as the need and value of such a service becomes generally appreciated. When, however, educators weigh the potential results of such a service, they may recognize that correct placement can reduce the need for some of the special services now necessary. Remedial work is often used in an effort to hold a child up to a level he cannot maintain. If he were placed where he could function, he might no longer need this extra help.

Many teachers of reading believe that the need for remedial reading help, for instance, could be greatly lessened if children were not forced to start reading before they were ready. If children could all wait till they were ready, they might not get into trouble with their reading in the first place.

The consideration of the load of examining which any school placement program will present must be faced early in such a program. Our own first year's load in our applied project in North Haven was entirely too heavy. We hoped to cover the first three grades in each school, which meant a basic 300 examinations plus an extra 100 when the kindergarten was reexamined in the spring. There was also the 10-minute spring screening test for the 100 next year's kindergarten applicants. Although an examination only takes around a half hour, four examinations a day with the needed time for evaluation and appraisal are all that most examiners will wish to undertake.

Our present thinking is that we would eventually like to see a developmental examiner be responsible for a school unit of around 600 children from kindergarten through fifth grade. The initial coverage of the entire school, providing for at least one developmental examination of each child, would be demanding, but it could be accomplished within the first two years of a concerted program.

A tentative examining schedule for a school starting in with such a program is shown in Table 92.

TABLE 92   *Examining Schedule*

	First Year	Second Year	Third Year
Kindergarten applicants (spring)	100[a]	100	100
Kindergarten (spring)	100	100	100
First grade (fall)	100	As needed	As needed
Second grade (winter)	100	As needed	As needed
Third grade (as needed)	As needed	As needed	As needed
Fourth grade (fall)	As needed	100	As needed
Fifth grade (winter)	As needed	100	As needed

[a]The arrow lines indicate the line of promotion and when traced back will reveal when the developmental appraisal was made.

In the first year of any full-scale program such as this, major emphasis should be placed on the first three classes, that is kindergarten through second grade. The screening test for kindergarten applicants could and should determine the grouping of the next year's kindergarten group. Also the spring examinations of the kindergarten subjects could determine their subsequent first grade grouping.

First and second grades would be more difficult to group without too much disruption, if they had already started school before the placement program began. Only obvious misplacements might at first be considered for examination, but on the other hand, some semblance of adjusted placement might not be too difficult following examining, especially if separate 5½-, 6½-, and 7½-year-old groups were established.

This first year examining program would include 300 examinations, plus 100 screening examinations for kindergarten applicants. Children in the upper grades (third, fourth, and fifth grades) could be examined when special needs or problems arose.

The fourth and fifth grade groups could be covered in the second year of examining, plus both the current kindergarten group and the kindergarten applicants. This would demand relatively the same number of examinations as in the first year of examining. The children in first, second, and third grades would have been covered by a developmental examination the previous year.

By the third year of our proposed program the entire school population through fifth grade would have been examined at least once, though the final kindergarten group would have had only a screening coverage. This kindergarten group will need to be examined in the spring along with the next year's kindergarten applicants.

Although we initially examined the kindergarten groups at North Haven in both fall and spring, we now feel that the kindergarten application screening examination in the spring before kindergarten entrance provides adequate coverage for the fall grouping. Only those kindergarten children who appear obviously misplaced should receive a full examination in the fall.

A very important part of any placement program should be the spring examination and plan for placement of the kindergarten group which will be entering school in the fall. Teachers need to have access to these records and time to discuss them with the examiner. Within the early weeks of school each teacher will be able to judge whether the placement of a child is correct. She should refer any questionable cases back to the examiner for a complete examination. Any shifts in placement should ideally be made early in the school year. As soon as the teacher has formed a judgment about each of the pupils, she should add this judgment to the child's developmental record during a conference with the examiner.

After a school placement program begins to move smoothly, there should be only a minimal need for replacement of children according to their developmental or behavioral age. The kindergarten screening test given in the spring preceding school entrance may not be adequate in some cases, and for these cases the information derived from a full developmental coverage as discussed above may be needed.

From first grade on, if the developmental findings, along with the teacher's realistic evaluation of each child, have really been followed, there should be little need for shifts after the initial group placement. There may be a few exceptions, as when a shift is indicated because of a child-teacher clash, or to give the child the security of being with a friend—or, of course, more basically, when a child's growth does not proceed in an even or predicted manner.

For those schools which may not be in a position to undertake a full and elaborate placement program, we might suggest as a starter confining the developmental examining to a preliminary examining of the incoming kindergarten group. The two-day spring registration period could be used. In most schools, however, this does not provide adequate time for tests. An individual appointment system is far better if it can be arranged. This past year, the North Haven schools arranged for appointments of prekindergarten children, at 20-minute intervals. The response of the parents was gratifying. They felt as if they were receiving the courtesy of private school attention. If the parent was needed to accompany the child during the 10-minute screening examination, this still gave her good time for registration, too.

Part of the smoothness of this prekindergarten examining program was that the examiner was always available. She could rearrange her schedule to fit in with appointments made. Since applicants came unannounced, this demanded some flexibility of scheduling. If a full-time developmental examiner is not available, some individual capable of doing the screening examinations should be made available for a period of perhaps a month in the spring when registrations are being made.

The screening examination as we use it is short and includes only such letters and numbers as the child can make, Copy Forms, and Incomplete Man. The examiner should summarize the examination results, including a thumbnail sketch of behavior, as soon as time is available. Pertinent material should then be transferred to a card for each child so that grouping can be facilitated.

In our first year of testing in the North Haven schools we found that the 100 kindergarten children in each of the two schools where we worked fell easily into four separate groups. These groups might quite naturally be called by numbers one to four, or they might be designated by age and qualitative level, from the most to the least mature as follows: 5A, 5B, 4½A, 4½B. This letter and number labeling is not as helpful in kindergarten as it is at later ages, when the quality level of performance becomes more defined, and a greater difference is evident between the A-quality and the B-quality children.

It is unfortunate when a school, because of parental sensitivity or prejudice, does not feel free to make this type of grouping. Grouping is, after all, determined by the developmental level and quality of performance of children in the class that is being grouped. It does not mean, as some fear, that a child is placed on a track and stays there. A good school and a perceptive developmental examiner are always alert to any relative changes in behavior, and are interested to see how children realign themselves over a period of, say, 3 years from kindergarten through second grade.

The age factor alone is more important at the kindergarten level than later. With kindergarteners more often than not the older child is most likely to land in groups one or two, the youngest children in groups three or four. However exceptions do show up strikingly, as when an older child fits best in the fourth group, as can be the case.

To give the reader some idea of the way grouping at the kindergarten level works, let us look at five thumbnail summaries of kindergarten applicants (all examined in the spring of the year preceding the fall of their entrance to kindergarten), and the potential grouping suggested for these children. It will be noted that these thumbnail sketches include only a total impression of behavior and do not give details of specific test performance which is, of course, available in the child's filed record.

TABLE 93 *Thumbnail Sketches of Kindergarten Applicants Made at the Time of the Spring Screening Examination*

Girl A 5⁰ (Birth date March) Group One

Nice performance; high tiny voice. A-quality. Copies divided rectangle; good obliques to triangle and vertical diamond.

Girl B 5¹ (Birth date February) Group Two; One alternate

Nice behavior coming into 5 years. B-quality. Is her motor performance ahead of her language? Advanced teething.

Boy A 4⁹ (Birth date June) Group Three

Nervous child, incessant talking. Behavior nearer 4-than 5-year level. Cannot imitate a triangle; copies only outside of divided rectangle, cannot reproduce the inside lines.

Boy B 4⁶ (Birth date October) Group Four; Reduced attendance

Can't wait to be examined. Lots of machine-gun noises. Messy behavior, though potentially good. Copies square at age level. Gross dashing strokes. Will need controls. On young side (October birthday). Should be on reduced attendance.

Boy C 4⁵ (Birth date November) Group Four; Three alternate

On too young side (November birthday). Stroke is soft and querulous. Has idea of triangle and good attempt at inside of rectangle, but has difficulty in executing. Behavior is at age. Good potential.

In reviewing these thumbnail sketches one can readily glimpse the behavioral level and potentials of each child. Girl A has both age (a March birth date) and good performance on her side. She is a real kindergartener, ready for an enriched program. She naturally falls into group one. It will be interesting to watch whether or not her high tiny voice turns out to be of real significance. Her adjustment in the group will also be interesting to follow.

Girl B also has age on her side (February birth date). Her behavior is well at age, but does not show the quality of that of Girl A. Her performance with paper and pencil appears to be at a higher level than her language output. With her advanced teething she is showing physical maturity. She may well be one of those salt-of-the-earth children who is such a nice addition to a group. She should do well in a regular kindergarten group.

Boy A was young when he was examined (4^9) which in one way put him at a disadvantage. His nervousness and incessant talking suggest potential adjustment difficulties. He is not coming into 5-year-old behavior though his behavior is relative to his age or a little below. He cannot, for instance, handle the complexity of the inside of the divided rectangle. His age is on the young side for a boy (June birth date). He is operating enough around a 4½-year level to adjust to a third kindergarten group which will allow him to progress at least 6 months more slowly than the top kindergarten group. All signs point to his need to progress at this slower rate. He will need either to repeat kindergarten or to be placed in a 5½-year-old group in his second school year.

Boy B is definitely on the young side for a boy (October birth date). He was 4^6 when examined and acted in general much more like an out-of-bounds 4-year-old. He needs to be placed in the fourth kindergarten group both because of his age and because of his behavior, although his behavior is potentially much better than it shows up here. With a slower course in school, along with good controls, it may be hoped that he will come into good line later on. He would be better off going to nursery school in the fall if a good 4-year-old group were available. Or he might be better off staying at home. If the school's cut-off date were September 1, they wouldn't have had to solve the problem. As it is the school needs to ask the parents to make some adjustment, as in having him come to school only twice a week. The amount of time at school can be increased as he improves. Any assistance the teacher can give to help the mother plan this boy's day will undoubtedly be welcomed. He will most probably need to repeat kindergarten.

Boy C was only 4^5 at the time of his spring examination and is definitely on the young side (November birth date). His behavior was at his age, but his stroke was soft and querulous and he had difficulty in executing his ideas. His maturity would place him in group four although his ability would make him eligible for group three. The good potential is here. Fortunately the parents, in going over the record with the examiner, realized it would be far better for him to go to nursery school in the fall, since otherwise he would need to repeat kindergarten the next year. If he waits another year to start kindergarten he will qualify either for the first or second group. It would be most helpful if there were more parents who could make this kind of good decision.

These thumbnail sketches give the reader a beginning idea of how developmental examination findings can be used for grouping. We are at the time of this writing two-thirds through our 3-year North Haven study in which we are applying our concepts of developmental grouping. Therefore at this time we can give only suggestions.

It was not until we examined and analyzed the North Haven first grade groups that we fully realized how clearly children showed half-year intervals of growth as well as the quality of growth which we have designated as A and B.[3] How useful these half-year levels will be in actual practice is still to be proven, but our present findings suggest that to add $4\frac{1}{2}$-, $5\frac{1}{2}$-, $6\frac{1}{2}$-, and $7\frac{1}{2}$-year groups[4] to the usual 5-, 6-, and 7-year-old groups might solve many of the in-between problems. This half-year grouping would allow for shorter intervals of promotion and thus would mean less need, if any, of keeping children back. Many children who do not seem ready for promotion from kindergarten to first grade might well be ready for the demands of a $5\frac{1}{2}$-year-old group, etc.

Considering half-year intervals of placement does not mean that there would be half-yearly promotions in February as was once the custom. Rather it suggests that the curriculum of a half-year group should be geared to having a $5\frac{1}{2}$-year-old group 6 months younger in behavior than the more typical 6-year-old first grade group. A child would remain in the class group labeled $5\frac{1}{2}$ or 6 for his entire school year, just as he would remain in the quality group A or B for an entire school year.

This extra step between grades can greatly facilitate a school's choice of placement by allowing a child who is not ready for full promotion to the next grade to move ahead by a half-year interval without having to repeat. Also, parents might find it much easier to accept the idea of their child's progressing 6 months slower instead of a whole year slower than might have been anticipated.

[3] Our use of the letters A and B differs from the traditional public school usage. We use these letters to make a qualitative differentiation between groups, Group A being made up of children who are of higher potential than those in Group B. Another basis of difference is that as we use these letters, children remain in Group A, or Group B, throughout the school year. According to traditional usage they are in Group B (5B, 6B) in the fall semester of any given school year and then are promoted to Group A in the spring semester.

[4] That is, we would suggest having more class divisions than are available in most schools at present. There would be, for the year following kindergarten, groups $5\frac{1}{2}$A and $5\frac{1}{2}$B for children not yet ready for first grade, and of either A-quality or B-quality in performance. Following first grade there might be groups $6\frac{1}{2}$A and $6\frac{1}{2}$B for those who do not need to repeat first grade, but who are not yet ready to be promoted into second.

Here again we depart from traditional usage since we label the group by the behavior age of the child. Thus 6 means a group for 6-year-olds not, as usually, sixth grade. And in our terminology, 6A means the top group of 6-year-olds, not the second semester of sixth grade.

If, as we have found in some schools, only 30% of the children are ready for the grade which age permits them to enter, and 20% should progress a year slower, this still leaves approximately 50% who do not fit either category. These may be the children who need to progress only 6 months slower than the regular rate. It would be unfortunate for such children, at the end of their kindergarten year, to have to repeat kindergarten needlessly. And it would be even more unfortunate if they were pushed beyond their limits of growth into first grade.

Growth Within a Placement Program

The initial approach of any school system to the use of the developmental examination will take different forms in different schools. The one essential universal need, as we see it, is that every kindergarten applicant should be screened prior to placement, and that he should also receive a full developmental examination in the spring of his kindergarten year. Any new child coming into a school system should have at least one full developmental coverage.

As for further examinations which could be so valuable, especially to help in evaluations of a child's process of growth, this would all depend upon the examiner's available time and the needs of the school. A re-examination program might be fitted into a teacher-training program, or some classroom teachers might like to try their hand at developmental examining under supervision.

Parent interviews should also be considered as an important supplement to any program of developmental testing, especially at the kindergarten level. The examiner, in addition to being trained in giving developmental examinations, should be able to conduct a developmental parent interview, which means that he would be able to explore pertinent areas of a child's life from his birth up to the present time. Any correlations between past behavior and present findings should be brought to the parents' attention. The examiner's own interpretation of the child is also enriched by knowing more about his background. This type of interview doesn't bring the parent to the school because his child is in trouble. Rather it has the potential of establishing a good working relationship between parent and school based on their common interest in the child's behavior and abilities. It is a pleasure for a parent in conversation with an interested professional person to think back and recapitulate the life of her child and to realize that all that has happened in the past is related to the child's life right now.

We have considered the possibility of calling the developmental examiner a developmental guidance coordinator, a term which suggests the multiple ramifications that such a position might include. Such an individual examines, guides, and coordinates. The job has many potentials. It can be as big or small as the examiner makes it, or is allowed to make it. The one thing that is certain, however, is that no one within a school population will be in a position to know so many children so intimately.

Such an individual can be invaluable to a principal who needs and desires this kind of knowledge about the children in his school. A developmental examiner can serve as a principal's right arm, thus releasing the principal for new activities that neither time nor setting could previously allow.

CHAPTER 25

THE PRINCIPAL

‖‖

Any school unit must have a central directing force. The principal is in a unique position to be this force. If he has come out of the teacher ranks, as is often the case, he has already had practice in knowing what is needed. What he thinks and believes becomes very important in determining the course his school will take.

His unique position is further supported by the fact that he is close to both the educative process in the classroom and also to the policy-making of the higher administrative personnel. He can thus become a force both in planning and in action.

Unfortunately any principal is running against an increasing number of problems. The size of the school population alone compounds his problems and can either distract him from important educational issues or hide them from view. A simple rule suggested by a principal himself is that a school population should be no bigger than the number of names a principal could remember. Five to six hundred was his limit. Thus, a unit of kindergarten through fifth grade, if held to 80 to 100 pupils per grade, could be within the power of one person's control.

Bigness is not the only problem of a principal. On the one hand, he is harassed by demands of parents, and on the other, he is discouraged by the results of his own school's handiwork as he sees an increase in the list of potential drop-outs. He is wrestling with entrance age and methods of initial placement and promotion. He is trying to figure out ways to handle the bright child who is failing, the less bright child who does no better when he is held back, and the disruptive child who makes life so hard for everybody including himself.

Each day new problems come to his attention. He can readily sense that something is not right with the child who, because of bad behavior, is required to sit out in the hall isolated from his classmates. He may note that this is more common at a third or fourth grade level and that one child may be apt to repeat this performance many times. Why is he there? Why hasn't he been able to adjust to the demands of the group?

What about the children who are sent to the principal's office either because it provides an isolated place where their teacher feels they can work, or to receive counsel from the principal? Should the principal be taking his time to do what should be done in the classroom by the teacher?

Somehow he needs to find a clearing house or channel through which all these and many other problems could be appraised. One of the most persistent ideas in modern education is that adequate grouping could solve many of our educational problems. We concur to this notion. In fact we believe that accurate grouping could solve a very large percentage of the problems, with which a school principal is now being faced.

However, the kind of grouping we recommend differs somewhat from traditional grouping in that we group on the basis of behavioral age and behavioral level rather than intelligence. Our experience suggests that if all the children who are behaving at, say, a 5-year level, or a 6-year level, are grouped together, all will be ready for the kind of instruction being given. With such grouping there will be many levels of *intelligence* represented by the children in any one class. They will not be "all too much alike" as some people seem to fear.

This kind of grouping, based on behavior age, seems to be preferable to grouping on the basis of intelligence alone, which so dangerously penalizes the superior immature child by putting him in with children whom he equals intellectually, but whose behavior and general ability and functioning level are far ahead of his own.

It is because of this that we recommend a developmental examining service for every school, through which each child's behavioral age could be determined. Such a service may not be available for some time in many schools, but generalizations which have come out of such developmental programs may be useful to all school principals. These generalizations may be listed as follows:

1. Boys in the early years develop more slowly than do girls. A 6-months lag should be considered for boys in the age zone of 5 to 7 years.
2. Age should be seriously considered in relation to grade placement. A child who is fully 5 by September 1 is, in most instances, more capable of adjusting to the demands of the kindergarten, and one who is fully 6 is more ready for first grade, than those who are younger.
3. Boys born even before this date, if their birthdays are as late as July or August, should be carefully screened to make sure they are ready for kindergarten by 5. (First grade by 6.)

4. Girls whose birthdays are in September and October should also be carefully screened to determine if they might not be ready for the grade in question, even though they miss the September 1 deadline.

5. Many boys need to progress 18 months slower than the average. At this slower rate they may be expected to keep up with a regular class group.

6. Few boys, or girls, who are more than 2 years behind, can be expected to keep up with a regular class group. Such children need to be sidetracked into an ungraded group in which they can receive individual attention and can progress both at their own rate and through their special interests.

7. Certain children who are advanced intellectually and who score high on both reading and achievement tests may still be functioning at an immature level and may need to progress at a slower rate than their chronological age would suggest.

8. A kindergarten teacher's judgment about a child and his readiness should be listened to. The judgment of most kindergarten teachers correlates very well with developmental findings.

9. Any mother who wishes a child to go at a slower rate should be listened to. No parent wishes to hold his child back without a good reason. Therefore, it may be assumed she must have real evidence to warrant this request to have her child held back.

10. The educator should also hold to his own decision about keeping a child back and should try to convince the parents of the wisdom of such a move if they should question it, as some do. When an educator feels that a child should be held back, the evidence for it is usually quite strong.

11. Any disruptive child should be placed on reduced attendance or removed from the group.

12. Decisions should be made as problems arise. If a child needs to be replaced, this replacement should not be delayed, especially in the early grades. Educators are too apt to put up with bad situations, blindly hoping for a change for the better.

These generalities, helpful as they may be, are still just generalizations. They do not and cannot answer the many problems which should and can be solved by individual developmental examinations given as part of a developmental placement program. The principal would find his load of determining placement greatly relieved if he could have available a preliminary developmental appraisal of each child, and the suggestion this gives as to potential group placement. If the groups could be divided into A and B or different quality levels he would no longer need to place the intellectually advanced or highly achieving child in a higher grade. Rather, this child could stay with the age group whose developmental level is comparable to his own, but receive the stimulation he needs from the stiffer demands of an "A" curriculum.

A by-product of a developmental placement program would be the possibility of caring for those individuals who do not move along with a group even at a slower pace. These are often what we call the reality-bound children who show such marked restriction in their behavior. They can be spotted in kindergarten and usually qualify for the lowest kindergarten group. Most should or could progress, by 6 years of age, into the second kindergarten (5B) group. By 7, they could progress to a 5½B group. It is at 8 years that a decision should be made as to whether these children should go into a first grade setting and might be capable of learning with a regular class group, or whether they should go into an ungraded class where they can receive more individual attention.

An ungraded class is a relatively small group of around 15 children from the ages of 8 to 13. We would anticipate the ratio of boys to girls in such a group to be quite high. We have seen such groups in a private boarding school and have been surprised by the success of these children in contrast to their earlier failure in a regular class group. Part of the success of such a group may be that a younger child might be able to relate better to an older child or vice versa. Another important aspect of such a group is that the different children would be allowed outlets through their interests which often verge on talents.

The main success of such a group, however, is due to its small size, which allows more individual attention from the teacher and permits a freer program. More equipment might be needed for this type of a setup, and more space. Equipment would shift according to the interests of the group, but in general woodworking facilities, mechanical outlets, and nature studies, including animals, would probably have continuous use.

The development of such units would depend upon the imagination of the staff and the use of these facilities in a learning situation. Schedules of visiting could be set up so that interested children from the regular classes could participate. This might increase the prestige of these groups so that rather than being looked down upon, children in them might even be looked up to because of their good fortune in being in such a group.

Not only would reality-bound children profit by such an ungraded grouping, but also those other children who are emotionally immature and who find it difficult to adjust to a regular class group. Such children may be achieving well. Reading may even be their best subject, but they, too, often have great difficulty in adjusting to the regular class group.

How many of these ungraded groups would be needed for a school population of 600 is hard to conjecture. The percentage would be low, but the relief of not having to carry these children in the regular classroom setup would be proportionately very high. There may not be more than 30 such children in a total school setup. Even the formation of one such group of 15 children could be tried to prove its usefulness and to remove the most difficult children from the regular class setups. The preventive value of such a program is immeasurable.

This type of grouping, which we propose to solve at least some of the special problems of the child who does not fit into the regular classroom, should not be confused with the kind of ungraded setup now being tried out in many schools, often including the entire group of kindergarten, first, and second grades as a somewhat free-floating ungraded primary unit.

In fact, our entire proposal for grouping children (both A and B quality groups for each grade, as well as the formation of a 5½-year-old class for those not ready for first grade, but too mature to need to repeat kindergarten, as well as the formation of these special ungraded classes), may seem to be moving in exactly the opposite direction from that being taken by many schools today with their new setups of an ungraded primary unit without class labels.

Actually both types of administrative solution are aiming at the identical thing—having each child taught at a level for which his abilities make him suited. However, the two methods of achieving this identical end are quite different.

Even teachers of so-called ungraded primary groups admit that they know very well what grade they are teaching, whether it has a label or not—so that in actual practice many so-called ungraded groups are not as ungraded as they are supposed to be.

While we agree that every child should be taught at the level for which his maturity suits him, we feel this goal is best reached by having class groups which are clearly labeled, and teachers who know very well what it is they are teaching. Then the child should be carefully fitted to the group for which he is best suited at the moment, by first determining his developmental level and quality of performance.

Flexibility in grouping allows for transferring the child quite readily from one group to another in the event that he has been misplaced or that his subsequent progress is either faster or slower than had originally been anticipated.

The speed and effectiveness with which most teachers can teach, and most children can progress *if* the grouping is right and if the group is not held back by children who do not belong with that group, would be a revelation to most school administrators.

Our suspicion, as we have already observed in our North Haven study, is that a good grouping can not only satisfy the individual child, but it can generate its own energy and suggest in what line more successful programming might be developed. It is one thing to place children correctly, but it is just as important to provide a meaningful experience for them once they have been placed. It is to this area of education that we would hope the principal could give major time and attention.

We would like him to try to find out why so many first and second graders dislike school. This information can best be secured from the parents, since a child does not necessarily reveal his dislike at school. Will proper placement allow for a child to relate himself more positively to his school experience? Also might not a more meaningful experience show up if the child truly enjoyed school?

With good grouping and good programming we would anticipate not only an enjoyment of learning, but also more rapid learning. Thus a child might accomplish in a half day what it had previously taken him a full day to accomplish. We are already receiving word from some preliminary grouping studies which have begun in different parts of this country that achievement levels are being advanced. Our North Haven study has also suggested this trend.

This more rapid learning at the child's own level could release time to put what he has learned to better use. Thus we might anticipate that only half of the day would be used for academic subjects in the earlier grades and that we might return to the old private school idea of school from 9 to 1 o'clock or thereabouts.

This would allow for a shortened day for the first and second graders which we have mentioned in the chapter for parents. From third grade on, a rich and varied extracurricular afternoon program could be provided. Fourth and fifth graders may wish to extend their time at school to include all of their various interests.

All of these ideas are suggested in hopes that they may be useful to the school principal in solving some of his many problems, some of which we fear may have developed because the need to place a child according to his behavioral age is not fully recognized in many schools.

As many experienced principals know, in the final analysis, effective teaching depends largely on a good teacher teaching a group of children who are ready for the level and kind of instruction being given. Sometimes it is as simple as that.

REFERENCES

BOOKS

1. Ames, Louise B., & Ilg, Frances L. *Mosaic patterns of American children.* New York: Hoeber-Harper, 1962.
2. Ames, Louise B., Learned, Janet, Métraux, Ruth, & Walker, Richard N. *Child Rorschach responses: developmental trends from two to ten years.* New York: Hoeber, 1952.
3. Conant, James B. *The education of American teachers.* New York: McGraw-Hill, 1963.
4. Gans, Roma. *Common sense in teaching reading.* New York: Bobbs Merrill, 1963.
5. Gesell, Arnold *et al. The first five years of life. A guide to the study of the preschool child.* New York: Harper & Row, 1940.
6. Gesell, Arnold, & Amatruda, Catherine S. *Developmental diagnosis: normal and abnormal child development.* (2nd ed.) New York: Hoeber, 1947.
7. Gesell, Arnold, & Ilg, Frances L. *The child from five to ten.* New York: Harper & Row, 1946.
8. Ilg, Frances L., & Ames, Louise B. *Child behavior.* New York: Harper & Row, 1955.
9. Ilg, Frances L., & Ames, Louise B. *Parents ask.* New York: Harper & Row, 1962.
10. Lowenfeld, Margaret. *The Lowenfeld mosaic test.* London: Newman Neame, 1954.
11. Monroe, Marion. *Growing into reading.* New Jersey: Scott Foresman, 1951.
12. Pitcher, Evelyn G., & Ames, Louise B. *The guidance nursery school: a Gesell Institute book for parents and teachers.* New York: Harper & Row, 1964.

ARTICLES

1. Ames, Louise B. The Gesell Incomplete Man Test as a differential indicator of "average" and "superior" behavior in preschool children. *J. genet. Psychol.*, 1943, **62**, 217–274.

2. Ames, Louise B. Usefulness of the Lowenfeld mosaic test in predicting school readiness in kindergarten and primary school pupils. *J. genet. Psychol.*, 1963, **103**, 75–91.

3. Ames, Louise B. Correlation between mosaic products and psychologists' judgments of 7- to 10-year-old children. *Int. ment. Hlth Res. Newsltr*, 1964, **6**, 2–6.

4. Ames, Louise B., & Ilg, Frances L. The Gesell incomplete man test as a measure of developmental status. *Genet. Psychol. Monogr.*, 1963, **68**, 247–307.

5. Ames, Louise B., & Ilg, Frances L. Age changes in children's mosaic responses from five to ten years. *Genet. Psychol. Monogr.*, 1964, **69**, 195–245.

6. Ames, Louise B., & Ilg, Frances L. Sex differences in test performance of matched girl-boy pairs in the 5–9 year old range. *J. genet. Psychol.*, 1964, **104**, 25–34.

7. Ames, Louise B., & Ilg, Frances L. Every child in the right grade: behavior age rather than age in years the best clue to correct grade placement. *The Instructor*, November, 1963, **LXXIII**, No. 3, 7 ff.

8. Ames, Louise B., Ilg, Frances, & August, Judith. Lowenfeld mosaic test: norms for 5- to 10-year-old American public school children and comparative study of three groups. *Genet. Psychol. Monogr.*, 1964, **70**, 57–95.

9. Baer, Clyde J. The school progress and social adjustment of underage and overage students. *J. educ. Psychol.*, 1958, **49**, No. 1, 17–19.

10. Gesell, Arnold, & Ames, Louise B. The development of directionality in drawing. *J. genet. Psychol.*, 1946, **68**, 45–61.

11. Ilg, Frances L., & Ames, Louise B. *Parents ask.* Daily Syndicated Newspaper Column. New York: Hall Syndicate, 1952—.

12. Ilg, Frances L., Ames, Louise B., & Apell, Richard J. *School readiness as evaluated by Gesell developmental, visual and projective tests. Genet. Psychol. Monogr.*, in press.

13. Jacobson, J. Robert. A method of psychobiologic evaluation. *Amer. J. Psychiatr.*, 1944, **101**, 343–348.

14. Jacobson, J. Robert, & Pratt, Helen G. Psychobiologic dysfunction in mental disease. *J. Nerv. and Ment. Dis.*, 1949, **109**, 6, 330–346.

15. King, Inez B. Effect of age of entrance into Grade I upon achievement. *Elem. School Journal*, 1954–55, **55**, 331–336.

16. Pauley, Frank R. Sex differences and legal school entrance. *J. educ. Res.*, 1951, **XLV**, 1–9.

17. Pelz, Kurt, Pike, Frances, & Ames, Louise B. A proposed battery of childhood tests for discriminating between different levels of intactness of function in elderly subjects. *J. genet. Psychol.*, 1962, **100**, 23–40.

18. Shaffer, Laurence F. Review of the California short-form test of mental maturity, 1950 S-Form. *J. Consult. Psychol.*, 1951, **15**, 516.

APPENDIX A

TABLES OF BASIC DATA RE SUBJECTS

||||||||||||||||||||||||||||||||||||||||||||||||||||||||||

TABLE 1   *Testing Schedule: Center and Montowese Schools, North Haven, Connecticut*

First Year: 1958–1959		
30 FIVES $(4^{11}-5^4)$	Group A	October
30 FIVE AND A HALFS (5^6-5^{10})	Group A	May, June
65 SIXES (6^0-6^8)	Group B	February
65 EIGHTS (8^0-8^8)	Group C	March, April
Second Year: 1959–1960		
65 FIVES	Group D	October
65 SEVENS	Group B	February
65 NINES	Group C	March
65 FIVE AND A HALFS	Group D	April
Third Year: 1960–1961		
65 SIXES	Group D	October
35 FIVES (random)	Group G	November
65 NINES (random)	Group F	January
65 EIGHTS	Group B	February
65 TENS	Group C	March
35 FIVE AND A HALFS (random)	Group G	May
Fourth Year: 1961–1962		
65 SEVENS	Group D	October
65 TENS (random)	Group F	January

355

TABLE 2 *Intelligence Scores for 25 Selected Girls Compared on the California Mental Maturity Scale and Wechsler Intelligence Scale for Children (or Stanford Binet)*

Name	Age	CMM	Intelligence Scores Compared for WISC or Stanford Binet
6 years			
Girl A	6^6	129	111
Girl B	6^5	122	92
Girl C	6^6	128	92
Girl D	6^6	110	103
Girl E	6^2	122	96
7 years			
Girl F	7^3	102	92
Girl G	6^{11}	107	97
Girl H	7^5	130	121
Girl I	7^3	132	108
Girl J	7^{10}	110	84
8 years			
Girl K	8^5	115	96
Girl L	8^1	125	100
Girl M	8^4	108	95
Girl N	8^7	121	123
Girl O	8^2	111	109
9 years			
Girl P	8^{11}	132	116
Girl Q	8^{11}	118	106
Girl R	9^0	119	126
Girl S	9^6	115	105
Girl T	9^5	120	89
10 years			
Girl U	10^2	119	125
Girl V	10^6	114	105
Girl W	10^0	128	115
Girl X	10^6	124	129
Girl Y	10^5	105	85

	Mean	Median	
CMM	118.7	122.0	
WISC	104.8	105.0	

TABLE 3 *Intelligence Scores for 25 Selected Boys Compared on the California Mental Maturity Scale and Wechsler Intelligence Scale for Children (or Stanford Binet)*

Name	Age	CMM	Intelligence Scores Compared for WISC or Stanford Binet
6 years			
Boy A	6^2	122	89
Boy B	6^6	122	100
Boy C	6^6	114	95
Boy D	6^5	124	110
Boy E	6^7	117	99
7 years			
Boy F	7^0	125	108
Boy G	7^0	126	110
Boy H	7^7	120	101
Boy I	7^0	134	103
Boy J	7^3	110	116
8 years			
Boy K	8^1	112	107
Boy L	8^1	112	104
Boy M	7^{11}	129	106
Boy N	8^9	127	125
Boy O	8^7	119	120
9 years			
Boy P	8^{11}	111	104
Boy Q	9^3	117	107
Boy R	8^{11}	111	111
Boy S	9^4	118	104
Boy T	9^8	115	109
10 years			
Boy U	9^{11}	120	105
Boy V	10^5	115	101
Boy W	10^1	116	111
Boy X	10^3	109	96
Boy Y	10^9	111	103

	Mean	Median	
CMM	118	118	
WISC	106	106	

TABLE 4   *Socio-Economic Status of Parents* (*North Haven*)
(Percentage)

Class	Current Government Scale	Minnesota Scale
I. Professional	34	5
II. Semiprofessional, managerial	13	22
III. Clerical, skilled labor, retail business	4	40
IV. Farmers	3	3
V. Semiskilled, minor business	26	10
VI. Slightly skilled	15	16
VII. Day laborers	5	5

A P P E N D I X   B

SEX AND GROUP DIFFERENCES

‖‖

SEX DIFFERENCES

There is general agreement among researchers, teachers, and parents that small but clear sex differences in rate of development do exist. Our own clinical impression is that these amount to about 6 months in favor of girls around the time of school entrance. This is why we have maintained that a girl should be, on the average, fully 6 before starting first grade while boys do better if fully 6½.

This is a small difference in rate of development, but an important one.

NORTH HAVEN SUBJECTS

Present data support this general finding that girls are slightly, but rather consistently, ahead of boys. A careful check of tables in this volume makes this evident. Sex differences for those tests where they appear to any appreciable degree are summarized here.

INTERVIEW

Differences are rather variable, but girls are slightly ahead of boys in performance, for most parts of the interview.

PENCIL AND PAPER

Writing name. Girls lead in writing letters of consistent size at every age. Differences in making an even base line are inconsistent, but from 7 years on favor the girls. Girls lead in correct use of capitals up till 7 years of age, after which all children respond correctly. Girls make fewer reversals than do boys at 5½ years of age. Cursive writing becomes normative for both at 8 years.

Girls tend to write slightly smaller and thus are considered advanced in this respect. Girls do slightly better at writing their first name at 5 years, the two sexes performing equally well thereafter. Girls do better than boys at writing their last name at 5 and 5½ years; performance is even thereafter.

Thus with minor exceptions, any differences in success of writing name are in favor of the girls.

Writing address.   Girls are a little ahead of boys in successful writing of number, street, city, and state, and success on all of these becomes normative in girls at 8 years, in boys at 9. A marked difference does appear at 9 years when 92% of girls, only 64% of boys, write their whole address without error. Here, again, differences throughout the age range are small, but definitely favor girls.

Writing numbers.   Girls are slightly ahead of boys in number of figures made (5 and 5½ years). Girls space numbers evenly before boys do. Over 50% of girls space evenly by 8 years of age. Boys do not reach this effectiveness till 9. Girls are also slightly ahead of boys as to evenness of figures in that 68% of girls, only 50% of boys make even figures at 7 years, when such performance is first normative. Girls are also somewhat ahead in using front of paper only for their figures.

Again, differences are small but in almost every instance they favor the girls.

COPY FORMS

Circle.   Differences here are fairly marked. Girls are considerably ahead of boys. Sixty-six per cent of girls start circle at the top at 5 years, 82% by 5½. Starting at the top does not become normative in boys till 5½ years (56%), and at every age through 8, more girls than boys start it at the top.

Also, more girls than boys use a CCW direction through 8 years. Girls predominantly use a CCW direction even at 5 years (58%). This direction is not normative in boys till 5½ years (58%).

Cross.   More girls than boys at both 5 and 5½ years draw V-line downward, H-line from L to R; girls achieve a qualitatively "good" cross at 8 years, boys not until 9.

Square.   In general more girls than boys draw the square CCW and start with the left side down. More boys draw CW, and their place of starting is much more varied.

Triangle.   More girls than boys use one line at 5, 5½, and 6 years; more boys than girls use one line only from 8 to 10 years. More boys than girls use three lines (presumably a less mature pattern) at 5, 6, and 7 years. However, all of these trends are highly variable.

At most ages more girls than boys start with left side down. Performance of boys is slightly more variable than that of girls. However at most ages boys make more continuous CCW lines than do girls and at every age through 8 years more girls than boys make immature or younger patterns.

Rectangle with diagonals.   So far as the outer part of this product (the rectangular shape) is concerned, performance of girls is ahead of that of boys at 5 years in that more girls than boys make a continuous single line. A continuous single CCW line occurs equally (44% of each) in girls and boys at 5½ years, but in more girls than boys at 6 years (56% girls, 44% boys). Thereafter trends are varied. In general girls seem to be slightly ahead of boys through 6 years; and boys slightly ahead of girls thereafter, but these trends are not clear-cut.

So far as the inside pattern of the rectangle with diagonals is concerned, the performance of boys is slightly ahead of that of girls through 5½ years, in that younger patterns drop out a little sooner in boys. Thereafter girls seem slightly more advanced than do boys though differences are slight and inconsistent.

Diamond—horizontal orientation. Younger patterns occur to a slightly larger extent in girls than in boys through 7 years of age. Horizontal or vertical split pattern, which appears to be the most mature response, occurs more in boys than in girls at 5½ and 6 years, but more in girls than in boys at 7 to 10 years. Drawing in a continuous single direction occurs more in boys than in girls throughout.

Diamond—vertical orientation. Sex differences are slight and somewhat inconsistent. Drawing one or more lines in a continuous direction comes in slightly sooner in boys than in girls. At the older ages a vertical or horizontal split pattern (the most mature pattern made) shows up a little more strongly in girls.

Three-dimensional forms. Girls are ahead so far as copying the cylinder is concerned, from 5 to 7 years of age. Boys are ahead from 8 to 10 years.

Boys, however, are slightly ahead throughout on copying the cube face-on, and definitely ahead throughout in copying the cube point-on.

Organization of Copy Forms on page. Girls are ahead of boys at every age so far as number of forms which are of an even size; and even size becomes normative in girls at 9 years, not quite normative in boys (46%) even by 10 years.

Girls are also ahead in that horizontal placement of forms on the paper becomes normative in girls at 7 years; in boys, not until 10 years.

As to placing forms in an orderly horizontal direction, girls are ahead of boys at 5, 7, 8, and 9 years. Orderly horizontal direction becomes normative in girls at 7 years; in boys not until 10 years.

INCOMPLETE MAN

Girls add more parts than boys do, on the average, from 5 to 8 years of age. Girls are also ahead of boys in achieving good length of leg, in adding a pupil to the eye, in completing the neck area, and in giving facial expression.

Boys are ahead of girls in placement and direction of arm, in making good fingers, and in placing the ear correctly. Other sex differences are small and variable.

RIGHT AND LEFT TESTS

Sex differences here are not particularly consistent, large, or interesting. Response to this group of tests appears to be a highly individual matter. It is of interest that in response to the Right and Left picture cards—the most difficult part of this test and given only from 8 to 10 years—boys are on the average rather quicker than girls in giving a verbal response to these pictures; girls are slightly quicker than boys in giving a motor response.

VISUAL ONE

Differences here are very slight. Choosing all forms correctly, starting more than half of the enclosing circles at the top, and drawing more than half the circles CCW become normative for both sexes at the same age. "Fair" closure of circles is normative for girls at 5 years, for boys not until 6 years, but here again differences in percentages are slight.

VISUAL THREE

Very few consistent sex differences appear, though the performance of girls is slightly ahead of that of boys in most respects at 5 and 5½ years.

NAMING ANIMALS

Sex differences as to number of animals named are very small. At 5½ years slightly more girls than boys can name animals for a full minute, but naming for a full minute becomes normative in both sexes at 6 years of age. At 6 years and thereafter at every age slightly more boys than girls can name for a full minute.

Mean number of animals named is the same in both sexes at 5 and 5½ years, higher in boys at other ages except at 9 years when girls lead. As to kind of animal named, at every age more girls than boys name domestic animals. At every age but 6 years more boys than girls name zoo animals; and at every age more boys than girls name fish and intermediate type animals. Difference in number of birds named is slight, but in general girls name more than boys.

At every age boys name more different kinds of animals than do girls.

HOME AND SCHOOL PREFERENCES

Likes best of all.   At every age, more boys than girls mention some kind of gross motor activity as a preference. An exception is winter or summer *sports,* mentioned more often by girls than boys at nearly every age.

Playing games is more popular with girls than with boys at every age; and coloring, drawing, and other creative activity, at nearly every age. At every age but 5½, more girls than boys mention specifically "doing something" with some other person. Doll play is, needless to say, more popular with girls; ball play with boys.

Indoor school preferences.   More boys than girls mention "play" at 5 and 5½ years when play is a strong preference. More girls than boys mention some kind of work activity from 8 to 10 years when work is such a strong preference. Creative activities are mentioned more by girls from 5 to 7 years, more by boys than girls from 8 to 10 years.

Outdoor school preferences. Boys appear to be more mature than girls in their outdoor school preferences. General gross motor behavior (seesaw, slide, swings, etc.) seems to be a less mature outdoor preference than playing games, since it occurs mostly at the younger ages. It occurs more in girls than in boys at 5 and 5½ years of age. Playing games occurs more in boys than in girls at every age except 5½ years.

Indoor home preferences. Sex differences are highly varied.

Outdoor home preferences. As at school, the preferences of girls seem slightly less mature than do those of boys. Gross motor activities in general appear to be less mature than playing games, and more girls than boys mention gross motor activities as preferences at every age. Conversely, at every age after 5 years more boys than girls mention a preference for playing games. More boys than girls mention ball play as a preference.

LOWENFELD MOSAIC TEST

As to level of maturity of performance, differences are slight. Five-year-old girls are a little ahead of boys, but 6-year-old boys are slightly ahead of girls. As to type of patterned structure, girls tend to make more nonrepresentational products with pattern (design) than boys do. Boys make more representational products.

Thus, as will be seen, sex differences are not entirely consistent. For most tests and most subtests, girls are at least slightly ahead at most ages, and this is especially true in the age zone from 5 to 6 years. Even when performance is rather similar over the total age period, girls tend to reach proficiency sooner.

In the following instances especially, successful response becomes normative in girls earlier than for boys.

Starting the circle at the top and drawing CCW.
Making the cross with two lines only.
Drawing the outside of the divided rectangle with a continuous CCW line.
Arranging Copy Forms in an orderly horizontal direction.
Writing name with a straight base-line, letters of consistent size.
Adding nine parts to Incomplete Man.
Adding a leg of good length and placed correctly to the Incomplete Man.
Adding neck, bow, and "neck and bow only" to Incomplete Man.
Giving facial expression to the man.
Achieving "fair" closure in the circles which encircle chosen responses in Visual One.
Naming animals for a full minute at 5½ years.

Exceptions to the more advanced behavior of girls, that is, instances where the performance of boys is more advanced, include:

Except for copy cylinder at 5 to 7 years, boys are outstandingly ahead of girls in copying the three-dimensional forms.

Some aspects of the Incomplete Man, as placement and direction of arm and placement of ear, see boys ahead of girls.

In some few aspects of the Right and Left tests, especially with relation to timing, boys are ahead of girls at some ages.

WESTON SUBJECTS

Since tables for the performance of Weston subjects[1] are not included in this volume, we include here tables which show the rather consistently advanced behavior of girls over boys in this particular group of subjects and which confirm the relative acceleration of girls suggested by North Haven figures.

A tabular summary of all those Weston subjects on whom our developmental ratings as to ready, questionably ready, or unready for the grade in which age had placed them were consistent from Test 1 to Test 4, shows (Table 5) that more girls than boys were fully ready (+), more boys than girls questionably ready (±), and more boys than girls not ready (−).

TABLE 5   *Sex Differences in Readiness for the Grade in Which Age Alone Placed Them of Subjects Who Remained Consistently Ready, Questionable, or Unready Over a Three-Year Period (Weston)*

| | Ready | | Questionable | | Unready | |
Original Group	Girls	Boys	Girls	Boys	Girls	Boys
54 Kindergarteners	22	9	6	11	1	5
21 First graders	6	6	3	4	0	2
23 Second graders	5	3	2	6	2	5
Total	**33**	18	11	**21**	3	**12**

A detailed study of sex differences in performance of these subjects on developmental, visual, and projective tests is reported elsewhere[2] and will be summarized here only very briefly.

From all Weston subjects, we matched as many girl-boy pairs as possible with relation to WISC IQ, age in months, and socio-economic status, and compared responses of each girl-boy pair on the Incomplete Man test, on Visual Three, and on the Mosaic and Rorschach tests. Table 6 shows the percentage of these matched pairs in which either girl or boy gives the better performance. As this table indicates, regardless of test used and regardless of age of subjects, for nearly every test at every age it is the scores of girls which are superior and which show greater maturity of response.

[1] See page 15 for description of Weston study.
[2] Louise B. Ames and Frances L. Ilg, Sex differences in test performance of matched girl-boy pairs in the 5- to 9-year-old age range. *J. genet. Psychol.*, 1964, **104**, 25–34.

TABLE 6 *Percentage of Matched Pairs in Which Either Girl or Boy Gives the More Advanced Performance (Weston)*

	Kindergarten Test Number			First Grade Test Number			Second Grade Test Number		
	1	2	3	1	2	3	1	2	3
Incomplete Man									
Number of pairs	18	18	17	6	6	6	7	7	7
Girls more advanced	**83**	**83**	**76**	**67**	**100**	**67**	**71**	**86**	**100**
Boys more advanced	17	17	24	33	0	33	29	14	0
Visual Three									
Number of pairs	16	15	14	6	6	6	7	7	7
Girls more advanced	**81**	**53**	**57**	**50**	**83**	**83**	43	28	**57**
Boys more advanced	19	47	43	**50**	17	17	**57**	**72**	43
Mosaic[a]									
Number of pairs	18	18	17	6	6		9	9	9
Girls more advanced	**72**	**55**	**53**	**50**	33		**66**	**55**	**66**
Boys more advanced	28	17	29	12	**66**		33	11	11
Rorschach									
Number of pairs	17			6			7		
Girls more advanced	**53**			**83**			**57**		
Boys more advanced	47			17			43		

[a]Not all percentages add up to 100% since performance of some pairs was judged to be equal.

GROUP DIFFERENCES

It is generally assumed that children of higher intelligence will give a superior response on tests other than intelligence tests as well as on intelligence tests. Present findings bear out this assumption.

The three groups compared here are (1) the basic group of 100 North Haven public school children at each age level; (2) subjects from Weston, Connecticut, fewer in number and ranging only from 5 through 9 years of age; (3) for some tests, New Haven private school research subjects used in earlier studies.

Mean intelligence rating for the three groups is as follows: for New Haven subjects mean IQ is 118; for Weston subjects, 109.7; for North Haven subjects, 105.4.

Socio-economic status (as measured on the Minnesota Scale) of parents of New Haven subjects was chiefly professional; of Weston parents, chiefly semiprofessional or managerial; of North Haven parents, chiefly clerical, skilled, and retail business.

FINDINGS

Most comparisons are given for Weston and North Haven subjects only. Since differences between these two groups are not large (though for the most part they favor Weston subjects) findings for Weston subjects are not given in this volume,[3] and differences between the groups will be summarized only briefly and only where some consistent or conspicuous differences exist.

PENCIL AND PAPER

Writing name. Weston subjects are slightly ahead of North Haven subjects in that a straight base line becomes normative in Weston children at 7 years, in North Haven children not till 9 years. In other aspects of writing name now one group, now the other, leads.

Writing numbers. For most aspects of writing numbers, North Haven subjects lead. Thus at 5 years, North Haven girls make numbers one through ten, Weston girls only through five. North Haven girls achieve even spacing by 8 years, Weston girls not till 9. Figures are of an even size in Weston girls earlier than in North Haven girls. Reversals drop out first in North Haven girls.

Thus for most aspects of writing numbers, North Haven girls are ahead of Weston girls, though performance of boys for the two groups is quite similar.

COPY FORMS

Differences are for the most part small and inconsistent. However Weston subjects are considerably ahead of North Haven subjects in their organization of forms on the page.

TABLE 7   *Organization of Copy Forms on Page, Two Groups Compared*

	Girls		Boys	
	Weston	North Haven	Weston	North Haven
Horizontal orientation	6 years	7 years	7 years	10 years
Even size	9 years	9 years	9 years	10 years
Less than one–half page used	9 years	10 years		9 years only

Three-dimensional forms. Responses of the two groups were compared at 9 years of age, the oldest age for which Weston data were available. Performance of Weston subjects is ahead for all three forms.

INCOMPLETE MAN

In every respect when differences occur between the two groups they favor the Weston subjects. Thus Weston subjects are ahead in number of parts added from 4 to 7 years. They add both arm and leg sooner. Good placement,

[3] All tables for Weston responses are on file and available at the Gesell Institute.

direction, and length of arm and leg become normative sooner in Weston than in North Haven subjects.

Weston subjects also achieve good placement and good size of ear, good placement, and good length of hair sooner.

An earlier study of difference between average and superior New Haven subjects showed clear differences between the two groups. Most parts are added earlier by superior subjects; more parts are added; parts come to be of the right size, placement, and direction sooner in superior than in average subjects. It was also clear that the superior child is not only more advanced than the average child of the same chronological age, but that his wider horizon may result in behavior never exhibited by average children, no matter how old. Thus the typical genetic gradation of behavior for the two groups appears to be somewhat distinctive for each.

Visual One and Visual Three

Results for Visual One are highly varied, now one group, now the other, giving the better response. On Visual Three, Weston subjects are slightly ahead at 5, 5½, 6, and 7 years. North Haven subjects are slightly ahead at 8 years.

Right and Left Tests

Naming parts, touching right ear, showing right thumb. Except for elbow and thumb, both of which are named correctly by both groups at 5 years, Weston subjects name parts earlier than do North Haven subjects.

Single commands. Differences in timing are small, but except for showing ring finger, North Haven subjects are quicker to respond.

Double commands. With the exception of "left ring–right eyebrow" and "left thumb–right ring" for which North Haven subjects are quicker, and "left middle–right index" where timing is equal, Weston subjects respond to double commands on the average more quickly than do North Haven subjects.

Naming Animals

More Weston than North Haven subjects can name animals for a minute, at 5 and 5½ years. Thereafter, more North Haven than Weston subjects name the more. However, the ability to name animals for a minute becomes normative in both at 6 years. Differences in mean number of animals named are variable. The largest differences are at 7 and 8 years when Weston subjects name the more.

Lowenfeld Mosaic

For this test, data are available for three separate groups of subjects— New Haven, Weston, and North Haven. New Haven subjects are definitely ahead of the other two groups as to level of maturity of product. Products of Weston subjects are more mature than those of North Haven subjects at 5½, 6, and to a lesser degree at 7 years of age. Differences between Weston and North Haven subjects after 7 years are small. The outstanding differences between the two latter groups is that nonrepresentational designs without pattern continue longer in North Haven than in Weston subjects. Table 8 gives these data.

RORSCHACH

For the Rorschach test we have data on the same three groups for which Mosaic data were available. Table 9 compares findings for these three groups on every Rorschach variable. As this table shows, for every variable except F + % and H%, New Haven subjects gave superior responses to those given by Weston or North Haven subjects. Differences in scores between subjects of the Weston and North Haven groups were small and variable.

Thus, in general, performance of Weston subjects, whose IQ and socio-economic status is on the average somewhat higher than that of North Haven subjects, is slightly superior to that of the North Haven subjects. New behaviors tend to come in sooner with Weston subjects.

This is especially true of the following test situations: writing name, organization of Copy Forms on page, copying three-dimensional forms, Incomplete Man, Visual Three, Right and Left naming parts, Right and Left double commands, Mosaic.

Exceptions are Writing Numbers and Right and Left single commands.

When these two groups of subjects are compared with a third group (from New Haven) on two of the tests—the Rorschach and Mosaic tests—subjects from New Haven (with a higher mean IQ and higher mean socio-economic status than either Weston or North Haven subjects) give a response superior to that of the other two groups.

Most differences are not great, but for the most part they consistently favor subjects with the higher IQ and higher socio-economic status.

TABLE 8 *Mosaic: Three Populations Compared—New Haven, Weston, North Haven*
(Percentage each group each type; sexes combined)

	5 years			6 years			7 years			8 years			9 years			10 years		
	N.H.	W.	No.H.	N.H.	W.	No.H.	N.H.	W.	No.H.	N.H.	W.	No.H.	N.H.	W.	No.H.	N.H.	W.	No.H.
A. Nonrepresentational without pattern																		
Drop or pile	0	0	0	0	1	0	0	0	0	0	0	0	0	0	0	0	0	0
Scatter	1	17	9	0	2	2	0	3	0	0	0	0	0	5[a]	0	0	4	0
Prefundamental	0	12	5	0	0	5	0	2	1	0	0	0	0	0	0	0	0	0
Slab	9	0	11	2	14	16	1	9	21	5	10	12	6	18	8	7	15	6
Overall	1	0	3	0	0	1	0	4	3	0	0	1	1	0	0	0	0	0
All A	11	29	28	2	17	24	1	18	25	5	10	13	7	23	8	7	19	6
All A without slab	2	29	17	0	3	8	0	9	4	0	0	1	1	5[a]	0	0	4	0
B. Nonrepresentational with pattern																		
Fundamental	0	8	3	0	2	2	0	6	4	2	0	4	0	0	3	0	4	0
Central design	15	8	9	13	20	9	13	12	14	13	12	11	18	5	19	14	8	15
Design along rim	4	0	0	2	0	0	0	0	0	0	0	1	4	0	0	0	0	0
Fills tray	4	0	2	2	0	1	11	2	1	11	0	2	8	5	2	12	4	1
Separate designs	5	0	0	7	3	3	6	0	0	1	0	2	2	0	4	4	0	2
All B	28	16	14	24	25	15	30	20	19	27	12	20	32	10	28	30	16	18
C. Representative																		
Object	51	50	53	47	35	47	29	40	34	34	45	53	35	40	48	30	46	49
Scene	8	4	4	22	18	9	33	22	18	25	28	11	20	27	14	27	19	26
All C	59	54	57	69	53	56	62	62	52	59	73	64	55	67	62	57	65	75
D. Mixed	2	0	1	0	5	4	4	0	4	3	0	3	1	0	2	2	0	1

[a] One girl only.

	5	5½	6	Years 7	8	9	10
			Number of Responses				
New Haven	13.9	13.6	15.8	18.3	16.0	18.6	16.3
Weston	10.7	11.3	12.8	13.7	14.0	12.9	14.8
North Haven	10.8	9.7	13.1	11.0	12.8	11.9	13.5
			W%				
New Haven	58	55	51	51	55	42	52
Weston	66	73	63	61	60	64	63
North Haven	65.5	67.5	70	67	58	62	58
			D%				
New Haven	34	33	34	41	37	48	40
Weston	30	25	31	32	35	31	31
North Haven	29.5	28.5	24.5	28	36.5	33	36
			Dd%				
New Haven	8	12	15	8	7	9	8
Weston	3.5	2	5.5	6.5	5	5	6
North Haven	5	4	5	5	5.5	5.5	6
			F%				
New Haven	70	62	60	52	58	67	63
Weston	75	73	65	67	69	74	72
North Haven	80.5	73.5	73	73	67.5	70	71.5
			F+%				
New Haven	78	84	81	82	87	84	89
Weston	77.6	83	87	89	89	92	92
North Haven	75	89	85.6	92	87	92	94
			M				
New Haven	.56	.44	1.0	1.4	1.3	1.4	1.7
Weston	.66	.63	1.0	1.0	1.0	1.1	1.0
North Haven	.32	.62	.4	.7	1.1	1.4	1.9

NOTE: Socio-economic status (by percent):
New Haven: 42 in I; 25 in II; 21 in III
Weston: 16 in I; 45 in II; 21 in III
North Haven: 5 in I; 22 in II; 40 in III

IQ:
New Haven—mean of 118
Weston—mean of 109.7
North Haven—Corrected mean of 105.4

TABLE 9 (*Continued*)

	5	$5\frac{1}{2}$	6	Years 7	8	9	10
				FM			
New Haven	1.08	1.26	1.62	1.88	1.54	1.62	1.74
Weston	1.00	.98	1.73	1.69	1.77	.86	1.80
North Haven	.56	.63	1.04	.99	1.77	1.27	1.73
				m			
New Haven	.16	.52	.44	.82	.40	.46	.36
Weston	.22	.38	.65	.54	.50	.40	.20
North Haven	.28	.17	.13	.70	.40	.40	.40
				sC			
New Haven	1.63	2.26	2.16	2.89	1.80	2.09	1.51
Weston	.44	.66	.94	.92	.64	.77	.45
North Haven	.78	.93	.98	.78	.87	.86	.55
				F(C)			
New Haven	.44	.60	.68	1.14	.92	.84	.62
Weston	.11	.06	.11	.17	.10	.13	.20
North Haven	.25	.25	.16	.11	.32	.19	.13
				A%			
New Haven	44	41	48	42	45	48	49
Weston	59	52	54	55	57	63	67
North Haven	47	53	52	57	53	55	56
				H%			
New Haven	9	11	11	14	17	16	16
Weston	13	12	14	15	17	16	16
North Haven	18	14	16	15	17	20	20
			Number content categories				
New Haven	4.7	4.9	4.8	5.2	4.7	5.2	4.8
Weston	3.8	3.7	3.9	4.2	4.4	3.8	3.5
North Haven	4.1	3.7	2.1	3.4	4.5	3.8	4.2

THE RORSCHACH TEST

||||||||||||||||||||||||||||||||||||||||||||||||||||||||||||||||||||||

The Rorschach test, the best known and most widely used of all so-called projective techniques, has proved remarkably useful in clinical practice, possibly far beyond even the most sanguine hopes of its author, Hermann Rorschach. Like most clinicians, we use it routinely with our clinical cases, where it proves time and again to be one of the most effective and revealing tools in helping to understand the individuality of the growing child.

However we do not recommend it as a basic and essential part of our proposed test battery for determining school readiness. An extremely delicate and technical test, it is not suitable for use except by individuals specially trained in its administration and interpretation.

In the hands of a trained individual it can be a most useful supplement to the usual battery of readiness tests. Its strong and weak points for such a purpose follow.

STRONG POINTS

1. The Rorschach constitutes an effective supplement to the recommended battery of tests in that it gives good clues to marked immaturity as well as to behavior which is conspicuously advanced.
2. More than other tests in the proposed battery it reveals the nature of a child's individuality.
3. It can spot emotional disturbance, especially in those children not suited for regular classroom attendance whose problem is emotional rather than one of low intelligence or immaturity.
4. It gives good clues as to the intelligence of subjects.
5. The Rorschach gives certain clues which in any 5- to 7-year-old suggest unreadiness for kindergarten and first grade. The most important of these is the relation of F% to F+%.[1] Our experience suggests that an F+%

---

[1] Technical scoring terms are not explained here. Any reader not familiar with these terms who wishes an explanation is referred to Louise B. Ames *et al.*, "Child Rorschach Responses," New York: Hoeber, 1952, pp. 41–44.

(or correct form percent) which is lower than the F% (form percent) is a clear warning sign that a child is not ready to start first grade.

WEAK POINTS

1. The fact that the Rorschach response requires interpretation by a highly trained person makes it not only impractical, but actually unsafe in un-skilled hands.
2. Even the skilled clinician may find it difficult always to distinguish be-tween a response which indicates immaturity and one which indicates merely a limited intelligence.
3. The qualitative aspects of the ages (which give the best clues as to age level of response) tend to show up only in superior or well-endowed children.
4. Unusually high F% or unusually high A% (animal percent), both sus-pect, may indicate immaturity or they may merely be a sign of a highly re-stricted individuality.
5. Because of normal variation from age to age, and especially because any given individual sometimes does less well at an older than at a younger age, it is not possible from a single test to be certain whether a given response has never come in, or may have come in at an earlier age and dropped out temporarily. This is especially true in the case of the human movement response on Card III. In some subjects, it is given at 5 years, drops out at 5½. In fact in 8% of present normative kindergarten girls, in 10% of kindergarten boys, and in 33% of first grade boys, the Ror-schach response on a second examination in sequence is less mature than on a first.
6. Thus a highly enlivened response to the Rorschach tells a good deal, for better or worse, but a record of from 8 to 10 responses with high F%, and high A%, tells relatively little with regard to school readiness, since this type of response may indicate low intelligence, a restricted psyche, or immaturity. It is often most difficult to make a clear and certain dis-tinction.
7. Also perhaps more than with other tests the expected Rorschach response at any given age differs markedly in subjects of different intellectual and social levels.

For those trained in the Rorschach who may be using it as part of a battery to assess developmental readiness, or for any who may be giving this test to a child within the 5- to 10-year-old age range, Table 9 on page 370 gives mean Rorschach scores for this normative population. It also compares scores for present subjects with those of subjects from two other groups of presumably somewhat higher intelligence levels.

UNREADINESS SIGNS

Rorschach examiners may also be interested in our list of possible "un-readiness signs"—kinds or levels of response which appear to be suggestive of unreadiness for first grade entrance and in some instances, even for entrance to kindergarten.

Of these signs, the single word response suggests not only unreadiness for starting first grade, but even for doing kindergarten work. Pure C (color unmodulated by form), C′ (black used as color), and Cn (color naming), single sentence responses, and perseveration occur in both ready and unready kindergarten subjects, but only in unready as opposed to ready first graders. Thus any of these responses suggest possible unreadiness for first grade.

Other signs of unreadiness for first grade, F% exceeding F+%, fewer than 10 responses, atypical concepts, and preschool confabulation or contamination, are found conspicuously in unready kindergarten subjects and also in unready first graders. A sC (sum of color responses) greater than M (sum of movement responses) is also suspect.

THE RORSCHACH AS PROGNOSTIC OF READING ACHIEVEMENT

A study by George Meyer in 1953[2] suggested that the Rorschach if given to kindergarten subjects could distinguish in many instances between those subjects who would later be good readers and those who would not, and also could provide data on first grade readiness.

We have checked Meyer's findings[3] on a group of 64 public school children for whom both kindergarten Rorschachs and fifth grade reading test scores were available. Comparison of the early Rorschachs of the later good and poor readers with IQ held constant supported Meyer's findings and added a few further distinguishing signs between the two groups.

Later good readers, as compared to later poor readers, give better quality W, have a lower W% (percent of whole responses) and higher D% (percent of detail responses), give more introversive responses, and more FM, have a lower F%, a higher F+%, and an F+% which exceeds the F%.

In general, we consider the Rorschach a useful supplementary test to a developmental battery chiefly in that it can provide important clues to a child's basic individuality structure, as well as spotting grossly immature or highly atypical children. It is most useful for this purpose in the 5- to 6-year-old range. By 8 years of age it seems less effective, though at any age it can spot the highly atypical personality.

As a rule the differences between a 7-, 8-, and 9-year-old performance (unless the subject is superior enough to show the characteristic qualitative signs of the age) are not great enough to be consistently helpful in determining developmental level.

Also owing to the fact that the Rorschach needs to be administered and interpreted by a highly trained person (and even then it is sometimes difficult to interpret just what it has to say about developmental level), we do not recommend that it be given routinely as part of a developmental battery.

[2] George Meyer, Some relationships between Rorschach scores in kindergarten and reading in the primary grades. *J. proj. Tech.* 17, 4, Dec., 1953, 414–425.

[3] Louise B. Ames and Richard N. Walker, Prediction of later reading ability from kindergarten Rorschach and IQ scores. *J. educ. Psychol.*, in press.

SAMPLES OF TEST RECORD FORMS

Final Thumb-nail summary of behavior   Name

                                                             Age

                                                             Date

                                                             School

                                                             Teacher

                                                             Group

Recommended group

Total impression and summary

Teachers comments

376

Initial Interview

How old are you?

When is your birthday? _____ Month? _____ Day? _____

Did you have a party? (who came)

What did you like to do best?

What was your favorite present?

How many brothers and sisters?
    (Names, ages)

What does your daddy do?
    (Where does he work?)

Write letters or name, last name (6-7 yrs), date (7-8 yrs),   Name
address (8-9 yrs)
1st name with non- dominant hand.   Age

Copy forms   R _____   L _____

Write numbers 1 to 20 -

Incomplete Man (look like; order of parts & comments)   Facial Expression (How can you tell?)

How does he look?

How does he feel inside?

Happy or sad?

How can you tell?

Form No. 103

Right and Left

Name

Age

Naming parts of body   Summary Comments:

   1. Eye

   2. Eyebrow

   3. Palm

   4. Elbow

Naming fingers () 5 yr. items

   (1) Thumb

   2 Index (pter)

   (3) Middle (2-2)

   4 Ring (wear)

   (5) Little

Naming R & L

R hand _____ (Show me your R hand)

How do you know?

L hand   R eye   L eye

L ear   R ear

Ex-er's R hand (How do you know?)

Single Commands () 5 yr. items

   (1) Eye   _____

   2 Index   _____

   3 Ring   _____

   4 Middle   _____

   (5) Cl. eyes,   _____
        bend head

   (6) Bend head,   _____
        tap fl.
        with heel

   7 Raise head, _____
        open mouth

   (8) R ear   _____

   (9) R thumb   _____

   (10) L index   _____
        (5 yrs-L
        big)

         Total _____   Av. _____

Double Command () 5 yr. items

   (1) R thumb-R little   _____

   2 L hand-L knee   _____

   3 L ring-R eyebrow   _____

   4 R elbow-palm L hand   _____

   5 R middle-L cheek   _____

   6 L thumb-R thumb   _____

   (7) R middle-L little   _____

   8 R little-L ring   _____

   9 L middle-R index   _____

   10 L thumb-R ring   _____

         Total _____   Av. _____

Pictures (8 yrs--)

Verbal

   1. _____

   2. _____

   3. _____

Total _____   Av. _____

Motor

   1. _____

   2. _____

   3. _____

Total _____   Av. _____

Form No. 104

380

GROUP TESTS

Visual Test 1

Memory of Orientation of Forms

Score.............

Visual I

Analysis of Projections

Visual III

1.

2.

3.

4.

Visual III Projections

Card 1.

Card 3.

Card 2.

Card 4.

Name

Age

Naming animals (60°)

Interests - what do you like to do best?

At school indoors:

At school outdoors:

At home indoors:

At home outdoors:

Tooth eruption

Physical items: (fat, muscular, slender, etc.)

R.   Upper   L.

12 6	2nd 1st		C	LI CI	CI LI	C	1st 2nd	6 12		
M M	B B						B B	M M		

Lower

Form No. 105

384

INDEX